To Barry from Sonny

LSTM 2009 - 2010.

Thanks for everything.

"IF YOU LEAVE US HERE, WE WILL DIE"

HOW GENOCIDE WAS STOPPED IN EAST TIMOR

HUMAN RIGHTS AND CRIMES AGAINST HUMANITY
Eric D. Weitz, Series Editor

Echoes of Violence: Letters from a War Reporter by Carolin Emcke

Cannibal Island: Death in a Siberian Gulag by Nicolas Werth. Translated by Steven Rendall with a foreword by Jan T. Gross

Torture and the Twilight of Empire from Algiers to Baghdad by Marnia Lazreg

Terror in Chechnya: Russia and the Tragedy of Civilians in War by Emma Gilligan

"If You Leave Us Here, We Will Die": How Genocide Was Stopped in East Timor by Geoffrey Robinson

"IF YOU LEAVE US HERE, WE WILL DIE"

HOW
GENOCIDE
WAS STOPPED
IN EAST TIMOR

GEOFFREY ROBINSON

PRINCETON UNIVERSITY PRESS

PRINCETON AND OXFORD

Copyright © 2010 by Princeton University Press

Published by Princeton University Press,
41 William Street, Princeton, New Jersey 08540
In the United Kingdom: Princeton University Press, 6 Oxford Street,
Woodstock, Oxfordshire OX20 1TW

Library of Congress Cataloging-in-Publication Data

Robinson, Geoffrey, 1957–
"If you leave us here, we will die" : how genocide was stopped in East Timor / Geoffrey
Robinson.
p. cm. — (Human rights and crimes against humanity)
Includes bibliographical references and index.
ISBN 978-0-691-13536-6 (hardcover : alk. paper)   1. Genocide—East Timor.   2. Political
violence—East Timor.   3. Genocide intervention—East Timor.   4. Humanitarian
intervention—East Timor.   5. East Timor—Politics and government—20th century.   6. East
Timor—History—Autonomy and independence movements.   7. East Timor—Relations—
Indonesia.   8. Indonesia—Relations—East Timor.   I. Title.
DS649.6.R63 2009
959.87'032—dc22   2009010313

This book has been composed in Bembo with Univers display

British Library Cataloging-in-Publication Data is available.

Printed on acid-free paper. ∞

press.princeton.edu

Printed in the United States of America

1   3   5   7   9   10   8   6   4   2

For Sofia

CONTENTS

CHAPTER ELEVEN

CONCLUSIONS

PREFACE

As I WRITE, the Lonely Planet guide lies open on my desk. My wife and daughter are eager to hear what I think of their plans for our summer vacation in East Timor. They are keen on the idea of a boat trip to the island of Ataúro off the north coast. But I can't help recalling that the island was the place where tens of thousands of East Timorese were detained, and many died, in the years after Indonesia's invasion in 1975. Nor can I forget that East Timor was the site of a genocide in which more than one hundred thousand people died in the first years of Indonesia's 24-year occupation. Or that in the aftermath of a UN-supervised vote for independence in 1999, the territory was once again consumed by violence so systematic that many feared it would degenerate into a second genocide. Is this really where we want to spend our family vacation? Still, I like to think it is a fitting choice. After all, the country is now independent and, despite its grinding poverty and the undeniable scars of the past, it is more peaceful now than it has been for 35 years. It is also fitting, I think, because our family history and East Timor's are so deeply intertwined. My wife and I met many years ago through our work on East Timor, I have been studying its history and politics for almost three decades, and this book about that history has taken its final shape in the years since our daughter's birth. Just as important, while East Timor's recent history has been characterized by extreme violence, it has also been filled with hope, and with evidence of the remarkable power of ordinary people to change the course of history for the better. Those are ideals that, however naively, I still believe, and that I hope my daughter will embrace too.

The idea for this book first came to me in the weeks immediately after the violence of September 1999, which I witnessed first-hand. On leave from my academic position as a history professor at UCLA, I had been working as a Political Affairs Officer with the United Nations Mission in East Timor (UNAMET) since June 1999. From that vantage point, I had experienced first the euphoria of the overwhelming vote for independence on August 30, followed by the quick descent into violence in which some 1500 people were killed, most of the buildings in the country were looted and burned to the ground, and more than half the population was forcibly displaced. I remained there until the final evacuation of UN personnel, and more than a thousand East Timorese refugees, on the early morning of September 14. Safely back in Los Angeles, but still troubled by what I had seen, I began to write. I did so partly as therapy, I suppose, but also to set down what I could recall before it disappeared or was hopelessly distorted through too frequent retelling. The idea then was to provide a first-hand account of the violence, and to offer some insight into why it had happened.

A few months later, in early 2000, I circulated a draft manuscript among a handful of colleagues, particularly those with whom I had worked at the UN in Dili. Their reaction was not encouraging. It was far too personal, they said, and in any case UN rules prohibited me from publishing any information I had gained while working with the organization. And so I set the manuscript aside. Over the next few years, I concentrated instead on writing scholarly historical accounts of the violence and, with the exception of a few short popular articles, I consciously left my own experiences and perceptions out of the equation. I also researched and wrote a report about the events of 1999 for the UN Office of the High Commissioner for Human Rights (OHCHR), which was finally published in 2006 by East Timor's Commission for Reception, Truth, and Reconciliation (CAVR), and by a group of Indonesian and East Timorese NGOs. Nevertheless, I remained frustrated that the story had not yet been told as fully as it might be; by setting aside the personal dimension, both the academic work and the human rights reporting, it seemed to me, left important pieces of the story untold. The problem was how to combine these very different sorts of writing into a single, satisfying whole. Then, quite by chance, in late 2006 I met Brigitta van Rheinberg and Eric Weitz, who were in Los Angeles to seek prospective authors for Princeton's new series on Human Rights and Crimes against Humanity. They encouraged me to submit a proposal for a book in which the two kinds of account would appear together. I did so, and this book is the result. Neither purely an academic treatise, nor simply a personal memoir, it combines elements of both in what, I hope, will be both good history and a good read.

The subject matter is admittedly rather grim. It is a history of East Timor's experience of violence since the period of Portuguese colonial rule, through the unlawful Indonesian occupation of 1975-1999, focusing on the events of 1999 and the years immediately thereafter. But if it is in large part a narrative and analysis of the violence in East Timor, it also tells the story of how that violence was finally brought to an end. In that sense, it is not a typical study of genocide and mass violence, but a contribution to a still rather small body of literature that seeks to explain how such forms of violence might be stopped. It is perhaps worth stressing that, while it provides a substantially new interpretation of East Timor's recent history, and offers what I believe are new insights into the conditions that give rise to genocide and other forms of mass violence generally, it does not propose new definitions. So, while I am aware of the debate surrounding the precise meaning of the term genocide, and of the various problems in the legal definition spelled out in the UN Genocide Convention of 1948, I nevertheless use that definition here.[1]

It goes without saying that, in writing this book, I have accumulated substantial debts of gratitude. Among the greatest are those I owe to friends in East Timor who have been so generous in sharing their knowledge with me, and who have shown such courage over the years in the face of threat and adversity. Among others, Fernando de Araùjo, José Antonio Belo, Estêvão Cabral, Sister Esmeralda, Bendito Freitas, Aniceto Guterres Lopes, José Luís de Oliveira, João Soares Reis Pequinho, Jacqueline Siapno, and Laurentina (Mica) Barreto Soares have been an inspiration. The same can be said of several Indonesian friends who, long before it was safe or popular to do so, dared to take a stand on behalf of East Timor. Yenny Rosa Damayanti, Arief Djati, Nug Kacasungkana, Coki Naipospos, Ibu Ade Rostina Sitompul, Titi Irawati Supardi, and Galuh Wandita, among others, stand out as examples of all that is good about Indonesia's civil society, and all that can be achieved through intelligent, transnational political action. For their friendship and courage in 1999 and since, and for their invaluable assistance in piecing this story together, I am also deeply grateful to several old UN colleagues and friends, in particular Nicholas Birnback, Patrick Burgess, Elodie Cantier-Aristide, Mandy Cordwell, Ric Curnow, Jim Della Giacoma, Siri Frigaard, Anthony Goldstone, Jenny Grant, Mark Harris, Ian Martin, Atanasia (Tata) Pires, Tamrat Samuel, Colin Stewart, and Francesc Vendrell.

Beyond Indonesia and East Timor, I owe a debt to the many human rights and political activists who worked tirelessly for so many years to document and draw attention to the plight of East Timor, and without whose efforts it would have been impossible to write this history.

Among many others, I particularly wish to thank Victoria Forbes Adam, Elaine Brière, Kerry Brogan, Carmel Budiardjo, Jean Pierre Catry, Kirsty Sword Gusmão, Jill Jolliffe, Sidney Jones, Arnold Kohen, Ed McWilliams, John Miller, Luisa Pereira, Charlie Schiener, Lucia Withers, and Pat Walsh. Special thanks are due to Arnold Kohen and Anthony Goldstone, among the first and most tireless of the old East Timor hands, who read the manuscript and offered many valuable suggestions for its improvement.

To my academic mentors at Cornell University, Benedict Anderson and the late George Kahin, I owe a special debt for their example of ethically responsible and politically engaged scholarship. I am also grateful to many other academic colleagues who, through their own scholarship, through their helpful comments on my earlier work, or through their kindness, have helped me complete this book. They include Peter Carey, Robert Cribb, Eva Lotta Hedman, Douglas Kammen, Gerry van Klinken, Joe Nevins, Nancy Lee Peluso, Samantha Power, Tony and Helen Reid, John Roosa, Michael Salman, John Sidel, Scott Straus, Richard Tanter, John Taylor, Nhung Tuyet Tran, David Webster, and Mary Zurbuchen. I am also grateful to several anonymous reviewers who provided constructive feedback on the proposal for this book and on the near-final manuscript.

For the generous fellowships that allowed me to carry out the necessary archival and field research, I am grateful to the American Council of Learned Societies, and the British Library's Endangered Archives Programme. I also wish to thank Professors Brenda Stevenson, Teo Ruiz, and Ned Alpers who, as successive chairs of UCLA's Department of History, granted me time off from teaching to serve with the UN for six months in 1999 and in later years to conduct research and write. As noted above, I am extremely grateful to Brigitta van Rheinberg and Eric Weitz at Princeton University Press, for encouraging me to write this book and for providing invaluable feedback and support along the way. No author could have asked for more. Leslie Grundfest, Clara Platter, and Cindy Milstein, have likewise been models of kindness and professionalism throughout.

Finally, a word of thanks to my family. My parents, Basil and Elizabeth, I thank for opening my eyes to a wider world. When I went to East Timor in 1999, it was at least in part because of them that I did so. And when I set about to write this book, they were the ideal readers for whom I wrote. My siblings, Katharine, David, and Ann, and my in-laws,

Henrik, Cecilia, and Hoffe Stannow, have been pillars of support, displaying a confidence in my abilities that I did not always share. I thank my wife, Lovisa, for her inextinguishable optimism even when it seemed unlikely that this book would ever see the light of day, for her sharp-eyed but always sympathetic editing, and for loving me in spite of my all too abundant flaws. A long-time human rights activist herself, she supported my decision to go to East Timor in 1999, and calmly reassured anxious friends and family as the situation in Dili grew increasingly dicey in early September. When I returned home, filled with terrible memories that would not go away, she convinced me that I should write this book, and she made it possible for me to do so by taking on far more than her share of family responsibilities despite the heavy burden of her own work. The simple truth is that, without her, this book would never have been written. Lastly, I thank my daughter, Sofia, because she laughs at most of my jokes and thinks I can fix anything, and because she is a constant reminder of the importance, maybe even the necessity, of believing that hope can triumph over despair.

NOTE

1. The UN Convention on the Prevention and Punishment of the Crime of Genocide, was approved by General Assembly Resolution 260 A (III) on December 9, 1948 and entered into force on January 12, 1951. The definition of genocide is spelled out in Article 2 of the convention, which reads: "In the present Convention, genocide means any of the following acts committed with intent to destroy, in whole or in part, a national, ethnical, racial or religious group, as such:

(a) Killing members of the group;

(b) Causing serious bodily or mental harm to members of the group;

(c) Deliberately inflicting on the group conditions of life calculated to bring about its physical destruction in whole or in part;

(d) Imposing measures intended to prevent births within the group;

(e) Forcibly transferring children of the group to another group."

LIST OF ABBREVIATIONS

ANP	Associação Nacional Popular (Portuguese National Union)
Apodeti	Associação Popular Democrática Timorense (Timorese Popular Democratic Association)
ASDT	Associação Social Democrática Timorense (Timorese Social Democratic Association)
BAIS	Badan Strategis Intelijen (Strategic Intelligence Agency)
BAKIN	Badan Koordinasi Intelijen Negara (State Intelligence Coordinating Agency)
BIA	Badan Intelijen ABRI (Armed Forces Intelligence Agency)
BRTT	Barisan Rakyat Timor Timur (East Timor People's Front)
CAVR	Comissão de Acolhimento, Verdade e Reconciliação de Timor-Leste (Commission for Reception, Truth, and Reconciliation in East Timor)
Civpol	United Nations Civilian Police
CNRM	Conselho Nacional de Resistência Maubere (National Council of Maubere Resistance)
CNRT	Conselho Nacional de Resistência Timorense (National Council of Timorese Resistance)
CRP	Community Reconciliation Process [of the CAVR]
CRRN	Conselho Revolucionária de Resistência Nacional (National Council of Revolutionary Resistance)
CTF	Commission of Truth and Friendship
DPA	United Nations Department of Political Affairs
DPKO	United Nations Department of Peacekeeping Operations
ELSAM	Lembaga Studi dan Advokasi Masyarakat (Institute for Policy Research and Advocacy)
Falintil	Forças Armada de Libertação de Timor-Leste (Armed Forces for the Liberation of East Timor
Fortilos	Forum Solidaritas Untuk Rakyat Timor Timur (Solidarity Forum for the People of East Timor)
FPDK	Forum Persatuan, Demokrasi dan Keadilan (Forum for Unity, Democracy, and Justice)
Fretilin	Frente Revolucionária de Timor Leste Independente (Revolutionary Front for an Independent East Timor)
Garda Paksi	Garda Pemuda Penegak Integrasi (Youth Guard for Upholding Integration)
GPK	Gerakan Pengacau Keamanan (Security Disruptors' Movement)
GRPRT	Gerakan Rekonsiliasi Persatuan Rakyat Timtim (East Timorese People's Reconciliation and Unity Movement)
Hansip	Pertahanan Sipil (Civil Defense)
ICRC	International Committee of the Red Cross
Interfet	International Force for East Timor
Kodim	Komando Distrik Militer (District Military Command)

Kodam	Komando Daerah Militer (Regional Military Command)
Komnas HAM	Komisi Hak Asasi Manusia ([Indonesian] Human Rights Commission)
Kopassandha	Komando Pasukan Sandhi Yudha (Special Warfare Force Command)
Kopassus	Komando Pasukan Khusus (Special Forces Command)
Korem	Komando Resor Militer (Resort Military Command)
Kostrad	Komando Cadangan Strategis Angkatan Darat (Army Strategic Forces Command)
KPS	Komisi Pengamanan dan Stabilitas (Commission on Peace and Stability)
LBH	Lembaga Bantuan Hukum (Legal Aid Institute)
MLO	United Nations Military Liaison Officer
NGO	Nongovernmental Organization
OPSUS	Operasi Khusus (Special Operations [Executive])
PIDE	Polícia Internacional e de Defesa do Estado (International and State Defense Police)
PKI	Partai Komunis Indonesia (Indonesian Communist Party)
PPI	Pasukan Pejuang Integrasi (Integration Fighters Force)
Ratih	Rakyat Terlatih (Trained Populace)
Renetil	Resistência Nacional dos Estudantes de Timor Leste (East Timorese National Students' Resistance)
Satgas P3TT	Satuan Tugas Pengamanan Penentuan Pendapat mengenai Timor Timur (Task Force for the Implementation of the Popular Consultation in East Timor)
SGI	Satuan Tugas Intelijen (Intelligence Task Force)
Solidamor	Solidaritas untuk Penyelesaian Damai Timor Leste (Solidarity for Peace in East Timor)
TBO	Tenaga Bantuan Operasi (Operational Auxiliaries)
TNI	Tentara Nasional Indonesia (Indonesian Armed Forces)
TP4 OKTT	Tim Pengamanan Pelaksanaan [or Penyuksesan] Penentuan Pendapat Otonomi Khusus Timor Timur (Team for the Security and Implementation [or Success] of the Popular Consultation on Special Autonomy in East Timor)
UDT	União Democrática Timorense (Timorese Democratic Union)
UNAMET	United Nations Mission in East Timor
UNTAET	United Nations Transitional Administration in East Timor

"IF YOU LEAVE US HERE, WE WILL DIE"

HOW GENOCIDE WAS STOPPED IN EAST TIMOR

CHAPTER ONE

INTRODUCTION

NINETEEN NINETY-NINE was a bad year in East Timor. Between January and late October, at least fifteen hundred civilians were killed among a total population of well under a million. Some of the victims were shot dead; others were decapitated, disemboweled, or hacked to death with machetes. Many were beaten or tortured, while women and girls were singled out for rape and other crimes of sexual violence. The vast majority of the victims were real or suspected supporters of East Timor's independence from Indonesia, including Catholic clergy, local UN staff, and political activists. The perpetrators were overwhelmingly members of armed East Timorese militia groups and their Indonesian army patrons.

The worst of the violence followed the announcement, on September 4, that 78.5 percent of the population had voted for independence in a UN-supervised referendum held just days earlier. Twenty-four years after invading and occupying the tiny former Portuguese colony, the Indonesian army and its local allies were not about to let it go without a fight. Over the next few weeks, the capital Dili along with many other towns and villages were burned to the ground. Warehouses, shops, and homes were looted, their contents loaded onto trucks and ships, and then taken to Indonesia. The systematic violence also fueled the displacement of the population on a massive scale. By the time it ended, at least four hundred thousand people had been forced to flee their homes, and an estimated 70 percent of the country's infrastructure had been burned or destroyed. For ten days in September, at the height of the violence, the UN compound in Dili where I worked became a place of refuge for some two thousand East Timorese and UN staff, and partly for that reason, came under siege.[1]

The swiftness with which the violence spread as well as its apparently

FIGURE 1.1. The market in Suai, December 1999. An estimated 70 percent of East Timor's infrastructure was burned or destroyed, at least four hundred thousand people were forced to flee their homes, and fifteen hundred were killed in the violence before and after the August 30, 1999 ballot. (Ross Bird)

orchestrated character led some observers to fear an impending genocide.[2] That was not an idle fear. In the late 1970s, at least a hundred thousand East Timorese, and perhaps twice that number, had died as a direct consequence of the Indonesian invasion and occupation.[3] Yet even as the possibility of a second genocide was being discussed, the tide suddenly turned. In response to mounting public outrage, in mid-September the United States and other key governments finally took steps to rein in the Indonesian army and its militia proxies, cutting military ties to Indonesia and threatening to suspend economic aid. Under this unprecedented pressure, Indonesian authorities agreed to accept international assistance to restore order. Then, in another unusual move, the UN Security Council authorized the deployment of a multinational military force under Chapter VII of the UN Charter. That force landed about one week later, and within a week or two of its deployment, the worst of the violence had stopped and the distribution of humanitarian assistance had begun.

This book tells the story of that terrible yet strangely uplifting year. It is a history not only of mass political violence that threatened to degenerate into genocide but also of a rare success in bringing such violence to an end. Viewing the events of 1999 against East Timor's longer history, this book examines the structural origins and logic of the violence, the historical conditions that shaped and ended it, and the related questions of personal and institutional responsibility. More specifically, it asks: Why did the violence of 1999 occur as and when it did? What best explains the central part played by East Timorese militias? What finally brought about the surprising international military intervention of late September? And finally, who was responsible for the violence, and what efforts have been or might yet be made to ensure that they are brought to justice?

The answers to these questions matter because they lie at the heart of the pressing moral, legal, and political problems with which East Timorese continue to grapple. They also matter because the story of East Timor is in some respects emblematic of many of the most important political and legal developments of the final decades of the twentieth century. Despite its small size, East Timor has lived in the crosshairs of the central ideological and geopolitical challenges of each of the last several decades, including the struggle for decolonization, the tragic consequences of cold war "realism," the problems of militarism and extreme nationalism, debates over humanitarian intervention and UN trusteeship, and the emergence of new regimes of international humanitarian law and justice.[4] For Americans, moreover, the violence in East Timor has a special significance because of the U.S. government's historical complicity in it. Against the backdrop of the war in Iraq and the wider "war on terror," a discussion of that history may help citizens and leaders alike as they struggle to make sense of their nation's place in the world, and the political and moral foundations of its public life.

Without suggesting that East Timor's experience is typical, I hope that this account may also contribute to broader scholarly and public debates about political violence, genocide, international humanitarian intervention, and transitional justice. More specifically, I believe it may shed new light on some of the following questions: Under what historical conditions are crimes against humanity and genocide most likely to occur, and under what conditions can they be prevented or stopped? Is armed humanitarian intervention an effective method of preventing mass violence, or stopping such violence once it has started? What role do human rights organizations, religious institutions, the media, and individuals play in the genesis and prevention of genocide? And is it possible to balance the pursuit of justice and reconciliation in a society that has experienced widespread and systematic violence?

My interest in the subject of this book is partly intellectual and partly personal. Most of my work as a scholar over the past twenty years or so has been devoted to understanding the history and dynamics of political violence, particularly in Indonesia and East Timor. Over the same period, I have been directly engaged in efforts to end such violence and to protect basic human rights in those places, among others. For several years in the late 1980s and early 1990s, I worked as the principal researcher for Indonesia and East Timor at Amnesty International's headquarters in London. From that vantage point, I became familiar not only with the seemingly intractable problem of violence in East Timor and the unusual brutality of Indonesia's New Order regime but also with the extraordinary courage of those inside East Timor who were fighting for their rights and independence. So when the opportunity arose in early 1999 to serve with the UN mission overseeing the historic referendum on the country's future, it is safe to say that nothing could have kept me from going. But if I felt honored to be part of that process, and if I felt reasonably well equipped to do the job, I was not fully prepared for the complexity or the sheer horror of what I witnessed there. That experience, more than any other, drove me to write this account.

In view of my somewhat unusual position as both a historian of and participant in the events described in this book, I have approached the subject from two complementary perspectives. On the one hand, in seeking to explain the origins and character of the violence, I have relied primarily on the methods and perspectives of the historian. Using a range of historical documents, interviews, and secondary sources, and informed by pertinent comparative and theoretical literature, I do my best to locate the events of 1999 in a broader historical and analytic framework, paying special attention to the legacies of Portuguese and Indonesian rule and to shifts in the international political environment. On the other hand, in examining the logic of events in 1999, I provide a detailed portrait from the point of view of those who were directly involved. Relying primarily on firsthand observations and interviews conducted during and after 1999—as well as contemporary UN and Indo-

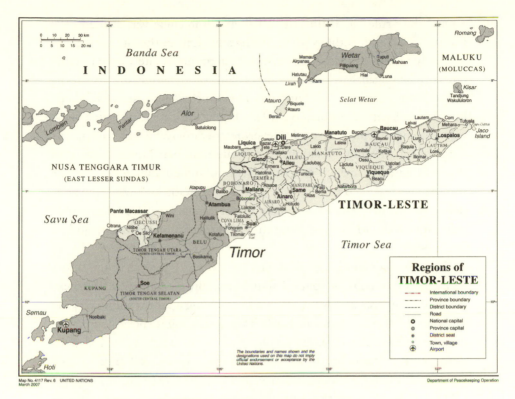

FIGURE 1.2. Map of East Timor. (UN Cartographic section)

nesian documents—I recount the actions and the apparent motives of militia members, soldiers, civilians, and UN officials, and explore the difficult moral and political dilemmas they faced. The book concludes with a discussion of the relevance of East Timor's experience for the larger debates to which I have referred.

My involvement in these events has undoubtedly affected my interpretation of them, and the more general conclusions I draw. Indeed, some might say that it has interfered with my capacity for objectivity. That may well be the case. If it is, I hope that there may nevertheless be some value in this account, and that others may treat it as one of many possible perspectives on the violence and its wider significance.

East Timor: A Brief History

For roughly three centuries, East Timor was a colony of Portugal. While Portuguese colonial authorities liked to imagine that East Timorese welcomed their rule, the truth was that their compliance was secured only through a series of ruthless pacification campaigns in the late nineteenth and early twentieth centuries. Those campaigns deliberately pitted "loyal" chiefs (*liurai*) against rebellious ones, laying the groundwork for deep-seated enmity among East Timorese. The same may be said of the brief but bloody Japanese occupation (1942–45), in the course of which some forty thousand Timorese died. Nevertheless, largely because of the absence of any meaningful nationalist movement in East Timor at the time, the Portuguese managed to return without much difficulty after the war. As the rest of the colonized world fought for and won independence from European powers, East Timor remained under Portuguese rule, and lived more or less harmoniously with its immediate neighbor, Indonesia.

That arrangement began to unravel in 1974 as Portugal, in the throes of its own momentous political transformation, set about to relinquish its colonies in Asia and Africa. Portuguese disengagement stimulated the growth of political parties in East Timor, including a social democratic party called Fretilin (Frente Revolucionária de Timor Leste Independente, or Revolutionary Front for an Independent East Timor), which advocated immediate independence, and a more conservative party, the UDT (União Democrática Timorense, or Timorese Democratic Union), which favored eventual independence but with continued ties to Portugal. Against that backdrop, Indonesia began to interfere in East Timorese politics by lending support to a small party called Apodeti (Associação Popular Democrática Timorense, or Timorese Popular Democratic Association), which advocated integration with Indonesia, and encouraging the UDT to fight against Fretilin. That meddling soon contributed to a growing hostility between Fretilin and the UDT, and to a coup by UDT forces in mid-August 1975. The UDT coup triggered a brief but intense civil war in which some two thousand Timorese died. Though Fretilin quickly emerged as the dominant party, it faced repeated cross-border attacks by Indonesia, and political sniping from both Apodeti and the UDT. Finally, anticipating a full-scale Indonesian invasion, in late November 1975 Fretilin declared East Timor's independence.

That declaration was the final straw for Indonesia's President Suharto, an army general who had seized power in an anti-Communist coup in October 1965. In the weeks and months after that coup, military forces under Suharto organized the killing of as many as one million real or alleged members of the PKI (Partai Komunis Indonesia, or Indonesian

Communist Party), a legal political party at the time. Another half a million people were imprisoned, the vast majority of them without charge or trial.[5] Claiming that an independent East Timor posed a threat of Communist insurrection and political instability on its border, and with the tacit support of the United States and other major powers, in early December 1975 Indonesia launched its invasion of East Timor. The UN Security Council and General Assembly passed several resolutions condemning the invasion, and East Timorese resisted with a tenacity that surprised Indonesian military officers. Indonesia responded by declaring East Timor its twenty-seventh province and launching a major counter-insurgency war, which led to massive displacement, disease, and death. That military campaign and the humanitarian crisis that flowed from it were greeted by silence and inaction by powerful states, most notably by the United States, Australia, and the United Kingdom. By the late 1970s, human rights organizations estimated that at least a hundred thousand people had already died, many of them due to starvation and disease, but a substantial number by summary execution or as the result of torture. At least in the colloquial sense of the word—and arguably even by its strict legal definition—this was genocide. For the next twenty-four years, Indonesia faced continued military and political resistance from East Timorese, but steadfastly rejected any suggestion that it should withdraw. Still, events on the ground in East Timor, widening fissures in Suharto's sclerotic New Order regime, and a gathering storm of international protest began gradually to weaken Indonesia's position through the 1990s.

The watershed event was the Santa Cruz massacre of November 12, 1991, in which as many as 270 East Timorese, most of them teenagers, were gunned down or beaten to death by Indonesian soldiers. Shocking video footage of the massacre was broadcast worldwide, prompting outrage and stimulating the formation of new East Timor support groups throughout the world. Under pressure from these groups and from international solidarity networks that had been forming since the invasion, as well as the media and the Catholic church, some Western governments voiced rare criticism of Indonesia and backed these with limited sanctions. A further critical development came in 1996 when two East Timorese, the international spokesperson for the resistance, José Ramos-Horta, and the bishop of Dili, Monsignor Carlos Filipe Ximenes Belo, were awarded the Nobel Prize for Peace. The Nobel Prize raised hopes for independence to unprecedented levels, and further increased the leverage of East Timor support groups and nongovernmental organizations (NGOs). Yet in spite of the widespread sympathy for the victims of human rights abuse, and the international legitimacy bestowed by the Nobel Prize, the prospects for East Timorese independence continued to appear bleak. Indonesian authorities were adamant that East Timor would remain a part of Indonesia, and key governments remained reluctant to criticize Indonesia, much less to insist on its withdrawal from East Timor.

All of this began to change in May 1998, when a surge of prodemocracy protest in Indonesia, coupled with a serious financial crisis and rioting in major cities, forced President Suharto to step down after more than thirty years in office. In East Timor, thousands of people took to the streets to demonstrate in favor of independence and against a proposal for "special autonomy" under Indonesian rule that had begun to be discussed in the context of UN-sponsored talks in New York. As details of the special autonomy proposal were being finalized, reports began to trickle out of East Timor about the mobilization of militia groups dedicated to maintaining the tie with Indonesia. And when Indonesia's new president, B. J. Habibie, unexpectedly proposed in late January 1999 that the East Timorese should be given a chance to vote for or against special autonomy, the trickle became a flood. More than a dozen militia groups appeared in a matter of months.[6]

It was soon evident that these groups were involved in a coordinated campaign of terror against supporters of independence. In February and March 1999, dozens of people were reported to have been killed, some in gruesome ways, and tens of thousands were forced to flee, after which their homes were burned to the ground. Many of those who fled sought refuge in nearby churches or the residences of prominent citizens. It was against these people, and in these places of refuge, that some of the most egregious acts of militia violence were committed in April. Against this inauspicious backdrop, the United Nations brokered a set of agreements with Indonesia and Portugal to conduct a referendum on the special autonomy proposal. The May 5 Agreements, as they were known, called for a vote to be held sometime in August, just three months away.[7] Regrettably, those agreements stipulated that security both before and after the popular consultation would be the responsibility of Indonesia, and that the United Nations Mission in East Timor (UNAMET) would be entirely unarmed. Despite well-founded concerns about that arrangement, the violence slowed somewhat with the arrival of UNAMET and other observers in May and June, lending some support to the view that the presence of hundreds of international observers would serve as an effective brake on the violence. Yet the violence continued in some form as the ballot day approached—and reached a terrible crescendo in the days and weeks after the results of the vote were announced in early September.

Certain distinctive patterns and variations in the violence were almost immediately evident. The clearest pattern was that notwithstanding claims of their independence, the militias operated with the full acquiescence and support of the military, police, and civilian authorities. A second pattern was that all of the militia groups adopted virtually identical rhetoric and repertoires of action, all mouthed the same slogans threatening violence against supporters of independence, and with a few exceptions, all were armed with an array of "traditional" weapons, including machetes, spears, and "homemade" guns. There were also some significant variations. For one thing, the worst of the violence was concentrated overwhelmingly in the western districts bordering Indonesia. The violence also varied substantially over time, with a peak in the first few months of the year, followed by a marked decline during the three months after UNAMET's deployment, and a dramatic spike in the immediate aftermath of the vote.

The postballot violence provoked outrage around the world, and led not only to the armed international intervention of late September 1999 but also to a round of international investigations and vows that the culprits would be punished. No fewer than six independent investigations concluded that crimes against humanity had been committed, that Indonesian authorities appeared to bear the primary responsibility for those crimes, and that they should be criminally prosecuted, if necessary before an ad hoc international tribunal. The international community, however, displayed a marked lack of resolve in seeing that the perpetrators of the violence were brought to justice. Indeed, some ten years later—and despite strong indications of their culpability—no Indonesian official had been successfully prosecuted for any crime related to the violence of 1999.

Understanding the Violence

Existing explanations of the violence of 1999 generally make one of three principal claims. The first, most commonly expressed by Indonesian military officials, is that the militias formed spontaneously in response to proindependence provocation in late 1998, and that their acts of violence were an expression of ostensibly traditional cultural patterns. The second, more common among Western journalists, NGOs, and scholars, is that the militias were formed at a stroke by the Indonesian army in late 1998, and that the violence was carefully orchestrated by high-ranking military commanders. The third, also stressed by outside observers, is that certain powerful states and the United Nations bear responsibility for the violence because of their failure to act decisively until it was too late.[8]

There is an element of truth in all of these claims, and my own approach draws in some way on all of them. In fact, without them I could scarcely have begun to make sense of what happened. Still, having examined the evidence carefully, and having viewed it in relation to my own experience and to the wider literature on genocide and mass violence, my sense is that most existing characterizations are in some important respects incomplete. Three problems stand out. First, with some notable exceptions, they tend to elide crucial historical questions about the violence. They often obscure the fact, for example, that the events of September 1999 were only the most recent act in a long history of state-sponsored violence in East Timor that included colonial pacification campaigns, civil war, and genocide. That history certainly casts serious doubt on the Indonesian claim that the violence of 1999 was purely spontaneous. But it also raises questions about the suggestion that the violence was solely the product of conscious official manipulation. The insistence that the militias and the violence of 1999 were created overnight by the army has meant that basic questions about the historical conditions that motivated the Indonesian army, and shaped the existence, character, and repertoires of the militias, have scarcely been asked. With that in mind, this book examines that history in some detail, considering in particular the legacies of Portuguese and Indonesian rule. Drawing on the wider literature on genocide and mass violence, it also considers the various ways in which states and state agencies played a role in shaping the violence.

Second, to varying degrees, existing explanations fail to take sufficient account of the changing international environment within which the longer history of violence played out, and that arguably both facilitated the violence of 1999 and brought it to an end. While critics have correctly noted that the violence was facilitated by the reluctance of powerful states to offend the government of Indonesia, they have generally failed to consider, much less explain, why those states ultimately decided to intervene militarily to stop the violence in late 1999. The fact is that without that unusual intervention, we might now be speaking of tens of thousands of casualties—and even genocide—rather than a terrible flurry of violence that was brought swiftly to an end. That key distinction requires some kind of explanation. Accordingly, this book devotes a good deal of attention to examining the logic and dynamic of international action with respect to East Timor, both in 1999 and in earlier decades. In doing so, it focuses not only on the self-interested behavior of powerful states that contributed so much to the violence but also on the counter-vailing tendencies that complicate the story of international complicity and ultimately brought about a critical, if short-lived, change in policy in mid-September 1999.

Finally, most explanations pay scant attention to the role of individual motives and actions, and the impact of unexpected events, in under-standing both the violence and its aftermath. My sense from having ob-served developments at close hand is that such individual actions and events were important not only in determining the course of the vio-lence but also the decision to stop it, and the subsequent failure to make good on promises to bring the perpetrators to justice. This book thus pays close attention to the motives and actions of individuals, not all of them powerful, and to the unusual conjuncture of historical events and trends that gave rise to the violence and ended it, while also shaping in-ternational action in the subsequent months and years. To gain a clearer sense of what I have in mind, it may be helpful to examine each of these themes in somewhat greater detail.

Culture and Violence

In an apparent effort to divert attention from their moral and legal re-sponsibility for the violence, Indonesian military officials have consis-tently claimed that their security forces behaved professionally and did their utmost to contain the regrettable violence among East Timorese.[9] From the outset, they have insisted that the militias formed spontane-ously in response to proindependence provocation, and acted violently out of an understandable but uncontrollable anger at alleged UN bias and cheating.[10] They have also argued that the violence in the postballot period was the result of timeless cultural patterns common among Indo-nesian peoples. In early 2000, for example, the senior Indonesian military officer in East Timor during the events, Major General Zacky Anwar Makarim, told journalists that the violence had been part of an Indonesian cultural pattern of "running amok."[11] In using this term, Makarim unwittingly evoked a common colonial caricature in which indigenous forces or individual assailants appeared to be in a state of "frenzy," and acting emotionally, uncontrollably, and without discipline.[12]

While they have been greeted with derision by many observers, official Indonesian claims are not wholly without foundation. East Timorese were divided, though by no means evenly, on the question of independence, and the tensions surrounding that division undoubtedly encouraged some to join the pro-Indonesian militias in late 1998 and 1999. Likewise, at least some part of the violence did stem from genuine anger at alleged UN bias and cheating in the course of the referendum. Moreover, as discussed in detail below, those militias did draw on or seek to replicate older traditions of warfare in the area, including head taking, house burning, and the amok style of attack. Nevertheless, such explanations are unsatisfactory for a number of reasons. For one thing, they seem deliberately to obscure the fact that the events of 1999 were only the final act in a story of systematic state-sponsored violence in East Timor that reached back at least to 1975—and earlier. They also take no account of the broader international political environment in which that long history of violence played out, and that arguably both facilitated it and brought it to an end. Perhaps most obviously, as discussed below, they ignore a substantial body of evidence demonstrating that the militias were mobilized and supported by Indonesian military and civilian authorities.

More generally, the contentions that lie at the heart of official Indonesian explanations share the shortcomings of most efforts to explain mass violence and genocide by reference to universal psychological conditions or cultural traits.[13] As I have argued at some length elsewhere, the principal problem with such explanations is their inability to account for variation across time and place.[14] If a people really are psychologically and culturally predisposed toward extreme mass violence, it must be asked why genocides and mass violence happen only in a few places and at specific moments. As the more sophisticated proponents of culturally based arguments acknowledge, the answer lies in the specific historical and political context within which any culture exists and evolves, and in the ways that it is deployed and understood by those who are part of it.[15] Similarly, those who have offered the most convincing accounts of the significance of psychological factors in the logic of genocide have been careful to note that these operate within a complex set of historical and political conditions. In his groundbreaking account of the murder of some fifteen hundred Jews committed by a German reserve police battalion in Poland in 1942, for instance, Christopher Browning maintains that those who killed were in fact "ordinary men" who had been conditioned to kill not only by certain universal sociopsychological tendencies but also by specific historical and political conditions, including war, officially sanctioned racism, propaganda, ideological indoctrination, and bureaucratization.[16] "If the men of Reserve Police Battalion 101 could become killers under such circumstances," he asks, "what group of men cannot?"[17] The relevance of this observation for the case of East Timor can scarcely be overstated. There, Indonesian soldiers, police, and above all East Timorese militias were quintessentially ordinary men, driven by fear, propaganda, the brutalization of war, and self-preservation, but also by ties of family, political patronage, and institutional culture, to become "willing executioners."

The wider implication of these arguments, I think, is that history itself has a defining importance in the dynamic of genocide and other forms of mass violence. Most obviously, perhaps, past violence can significantly increase the likelihood of future violence. That is partly because the experience or memory of violence can help to create or deepen a sense of group identity and enmity. In part too it is because history, including memories of past violence, provides the essential raw material for political leaders seeking to mobilize populations to take part in or at least acquiesce to mass violence.[18] Crucially, historical experience and memory also provide the organizational and behavioral models as well as the rhetorical tool kit that are the foundation of future violence, and shape its character.[19] These observations certainly appear to make sense for East Timor, which has had a long history of violence, where political leaders on all sides have appealed to that history in mobilizing their followers, and where both identities and enmities appear to have stiffened through the long experience of violence.

States and Violence

Perhaps not surprisingly, many scholars and human rights advocates have taken issue with the official Indonesian position. Far from being spontaneous, they have claimed, the violence was deliberately organized and encouraged by army officers and civilian officials at the highest levels. Some of these accounts in fact have claimed that the violence was planned and orchestrated in its entirety by military officials. In November 1999, for example, the Indonesian Human Rights Campaign (Tapol) wrote that "there is overwhelming evidence that the destruction was a well-prepared military operation."[20] Virtually all independent investigations of the violence have reached similar, if somewhat less categorical, conclusions. Even pro-Indonesian militia leaders have taken up this refrain, declaring that the postballot violence was explicitly ordered by President Habibie at a meeting less than two weeks before the vote.[21]

The idea of a centrally ordered plan certainly comes much closer to the truth than the claim of a spontaneous, culturally rooted eruption of violence. Indeed, as discussed in some detail in this book, there is now a substantial body of documentary and circumstantial evidence demonstrating that the pro-Indonesia militias were mobilized, armed, trained, supplied, and financed by Indonesian military and civilian officials. A careful analysis of that evidence leaves little room for doubt that several dozen high-ranking military, police, and civilian officials bear either individual or command responsibility for crimes against humanity committed in 1999.[22] That conclusion, moreover, is consistent with a common pattern in the general history of mass violence: that it is more often the result of deliberate calculation by state leaders than the consequence of spontaneous action by individuals or groups. Benjamin Valentino has argued that mass political killing is *always* the product of a conscious strategic decision on the part of political leaders to achieve political or military goals, such as the defeat of an insurgency, the revolutionary transformation of class relations, or territorial expansion.[23] That insight helps to explain the otherwise puzzling fact that mass violence and genocide have been perpetrated by regimes with different political ideologies, and in a wide variety of cultural, social, and economic contexts.

Nevertheless, the suggestion that the violence of 1999 was planned in its entirety by high-ranking military authorities has tended to obscure the possibility that there were other historical or political dynamics at work. Most important, the insistence that the militias and the violence were manufactured at a stroke by the TNI (Tentara Nasional Indonesia, or Indonesian Armed Forces) has meant that basic questions about the motives and methods of the Indonesian army, and the historical origins and internal dynamics of the militias, have scarcely been asked. Why, for instance, would the Indonesian army have decided to encourage violence in the context of the UN-sponsored referendum, especially one year after the authoritarian Suharto regime had been swept away on a tide of prodemocracy and antimilitary protests? And having opted for a policy of violence, why would the army have chosen to deploy a network of local militias armed mainly with traditional weapons? As for the militias themselves, how were they mobilized so quickly? Why did they act in the ways that they did? And what accounts for the significant geographic and temporal variations in the violence they committed? I believe that a satisfactory answer to these questions requires a careful examination of the history of the Indonesian military, including its institutional culture and patterns of behavior, and of militia formations, both in East Timor and Indonesia. It also requires a close-grained analysis of the actual patterns of violence in 1999, with a view to understanding both its patterns and variations.

Some clues to these questions may also be found in the wider literature on mass violence and genocide. That literature suggests, among other things, that the nature and relative power of key state institutions—such as the military and police—and the distinctive qualities of those institutions, can have a profound impact on the likelihood and patterns of violence.[24] For example, as human rights organizations have long recognized, where states are dominated by military institutions, the likelihood of mass violence increases dramatically. That pattern stems partly from the fact that in such regimes, the military tends to have broad autonomy and to exist beyond the control of other state institutions. In those circumstances, commanding officers—and other authorities—commonly fail to control or punish unlawful or exceptionally brutal behavior. That failure invariably leads to a climate of impunity, which in turn makes future unlawful violence far more likely to occur. These general patterns are arguably compounded in the context of war, partly because of war's brutalizing effects on soldiers and civilians alike, and partly because it provides both the opportunity and rationale for the use of extreme violence.[25] In such contexts, furthermore, military and police forces—and their proxies—frequently develop distinctive institutional cultures that can make the resort to unlawful violence by their members more likely.

These general arguments square well with the evidence from East Timor, where military dominance of the state after 1965, and a long-standing pattern of impunity, gave rise to what I call a "culture of terror" within the Indonesian army and its affiliated institutions. In addition, during the decades of its dominance, the Indonesian military developed a distinctive approach to handling opposition, which entailed the systematic use of violence and the mobilization of local militia forces as provocateurs and enforcers. All of these tendencies, moreover, were exacerbated by the context of more or less constant war between 1975 and 1999. Given these historical patterns, the extreme brutality of Indonesian forces, the deployment of militias in 1999, and their use of violent methods to achieve the desired result in the referendum made perfect sense.

The literature also suggests that mass violence and genocide are shaped significantly—though not always in obvious ways—by the degree of centralization of power in a given state. There is broad agreement, for example, that genocide is most likely to occur under the aegis of a centralized authoritarian state—as it did in East Timor in the late 1970s.[26] On the other hand, some recent scholarship has suggested that other forms of mass violence—including mass killing, riots, and pogroms—may be more common in newly democratizing or decentralizing states—a fair description of Indonesia in 1999.[27] One explanation for this pattern is that the processes of democratization and decentralization constitute "critical historical junctures," in which the accepted rules of the political game are suddenly open to question and debate. In such circumstances, the leaders and members of different political, ethnic, or religious communities have reason either to worry about losing past prerogatives or hope that they may gain new ones. That in turn creates the conditions in which leaders have both an incentive and an opportunity to mobilize their communities, sometimes through resort to violence. This contention may offer some insight into the violence in East Timor in 1999, which came precisely at the moment when Indonesia's claim to East Timor faced its most serious challenge.

Finally, the wider literature points to the importance of state ideology in fueling genocide and mass violence. While some scholars have sought to portray genocide as a direct and perhaps inevitable by-product of either communist or fascist ideology, most paint a more complex picture. Some have argued, for example, that the critical variable is not the specific content of an ideology, but its utopian or revolutionary quality, and the degree to which state leaders have the will and capacity to carry out their vision. Eric D. Weitz, for instance, has highlighted the significance of a utopian vision and state power in four of the twentieth century's worst genocides.[28] The evidence from East Timor lends some support to that view, but also suggests the need for its refinement.[29] Even though the ideology of Indonesia's New Order evinced a strident anti-Communism and contained a powerful undercurrent of racism, it could hardly be characterized as utopian or revolutionary. Indeed, if any ideology can be said to have driven the genocide in East Timor in the late 1970s and the mass killings of 1999, it was the ideology of an arrogant, bellicose militarism, wrapped in the guise of a benign nationalism and a commitment to economic development.[30]

International Context

Without ignoring the part played by the Indonesian Armed Forces and its militia proxies, some observers have stressed the role of powerful states and international institutions in facilitating the violence in 1999. They have maintained in particular that the violence was made possible by the self-serving policies of the United States, Australia, and other Western governments, which were reluctant to offend the government of Indonesia, and so resisted calls for peacekeepers or armed intervention both before and immediately after the vote.[31] Similarly, a number of commentators have blamed the violence on the incompetence and hubris of the United Nations, noting especially its failure to heed credible predictions that there would be widespread violence after the vote.

There is a good deal of truth in these charges. As discussed in some detail in this book, the weak posture of the United States and other powerful states in 1999 had roots in a long tradition of active international support—on the part of the same governments—for Indonesia's unlawful invasion and occupation of East Timor, and near-total silence in the face of its appalling human rights record. The repeated assurances of U.S. understanding given to President Suharto by President Gerald R. Ford and Secretary of State Henry Kissinger on the eve of the 1975 invasion are only the most obvious in a long pattern of such support.[32] And it is true that the United Nations—or at least its most powerful body, the Security Council—failed to enforce its condemnation of Indonesia's invasion and occupation, and declined to act decisively to stop the violence of 1999 even when presented with compelling evidence that it was being organized by Indonesian authorities, and that worse was likely to come.

Such criticisms are, moreover, broadly consistent with a substantial body of literature that has highlighted the role of powerful states and the

United Nations in facilitating mass violence and genocide.[33] That literature argues, for example, that powerful states have historically contributed to genocide and mass violence not only by providing direct military or economic assistance to those responsible for it but also by remaining silent as the death toll mounts. Scholars assert that such support gives genocidal regimes, and perhaps even individual perpetrators, confidence that they may pursue their campaign without fear of penalty or punishment. In a similar vein, the reports on UN failings in Rwanda in 1994 and Srebrenica in 1995 as well as the Brahimi report on UN peacekeeping operations have made it abundantly clear that there is much room for improvement in the United Nations' handling of major humanitarian and political crises, and that it has often shared responsibility for allowing such violence to happen.[34]

And yet, this simple portrait of national self-interest and UN incompetence cannot easily explain why the most powerful states and the UN Security Council ultimately decided to intervene militarily in East Timor in mid-September 1999 to stop the violence. In that respect, East Timor in 1999 was fundamentally different from East Timor in 1975–79, when forced displacement and genocide were met with silence and inaction on the part of the world's major powers, and the United Nations was rendered powerless to act. It was also different from most other cases of genocide and mass violence in the twentieth century. Such differences require some kind of explanation.

Here again, the wider literature on genocide and mass violence provides some helpful clues. Against the tide of scholarship that has described the apparent inevitability of genocide and mass violence in certain historical conditions, a number of scholars have highlighted the ways in which the choices and acts of individuals and groups did, or might have, mitigated the killing. In his harrowing account of the massacre of sixteen hundred Jews by their Polish neighbors in July 1941, for example, Jan Gross has stressed that the terrible outcome in the town of Jedwabne, and in Europe more widely, was in part the consequence of individual choices: "And thus it is at least conceivable," he observes, "that a number of those actors could have made different choices, with the result that many more European Jews could have survived the war."[35] Other scholars have pointed to the possibility that acts of conscience on the part of a wide range of nonstate actors—including the media, religious groups, and NGOs—might prevent, stop, or at least slow the dynamic of mass violence.[36] Finally, some scholars have drawn attention to the ways in which shifts in international norms and legal regimes might affect the prospects for intervention to stop mass killing and genocide.[37] Whether they focus on the acts of individuals and groups, or on the more amorphous realm of international norms, these approaches all stress the essentially contingent quality of genocide and mass violence, and thus reject any notion that they are inevitable or unstoppable.

A careful reconstruction of the decisions and events of mid-September 1999, against the background of this literature, suggests that the intervention was the result of an unusual conjuncture of historical trends and events that distinguished that moment decisively from the situation in the late 1970s. These included: the presence of a good many foreign observers and journalists in the midst of the postballot violence; the credibility and strength of the international NGO and church networks that exerted influence on their governments, and mobilized popular demonstrations around the world, most notably in Canberra and Lisbon; the impact of myriad acts of conscience and extraordinary courage by East Timorese; a temporary shift in prevailing international norms and legal regimes that strongly favored humanitarian intervention in cases where national governments commit crimes against their own populations; the presence in a position of power of a strong proponent of humanitarian intervention in such circumstances—UN Secretary-General Kofi Annan; and the recent memory of egregious UN failures to protect civilians from mass killing in comparable situations, notably in Rwanda and Srebrenica.

What I am suggesting, then, is that the decision to intervene militarily in East Timor in mid-September 1999 stemmed from an unusual, but temporary, confluence of historical trends and political pressures that briefly altered the calculus by which key states assessed their national interest, making inaction more costly than humanitarian intervention. That view accords well with Samantha Power's argument about the reasons for U.S. inaction in the face of genocide in the twentieth century. U.S. failure, she argues, can be traced to the fact that there have been no significant domestic political costs to such inaction.[38] It follows that where, as in East Timor, there was some clear domestic political cost for inaction, one should expect to see a change in that posture of indifference.

Paradoxically, the historical conjuncture of September 1999 may also offer the best explanation of the curious ambivalence of the international community with respect to the question of justice for East Timor. Within a few months of the international intervention—and by some accounts, within a matter of weeks—the unique combination of forces and trends that had made it possible had largely dissipated, allowing major powers to return to a more conventional calculus of their national interests. As far as powerful countries like the United States were concerned, that meant a return to strong ties with Indonesia, especially its military, and away from any policy or action that would offend them. That logic was further reinforced after the attacks of September 11, 2001, and the U.S. declaration that Indonesia was an essential ally in the "war on terror." The U.S. shift, in turn, destroyed any chance of a consensus on the Security Council, and rendered moot the possibility of an international criminal tribunal for East Timor for at least the next decade.

These, then, are the main contours of the story and the argument that I hope to convey in this book. In its simplest form, my contention here is that the violence of 1999 in East Timor was neither spontaneous, nor conditioned primarily by psychological urges, ancient hatreds, or cultural predispositions or traditions, as Indonesian authorities have claimed. Nor do I find much support for the idea that it stemmed from long-standing ethnic, religious, or socioeconomic conflicts among East Timorese, or between them and Indonesians. Rather, I maintain that the violence was shaped by the long history of Portuguese and Indonesian rule that served to structure political identities and tensions; by the decision of those in positions of power in Indonesia and East Timor to deploy violence for strategic ends; by the violent institutional culture of the Indonesian army and its militia proxies; and by the complicity or acquiescence of powerful states both in the genocide of 1975–79 and in the subsequent occupation. In seeking to explain the unexpected intervention that brought the violence to an end in September 1999, and the subsequent failure to make good on the promise to bring the perpetrators to account, I draw particular attention to shifts in international context and norms over the final decades of the twentieth century, to many individual acts of conscience and courage inside East Timor and abroad, and more generally to a unique and unpredictable concatenation of historical events and trends in late 1999 that distinguished that moment from all that came before and all that followed.

CHAPTER TWO

COLONIAL LEGACIES

TIMOR HAS LONG HAD A REPUTATION among foreign observers as a place of endemic violence. From the time of their earliest encounters, Portuguese officials described the Timorese as "warlike" and cataloged their frequent battles and methods of warfare.[1] Drawing on early Portuguese impressions, in 1869 the naturalist Alfred Russel Wallace wrote that Timorese "fight continually among themselves, and take every opportunity of kidnapping unprotected people of other tribes for slaves."[2] A century later, the colonial historian C. R. Boxer commented that "there seems to have been something about the atmosphere of Timor which was conducive to violence . . . for sudden death was the order of the day amongst its unruly inhabitants."[3] And as we have seen, Indonesian authorities claimed that the postballot violence in 1999 was the result of age-old divisions among Timorese and an ostensibly timeless cultural pattern of running amok.

There is certainly no denying that violence has a long history in East Timor. There are, moreover, some striking similarities between the patterns of violence in 1999 and those of earlier centuries. The weapons used by Timorese warriors from the seventeenth century onward, and their methods in battle, appear to foreshadow those used by the modern militias. Timorese fighters typically carried swords (*catana*), spears (*assegai*), rocks, and flintlock guns, almost exactly the same array of weapons used in 1999.[4] Likewise, the practice of head taking and display, a common feature of battle and customary law as early as the eighteenth century, reappeared as a militia tactic in modern times. A Dutch account of a battle in 1749 describes, for example, how the Timorese allies of the Dutch "carried off in triumph approximately a thousand heads and at least as many again in the course of the next two days."[5] Accounts from the seventeenth through to the early twentieth century also indicate that Timorese preferred the apparently frenzied, amok style of attack employed with such frightening effect by East Timor's modern militias. In a passage that might have been a description of the events of September 1999, a Portuguese army captain wrote of a battle in 1896: "It was a vision of hell with cries of anguish mixed with the shouts of the victors against the backdrop of burning bamboo. . . . In the morning the central square was strewn with more than one hundred bodies, stripped, decapitated and horribly mutilated."[6] Such antecedents and models of violence—or the rekindled memory of them—may well have influenced the character and behavior of the militias of 1999.

Yet there is reason to doubt that the late twentieth-century conflict in East Timor was rooted in a natural propensity toward violence among its people. A closer look at the history of violence on the island reveals that the similarities between the old and new forms do not reflect a simple, uninterrupted continuation of an immutable Timorese tradition. On the contrary, it makes clear that the very existence of the local militias as well as their weaponry and behavior were shaped by the presence, and indeed the sponsorship, of Portuguese, Dutch, and other foreign powers. More broadly, that history reveals that the political conflict and violence of the late twentieth century had their origins in the unique patterns of Portuguese colonial policy and practice in the territory, and the distinctive cultural and political forms that emerged in that context. The violence was also a consequence of the disgraceful meddling in the process of decolonization by Indonesian military authorities and their international supporters in the years before the 1975 invasion.

The Portuguese Legacy

The deepest roots of the conflict between East Timor and Indonesia, and the violence that attended it, arguably lie in the history of European expansion in Southeast Asia from the sixteenth through the twentieth century. Portuguese missionary and trade efforts, and later colonial control, stimulated changes in cultural patterns and administrative practices among the peoples of the territory, and these changes much later formed the basis for a distinctive national consciousness.[7] The division of the island of Timor into two separate colonial entities, Portuguese and Dutch, from the eighteenth century also gave geographic expression to the national identities that emerged in each. Thus, when the Netherlands East

Indies became the independent state of Indonesia in 1949, the western half of Timor became Indonesian territory, while the eastern half of the island, plus the enclave Oecussi, remained a colony of Portugal. As in most instances of anticolonial nationalism, East Timor's nationalists accepted without question the political boundaries created by the colonial power. The same artifact of colonial bargaining formed the territorial basis of what Indonesian authorities called the province of East Timor, and later of the independent state of Timor-Leste.

Despite its importance in shaping the geographic parameters of a later East Timorese political identity, the Portuguese presence in the eastern half of Timor was relatively unobtrusive, culturally and politically, at least until the twentieth century. Portuguese colonial administration of the eastern half of the island did not begin until 1769, when the capital was moved hastily to Dili in the face of constant rebel attacks at Lifao.[8] Even then, with only a tiny contingent of soldiers and officials through much of the eighteenth and nineteenth centuries, Portuguese authority was hardly overwhelming, and relied to a great extent on a network of informal alliances with friendly chiefs or liurai.[9] Indeed, Portugal did not manage to "pacify" the half island until 1913, when with the assistance of some loyal chiefs and an infusion of troops from Mozambique, it managed finally to put down a rebellion that had simmered for almost two decades.[10]

In contrast to the vigorous policies of colonial state formation undertaken in neighboring colonies by the Dutch, the French, and the British in the late nineteenth and early twentieth centuries, the Portuguese never extended their administrative reach far beyond the capital Dili.[11] Having been governed jointly with Macau since 1844 the territory was made a separate colony in 1896, but by 1928 there were still only two hundred Portuguese civilians and three hundred soldiers living there.[12] Relatively weak militarily, and no longer the major trading power that it had been in the sixteenth and seventeenth centuries, Portugal also devoted little energy and capital to the economic development of its distant colony. Following a visit to the island in 1861, Wallace wrote, with only slight exaggeration, that

> Delli is a most miserable place compared with even the poorest of the Dutch towns.... The whole aspect of it is of a poor native town, and there is no sign of cultivation or civilization round about it.... Nobody seems to care the least about the improvement of

FIGURE 2.1. Three men on a mountain pass in East Timor, 1974. Although the Portuguese presence in East Timor dated from the early sixteenth century, colonial political and cultural influence was relatively unobtrusive, especially in the remote, highland areas outside the capital Dili. By contrast, Indonesia's occupation of 1975–99 entailed aggressive military campaigns that disrupted social, cultural, and economic life throughout the territory. (Elaine Brière)

> the country, and at this time, after three hundred years of occupation, there has not been a mile of road made beyond the town, and there is not a solitary European anywhere in the interior.[13]

The simple truth was that Portuguese Timor was a colonial backwater of little economic value, useful primarily as a place to which undesirable elements could be deported.

The late nineteenth and early twentieth centuries saw some modest changes in the direction of "progress," with the opening of coffee plantations in the more fertile western regions of the colony, the establishment of a rudimentary administrative presence in the interior, and the opening of a few dozen schools and medical posts.[14] However, the Japanese invasion in February 1942 and the fierce battles with Allied troops that followed destroyed what little had been created, and left between forty thousand and sixty thousand Timorese dead.[15] On their return to the island after the war, a nearly bankrupt and understaffed Portuguese administration faced a monumental task of reconstruction.[16] Despite some efforts by Portuguese authorities, such as the building of new primary schools and the provision of clean water to some villages, by 1975 they had scarcely made a dent in that huge task. As Indonesian officials were later fond of noting, during the whole period of Portuguese rule in Timor, the colonial authorities had built only 12.5 miles of paved road, opened only 50 schools, and left behind a population that was still 80 percent illiterate.[17] Political developments were equally slow in coming. The territory was declared an "overseas province" of Portugal in 1951, and in 1972 it became an "autonomous region of the Portuguese Republic," but for all practical purposes it was governed from Lisbon and remained "a backwater of Portugal's colonial empire."[18]

One consequence of the "lightness" of Portuguese rule in Timor was the relatively late development there of the anticolonial nationalist consciousness that accompanied the newly invasive style of colonial rule elsewhere in the region.[19] While East Timor had its share of rebellions and uprisings in the late nineteenth and early twentieth centuries—including the serious anti-Portuguese rebellion crushed in 1913, and a less serious uprising in 1959—it is not possible to speak in any meaningful sense of a nationalist movement there before the early 1970s. This relatively late development helps to explain the odd durability of Portuguese rule in the immediate postwar years, when much stronger colonial powers were systematically swept away by popularly based nationalist movements and guerrilla forces.

Yet if Portuguese rule was, by some measures, less intrusive than that of other colonial powers in the region, it would be wrong to suggest that nothing changed as a result of the long colonial presence. For one thing, the authoritarian Portuguese colonial administration introduced new methods and institutions of warfare and policing, thereby providing many Timorese with military and paramilitary training, and laying the groundwork for the security forces that began to emerge alongside the new political parties in 1974–75 and the militias that flourished under Indonesian rule. Timorese experience with colonial security forces took various forms. Some local men joined the Portuguese colonial army (Tropas) as volunteers, while others were conscripted. Until the final years of Portuguese rule, all Timorese men were required to do thirty days of military service. By the early 1970s, at least two thousand Timorese were serving as soldiers in the regular colonial army. Most of those were deployed in Timor, where they served alongside a smaller number of Portuguese and African soldiers maintaining security on behalf of the colonial authorities; others were deployed to distant parts of the empire, notably to Angola and Mozambique, where they assisted in putting down anticolonial rebellions. As the Portuguese military began to abandon its colonial mission in 1974, the size of the European component of the army in Timor was dramatically reduced, leaving a force comprised overwhelmingly of local soldiers.[20] In mid-1975, as Portuguese authority unraveled, a great many of these soldiers deserted and lent their services to one or another of the new political parties.

Many local people also had experience with the PIDE (Polícia Internacional e de Defesa do Estado, or International and State Defense Police), the formidable Portuguese secret police.[21] While relatively few Timorese actually served with the PIDE, except perhaps as informers, most knew of its existence and its fearsome reputation. Indeed, more than the colonial army, for most of the twentieth century it was the PIDE that kept a lid on political dissent and ensured that political activity remained virtually invisible, at least until 1974. Like secret police forces in other colonies, the PIDE was not averse to using harsh methods, including torture and intimidation, to achieve its objectives. As one Timorese woman who later joined the resistance recounted in 1999: "We knew, or at least my parents knew, that if we discussed politics that could be dangerous. [My parents] were afraid that if they spoke of such things, the children would talk about them outside and they themselves would come under the surveillance of the PIDE."[22] That lesson might well have influenced the methods adopted by the new political parties, and their security forces, in dealing with enemies and internal dissent after 1975. It also meant that Timorese had ample experience in serving as police informers—known as *Bufos* or snitches—long before Indonesian intelligence officers arrived on the scene.

Perhaps most important for understanding the later history of violence, many thousands of Timorese served in Portuguese auxiliary or militia forces. Known as *moradores* and *arraias*, these "second-line" troops were mobilized by Portuguese authorities to provide security for the colonial community and to suppress opposition.[23] In 1912–13, for example, the Portuguese successfully crushed the most serious rebellion of the colonial period—led by the liurai of Manufahi—by enlisting the forces of several other liurai who had sworn vassalage to the government.[24] This was only the best-known instance of a more general pattern in which liurai were induced or compelled to support the Portuguese, and were then employed to raise troops to fight against others less loyal.[25] The Portuguese authorities were still employing that strategy at the outbreak of the Second World War. Australian soldiers who were there in 1942 gave the following description of the Portuguese response to an uprising: "Their army was collected; it consisted of two companies. . . . The troops were Timorese, and the non-commissioned officers and officers were Portuguese. . . . At the same time the natives in the surrounding areas were ordered to arm themselves and prepare for war."[26] The end of the war did not bring an end to the Portuguese practice of mobilizing local auxiliaries. Despite changes in colonial policy in the 1950s and 1960s, the authorities were careful to maintain native forces under the command of loyal liurai.[27]

The political and military logic behind the Portuguese reliance on indigenous troops is worth spelling out briefly. First, the norms that shaped colonial policy in Timor were basically those of military officers that prevailed throughout Portugal's colonial domains, and these called, as in many colonies, for the use of native forces in maintaining security and order.[28] Second, like most nonsettler colonial powers, Portugal simply did not have the financial or human resources to field a full army of European (or African) troops. In the late nineteenth century, in fact, the government could seldom afford to deploy more than two hundred regular soldiers in Timor, and even these were frequently of a poor quality.[29] In 1910, even as Portugal conducted pacification campaigns in its various colonies, there were only some thirteen thousand soldiers in the entire colonial army, and of these fewer than four thousand were Europeans.[30] Third, local troops invariably knew the terrain, and tolerated the climate, food, and diseases better than any foreign troops could. And finally, the policy of mobilizing some Timorese against others served a useful—if not always intended—political purpose of minimizing the likelihood of concerted anti-Portuguese action.[31] For similar reasons the Japanese forces that occupied the territory from 1942 to 1945 also relied on local auxiliaries, using the followers of "loyal" liurai against those of disloyal ones. So too did the Australian commandos that fought the Japanese in Timor during the war.[32]

To sum up, there would appear to be some basis for the claim that the militias that emerged in East Timor in 1999 reflected, or were drawing on, uniquely Timorese historical models and traditions. The evidence that Timor's militias were consciously cultivated and used by a succession of outside powers over three centuries suggests, however, that the parallels constituted something more than a simple transmission of an unchanging tradition. Without the encouragement of those foreign state

FIGURE 2.2. Easter Sunday, Baucau. Introduced by Portuguese missionaries in the sixteenth century, by the 1970s Catholicism had become a cultural focal point for East Timorese of all political persuasions. The influence of the church grew markedly after the invasion of 1975, as local priests and nuns protected the population from Indonesian attacks, and defended their cultural and political rights. Viewed by Indonesian authorities as a center of support for independence, the church was targeted by prointegration forces in 1999, and several Catholic priests and nuns were killed. (Elaine Brière)

authorities—which were in turn driven by a common political logic of scarce resources, a need for local knowledge, and the dominance of military norms—it seems doubtful that the modern militias would have existed or would have adopted the traditions that they did.

Portuguese influence brought important changes in the religious sphere as well, notably through the introduction of the Catholic faith to a population that was predominantly animist.[33] It is true that no more than one-third of the population officially converted to Catholicism under Portuguese rule.[34] Yet by 1975, the church had nevertheless become so sufficiently embedded in popular consciousness and cultural practice that it was a spiritual and symbolic focal point not only for those who favored continued ties to Portugal, but also for those demanding immediate independence. One reason for that pattern was that throughout the colonial period, the Catholic Church had been the primary provider of education to Timorese.[35] As a consequence, most of

Timor's early political leaders—both nationalist and loyalist—had been educated in Catholic schools or Jesuit seminaries, particularly at the Catholic school in Soibada, a stronghold of conservative Catholic values and Portuguese culture, and at the more liberal seminary in Dare in the hills south of Dili.[36]

Finally, the Portuguese presence gave rise to a new and distinctively colonial pattern of social relations—most notably in the formation of a small, largely mestizo, cultural elite. A significant degree of intermarriage among different "racial" groups had long been a feature of colonial life in Timor—a subject much commented on by late nineteenth-century observers.[37] According to official census data, however, the number of mestizos grew substantially through the twentieth century, with 375 in 1927, 689 in 1936, and 2,022 in 1950.[38] These were most often the children of Portuguese fathers—some of them *deportados*—and indigenous mothers. Over time these elites, and to some extent the small group of "civilized" natives who lived in the towns, became absorbed in or saw themselves as part of a broader Portuguese cultural world. Educated according to Portuguese standards, speaking Portuguese from an early age, and reading Portuguese history and literature, their ties were not with their immediate neighbors in Southeast Asia—nor even with the vast majority of Timorese—but with others of a similar status within the Lusophone world. Even as the empire began to crumble, they listened to the great Portuguese fado artist Amalia Rodriguez, Brazilian singers like Roberto Carlos, and "the mournful music of Mindelo." They played on soccer teams with names like Benfica and Sporting, and waited eagerly for the latest scores from Portugal.[39] And when they had the chance to study or work abroad, it was invariably to Lisbon, Macau, Luanda, or Maputo that they went.

Decolonization and Civil War

As in many other colonial settings, members of this elite mestizo group were among the first nationalists in East Timor, and joined the early core of political leaders demanding independence from Portugal in some form. But that process was not automatic. A critical impetus to change came in late April 1974 when Portugal's authoritarian Caetano regime was overthrown in a bloodless officer's coup dubbed the "Carnation Revolution." Among other changes, the new regime set about to relinquish control of the colonies. As part of that process, it permitted the formation of new political parties in East Timor, ending the decades-long monopoly of the ruling ANP (Associação Nacional Popular, or Portuguese National Union).[40] Those new parties formed the ideological and institutional framework for much of the conflict and violence that followed.

An influential strain of thought among the small cultural elite was the view that Portuguese Timor should seek independence, but only after a period of transition under Portuguese tutelage. These were the guiding principles of the UDT, which was founded on May 11, 1974. The UDT leaders tended to be drawn from the wealthier landowning families and employees in the higher echelons of the colonial civil service as well as some liurai and Chinese who had done well under Portuguese rule. Geographically speaking, the UDT's support was strongest in the agriculturally rich, coffee-growing areas of Ermera, Maliana, and Maubara, in the western part of the territory, near the Indonesian border.[41]

Among the more prominent UDT leaders were the Carrascalão brothers (Manuel, Mário, and João), whose father was a rehabilitated deportado who had married a Timorese woman and had become a prosperous coffee planter. Two of the three brothers, Mário and João, had received a higher education, and in 1975 held important positions in the colonial bureaucracy. Mário, a founding member of the UDT, had studied in Portugal, had been active in the ruling ANP, and in 1975 was chief of the Agriculture and Forestry Department.[42] He later served in the Indonesian Foreign Ministry (1977–82), and then as governor of East Timor (1982–92) under Indonesian rule, before eventually becoming a moderate advocate of independence.[43] Another key figure in the UDT was Francisco Lopes da Cruz, who had attended the Catholic school in Soibada, and had studied theology and philosophy in Macao, before joining the colonial army, with which he fought in Mozambique. Returning to Timor "with a reputation as a fighter of terrorists," he became director of East Timor's only newspaper, *A Voz de Timor*, and in 1975 held a respectable position in the colonial Ministry of Customs and Excise.[44] A vehement critic of Fretilin, he became a strong advocate of Indonesian rule and served as deputy governor for several years (1976–82). He subsequently joined the Indonesian Foreign Ministry, and in 1999 served as Indonesia's roving ambassador for East Timor. In a slightly different mold was João Tavares, a wealthy landowner who served as bupati of the border district of Bobonaro for more than a decade (1976-89). In 1999 he was appointed overall commander of the PPI (Pasukan Pejuang

Integrasi, or Integration Fighters Force), the pro–Indonesian militia forces responsible for the widespread violence and intimidation before and after the referendum.

A more radical political viewpoint was expressed by a small group of mostly younger, educated Timorese, some of whom had studied or worked abroad in the 1960s and early 1970s. Strongly influenced by the rise of the Left in Portugal, on May 20, 1974, they established the ASDT (Associação Social Democrática Timorense, or Timorese Social Democratic Association), which advocated immediate independence.[45] The party drew its early support from students, teachers, and low-ranking civil servants, but soon expanded its base to include a substantial majority of the country's overwhelmingly rural population. Reflecting the influence of the national liberation movements then flourishing in Africa—notably Frelimo in Mozambique and PAIGC in Cape Verde and Guinea-Bissau—in mid-September 1974 the ASDT changed its name to Fretilin.[46] While some party leaders, particularly those who returned from Lisbon in late 1974, adopted an avowedly leftist posture and borrowed freely from the lexicon of other liberation movements, Fretilin was primarily a nationalist party, seeking not revolution but independence.[47] A pamphlet outlining the Fretilin platform in late 1974 stated its position plainly: "At the moment, East Timor is a colony and as a colony the immediate and only objective is the struggle for national independence and liberation of the people."[48]

Exemplifying this nationalist current was one of the party's founders and early leaders, Ramos-Horta. The son of a deportado father and Timorese mother, he attended the Catholic school in Soibada and the elite secondary school in Dili. In the early 1970s, he was exiled to Mozambique for his anticolonial writings and activities, but used his time to learn and write about the liberation movement there and in Angola. On his return to Timor in 1974 he helped to establish the new party. After a brief stint as foreign minister in Fretilin's provisional government, established in September 1975, he left the country and thereafter served as the international representative of the resistance for more than twenty years. In 1996, together with East Timor's Bishop Belo, he was awarded the Nobel Prize for Peace. Two other founding members of note were Nicolau Lobato and Francisco Xavier do Amaral, the party's first president. Both men were respected intellectuals, but do Amaral was also "immensely popular, an orator who knew how to move crowds."[49]

Another leading Fretilin figure, though not one of its founders, was

José Alexandre (Kay Rala Xanana) Gusmão.[50] Educated at the Jesuit seminary in Dare, Gusmão had a reputation as a poet rather than a revolutionary.[51] By his own admission, he hesitated before joining Fretilin, but after he did so he emerged quickly as a leading figure, serving as a member of the party's Central Committee, a commander of its armed wing, Falintil (Forças Armada de Libertação de Timor-Leste, or Armed Forces for the Liberation of East Timor), and after 1981 overall commander of both the political and military wings of the resistance. Captured by Indonesian forces in 1992, and subsequently sentenced to life in prison for subversion, he remained as leader of the resistance and earned a reputation as the "Nelson Mandela" of East Timor. Following his release in September 1999, he returned to East Timor, and in 2002 was elected president of independent Timor-Leste.

The third, and by far the smallest political party of any significance, was Apodeti, founded on May 27, 1974.[52] If the UDT leaders preferred, at least initially, to maintain cultural and political ties with Portugal, Apodeti took the view that East Timor would be better off becoming a province of Indonesia. The party was openly supported by Indonesian authorities, and its leaders received funds from Indonesian sources.[53] The party's leaders, like those of the UDT, tended to be wealthy landowners and disgruntled members of the local social elite. For example, one of the party's founding figures was Arnaldo dos Reis Araújo, who had been imprisoned by the Portuguese for twenty-nine years for his admitted collaboration with the Japanese during the Second World War.[54] Following the 1975 invasion, he was appointed governor of the provisional government of East Timor. Another leading figure in the party, José Osório Soares, was likewise angry with the Portuguese for sending his uncle into exile in Angola.[55] He was killed by Fretilin forces in early 1976, but other members of his family followed in his footsteps and became staunch supporters of Indonesian rule. The most important among them was his brother, Abílio Osório Soares, who was appointed governor of East Timor in 1992—a position he still held in 1999.[56] The party's leadership also included a number of liurai from the western border areas. Among the most prominent of these was the liurai of Atsabe, Guilherme Maria Gonçalves, and his son, Tomás Gonçalves. Gonçalves the elder was a coffee planter and reputed to be one of the wealthiest chiefs in Portuguese Timor.[57]

We know something about the relative popularity of these three parties from the scattered elections for liurai that were held in early 1975 as part of Portuguese decolonization plans. Although the conditions under which the elections were held made a precise count impossible, it appeared that a substantial majority had favored Fretilin, with the UDT coming in second, and Apodeti a distant third.[58] Fretilin's popularity has been attributed to the fact that it developed, and by late 1974 had begun to implement, serious social and economic programs in the country's rural areas, where most of the population lived. Among others, its campaign to eradicate illiteracy, based on the teachings of Paulo Freire, and programs to improve health care and food production in rural areas have been cited as reasons for its greater appeal with ordinary voters.[59] By contrast, while it had benefited from early logistical support from Portuguese authorities, and its association with symbols of Portuguese rule—like the flag, which some Timorese considered sacred—the UDT had relied heavily on conventional patron-client networks, without making any serious effort to assist or mobilize the population.[60] The result was that by mid-1975, it had lost a great deal of its early support among the population.

Whatever they may have demonstrated about popular preferences, however, the elections did not end the struggle for political dominance between the proindependence Fretilin and the more conservative UDT. Indeed, the tension between the two parties grew. A tenuous coalition, hammered out in January 1975 by moderates in both parties, fell apart in late May as conservative elements in the UDT sought to distance the party from Fretilin, and began to collaborate instead with Apodeti and Indonesia.[61] The split was exacerbated in June, when Fretilin decided to boycott all-party talks in Macau that had been intended to work out a formula for decolonization. Then, in mid-August, the tension degenerated into armed conflict, which has been described as a civil war. The violence, which left an estimated two thousand people dead, was triggered by a UDT attempt to seize power in Dili on August 11.[62]

Responding to the coup attempt, Fretilin mobilized its forces into an armed wing called Falintil and attacked UDT positions. The Portuguese governor, Colonel Lemos Pires, having ordered his troops not to take sides in the fighting, then fled with a small group of officials to the island of Ataúro, some ten miles off the coast. By early September 1975, Fretilin had regained control of Dili and consolidated its position in the rest of the country. With the Portuguese authorities still on Ataúro, in mid-September Fretilin announced the formation of a provisional government, which aimed to govern the territory while awaiting formal decolonization. In the face of Fretilin's superiority, key UDT and Apodeti leaders, together with several hundred of their immediate followers, fled to the western districts of Liquiçá and Bobonaro, and then across the border into Indonesia. There, egged on by Indonesian military operatives, the UDT and Apodeti began to make common cause, denouncing Fretilin as Communist and calling for integration with Indonesia.[63]

Indonesian authorities were quick to portray the 1975 civil war and its aftermath as proof that East Timorese were not ready for independence, but it is clear that the war was fueled as much by the actions of outside parties, especially Indonesia, as by any lack of political maturity on the part of Timorese. While maintaining a public pretense of noninterference in East Timor's internal affairs, Indonesian military authorities had begun as early as September 1974 to mount a covert operation designed to bring about East Timor's eventual integration with Indonesia.[64] Code-named Operasi Komodo, the campaign was spearheaded by General Yoga Sugama, head of BAKIN (Badan Koordinasi Intelijen Negara, or State Intelligence Coordinating Agency), and his deputy, General Ali Murtopo.[65] Murtopo also served at the time as the informal chief of OPSUS (Operasi Khusus, or Special Operations), a unit tasked with conducting covert operations on presidential order.[66] A key role was also played by Liem Bian Kie (aka Jusuf Wanandi), the head of Indonesia's Center for Strategic International Studies, an ostensibly civilian think tank with close ties to the military. Borrowing from a wide repertoire of intelligence and psychological warfare techniques that had proven effective in other theaters, the campaign began with the gathering of political intelligence inside Timor and with "soft" efforts to encourage support for integration with Indonesia. Initiatives included the formation and bankrolling of Apodeti, and the dissemination of anti-Fretilin propaganda through radio broadcasts and print media.[67] The propaganda campaign relied heavily on the demonstrably false claims that Fretilin was a Communist party, and that it was receiving military backing and advice from China and Vietnam.[68]

In January 1975, Operasi Komodo was expanded to include a more aggressive dissemination of pro-Indonesian and anti-Fretilin propaganda.[69] The campaign was intended, in part, to drive a wedge between Fretilin and the UDT, whose new coalition was seen as disrupting Indonesian plans for integration.[70] As part of the same effort, the UDT and Apodeti leaders were invited to Jakarta to speak with high-ranking Indonesian military officials, who warned them of Fretilin's Communist tendencies, and promised them Indonesian political and military support.[71] After one such visit, in April 1975, the UDT leaders announced that they would work with Apodeti against Fretilin.[72] During another meeting in early August 1975, Murtopo reportedly warned the UDT leaders that Fretilin was planning to stage a coup in mid-August, and urged them to take preemptive action before it was too late. The UDT's own coup was launched just a few days later.[73]

With the collapse of the UDT coup and the sudden emergence of Fretilin as the dominant political force in East Timor, Indonesian military authorities looked for new ways to achieve their goal of integration. Their solution was a campaign of covert military operations inside East Timor, which began in earnest in late August 1975. The fact that Kopassandha units had already been trained and deployed to West Timor for the purpose made that solution possible.[74] The initiative had come from the powerful General Benjamin (Benny) Murdani, the recently appointed assistant for intelligence in the Department of Defense and Security.[75] With the ear of the president and help from his Kopassandha colleagues, in early 1975 Murdani had quietly set in motion a second covert operation, code-named Operasi Flamboyan.[76] In contrast to the soft approach of Operasi Komodo, Murdani's operation focused on paramilitary training and combat, and relied on Kopassandha forces with expertise in special warfare. Mobilization and training for the operation began in March 1975, and by April the first of several Kopassandha combat units had been deployed to Atambua, on the Indonesian side of the border. Their initial mission was to arm and provide paramilitary training to some four hundred Apodeti recruits who had been gathered there.[77] With the defeat in August of the UDT forces, the mission was expanded, and in September Kopassandha units commenced the first of many covert military operations inside East Timor.[78] The most notorious of those raids concentrated on the town of Balibo, where Falintil had established an encampment. In the course of the fighting, on October 16, 1975, five foreign journalists who had gone to the area to investigate rumors of Indonesian incursions were killed, and their bodies burned by Indonesian forces.[79]

The purpose of these military operations was to establish forward guerrilla bases, carry out acts of sabotage, attack Fretilin forces, spread propaganda, and perhaps most important, create the impression that the attacks were being conducted by UDT and Apodeti "partisans."[80] To that end, the Kopassandha troops involved grew their hair long, donned blue jeans and T-shirts, and carried AK–47s and Yugoslavian rocket launchers. Apart from its propaganda value, the ruse was intended "to give Jakarta plausible deniability and to avoid any protests from the U.S. for using American weapons."[81] In Jakarta, civilian and military authorities flatly denied that Indonesian forces were operating inside East Timor, falsely claiming that reported attacks on Fretilin were the work of UDT and Apodeti fighters.[82]

In many respects, then, these operations foreshadowed the methods used by anti-independence forces in 1999: they were covert military operations, designed to disguise Indonesian involvement and create the impression that East Timorese were fighting among themselves. It is also noteworthy that some of the key figures involved in these events appeared again as pivotal figures in 1999. They included, for example, Yunus Yosfiah, the Kopassandha company commander who is said to have ordered the killing of the five journalists at Balibo in October 1975. In 1999, after a long military career, Yosfiah was Jakarta's minister of information and reportedly played a central role in arranging funding for the pro-Indonesian militias.[83]

If the UDT and Apodeti were egged on to violence by Indonesian military authorities, Fretilin was emboldened to use force by the disintegration of the Portuguese colonial army in mid-1975 and by the inaction of colonial authorities in the face of the UDT coup. The crucial turning point came less than two weeks into the civil war. On August 19–20, 1975, Fretilin forces seized the colonial army headquarters and weapons depot in Dili, and called on Timorese army members to join them, which most did.[84] In addition to securing some two thousand trained soldiers, in this way Fretilin also gained control of a full arsenal of Portuguese weapons and equipment, including G–3 rifles, some artillery pieces, and Mercedes Unimog vehicles.

More generally, the ambivalence of Portuguese authorities in the face of the dramatic political changes in Dili in mid-1975 created conditions that encouraged both sides to resort to force, and provided Indonesia with an ideal pretext for intervention. Most notably, Governor Pires's withdrawal to Ataúro in late August 1975 allowed Indonesia to claim that Portugal had failed in its responsibility to arrange an orderly decolonization process.[85] In the face of mounting criticism of its own role in East Timor many years later, Indonesia again drew attention to Portugal's alleged irresponsibility: "What is described as a 'process of decolonization' by Portugal," an official pamphlet declared, "deserves rather to be termed a record of failure and ineptitude. In August 1975, the colonial authorities in Dili, in a most irresponsible manner, simply packed up and left East Timor, after allowing the situation in the territory to deteriorate to the point of civil war."[86]

Finally, and crucially, the permissive posture adopted by a number of powerful states contributed to both the civil war and the ensuing conflict by giving Indonesia reason to believe that its unlawful intervention would bear no serious political or economic cost.[87] As a number of authors have shown, both the United Kingdom and Australia knew of Indonesian intentions, Operasi Komodo, and the cross-border paramilitary operations, but did nothing to stop them.[88] In fact, in a meeting with President Suharto in early September 1974, Australian prime minister Gough Whitlam reportedly expressed the view that "an independent Timor would be an unviable state and a potential threat to the area," and that Australia would have no objection if Timor chose to integrate with Indonesia.[89] While subsequent government statements sought to address public concern in Australia about an Indonesian takeover, noting that the Timorese would need to be consulted on the matter, Australia's preference for integration with Indonesia as opposed to independence remained unchanged. Speaking in parliament in late August 1975, as the civil war raged, Whitlam rejected a suggestion that Australia should convene a meeting of the warring parties and foreshadowed what would soon become Indonesia's rationale for armed intervention: "We, for our part, understand Indonesia's concern that the territory should not be allowed to become a source of instability on Indonesia's border."[90]

Some of the clearest evidence of Australia's craven support for Indonesia, however, came in its response to the killing of the five Western journalists at Balibo in mid-October. Through their monitoring of Indonesian military radio traffic, Australian intelligence authorities knew almost immediately what had happened and that the attack had been carried out by Kopassandha troops. Nevertheless, far from criticizing Indonesia or demanding a proper investigation of the killings, Australia sought to deflect attention from the available evidence, publicly accepting the false Indonesian claim that the "Balibo Five" had been caught in the crossfire during a battle between Fretilin and UDT forces.[91] In that dishonest posture, the Australian authorities were joined by virtually all of their major allies. The British authorities in particular sought deliberately to silence discussion and debate on the matter.[92]

The United States also knew about Indonesia's real intentions with respect to East Timor, but expressed no disapproval or concern, even when such a message could have prevented Indonesian military intervention.[93] At a meeting at Camp David in July 1975, for instance, U.S. president Ford said nothing when President Suharto described the supporters of independence as "Communist-influenced" and told him that the only viable option for East Timor was integration with Indonesia.[94] That acquiescent silence came at a time when Suharto was personally ambivalent about taking military action in East Timor. As the Central Intelligence Agency reported in mid-1975, and as Ford and his advisers certainly knew, Suharto was then still "concerned about the impact on Indonesia's bilateral relations with Australia and the United States. In both cases, he is worried about the loss of military assistance, which he badly wants to improve Indonesia's outdated equipment."[95] Under the circumstances, a word of caution from Ford might easily have tipped the balance against invasion in Suharto's mind. Ford's silence instead gave Suharto precisely the reassurance he needed that a move against East Timor would not disrupt relations with the United States. Little wonder, then, that just a few weeks later, in early August 1975, Indonesian military authorities stepped up their involvement to the point of fomenting the UDT coup attempt. Little wonder, too, that when that coup failed, Indonesian military authorities launched a campaign of covert military action designed to create a pretext for intervention.[96]

Although it was fueled by outside parties and events, and lasted a mere three weeks, the civil war of August 1975 left a powerful legacy of distrust among East Timorese, and hardened political loyalties and enmities that had until then appeared somewhat malleable.[97] Reflecting on the speed with which such enmity had arisen, Ramos-Horta later wrote: "I was discouraged at how we had turned against each other overnight, we who had been friends, neighbors, and relatives, just yesterday."[98] In that way, the civil war of 1975 helped to create and solidify precisely the kinds of divisions that Indonesia sought to use as a justification for its intervention, and that contributed to much of the violence of the next twenty-four years. The significance of the 1975 civil war became clear in 1999 as key figures from the 1975 conflict once again lined up on opposite sides of the issue of independence,[99] and locales that had been the center of tensions in 1975—places like Maliana, Batugede, Atsabe, and Maubara—reemerged as key battlegrounds. The importance of the civil war also surfaced after independence when, in the context of public hearings about past violence, East Timorese focused to a surprising degree on those few weeks, often expressing deep anger about the behavior of UDT or Fretilin forces.[100] The tensions that surfaced during those hearings were so great that they forced the country's leading political figures—including President Gusmão and Prime Minister Mari Alkatiri—to offer what appeared to be sincere public apologies for their past crimes.

But the violence after 1975 was not solely or even primarily the result of the brief civil war of August. It was also a legacy of the distinct cultural and political imaginings that emerged in the course of Portuguese rule—including the very notion of an East Timorese nation, and the bundle of ideas, institutions, and modes of action that are everywhere part of the nationalist repertoire. Though seldom mentioned by historians, moreover, a strong case can be made that the violence was fueled by Timorese experience serving in, or fighting against, colonial military, police, and militia forces. For good and ill, that experience provided a template for the use of violence for political ends, and the skills needed to do so. Finally, and perhaps most important, the post-1975 violence was the result of the deceitful and provocative meddling of Indonesian military authorities determined to prevent a Fretilin victory in East Timor, and the willful participation in that game by some of the most powerful states in the world.

CHAPTER THREE

INVASION AND GENOCIDE

UNDER CONSTANT PRESSURE from cross-border raids and anticipating a major Indonesian assault, on November 28, 1975 Fretilin declared East Timor's independence. Just over one week later, in the early morning hours of December 7, Indonesia launched a combined land, sea, and air invasion of East Timor. Accompanied by thousands of civilians, Fretilin and its armed wing Falintil withdrew from the towns into the hills, and began a campaign of guerrilla resistance. Thousands of real or alleged Fretilin sympathizers were summarily executed or "disappeared" by the Indonesian army and its proxies over the next several years, and countless others were subjected to interrogation under torture or detained without trial. Indonesian forces, using U.S.-supplied OV-10 "Bronco" warplanes, conducted large-scale aerial bombardment of the countryside. Those believed to be lending support to the resistance—eventually, more than half the total population—were forcibly resettled in an Indonesian version of the strategic hamlets used in South Vietnam. By late 1978, the bombing and forced relocations had led to widespread famine and disease, and church and human rights organizations estimated that as many as 100,000 of a preinvasion population of about 650,000 had died.[1]

Why did Indonesia's leaders decide to invade East Timor in December 1975? And why did that invasion lead to genocide? These questions have no simple answers, but some things can be said with certainty. First, the invasion and genocide were emphatically not the consequence of long-standing political or economic differences between the people of East Timor and Indonesia. In fact, until 1974–75, political relations between Indonesia and Portuguese Timor had been cordial, and efforts had been undertaken to improve both economic and cultural ties. Nor was the conflict the result of deeply rooted cultural or religious antagonisms between East Timorese and Indonesians. For despite the differences that had developed as a consequence of colonial rule, there was no history of serious animosity or hostility between the two peoples. A careful reading of the history of these events suggests that both the invasion and the genocide stemmed instead from certain distinctive features of the Indonesian state, and from the strategic approach to crushing the opposition adopted by army leaders. That approach simultaneously galvanized demands for independence, and deepened divisions between East Timorese who favored that outcome and those who chose to collaborate with the occupying power. Crucially, both the invasion and the genocide were also the product of decisions taken by powerful states to lend their support to Indonesia's vision of an "integrated" East Timor, and to acquiesce in all that was done in its name.

A Culture of Terror

The approach adopted in East Timor was the product of Indonesia's own history and especially of the rise to power of the Indonesian army after the declaration of independence in 1945. In the two decades that followed that declaration, the army came to play an increasingly important role in Indonesian political life.[2] During the same period, it was centrally involved in a variety of efforts to suppress internal dissent and rebellion—against an alleged Communist uprising in East Java in 1948, a separatist rebellion in South Sulawesi in the early 1950s, a geographically dispersed Islamic movement known as Darul Islam from 1948 to the early 1960s, and then against an emerging nationalist movement in West Irian (later renamed Irian Jaya and West Papua), which had remained under Dutch control after Indonesian independence. In the process, the army gained considerable experience in the use of unconventional counterinsurgency techniques, including the use of terror and forced displacement, while also developing a distinctive territorial command structure and a doctrine that emphasized the mobilization of civilian militias in the suppression of internal dissent. All of these were critical in laying the foundations for the later invasion and occupation of East Timor.

The crucial turning point, however, came on October 1, 1965, when an unsuccessful officers' coup was crushed by the army high command, which used the event as a pretext to wipe out its political opponents and seize power. Debate continues over the motives of those responsible for the initial coup attempt, but there is no doubt about the identity of the man who launched the countercoup the same day, or about the consequences of his actions.[3] He was Major General Suharto, the man who would eventually remove his military regalia and serve as president of Indonesia until May 21, 1998. Within hours of the October 1 coup, forces under Suharto organized and encouraged the killing of as many as one million real or alleged members of the PKI and its affiliated organizations, all of which were legal organizations at the time.[4] Another half a million people were imprisoned, the vast majority of them without charge or trial. In the wake of the killings, Suharto maneuvered to remove the sitting president, Sukarno, and established a new regime that became known as the New Order.

Significantly, Suharto's seizure of power was warmly welcomed by the United States and other Western governments. There is now substantial evidence that the United States and its allies encouraged army officers to seize power and crush the PKI, and then provided material and political support to help them consolidate their victory.[5] In the years after 1965, moreover, Western governments supplied vast quantities of economic and military assistance—including military training—that substantially buttressed the power of the army. That support established the important precedent that powerful Western states would turn a blind eye to even the most egregious of the New Order regime's violations of human rights, provided they were committed in the name of some ostensibly greater good, like the annihilation of Communism or the preservation of regional stability.

The New Order state that emerged after 1965 had certain distinctive features that help to explain both the decision to invade East Timor in 1975 and the genocide that followed. The first and most obvious of these was the unquestioned political power of the military, and in particular the army. That power was evident in many spheres, but perhaps most clearly in the "territorial" structure of the armed forces.[6] Roughly two-thirds of the military forces were dispersed throughout the country in a network that extended down to the village level.[7] That system effectively ensured military involvement in, and usually dominance over, the formulation and implementation of policy. It also permitted the armed forces to intervene directly in all kinds of political, social, and economic matters.

Military power was also manifest in the dominance and autonomy of various centrally commanded elite combat units that were deployed to crush perceived security threats, particularly in areas considered *rawan* or "troubled." Chief among these units were Kostrad (Komando Cadangan Strategis Angkatan Darat, or Army Strategic Forces Command) and Kopassandha, later renamed Kopassus.[8] Established before the 1965 coup, and led at that time by Major General Suharto, by 1975 Kostrad had evolved into a formidable mobile strike force with airborne capability, allowing its units to be deployed swiftly in response to perceived threats to internal security across the country. Despite a reputation in some quarters for professionalism, however, Kostrad units were accused of serious human rights violations. Like Kostrad, Kopassandha (and its successor Kopassus) had a reputation for expertise in methods of unconventional warfare, but also for brutality and abuse of authority. Indeed, the name Kopassus soon became synonymous with the practice of torture, extrajudicial killing, and the deliberate use of terror against rebel groups and civilians alike.

Finally, military dominance in the New Order found expression in the pervasive domestic intelligence network that with only minor exceptions, was controlled by the armed forces.[9] That apparatus operated formally through the Ministry of Defense and Security, and extended through the territorial structure to every village and neighborhood in the country. In addition, several other units were tasked with some kind of intelligence or counterintelligence responsibility. These included the ostensibly civilian intelligence body, BAKIN, and the informal "Special Operations" outfit, OPSUS, which conducted covert operations for the president. It also included Kopassandha/Kopassus, which operated its own intelligence network, and tended to dominate intelligence operations in areas considered troubled. Taken together, this apparatus provided the armed forces with an unequaled system of surveillance and control. Intelligence officers and officers with intelligence backgrounds, moreover, were disproportionately well represented in positions of power within the army, and invariably had the attention of the president.

The New Order state was also notable for its definition of national security, which focused on the danger of internal subversion by a resurgent Communism or by extremist religious movements, and the threat to national unity and stability posed by regional rebellions, such as those in Aceh, Irian Jaya, and East Timor. These preoccupations help to explain a good deal of the New Order's extreme intolerance of dissent and in particular its bellicose attitude toward the emergence of a moderately leftist independence movement in East Timor in 1974–75.

A related and equally significant feature of the New Order state was its doctrine of "total people's defense."[10] A legacy of the guerrilla struggle against the Dutch, that doctrine called for the close cooperation of regular military forces and the civilian population in defending the country against both external and internal threats. The doctrine provided the rationale for the mobilization of a wide variety of official and semiofficial gangs, militia groups, and paramilitary units. The mobilization of militia groups by military leaders had a long history in Indonesia, but it was not until 1965 that these groups were systematically integrated into the state apparatus, ready to be deployed in a coordinated fashion under strict army control.[11] Thereafter, the deliberate mobilization of civilians into armed militia groups became a central component of the government's strategy for dealing with political dissent. Often justified as a means to maintain order and stability, such groups were frequently used to intimidate political opponents, provoke violence to achieve political ends (especially around election time), and take part in military operations aimed at detaining or killing alleged opponents of the regime.

Finally, in the post-1965 period, both the military and the militias adopted far more brutal repertoires of action. Many of these were modeled on actions taken during the pogrom of 1965–66, though these were themselves sometimes adaptations of methods developed during earlier counterinsurgency campaigns. One of the clearest examples of this pattern was the so-called fence of legs (*pagar betis*) tactic, in which civilians were made to form a protective boundary behind which army troops could safely move into rebel territory. First used against Darul Islam in the early 1950s, it was used to more terrible effect in 1965, in East Timor after 1975, and later in Aceh. Under army guidance, after 1965 militias and paramilitary forces were also increasingly deployed to carry out a range of "dirty tricks" and covert operations, including assassination, torture, public execution, decapitation, and rape, as mechanisms of political control.

The manner in which Suharto and his army allies destroyed the PKI and consolidated their power after 1965, in short, prefigured a new style of governance that profoundly affected political life in Indonesia, and eventually East Timor, for at least the next thirty years. More precisely, it led to the unquestioned political dominance of the army, and especially its intelligence and counterinsurgency branches; the entrenchment of a state ideology preoccupied with security and national unity; the articulation of a military doctrine of total people's defense that entailed the mobilization of the civilian population to wage war on the state's internal enemies; and the systematic deployment of terror—including public executions and torture—for maintaining internal security. The coup and massacre also marked a normative and legal turning point, in the sense that such strategies were implicitly legitimized, not only because they were carried out by state authorities and their allies, but also because they were never punished. These were the defining features of the Indonesian state in 1975, as military and political leaders prepared to invade East Timor, and in the years immediately after the invasion. More than any other factor, they explain the Indonesian decision to invade, and the genocide of 1975–79.

These general features of the New Order state were compounded by a number of factors that were arguably distinctive to East Timor and other areas that became the target of full-scale military operations, like Aceh and Irian Jaya. Easily the most powerful political institution in the country, in East Timor the army—and more specifically, the counterinsurgency force Kopassus—operated with almost complete autonomy, with no meaningful oversight from other branches of government, or from a weakened and intimidated civil society. That combination ensured that at least until the 1990s, the army was not held to account for the extreme acts of violence it committed in East Timor. The result was a climate of impunity—a well-founded belief among officers and soldiers that they were beyond the reach of the law—in which extreme violence was almost inevitable. These circumstances virtually guaranteed the abuse of power, and the perpetration of extreme acts of violence by all those deployed in East Timor and those who fell under their influence.[12]

The problem was further exacerbated in East Timor by the imperious attitudes of the army's commanding officers as well as police and civilian officials toward the local population. In important respects, these were the attitudes of colonial authorities everywhere—a sense of superiority, fueled by the notion that the local people were backward and in need of civilization. As the author of a strategic police plan wrote in 1978, "The people of East Timor are for the most part (65%) still primitive, with a very low level of thinking."[13] Like colonial authorities elsewhere, too, Indonesian officials expressed impatience with local people, especially those who resisted their civilizing intentions, and complained that they were "ungrateful" for the sacrifices being made on their behalf. In other

respects, Indonesian attitudes differed from those of most colonial powers, while bearing intriguing similarities to that most powerful of "second colonizers"—the United States. Like Americans, Indonesians saw
themselves as an anticolonial people, incapable of imperialism, and grew
angry and defensive at any suggestion that their rule in East Timor was
colonial in nature.

Taken together, these features of the Indonesian state fostered what I
think can best be described as an institutional culture of terror within
the Indonesian army and its proxy forces in East Timor. In using this
phrase, I do not mean to imply that the peoples of Indonesia and East
Timor are inherently violent or prone to terrorism. Nor do I mean to
suggest that culture is something uniform or unchanging. Rather, I use
the phrase to describe a complex and evolving system of norms, discourse, and behavior *within an institution*, in which extreme violence or
terror is a defining feature. Not only did that institutional culture inform
the policies of military commanders but through a process of socialization and indoctrination, it also shaped the attitudes and actions of individual soldiers and those belonging to its affiliated organizations. Understood in this way, I believe the notion of an institutional culture of terror
helps to elucidate the causes and dynamics of the violence in East Timor,
and perhaps in other places as well.

Invasion

In the months before the December 1975 invasion and for many years
afterward, Indonesian authorities insisted that they had no territorial
ambitions in East Timor. Their main concern was that the territory
should be freed from Portuguese colonial rule and that the process of
decolonization should be done in accordance with the wishes of the Timorese people. At the same time, they acknowledged that they would
certainly not object if their "brothers" in East Timor—so cruelly separated from them by centuries of colonialism—asked for Indonesian assistance in their struggle to be free or if Indonesian "volunteers" provided such help. President Suharto expressed all of these honorable
themes in his memoir, published in 1988:

> To the people of Indonesia, who were permeated with the endless
> problems of colonialism in this world, East Timor should no longer
> remain under Portuguese rule. Meanwhile, of course, we consid-

ered the best way for Portuguese Timor to become independent was to integrate with Indonesia, but this had to be decided by the people themselves.... . Our volunteers supported those who regarded us as brothers. . . . We believed that the people of East Timor should be given the opportunity to decide on their own destiny in a fair manner. However, we must make it clear to ourselves and to the world that we had no territorial ambitions whatsoever.[14]

Some variation on this story was carefully disseminated through the Indonesian media from early 1975 and in the days after the invasion itself.[15] Lacking any alternative source of information about the situation in East Timor, it is quite likely that many Indonesians actually believed it. There may even have been some Indonesian officials who did so. But that does not mean it accurately explains why the invasion happened.

A more plausible explanation is that the invasion was driven by the anxieties, interests, and power of the military officers who plotted it— Murtopo, Sugama, and Murdani—and their civilian sidekicks, including Murtopo's special assistants, Liem Bian Kie and Harry Tjan Silalahi. It is also possible that the plan to invade reflected the unique and somewhat surprising power within the New Order of a small group of Catholic army officers and intellectuals, including Murdani and Liem Bian Kie. For this group, the incorporation of predominantly Catholic East Timor might well have been viewed as a pet project for which they could take special responsibility and claim a kind of sovereign power by virtue of their Catholic faith.[16]

Because of their zealous anti-Communism and obsession with order, it appears that these men were genuinely worried about what they saw as Fretilin's Communist inclinations and about the possibility of political disorder in the region.[17] Their anxiety about Communism and disorder stemmed partly from their training and socialization as military officers, and partly too from a concern that an independent East Timor might encourage separatist movements and regional instability. But it was also shaped by a unique conjuncture in world affairs that played into their worst fears. The turmoil in East Timor coincided, after all, with the victory of Communist forces in Vietnam, Cambodia, and Laos in April 1975, with the leftward shift of the new government in Lisbon, and with the rising popularity and in some cases victory of leftist movements in Africa, notably those in former Portuguese colonies. Under the circumstances, Indonesian officers quite naturally believed that the tide of history was turning against them. They were undoubtedly also attracted by East Timor's substantial offshore oil reserves, especially in light of rapidly rising oil prices in late 1973 and the spectacular $10 billion bankruptcy of Indonesia's state oil company, Pertamina, in early 1975.[18]

Yet perhaps the simplest reason for the invasion, as Benedict Anderson has suggested, was that the key military officers and civilian advisers believed that it could be accomplished quickly and without fuss.[19] They were not alone. Outside observers of varied political persuasion shared the view that an Indonesian military intervention would meet little meaningful resistance. In early 1975, for example, Grant Evans concluded that "if Indonesia takes over Timor within the next six months, they will be irremovable, and any local resistance will be quickly and easily crushed."[20] Perhaps aware of such assessments, Indonesia's military planners confidently predicted that the operation would take a matter of a few weeks and that East Timor's population would offer only token resistance before succumbing.[21]

They were mistaken. The initial invasion was a fiasco, a picture of poor planning and muddled leadership, marked by indiscipline and many instances of friendly fire, all contributing to what one military historian has called "bloody mayhem."[22] Even those directly involved in the planning and execution of the operation later acknowledged that it had been a disaster. Murdani, one of the principal advocates and architects of the invasion, later described the operation as "an embarrassment."[23] It was against this backdrop and in the face of continuing UN criticism that it had unlawfully annexed the territory that Indonesian authorities set up a puppet Regional People's Assembly in Dili. At its first and only meeting, on May 31, 1976, the assembly—ostensibly speaking on behalf of the people of East Timor—unanimously approved a petition requesting integration with Indonesia, and on July 17, 1976, President Suharto duly signed Law 7/76, incorporating East Timor as Indonesia's twenty-seventh province.[24]

That political charade did nothing to change the situation on the ground. Much to the chagrin of Indonesian officers and soldiers, for a time East Timorese resisted the invading force with great tenacity and skill. Provided with food, shelter, and intelligence by the local population, Falintil managed to hold out far longer than Indonesian military planners had anticipated. For two years (1975–77), in fact, Fretilin claimed that some 80 percent of the population was living under its protection in "liberated zones" in the mountainous interior of the country.[25] Although the precise figure cannot be verified, it is certainly true that Indonesian forces had great difficulty extending their control beyond the main towns and coastal areas.[26] Army plans to reduce troop levels in 1976 had to be abandoned in the face of Falintil successes, and in 1977 still more combat troops were deployed to "crush the remnants of the Fretilin gang."[27] Even after most of the top resistance leaders had been killed in late 1978 and early 1979, and tens of thousands of people had surrendered, Indonesian military planners felt it necessary to maintain some thirty combat battalions in East Timor.[28] Despite its tenuous hold on the territory, Indonesia insisted that the majority of East Timorese favored integration and that life was quickly returning to normal. But both the military campaign and the resistance to it continued, and the human toll mounted.

Counterinsurgency

There is no evidence that the Indonesian army commanders who planned the operations in East Timor intended to kill one-third of the population. Their principal aim was to quell resistance to their rule. A secret military document dated May 17, 1976, for instance, stated that "the main objective in the next phase of the operation is to secure the integration of the territory and the people of East Timor into the Republic of Indonesia."[29] But the strategies and practices adopted to achieve that end—together with the prevailing culture of terror in the army, the imperious attitude of its officers, and the complete lack of accountability—led inevitably and predictably to a massive loss of life. An order issued by the minister of defense and security in October 1978 establishing a new military command structure (Kogasgab "Seroja") for East Timor gave some sense of the means by which integration was to be achieved: "In the shortest possible time, Kogasgab 'Seroja' will destroy and cleanse the remaining armed terrorist elements."[30]

A crucial element of the effort to destroy the resistance—and the one that led most decisively to genocide—was the massive, forced displacement of the civilian population from 1975 to 1979. The clearest manifestation of that strategy, and not by chance the period of greatest displacement and death, began in mid-1977 with the start of a new Indonesian military campaign that continued through 1978. The campaign—dubbed "encirclement and annihilation" by the resistance—entailed the deployment of some forty thousand combat troops.[31] It also included the intensive aerial bombardment of one Fretilin base area after another, using low-flying counterinsurgency aircraft, such as the U.S.-supplied OV-10 Broncos.[32] Houses were burned to the ground, livestock were killed, and both crops and food stores were destroyed or stolen. In the face of these sustained attacks, the population abandoned what had been relatively safe and productive areas of the country, moved progressively into more remote and less productive areas, and finally surrendered.[33] The following account, by a woman named "Edhina" (who like many East Timorese refers to Indonesian soldiers as "the Javanese"), captures some sense of the sheer desperation felt by many civilians at this time:

> The Javanese kept attacking and dropping bombs and we were like animals running from one place to the other carrying our children, going this way and that. We slept anywhere, in the rain, in the mud, even near the dead animals. The bombs would come and we would stand up and run again. On the way we ate anything growing, anything we could find. In the daytime we went into caves or under rocks to hide.... If the babies cried you put some clothing inside their mouth to stop the noise, because the enemy could hear us and find us—the sound echoed in the mountains.[34]

The encirclement campaign took a terrible toll. By early 1978, large numbers of people were suffering serious food shortages and illnesses, Fretilin's structure had started to break down, and tens of thousands of civilians had either been captured or had surrendered. The campaign reached its culmination in October and November 1978, in a final massive assault on Mount Matebian in the eastern part of the country, where most of those under Fretilin control had fled. In late November, as Indonesian forces closed in, Fretilin's Central Committee decided finally to abandon its policy of holding civilians in the base areas.[35] In the following weeks, thousands of civilians and a good many resistance fighters came down from Mount Matebian and surrendered to Indonesian authorities.[36]

Surrender, however, did not bring an end to the suffering or dislocation. Those who surrendered were immediately placed into scores of military-run "transit camps." All told, the campaign of encirclement and annihilation resulted in the forcible relocation of at least three hundred thousand people into these camps.[37] In the transit camps, the surren-

dered were registered and interrogated, often under torture. Those believed to be members of Fretilin or Falintil were detained and sometimes
killed.[38] From the transit camps, the civilians were sent to "resettlement
areas," of which there were well over one hundred.[39] Known locally as
"concentration camps" (*campos de concentração*), the resettlement areas
were akin to the strategic hamlets used by U.S. forces in Vietnam, and
their purpose was similar: to control the population and separate it from
the insurgents, whatever the cost.

The objective of separating the population from the guerrillas was
clearly spelled out in army operational plans and training manuals for
East Timor. The general approach was articulated in a May 1979 operational order from the Department of Defense and Security. Using the
official term GPK (Gerakan Pengacau Keamanan, or Security Disruptors' Movement) to describe the guerrillas, the order called for "the destruction of the armed elements of the GPK by separating them from
the population."[40] A training manual offered more specific guidance, in-
structing field officers in East Timor to "physically separate GPK support by . . . moving to another place people with relatives who are GPKs
still active in the bush, particularly those classified as leaders."[41] The manual further explained that those separated were to be moved to various
secure locations, including the prison island of Ataúro: "Evacuate to
Ataúro and other designated places the network of GPK support in the
settlements as well as families of GPK not yet evacuated."[42]

The conditions in the resettlement areas were appalling. Supplies of
food and medicine were minimal, and residents were prevented from
venturing outside a limited area to tend crops or harvest wild food. As a
consequence, malnutrition and disease were rampant, and many thousands died. Members of a delegation of diplomats and journalists who
visited a resettlement camp in Remexio in early September 1978 were
shocked by what they saw. One of the journalists wrote:

> In Remexio as in most other towns the people are stunned, sullen,
> and dispirited. Emaciated as a result of deprivation and hardship,
> they are struggling to make sense of the nightmarish interlude in
> which as much as half the population was uprooted. . . . The towns-
> people are undernourished and desperately in need of medical at-
> tention. . . . The children in Remexio are so undernourished that
> one ambassador said they reminded him of the victims of an Afri-
> can famine.[43]

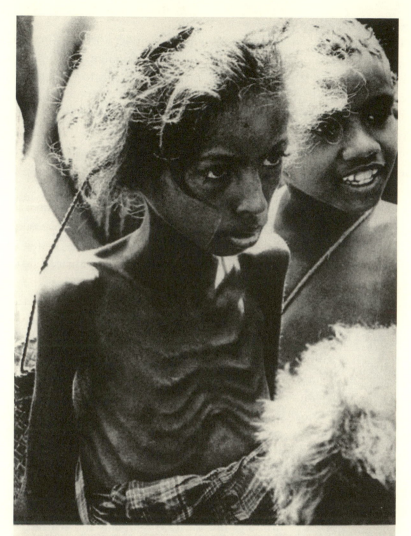

Muda obrigatóriu, rende no hamlaha
Surrender, resettlement & famine
1977-79

FIGURE 3.1. Victims of forced relocation and famine, 1979. Indonesian counterinsurgency operations against East Timor's independence movement in the late 1970s resulted in a massive displacement of the civilian population along with widespread starvation and disease. Human rights and church organizations estimated that at least one hundred thousand people died during this period. Photos like this one prompted a brief outcry and a program of humanitarian assistance, but did not result in any serious international challenge to Indonesia's occupation of East Timor. (CAVR)

These revelations prompted calls for urgent international relief operations and stimulated small-scale humanitarian efforts by church groups. But it was another full year before two international agencies—Catholic Relief Services and the International Committee of the Red Cross (ICRC)—were permitted to commence meaningful relief efforts in the area.[44]

When it finally began in September 1979, the humanitarian intervention brought significant results, effectively ending the famine and dramatically reducing death rates. This vital work, however, was carried out in the face of continuing restrictions by the Indonesian military authorities, who considered the control of humanitarian supplies to be vital to their strategic and political objectives. The decision to grant limited access to international relief agencies in September 1979 was part of the same dynamic. With more than half of the population secured in camps and the armed resistance severely weakened, by late 1979 the military had achieved its main strategic objectives and no doubt believed it could earn credit for assisting the suffering, without risking much in the way of outside scrutiny or criticism.[45]

Yet it is worth stressing that the humanitarian crisis would have been far worse had it not been for an unusual flurry of media coverage in 1979, the insistent pressure of international NGOs and church groups, and the critical interventions of a handful of scholars—notably linguist Noam Chomsky, political scientist Benedict Anderson, and anthropologist Elizabeth Traube. Shocking photographs of emaciated East Timorese children, taken by the Australian journalist Peter Rodgers in October 1979, stimulated a series of critical newspaper reports in the United States, the United Kingdom, and Australia, many of which compared the situation in East Timor with the war-related humanitarian disasters in Cambodia and Biafra.[46] Editorials in the *Christian Science Monitor*, the *New York Times*, and the *Washington Post*, among others, excoriated key governments for their complicity in the crisis, and their silence and inaction in the face of humanitarian catastrophe.[47] These media reports helped to buttress the work of existing church and solidarity groups as well as scholars in their efforts to influence the Australian and British parliaments and the U.S. Congress.[48]

It was largely due to these efforts that the U.S. Congress briefly demonstrated serious concern on the issue and threatened a reevaluation of U.S. policy. In 1979–80, for example, Congress held three separate hearings on East Timor, highlighting the duplicitous role of successive U.S.

administrations in the invasion and genocide, and providing the essential, albeit short-lived, political pressure that permitted the ICRC and other agencies to conduct their humanitarian work.[49] While the election of Ronald Reagan in 1980 effectively put an end to demands for meaningful change in U.S. policy on East Timor, the work of church and secular solidarity groups at this juncture bore long-term dividends. Crucially, these groups, and the political and media networks they had forged, laid the groundwork for a continued awareness of East Timor during the lean years of the 1980s, and for the groundswell of international criticism that grew in strength in the 1990s.[50]

People's War

A central element of Indonesia's counterinsurgency strategy in East Timor was the mobilization of local people into militia and paramilitary forces. By drawing tens of thousands of East Timorese directly into the war against Fretilin, Indonesian authorities, perhaps deliberately, deepened divisions among East Timorese, and contributed directly to the genocide and the persistent violence of later years. The story of an East Timorese conscript named "Jorge" eloquently captures both the unanswerable logic and terrible consequences of that strategy:

> I was in high school, a student, when the war started in Timor. I had no political ideas, didn't belong to any party. My friends and I were forced to join the Indonesian army. We were warned; all who didn't join their army had to take the consequences. That means they say you are Communist. None of us wanted to but there was no way not to fight. If you don't fight you get killed yourself. I went on operations to kill other Timorese, ordinary people. Then I felt strange. None of us felt good. At first we were sad, we have [sic] remorse, but after two or three years it was easy. You get used to killing.[51]

Even before the December 1975 invasion, as we have seen, Indonesian strategy entailed the mobilization of East Timorese into rudimentary militia forces. Although those forces took part in combat missions in 1975, their main purpose had been political: they were intended primarily to provide cover for Indonesian military intervention. Once their essentially political purpose had been served, the militias began to be regrouped and organized to perform more conventional militia functions,

as guards, auxiliaries, and so on. An Australian Embassy official who visited East Timor in mid-1976 reported some of the first evidence of this
militia mobilization: "Indonesian 'volunteers' in charge of these groups
drilled them in military fashion. (A platoon of men in traditional costume in Viqueque drilled with some precision using wooden rifles
capped with Indonesian flags.) Light blue uniformed 'partisans'—ex-
Apodeti and UDT soldiers—acted as guards and controlled crowds.
They formed a Timorese militia force."[52] With the start of the new encirclement military campaign in August 1977, the Indonesian army
began even more energetically to recruit local people to fight on its side.
Following the model used by Indonesian forces to crush the PKI in
1965, thousands of ordinary Timorese were now conscripted to join
military operations against Fretilin. Eyewitness accounts from this period
describe villagers being forced at gunpoint to beat or kill other members of their community.[53] Some who witnessed such operations described them as the "mass mobilization of citizens to make war on each
other."[54]

The mass mobilization of civilians to make war was precisely what
Indonesian military leaders had in mind—and increasingly so as the occupation wore on and combat troops were needed elsewhere. A secret
military order from May 1979 clarified that one of the principal methods to be used in destroying the armed resistance was to "develop the
capacity of the people to fight the enemy." To that end, the army should
work to "create awareness among the people of the need to assist in the
effort to completely destroy the GPK."[55] In mid-1981, that approach was
put into effect in shocking fashion, as the army mobilized tens of thousands of civilians to take part in a massive fence of legs operation intended to capture or kill the remaining Falintil troops and their commander, Gusmão. Backed by at least 12,000 soldiers, and probably many
more, the civilians were made to form human fences extending many
miles and then to march in lines ahead of Indonesian soldiers sweeping
the ground for Falintil forces. A 1982 army document said that the campaign, code-named Operation Security, involved more than 60,000 civilians, while a Marine source gave a figure of 145,000.[56] Despite its
massive size, the operation resulted in the capture of few Falintil members, at least in part because many civilians allowed resistance fighters to
pass unscathed through their human fence. Nevertheless, the operation
did result in the capture of some 4,500 people, most of them women,
children, and the elderly who had been hiding in the bush. It also culmi-

nated in a notorious series of mass killings near Lacluta in September 1981, in which at least 70 people and perhaps as many as 500 were killed.[57] An East Timorese man who was fighting on the Indonesian side gave the following account of killings that took place at a military headquarters nearby:

> When we arrived at the Kotis [military] headquarters, we saw lots of bodies without heads on the floor, in several lines. I couldn't count them. Many civilians who had survived were summoned to the headquarters. They said that these people would be put in a helicopter, but this didn't happen. They were shot dead with a machine gun and none survived.[58]

So began the shift away from what may be called the traditional pattern in East Timor—in which auxiliary forces were mobilized primarily through liurai, and maintained a degree of local autonomy—in the direction of a more bureaucratized arrangement, shaped by modern Indonesian counterinsurgency doctrine and the brutalizing experience of 1965. Semipermanent militia forces were now spread throughout the entire territory, with a certain number in every village and town; and they were tightly controlled not by liurai but by Indonesian military officers and other government officials.

Secret army documents from 1982 provide important details on the nature of these militia units and their role in the army's counterinsurgency strategy.[59] The documents make it clear that an essential starting point for Indonesian military strategy in East Timor was the doctrine of "total people's defence."[60] They also show that in practice, this meant that East Timorese could expect to be called on to fight "the enemy" at a moment's notice. Most local conscripts and volunteers were grouped into one of two official bodies: Ratih (Rakyat Terlatih, or Trained Populace) and Hansip (Pertahanan Sipil, or Civil Defense). Both were village-based auxiliary units, designed to assist the armed forces in detecting and combating the enemy. Both were organized along military lines, divided into companies, platoons, and teams, and were guided by an assortment of military figures, including the subdistrict military commander, and representatives of the powerful intelligence outfit, SGI (Satuan Tugas Intelijen, or Intelligence Task Force).[61] Members of both were to be stationed at military command posts, so that they would be ready for deployment at short notice.[62] In addition to these formally constituted units, hundreds of individual East Timorese, some of them boys as young as twelve, were brought along on combat missions at the request of a military unit. Officially dubbed TBO (Tenaga Bantuan Operasi, or Operational Auxiliaries), these men provided the same sort of invaluable service as the guides or *criados* who had operated alongside Australian forces during the Second World War.[63]

The use of local people to assist in pacification had some obvious military and political advantages. Unlike most Indonesian soldiers, local people knew the terrain and language—crucial qualities in fighting a counterinsurgency war. They cost little to maintain while alive, and did not require much in the way of compensation when they were killed or wounded.[64] Importantly, they allowed the Indonesian army to pretend that it was not, in fact, an invading or occupying force. But the strategy also had serious drawbacks. Most pressing was the problem of disloyalty, a subject to which the 1982 army documents repeatedly returned.[65] One document stated plainly that there was always a danger that the local auxiliaries might use their guns against Indonesians, and suggests strategies for minimizing that possibility.[66] Indonesian fears came to pass in mid–August 1983, when a joint Hansip/Ratih patrol attacked and killed fourteen Indonesian soldiers at Kraras, near Viqueque, before fleeing with captured Indonesian weapons to join Fretilin. The attack led to bloody reprisals by Indonesian forces, which killed as many as three hundred villagers over several days in September 1983, in what came to be known as the Kraras massacre.[67]

Notwithstanding these problems, the network of militia organizations established in the late 1970s and early 1980s came to form an essential bulwark in the Indonesian occupation and counterinsurgency campaign for the next two decades. The Hansip and Ratih infrastructure continued to function throughout this period, and provided the model for the basic repertoire of militia training, marching, and patrolling that were common elements throughout the territory in 1999. Moreover, many of the units that seemed to appear out of nowhere in 1999 were in fact the remnants of much older paramilitary outfits set up in the late 1970s that had continued to function in the intervening years. Likewise, at least some of the militia members and leaders in 1999 were former TBOs with long and close attachments to Indonesian army officers and units.

Thus, just as the Portuguese period left a legacy of practices and norms that reappeared in 1999, so the Indonesian occupation introduced models that powerfully influenced the style and organization of the later

militia formations. They also entangled tens of thousands of East Timorese directly in the fight against the resistance, thereby worsening dramatically the effects of the war, while creating both bonds of loyalty and
patterns of enmity that would prove difficult to untangle.

A Blind Eye

The news of Indonesia's invasion of East Timor and its counterinsurgency operations there were condemned by the United Nations, and
met with angry protests and demonstrations by church groups, trade
unions, and NGOs, especially in Australia, Portugal, the Netherlands, the
United Kingdom, and the United States. To a remarkable degree, however, Indonesia managed to conceal the nature of its operations and the
extent of the humanitarian crisis that was the result. It did so in part by
preventing visits to the territory by any international media or independent observers. Indonesian authorities were also ably assisted by powerful international allies, most notably the United States, Australia, and
Britain, but many others besides. Without the conscious support of these
states, it is safe to say that the invasion and the genocide would never
have happened.[68]

On December 22, 1975, the UN Security Council unanimously passed
resolution no. 384 "deploring" the invasion of East Timor and calling on
Indonesia "to withdraw without delay all its forces from the Territory."
The resolution also called on all states to respect East Timor's territorial
integrity and "the inalienable right of its people to self-determination."[69]
In keeping with that resolution, and several others passed by the Security Council and the General Assembly, the United Nations continued
to regard Portugal as the "administering power" in the territory, and refused to recognize Indonesian sovereignty in East Timor when it was
declared in July 1976. The problem was that no concrete action was
taken by the Security Council or member states to give effect to these
laudable principles. The reason was rather simple. No state with any real
power within the United Nations had the inclination to challenge so
important a political and economic player as Indonesia—the fifth most
populous country in the world, a bastion of anti-Communism in Asia,
and an enviable economic prize—over a half island the size of New Jersey. On the contrary, those best placed to help, such as the United States
and Australia, simply declined to do so.

The December 1975 invasion, for example, was launched less than twenty-four hours after a meeting in Jakarta between President Suharto and U.S. president Ford and Secretary of State Kissinger. For years, Kissinger steadfastly denied that he and Ford had given a "green light" to the invasion at that meeting. Questioned about the meeting in 1995, Kissinger said: "Timor was never discussed with us when we were in Indonesia. . . . At the airport as we were leaving, the Indonesians told us that they were going to occupy the Portuguese colony of Timor. To us that did not seem like a very significant event."[70] For more than twenty-five years, the detailed transcript of the Ford–Suharto meeting was either kept secret or was so heavily censored—in official parlance, "sanitized"—before declassification that it was difficult to know with any certainty whether Kissinger was telling the truth. When the document was finally released in uncensored form in late 2001, it confirmed what most critics had already surmised on the basis of the existing evidence. It revealed that Kissinger and Ford gave Suharto repeated assurances that the United States understood Indonesia's "problem" and "intentions" in East Timor, and would not object if Indonesia found it necessary to take "drastic action" there. "Whatever you do," Kissinger stressed, "we will try to handle in the best way possible." The transcript also showed that Kissinger and Ford asked that any Indonesian action be delayed until they had returned to the United States, so that they could prevent people from "talking in an unauthorized way." Finally, the transcript made it clear that Kissinger advised Suharto on how "we" might evade provisions of U.S. law that explicitly forbade the use of U.S.-supplied weapons for purposes other than self-defense.[71] Considering that U.S. arms sales to Indonesia quintupled from 1974 to 1975, and that roughly 90 percent of the military equipment used in the invasion was supplied by the United States, Kissinger's concern about legality was not an idle one.[72] The full exchange follows:

> Suharto—I would like to speak to you, Mr. President, about another problem, Timor. . . . It is now important to determine what we can do to establish peace and order for the present and the future in the interest of the security of the area and Indonesia. These are some of the considerations we are now contemplating. We want your understanding if we deem it necessary to take rapid or drastic action.

> Ford—We will understand and will not press you on the issue. We understand the problem you have and the intentions you have.

Kissinger—You appreciate that the use of U.S.-made arms could create problems.

Ford—We could have technical and legal problems. You are familiar, Mr. President, with the problems we had on Cyprus, although this situation is different.

Kissinger—It depends on how we construe it. Whether it is in self-defense or is a foreign operation. It is important that whatever you do succeeds quickly. We would be able to influence the reaction in America if whatever happens, happens after we return. This way there would be less chance of people talking in an unauthorized way. The President will be back on Monday at 2:00 pm Jakarta time. We understand your problem and the need to move quickly but I am only saying that it would be better if it were done after we returned.

Ford—It would be more authoritative if we can do it in person.

Kissinger—Whatever you do, however, we will try to handle in the best way possible.

Ford—We recognize that you have a time factor. We have merely expressed our view from our particular point of view.

Kissinger—If you have made plans, we will do our best to keep everyone quiet until the President returns home.

Ford—Do you anticipate a long guerilla war there?

Suharto—There will probably be a small guerrilla war. The local kings are important, however, and they are on our side. The UDT represents former government officials and Fretelin [sic] represents former soldiers. They are infected the same as is the Portuguese army with communism.[73]

The significance of this exchange can scarcely be overstated. At least until August 1975, President Suharto had been ambivalent about the wisdom of military action in East Timor and, by some accounts, he had hesitated to give his final approval until much later.[74] As noted earlier, the main reason for his hesitation was that he feared the criticism of key allies, and especially the United States, on which Indonesia then relied heavily for its military hardware.[75] By saying clearly that the United States understood Indonesia's "problem" and "intentions" in East Timor

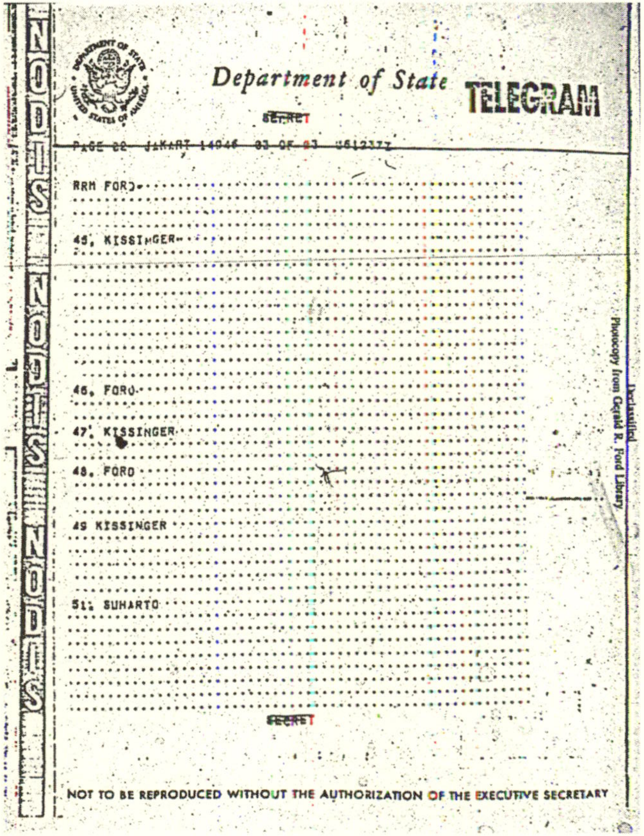

FIGURE 3.2. The December 7, 1975 invasion of East Timor began less than twenty-four hours after President Gerald R. Ford and Secretary of State Henry Kissinger met President Suharto in Jakarta. For more than twenty-five years, the memorandum of their conversation was heavily "sanitized" (see image on left), and U.S. officials denied allegations that they had given Suharto the "green light" to invade. When an uncensored version of the memo was finally made public in 2001 (see image on right), it revealed that Ford and Kissinger had given Suharto repeated reassurances that the United States would understand should Indonesia choose to take "drastic action" in East Timor.

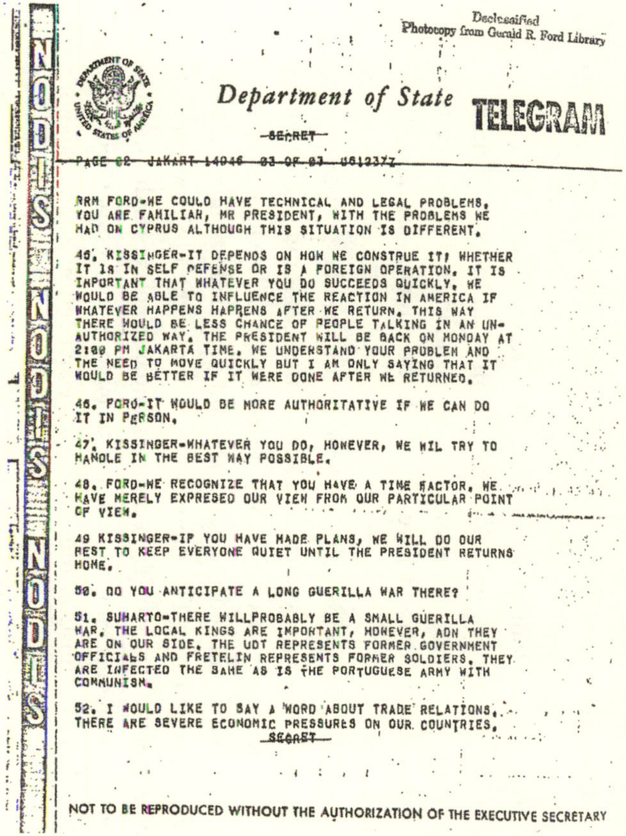

offering advice about how an invasion should be portrayed to avoid legal and political problems, promising to "handle" any unwelcome publicity in the United States, and urging that it be "done quickly," Kissinger and Ford removed any possible doubt that may have remained in Suharto's mind about the wisdom of an invasion. Had Kissinger and Ford delivered instead a clear message of U.S. opposition to an Indonesian military adventure in East Timor, it is quite possible—and indeed it is more than likely—that Suharto would have called off or substantially altered the operation.

Given the terrible consequences of the invasion and especially its slide into genocide, it is hardly surprising that Kissinger sought to cover his tracks. Still, Kissinger was only a small part of a much wider pattern of U.S. action that facilitated the genocide and provided essential political cover to its perpetrators. The supportive posture of the U.S. government, already evident in mid-1975, became abundantly clear in the months and years after the invasion, even as the terrible human consequences of the Indonesian occupation mounted. Successive administrations—both Democrat and Republican—funneled hundreds of millions of dollars of economic and military aid to the Suharto regime, and consciously protected it from any serious political challenge to its illegal occupation of East Timor.

U.S. military assistance sent an especially clear message. Between 1975 and 1979, U.S. arms sales and transfers to Indonesia totaled more than $318 million, and in 1978, the year of the deadly encirclement and annihilation campaign, it spiked to more than $129 million.[76] In addition to thousands of M-16 assault rifles and other small arms, the U.S. weapons systems transferred to Indonesia in these years included, among others, sixteen Rockwell OV-10 Bronco counterinsurgency aircraft, three Lockheed C-130 transport aircraft, and thirty-six Cadillac-Gage Commando armored cars.[77] Especially important were the versatile, low-flying OV-10 Broncos, which were ideal for counterinsurgency operations in East Timor's difficult terrain.[78] In early 1978, as the deadly encirclement and annihilation campaign was gathering steam, the U.S. government offered to sell Indonesia 16 A-4 Skyhawks, counterinsurgency aircraft used by U.S. forces in Vietnam, to be followed by sixteen Bell UH-1H Huey helicopters.[79] By any reasonable measure, the introduction of these weapons systems at this critical juncture contributed directly to the massive forced displacements of 1977–79 in East Timor and therefore also to the genocide.[80]

Meanwhile, the United States worked assiduously to block meaningful international action in response to the invasion and to conceal the truth about its human consequences. As Daniel Patrick Moynihan explained in his memoir, as the U.S. ambassador to the United Nations in 1976, he played a central part in that effort: "The United States wished things to turn out as they did, and worked to bring this about. The Department of State desired that the United Nations prove utterly ineffective in whatever measures it undertook. This task was given to me, and I carried it forward with no inconsiderable success."[81] Other U.S. officials contributed by consistently, and knowingly, understating the number of dead. In 1977, for example, a senior Department of State official in the Carter administration, Robert B. Oakley, suggested that the total number of casualties in East Timor was "probably under ten thousand," and that "most of the violence in which there were major losses of life or wounded, took place during the period between August 1975, and March 1976."[82]

Of course, the United States was not alone in lending its support to Indonesia at this crucial stage. As noted earlier, British authorities were well aware of Indonesia's covert incursions into East Timor in 1975, but sought deliberately to silence discussion and debate on the matter. The British government later worked effectively to keep news of the invasion out of the press, and to limit criticism and action against Indonesia at the United Nations.[83] Australia was also privy to Indonesian plans to invade in 1975—and had details of atrocities committed by Indonesian before, during, and soon after the invasion—but chose not to speak out or interfere.[84] Anxious not to alienate an important neighbor and eager to exploit the new economic opportunities that might follow, Australia later became the first and only major power to accept Indonesia's disputed claim over East Timor.[85] In 1989 it reaped its reward, signing the Timor Gap Treaty, an agreement with Indonesia for the joint exploitation of the substantial oil and mineral wealth lying beneath the sea off East Timor's coast. For most of the twenty-four-year occupation, moreover, a succession of Australian governments sought to deny or downplay reports of gross human rights violations in the territory, consistently casting doubt on the credibility of the sources. Australia also provided substantial military training to Indonesian forces, including the notorious Kopassandha and Kopassus. In a 2001 mea culpa that came too late to make any difference, the foreign minister from 1988 through 1996, Gareth Evans, admitted that much of Australia's military training had "helped only to produce more professional human rights abusers."[86]

Key states also abetted the genocide by aiding the Indonesian army's cynical manipulation of information, humanitarian assistance, and access to the territory. Pursuing a policy of deliberate silence and obfuscation, the United States, Britain, Australia, and other states sought to suppress or dismiss information regarding the widespread dislocation and famine in East Timor.[87] According to one reliable account, for example, the U.S. ambassador to Indonesia, Edward Masters, failed to report the famine in East Timor for a full nine months after he had witnessed it firsthand.[88] When he was finally compelled to do so by Congress, Masters sought to attribute the famine to "backward" East Timorese agricultural practices, erosion and drought, and Portuguese colonialism.[89] And when the program of humanitarian assistance was finally set in motion in late 1979, key states sought disingenuously to portray it as evidence of Indonesia's sincerity in assisting the people of East Timor. Testifying before Congress in June 1980, the then U.S. assistant secretary of state for Asia and the Pacific, Richard Holbrooke, said of the humanitarian situation in East Timor: "I am pleased to be able to report dramatic improvement in conditions with many areas returning to normal, and I wish to acknowledge and commend the excellent efforts of the international agencies, the Indonesian Government and all those who have contributed to this effort which has resulted in the saving of many lives."[90]

Holbrooke was certainly correct in saying that the humanitarian situation had improved after the start of the relief operation. Although many East Timorese continued to suffer hunger and disease, by late 1980 the worst of the famine had ended. As noted above, however, that success was primarily the work of the international humanitarian agencies and their supporters—not of the Indonesian government. More to the point, it had been achieved *in spite* of the restrictions imposed by Indonesian military authorities and the disgraceful code of silence maintained by its international allies. To suggest that the Indonesian government deserved any credit for the improvement diminished the achievement of the international agencies while also obscuring the fact that the Indonesian military had been responsible for the humanitarian crisis in the first place. It was also noteworthy that in all the ostensible concern expressed by Western governments about the humanitarian situation—a concern voiced only after intense political pressure from solidarity groups, the media, and some scholars and legislators—not a critical word was spoken about the unlawful Indonesian occupation itself.

It is hardly surprising, under these circumstances, that for more than twenty years, Indonesia refused to contemplate any challenge to its claimed sovereignty in East Timor—whatever the United Nations may have said about it. As a consequence, the violence continued and the patterns of enmity deepened. Nevertheless, as we shall see, developments on the ground in East Timor, including changes in the strategy of the East Timorese resistance and significant shifts in the international environment in the 1990s, began gradually but inexorably to weaken Indonesia's position and open the possibility of a political solution.

CHAPTER FOUR

OCCUPATION AND RESISTANCE

WITHOUT QUESTION the critical turning point in East Timor's path to independence was the massacre at the Santa Cruz cemetery in Dili, on November 12, 1991, in which as many as 270 young people were killed by Indonesian troops.[1] The victims, most of them teenagers, were among some 2,000 people who had marched through Dili to the cemetery to honor a young man shot dead two weeks before by pro-Indonesian militias. What distinguished this massacre from others in East Timor's modern history was the fact that it was captured on video by a British filmmaker and broadcast a few days later around the world.[2] The video showed scores of terrified youngsters fleeing into the cemetery, some of them already badly wounded, hiding behind tombstones and in chapels, the red dust swirling as automatic weapons fired and sirens screamed. It also showed Indonesian security forces beating some who had escaped the shooting. Eyewitnesses, both East Timorese and foreign, later said that combat troops had arrived at the cemetery in several trucks, marched into position, and then without warning, opened fire on the unarmed protesters. They also reported that many of the wounded had been taken away in trucks and killed in other locations, including the hospital, before being buried in unmarked graves.[3]

Indonesian authorities sought to downplay the seriousness of these events and shift responsibility for the violence to those who had been its victims. Characterizing the peaceful demonstration as a violent riot, they insisted that military and police authorities had acted appropriately. Disputing well-founded claims that more than two hundred had been killed, they asserted that "only" nineteen people had died. They also sought to blame foreigners—journalists, human rights activists, tourists, and others—for encouraging the demonstrators. Several East Timorese youths

FIGURE 4.1. Scene from the Santa Cruz massacre. As many as 270 young people were killed by Indonesian army troops during and shortly after a peaceful proindependence demonstration at the Santa Cruz cemetery in Dili, November 12, 1991. Still and video images broadcast around the world provoked a groundswell of criticism of Indonesia's human rights record and stimulated the growth of international solidarity groups supporting demands for East Timorese independence. (By kind permission of Continuum International Publishing Group. Photo by Steve Cox)

were sentenced to long prison terms for "provoking" the violence and disseminating information about it to human rights organizations abroad.[4] Perhaps most disturbing to many observers, the military authorities appeared to show no remorse for the killings. One day after the massacre the commander of the Indonesian Armed Forces, General Try Sutrisno, said that people in the procession had "spread chaos" and had shouted "many unacceptable things." In the end, he said, "they had to be shot. These ill-bred people have to be shot . . . and we will shoot them."[5] Several months later, the regional military commander, Major General Mantiri, offered the following remarks about the massacre:

> We don't regret anything. What happened was quite proper. . . . They were opposing us, demonstrating, even yelling things against the government. To me that is identical with rebellion, so that is why we took firm action. . . . [T]heir theme was opposing the government. Long Live Fretilin. Long Live Xanana, waving Fretilin flags. If they try that now, I will not tolerate it. I will order strong action. . . . I don't think there's anything strange in that.[6]

The massacre and the callous Indonesian response to it prompted un-precedented international condemnation, and placed Indonesian authori-ties firmly on the defensive for the first time since the invasion of 1975. It also stimulated important changes in the strategy of the resistance.

Yet while it is true that the Santa Cruz massacre marked a turning point, it was also the culmination of military, political, and social trans-formations—both inside East Timor and abroad—that had been under way for more than a decade. Some of those transformations were the result of adjustments in Indonesia's strategy of occupation, while others stemmed from reassessments and realignments within East Timorese and Indonesian society. The unusual reaction to the Santa Cruz massacre also stemmed from the gathering strength of the international solidarity movement through the 1980s, and changes in the international environ-ment set in motion by the collapse of the Berlin Wall in 1989, which had signaled the start of a period in which most Western states declared their unqualified support for the idea of the universality of human rights. Taken together, these changes influenced the course of the struggle for independence and shaped the patterns of violence in the years leading up to the cataclysm of 1999.

Repression and Development

For some time after its apparent victory in late 1979, Indonesia contin-ued to rely primarily on overt repression to engage and contain Falintil. Even as military authorities declared that the resistance had been re-duced to a few hundred fighters, Indonesian commanders maintained between fifteen thousand and thirty thousand troops in the field. Not-withstanding a brief cease-fire in 1983, Indonesia continued for several years to mount major military campaigns aimed at wiping out the final remnants of the resistance and subduing the civilians thought to be sup-porting it. The predictable result was a steady stream of casualties, punc-tuated by instances of extreme violence against civilians. In September 1981, as we have seen, as many as five hundred people were killed by Indonesian forces in the village of Lacluta, and in September 1983 some three hundred civilians, including women and small children, were killed near the village of Kraras. Against this background, the Santa Cruz mas-sacre of 1991 was hardly an anomaly. It was simply the most recent in a long-standing pattern of brutality against civilians perpetrated by Indo-nesian forces.

Yet in one sense Santa Cruz was unusual. For while Indonesia never stopped its military campaign against the armed resistance, by the mid-1980s it had begun to shift away from a strategy of direct combat and toward more "subtle" techniques, including the selective detention, interrogation, and torture of alleged members of the resistance, the promotion of a program of economic development intended to undermine support for the resistance, and a further refinement of the system of militia mobilization initiated in 1975. The consequence of the new strategy—together with significant adjustments made by the resistance over the same period—was an overall decline in the levels of deadly violence from 1985 through 1998.[7] That did not mean an end to conflict and violence but rather a change in their *patterns*, which with the exception of the Santa Cruz massacre would continue until 1999.

At the heart of this repressive apparatus was the elite counterinsurgency force, Kopassus. Involved in East Timor operations even before the 1975 invasion, by the 1980s Kopassus had established something like a fiefdom in the territory. Though virtually invisible, it effectively dominated both the civilian administration and the regular territorial and combat troops stationed there. Through its extensive intelligence apparatus—known locally simply as "Intel"—it tracked the movements of resistance figures, detaining, torturing, or killing them as it deemed appropriate. Effectively beyond the control of any other authority, Kopassus also became the central player in what has been described as a "local mafia."[8] That mafia, which included members of the East Timorese political elite, dominated political and economic life in the territory, and sought to expand and defend its control through resort to intimidation and violence.[9]

A central figure in this configuration of power was an officer named Prabowo Subianto Djojohadikusumo, who served several tours of duty in East Timor in the 1970s and 1980s.[10] The son of a noted economist and politician, Prabowo married the daughter of President Suharto in 1983 and thereafter became something of a golden boy, rising to the rank of lieutenant general and commander of Kopassus in 1995–98. Educated abroad, and the recipient of military officer's training in the United States and Germany, he spoke good English and was viewed in Western capitals as the ideal of a "professional" soldier. His reputation in East Timor was rather different. There, he was regarded as an unusually ruthless counterinsurgency commander, known for his involvement in the terrible Kraras massacre of 1983. He was also credited with establishing the first elite paramilitary units in the territory.

The centerpiece of the new Indonesian strategy in East Timor was a program of selective detention, interrogation, and torture. A central purpose of that program was to gather intelligence about the armed and clandestine resistance. While regular army units generally played a role in such operations—providing armed support, transportation, and detention facilities—East Timorese soon came to understand that they had most to fear from the smooth-talking, plainclothes-wearing Intel agents, most of whom were under Kopassus command, rather than from regular soldiers or police. Suspects were typically held in one of many secret interrogation centers, where they were subjected to all manner of extreme treatment, including mock execution, electrocution, beating, and so on.[11] One of several secret Indonesian army intelligence documents leaked in 1983 revealed, moreover, that the torture and ill-treatment of political detainees was not incidental or, as authorities often claimed, the work of "rogue elements" but a matter of policy. The document, titled "Procedures for the Interrogation of Detainees," offered the following guidance on the use of force and torture of suspects:

> It is hoped that interrogation with the use of force will not be implemented except in those situations where the person examined is evasive. However, if the use of force is required, a member of the local population ... should not be present to witness it, in order to avoid arousing the antipathy of the people.... Avoid taking photographs showing torture (of someone being given electric shocks, stripped naked and so on).[12]

Indonesian authorities also sought during these years to demoralize and thereby weaken the resistance by placing its leaders on public trial, and sentencing them to long prison terms. Between 1983 and 1986, more than three hundred resistance figures were tried and convicted on charges of subversion and/or treason.[13] This approach offered distinct advantages over the earlier strategy of killing top leaders. For one thing, it effectively demonstrated the far-reaching authority of the Indonesian state, while offering fewer opportunities for the accused to be raised up as martyrs. It also helped to buttress the Indonesian claim that in East Timor as elsewhere, the regime was not an arbitrary one but instead adhered strictly to the rule of law.

The actual conduct of the trials belied such claims. By any reasonable standard, these were show trials, in which the guilt of the accused was decided in advance, and the judiciary served as a rubber stamp for the intentions of the military authorities.[14] Nevertheless, the superficial adherence to the formal procedures of interrogation, trial, and sentencing provided useful political cover for Indonesia and its international allies. Thus, when political prisoners began to be sentenced to long prison terms in 1983–84, Indonesia's allies portrayed it as a sign of progress and "normalization" of conditions in the territory. And when some prisoners began to be released in 1988–89, after serving their sentences, those supporters concluded disingenuously that the human rights situation in East Timor had improved dramatically and that the argument for independence had therefore been rendered moot.

Other changes in Indonesia's approach initiated in the 1980s were likewise intended to silence the critics of occupation and remove East Timor from the international agenda. Following a visit to East Timor by President Suharto in late 1988, for example, Indonesia announced that much of the territory, which had been entirely closed to outsiders since 1975, would be opened up to tourists and journalists. The opening up of East Timor was clearly designed to create the impression that the process of integration was complete and that life had returned to normal. The truth was that East Timor remained closed in anything but the most superficial sense. Visitors were closely monitored by Indonesian intelligence agents, who diligently recorded where they stayed, what they ate, and with whom they spoke. The vast majority of East Timorese knew very well that to speak to such visitors would be to invite suspicion and likely arrest. The threat was compounded by the existence of an extensive network of local spies. Organized by army intelligence, with substantial control exercised by Kopassus, the internal spy network eventually reached into every village, neighborhood, and organization in the country. East Timor's Bishop Belo summarized the problem succinctly in late 1991, describing East Timor as a society in which "half of the population is paid to spy on the other half."[15]

It was not surprising, then, that in the years after the opening up, Amnesty International consistently reported a pattern of systematic human rights violations in the territory.[16] Dozens of proindependence figures were killed, while scores of others were detained, tortured, or seriously ill-treated. Political show trials also returned as a favored tactic, with several dozen young people being tried and imprisoned in the early 1990s. The courts imposed especially harsh sentences on those who had organized demonstrations or had communicated with international human rights organizations.[17] In some cases, the terror worked, leading members to step back from the movement, or even switch sides and work for the Indonesians.[18] For many more, however, the experience of arbitrary detention and torture, or the execution of a friend or family member, served only to renew and deepen their commitment to the cause.[19]

Indonesia also embarked in these years on a concerted program of economic development in the territory. Fueled by surging revenues from oil and gas, and by the mantra that development would bring prosperity and stability, the New Order regime invested substantial sums in East Timor.[20] Indeed, as government authorities liked to point out, Indonesia had achieved far more development in twenty years than the Portuguese had in four hundred. As an Indonesian diplomat wrote in November 1996:

> And now, rather than political incitements and awards, progress is measured in churches, schools and health care facilities. In 20 years, the number of new churches on East Timor has risen to more than 800, from 100 in 1974. . . . The number of schools has also risen since the departure of the Portuguese from 50 to more than 800 including, for the first time, four colleges. Hospitals and village healthcare facilities have increased from two and 14, respectively, in 1974 to more than 11 hospitals and 330 health care centers throughout the province.[21]

Critics countered with some justification that these development projects served mainly to benefit the Indonesian army, by simplifying the task of maintaining security and by providing authorities with ample opportunities for graft and corruption. They also charged that economic development was designed to benefit the many Indonesian migrants, chiefly from Bali and Sulawesi, who increasingly dominated the local economy.

Like many colonized peoples, East Timorese were especially suspicious of the colonizing power's initiatives in the fields of education and health. While acknowledging that Indonesia had built many schools, they noted bitterly that schoolchildren were now taught only about Indonesian history and culture, and were required to study Indonesian rather than local languages like Tetum. In their view, and in the view of many supporters abroad, this was a deliberate attempt to "Indonesianize" the population, and wipe out any trace of East Timorese culture and identity. A 1985 statement by East Timor's Council of Diocesan Clergy suggested that Indonesian rule was tantamount to cultural genocide:

> We are witnessing an upheaval of gigantic and tragic proportions in the social and cultural fabric of the Timorese people and their identity is threatened with death.... An attempt to Indonesianise the Timorese people through vigorous campaigns to promote Pancasila [the state ideology], through schools or the media, by alienating people from their world view, means the gradual murder of Timorese culture. To kill the culture is to kill the people.[22]

Similarly, East Timorese expressed deep suspicion about the network of clinics and hospitals that had been established under Indonesian rule. Rumors circulated of patients being deliberately poisoned or ill-treated while at these institutions, and Indonesian doctors and nurses were routinely accused of working for military intelligence. Indonesia's national family planning campaign, which had been praised by the World Bank, was met with especially strong criticism, and not only because it was inconsistent with Catholic teachings. Why, critics asked, was Indonesia seeking to limit the number of children born in a territory that had recently lost such a large part of its population through famine and war? The widely accepted answer was that Indonesia was seeking to destroy the East Timorese people and replace them with a population of Indonesian migrants.

The 1980s and 1990s also brought significant adjustments in the strategy of mobilizing East Timorese to fight the resistance. In addition to the basic auxiliary forces established earlier, in the mid-1980s the army began to create a small number of highly trained paramilitary units.[23] The first three, established by a special task force code-named Railakan, were Team Alfa, Team Sera, and Team Saka. These units performed important reconnaissance, intelligence, and combat roles, and took part in special counterguerrilla operations. Formally coordinated at the level of the District Military Command, in practice they were under Kopassus control. In fact, like similar formations used by U.S. Special Forces in Vietnam, each of these units included a number of Kopassus officers. More surprising, perhaps, most of the Timorese recruited to serve in them were former Falintil guerrillas. Team Alfa and Team Sera, for example, were each comprised of twenty-one ex-Falintil fighters and nine Kopassus soldiers. Significantly, all three units resurfaced as militia groups in 1999, highlighting the critical continuity of these formations and their continuing link to Kopassus.

In the early 1990s, a rather different sort of group—more like urban death squads than counterguerrilla units—began to make its presence felt in East Timor. The best-known manifestations of the new type were the so-called Ninja gangs, first reported abroad in 1991, but likely in existence a year or two before that.[24] Also known as Bufo, these gangs roamed the streets at night, dressed in black, their heads covered with dark balaclavas, harassing, kidnapping, and sometimes killing supporters of independence, leaving their dead bodies in public places. For Indonesians, and probably also for East Timorese, the Ninjas evoked memories of the terrifying state-sponsored killing of at least five thousand alleged petty criminals in the mid-1980s in Indonesia, known by the acronym Petrus (*penembakan misterius*, or "mysterious shootings").[25] Those executions were often carried out by men in plainclothes and balaclavas, and the victims' bodies were usually left in full public view. At the time, officials denied government responsibility. Yet in 1988 President Suharto boasted in his memoirs that the killings had been deliberate government policy—a form of "shock therapy" to bring crime under control.

> The peace was disturbed. It was as if there was no longer peace in this country. It was as though all there was was fear. . . . We had to apply some *treatment*, to take some stern action. What kind of action? It had to be with violence. . . . Those who tried to resist, like it or not, had to be shot. . . . Some of the corpses were left [in public places] just like that. That was for the purpose of *shock therapy*. . . . This was done so that the general public would understand that there was still someone capable of taking action to tackle the problem of criminality.[26]

By one account, the Ninjas and Bufos were the brainchild of the local mafia of military and civilian officials in East Timor noted earlier.[27] According to this interpretation, the mafia created these groups on the basis of existing criminal networks, and used them to terrorize the proindependence resistance and as agents provocateurs. Among other things, the mafia was said to have infiltrated its vigilantes into the procession to the Santa Cruz cemetery on November 12, 1991, in order to provoke an incident that could be used to justify a "firm" military response.[28] Whether it was the result of provocation or not, the massacre solidified the position of this mafia and cleared the way for the removal of those who had expressed opposition to its tactics. Mário Carrascalão, for example, who had been openly critical of the Ninja, was replaced as governor in October 1992 by Abílio Osório Soares, the notorious Apodeti figure who had been the mayor of Dili in the late 1980s when the Ninjas first appeared in the city. It is perhaps not surprising, then, that after a brief lull, there was a resumption in the activities of these groups and other militias, even if they now began to operate under different names.

For instance, in the countryside the military set about reactivating and recasting its militia forces. In October 1993, an army spokesperson announced that some 3,844 young East Timorese men had recently been sworn in as auxiliaries. Rather than calling them Ratih and Hansip, however, the spokesperson referred to them as "Traditional Forces" (Pasukan Adat).[29] In all likelihood, the decision to mobilize these auxiliaries, and the odd choice of name, was related to the fact that Indonesia was at the time under unusual international pressure to reduce its troop presence in East Timor and to show progress on the human rights front. No doubt some military strategist or public relations expert believed that in those circumstances, the invocation of tradition would provide a veneer of deniability and cause less trouble.[30]

But the real action was in the towns and especially in Dili, where the underground resistance was regrouping after the catastrophe of Santa Cruz. In early 1995, for example, there were reports that Ninja gangs were operating again. Amnesty International reported in February that groups "referred to as 'Ninja' gangs ... have been roaming the streets at night, stoning and burning houses and attacking residents of Dili. Their primary objective seems to be to target pro-independence activists and to create an intensified atmosphere of fear for those opposed to Indonesian rule."[31] Later the same year, a new pro-Indonesian group had emerged with many of the hallmarks of the earlier Ninjas—but now mixed with characteristics of the notorious thugs of Java and Sumatra, known as *preman*. The new group was called Garda Paksi (Garda Pemuda Penegak Integrasi, or Youth Guard for Upholding Integration).[32] Like the Ninjas, members of Garda Paksi appeared to be drawn largely from unemployed East Timorese youth. The pretext for their formation, in fact, was that they would be given job training and assistance in finding employment, not only in East Timor, but also in Java.[33] Like the Ninja, Garda Paksi members and leaders appear to have had links to criminal networks and Kopassus.

Garda Paksi is usually described as the brainchild of Prabowo Subi-anto, the son-in-law of President Suharto notorious for his role in spe-cial operations in East Timor. Yet the group could have been set up by any number of powerful military officers. One likely candidate is Kiki Syahnakri, who became East Timor military commander in late 1994, just a few months before Garda Paksi appeared on the scene (and who reappeared as martial law commander in early September 1999). His tour of duty was noted for a serious deterioration in the human rights situa-tion. In response to a series of protests in Dili in November 1994, for example, he reportedly said, "We will not tolerate any more disturbances or demonstrations in East Timor. . . . If it happens again, the armed forces will not hesitate to cut them down, because we have pleaded with them enough and our patience has run out."[34]

Judging from its activities, Garda Paksi's assigned role was to infiltrate the underground resistance and provoke disturbances among East Ti-morese. Dressed in black and armed with knives, its members terrorized Dili, throwing rocks, burning houses, setting up roadblocks, and abduct-ing and occasionally killing independence activists. It was in essence a gang of toughs similar to the preman of the major towns and cities of Java and Sumatra. And like the preman, its purposes were not by any stretch strictly criminal. As Bishop Belo remarked to an Indonesian jour-nalist in 1996, "The Governor has said [Garda Paksi] is for training pur-poses . . . but they are the ones who are always causing disturbances. . . . They are *intel* agents."[35] In this sense, Garda Paksi was simply one mani-festation of a model that was characteristic of the final years of the New Order. Whether in Jakarta, Medan, or Dili, by the mid-1990s the pres-ence of easily mobilized thugs had become an integral element of Indo-nesian political life.

In fact and perhaps not coincidentally, Garda Paksi was also the pre-decessor of one of the most violent militia groups of 1999, Aitarak. Al-most overnight, in early 1999, Garda Paksi disappeared and Aitarak emerged in its stead. The link between the two was personified by the career path of one of the most notorious of East Timor's militia leaders, Eurico Guterres.[36] A protégé of Prabowo from the late 1980s, between 1995 and 1998 Guterres was the de facto leader of Garda Paksi.[37] When the new militias were mobilized in late 1998 and early 1999, he was re-warded for his loyalty by being made commander of Aitarak and later deputy commander of the PPI. His selection for this powerful position at the age of twenty-eight spoke volumes about the nature of Indonesian rule and the quality of its local support base in 1999. "After twenty-four years," one observer has aptly noted in reference to Guterres, "the best example of a 'good patriotic Indonesian' in East Timor was some bombastic, half-wit junior mafia boss."[38] With his penchant for brandishing weapons and uttering threats, and his trademark mullet hairstyle, Guterres was without question one of the most obnoxious militia leaders around, and his style seems to have reflected his preman roots. These links were further emphasized by the fact that after being flushed out of East Timor in 1999, Guterres moved to Indonesia, where in 2000 he became a key figure in the preman-style youth movement of President Megawati Soekarnoputri's political party, the PDI-P.

In short, from the early 1980s to the late 1990s, Indonesian strategy evolved in significant ways. The military continued to dominate, and regular combat never ceased entirely, but it was increasingly disguised beneath a veneer of normalization and the rule of law—with economic development programs, political trials, and the mobilization of local proxies to fight the war. In these ways, Indonesian strategy exacerbated conflicts among East Timorese and laid the essential groundwork for the violent anti-independence campaign of 1999.

The Resistance

Indonesian military strategists were not alone in seeking new approaches during these years. East Timor's resistance movement, which had come close to total collapse in 1979, also scrambled to find a more viable strategy. With the help of a new generation that had studied Indonesia's own nationalist history, the resistance charted a new approach that shaped the path to independence and foreshadowed the strategic posture that would be adopted in 1999. While never completely forsaking the armed struggle, the new approach relied increasingly on clandestine political organization, nonviolent mobilization, and international diplomatic initiatives.

With the disastrous defeat of Falintil forces at Mount Matebian and the death of Commander Nicolau Lobato, it seemed by 1979 that the resistance had reached a dead end. For the next two years at least, there was uncertainty and disagreement about the strategic direction that should be taken. Some of that confusion was resolved in March 1981, at a meeting of surviving resistance leaders near the village of Lacluta.[39] The meeting resulted in a major reorganization of Falintil, which instead of maintaining fixed bases would now operate in small, mobile guerrilla

FIGURE 4.2. Xanana Gusmão, East Timor, October 1999. One of a handful of
resistance figures to survive Falintil's near total defeat in 1978–79, Gusmão became commander of both the political and military wings of the resistance. He
was captured by Indonesian forces in 1992 and imprisoned, but remained as
overall leader of the resistance and gained a reputation as the "Nelson Mandela"
of East Timor. Following his release from captivity in September 1999, he returned to East Timor and was elected its first president in 2002. (Eddy Hasby)

units; the creation of a clandestine underground network in Indonesian-occupied territories; and the establishment of an overarching organization to lead the resistance, called the CRRN (Conselho Revolucionária de Resistencia Nacional, or National Council of Revolutionary Resistance). At the apex of both the CRRN and Falintil was Gusmão, one of only a handful of the first generation of Fretilin leaders to have survived the first four years of the war.[40]

This was the first in a series of strategic reorientations that took place over the next two decades under Gusmão's leadership. While never abandoning the armed struggle or the ultimate goal of independence, the general direction of those changes was, first, toward a more broadly based nationalist front, and, second, toward an approach centered on clandestine and diplomatic work directed at an international audience.[41] The first signs of change came in early 1983 when Gusmão negotiated a controversial cease-fire with Indonesian military authorities. Although the cease-fire collapsed amid renewed violence in August 1983 and led to bitter recrimination by some within the resistance, it arguably signaled the beginning of a shift away from direct armed confrontation and toward a more inclusive political strategy.[42] That shift was reinforced in December 1987, when Gusmão formally resigned from Fretilin and declared that Falintil was not aligned with any political party.[43] Despite strong resistance from some quarters—most notably from Fretilin leader Abílio Araújo in Portugal and some Falintil commanders—those crucial changes were formalized in 1988 with the creation of the CNRM (Conselho Nacional de Resistência Maubere, or National Council of Maubere Resistance). The CNRM was intended to overcome the many differences among Timorese—including loyalty to different political parties—that in Gusmão's view still hampered the quest for independence.

The new approach was stimulated, among other things, by a growing awareness among some resistance leaders that its strategy of armed resistance and the language of militant anticolonialism had failed to win the sympathy of the wider international community, and may even have undermined it.[44] Through the 1980s, the most powerful states, including the United States, Australia, Japan, the United Kingdom, and much of Europe, had maintained a familiar posture of indifference toward claims of Indonesian brutality in East Timor. Claiming either that the situation in East Timor was gradually improving or that the evidence of serious human rights violations was not credible, they continued to sell arms and provide military training to Indonesia, and provide its government with political cover and valuable economic assistance. Indeed, by the late 1980s, many states—and some international organizations—had begun to suggest that it was time to accept Indonesia's occupation as a fait accompli. Those who continued to criticize Indonesia and support demands for independence, they said, were simply making things worse, by giving East Timorese false hope and encouraging them to take fruitless risks. Even Amnesty International, which had long been at the forefront of international criticism of Indonesia's human rights record in East Timor, contemplated ending its annual testimony to the United Nations' Decolonization Committee in 1989.[45]

The change in strategy was also stimulated by a new generation of East Timorese. Educated in Indonesian schools and fluent in the Indonesian language, this was the first generation to have no real memory of life under Portuguese rule. Indonesian authorities—like most colonial authorities—had hoped that this new generation would embrace integration, and would go on to become the collaborating political and bureaucratic leaders of the province. They were to be sorely disappointed. For many of East Timor's young people, the experience of living under Indonesian rule—which often meant having witnessed or experienced the extreme brutality of the Indonesian armed forces—had served to galvanize their sense of national identity.[46] That experience was not limited to those whose older relatives had long supported the resistance.[47]

Moreover, as Indonesia's own young nationalists had done in the 1920s and 1930s, the young people in East Timor took advantage of the new educational opportunities made available to them by the colonial power, and used them as a springboard for a revitalized movement of national resistance. Many attended universities in Indonesia from the mid-1980s through the 1990s. By chance, their arrival in Indonesia in these years coincided with a renaissance of Indonesia's own student movement. Despite the dangers of open opposition to the New Order, Indonesian students began to show a measure of political courage and intellectual sophistication that had not been evident for almost a decade. They began to build a network of student groups across the country and link up with NGOs, many of whose members were former university students. They also sought out international contacts, and began to read whatever critical scholarship and reporting was available.[48] In this context, East Timorese students had an opportunity not only to speak freely among themselves about East Timor but also to discuss a wide range of subjects and issues with Indonesian students and activists. Almost without exception, the younger generation of East Timorese point to that experience as an essential turning point in their nationalist consciousness and their search for an effective political strategy to achieve independence.[49] The similarities with Indonesia's historical experience, furthermore, were not lost on East Timor's students. Indeed, they consciously compared their struggle to Indonesia's quest for independence from the Dutch. As Donaciano Gomes, a student activist, wrote in 1995: "The Indonesian military and the people of Indonesia should both remember their own arduous struggle against Dutch colonialism in the late 1940s. They should remember that we . . . have the same rights as they do."[50]

This was the background to the formation in 1988 of Renetil (Resistência Nacional dos Estudantes de Timor Leste, or East Timorese National Students' Resistance), which quickly became one of the most important organizations in the clandestine resistance. According to one of its founding members, Fernando de Araújo, the idea for Renetil did not come from the older generation of leaders but rather from the students themselves. "We considered Xanana Gusmão our leader, but Renetil was our idea. He later gave his approval."[51] Renetil provided a crucial link not only between East Timorese students and the armed resistance but also with Indonesian and international human rights organizations and solidarity groups. From his small student room in Denpasar, Bali, for example, de Araújo sent carefully drafted messages about recent human rights and political developments inside East Timor, to a wide range of international contacts, including Amnesty International and the ICRC. And when new information arrived from abroad, he would send it by Renetil courier back to East Timor for further distribution within the resistance.[52]

This new cohort burst loudly onto the political scene in October 1989 on the occasion of a visit to East Timor by Pope John Paul II. As the pope concluded his celebration of a huge outdoor mass, before the largest contingent of foreign media since the invasion, several young people began to shout and unfurl hand-painted banners bearing proindependence slogans, most of them in English.[53] The reaction of Indonesian security forces was swift and harsh. The suspects were detained by the military and badly beaten in custody. But the message had been sent. Virtually all of the media coverage of the visit was devoted to the act of defiance, and most featured a photograph of security forces hurling metal chairs at the protesters. While it unsettled many in the older generation and arguably resulted in more casualties in the short term, the public demonstration had the important effect of showing Indonesia and its allies as well as other East Timorese that the resistance was not dead. The pope's visit also sent a clear signal to Catholics around the world that it was right to support the cause of human rights in East Timor.[54]

The incident marked the start of a new approach by the resistance. Frustrated by the continued military stalemate, and impressed by the courage and creativity of the new generation, Gusmão endorsed their plans for direct, nonviolent action aimed at an international audience. And after the pope's visit, no opportunity was missed to carry out that strategy. Virtually every foreign delegation that visited the territory after 1989 was met by a brief, often frantic demonstration. One such protest was staged during a visit of the U.S. ambassador to Indonesia, John Monjo, in January 1990. Another took place in early September 1990, during a celebration of the fifth anniversary of the diocese of Dili. In both cases, Indonesian military authorities responded with the arrest, torture, and ill-treatment of the alleged organizers.[55]

The new strategy reached its tragic apex in the demonstration of November 12, 1991, which culminated in the massacre at Santa Cruz. The massacre dealt a terrible, if temporary, blow to the proindependence movement. Apart from the estimated 270 who were killed, many young leaders of the underground resistance were jailed, while others were compelled, sometimes under torture, to provide information to their captors. At the same time, the shocking footage and witness testimony of the massacre, and the callous indifference of Indonesian military authorities, stimulated a number of key developments.

Internationally, governments that had consistently dismissed reports of atrocities in the territory as unfounded simply could not do so in this case. Moreover, because the massacre came at a time when human rights were becoming an increasingly important focus of foreign policy for many Western states, and because international solidarity and church groups were simultaneously redoubling their efforts, it was virtually impossible for these states not to do or say something. The result was an unprecedented international condemnation of Indonesia's human rights record in East Timor and the initiation of some of the first concrete measures designed to compel the Indonesian government to clean up its act.[56] Several governments temporarily suspended development assistance to Indonesia and put Jakarta's leaders on notice that the resumption of assistance as well as future military ties would be jeopardized if they did not take decisive action. In response, for the first time in two decades, senior Indonesian army officers were held to account—albeit somewhat obliquely—for acts of violence against civilians committed by their troops, and some junior officers were tried.[57] After Santa Cruz, in fact, Indonesia remained permanently on the defensive with respect to East Timor, leading its foreign minister, Ali Alatas, to describe the territory famously as "a pebble in our shoe."[58]

The massacre and the unusual international response to it also stimulated critical adjustments in the strategy of the resistance. Without ever renouncing the armed struggle, it began to focus more systematically on diplomatic and political efforts. Ramos-Horta was encouraged to redouble his diplomatic efforts at the United Nations and in capitals around the world. The leadership also sought consciously to broaden the political base of the movement, urging former UDT and Apodeti members to join in forming a broad nationalist coalition. Encouraged by the more open attitude adopted by the resistance and shocked by the events at Santa Cruz, some who had previously cooperated with Indonesia now began to contemplate support for the independence movement.[59] In the same spirit, East Timorese living in exile organized a series of meetings aimed at finding a political solution to the conflict, while inside the country former UDT figures—notably Manuel Carrascalão—formed a new moderately proindependence organization, the GRPRT (Gerakan Rekonsiliasi Persatuan Rakyat Timtim, or East Timorese People's Reconciliation and Unity Movement), seeking a similar goal.

The changes in the strategy of the resistance were also the result of the development in the preceding years of a worldwide network linking the resistance to human rights organizations, the United Nations, solidarity groups, and the Catholic church. Through the 1980s, a unique relationship had developed among these groups that focused on the gathering and dissemination of accurate information on the political and human rights situation in the country. That network, and the steady flow of credible information that it generated, made life increasingly difficult for the Indonesian government and raised the political stakes for its main international supporters through the 1990s.

The alliance with international human rights organizations was a natural one. Amnesty International had been reporting on the human rights situation in East Timor since the late 1970s, and in 1985 had released a major report that drew together most of what was then known about human rights conditions in the territory.[60] For those who had decided that East Timor's best hope lay in gaining the sympathy and support of the international community, it made sense to reach out to these organizations and channel information to them. As the lines of communication developed, those involved learned how to frame their information in a language that would be most readily absorbed and understood by an international audience. Overwhelmingly, the language they adopted was that of universal human rights.[61] Even members of the armed resistance began to adopt it. In 1994, for example, a former Falintil commander, Paulino Gama, wrote:

> We members of the East Timorese resistance are not murderers as some people have tried to depict us, but simply nationalist soldiers dedicated to the defence of our country in the face of Indonesian invasion, occupation, and genocide. We are dedicated to upholding the fundamental principles of the Universal Declaration of Human Rights (1948), such as the avoidance of arbitrary violence and arrest, respect for human life, and the protection of the lives and dignity of all prisoners of war.[62]

By casting its demands in the language of human rights, the East Timorese resistance and its allies succeeded in reaching a far broader international audience than it had done when the movement was seen as being engaged primarily in armed struggle. The audience grew still larger after the Santa Cruz massacre, mainly because that event led to the emergence of dozens of new advocacy groups, and gave a new visibility and cachet to the work of older organizations.[63] Together, these organizations worked aggressively to raise public awareness about the situation in East Timor and to demand that key decision makers in their own countries adopt policies consistent with their rhetorical support for human rights.

Crucially, after 1991 the resistance also began to win support from the growing number of Indonesians who were critical of their own government. Comprised mainly of younger, middle-class human rights activists and students—some of whom had suffered ill-treatment and imprisonment by Indonesian authorities—this group proved to be a vital ally in weakening the Suharto regime at home and exposing the reality of its history in East Timor. As early as the mid-1980s, they began to see the illegal occupation of East Timor as an emblem of all that was wrong with the New Order, and to believe that it was strategically important to their own cause.[64] Part of their calculation was that as an international issue, East Timor's status presented a significant strategic opportunity for those seeking change in Indonesia.[65]

Already underway informally by the late 1980s, the Indonesian solidarity movement for East Timor began in earnest shortly after the Santa Cruz massacre. Almost immediately, Indonesian activists began to form solidarity groups of various persuasions to protest the massacre and to defend the East Timorese in Indonesia and East Timor who had been detained for organizing demonstrations in the weeks thereafter. These groups linked up with existing NGOs, like LBH (Lembaga Bantuan Hukum, or Legal Aid Institute) and ELSAM (Lembaga Studi dan Advokasi Masyarakat, or Institute for Policy Research and Advocacy), under an umbrella organization called the Joint Committee for East Timor. Eventually the Joint Committee was disbanded, but the cause continued to be supported by a wide range of independent groups, the most prominent of which were Fortilos (Forum Solidaritas Untuk Rakyat Timor Timur, or Solidarity Forum for the People of East Timor) and Solidamor (Solidaritas untuk Penyelesaian Damai Timor Leste, or Solidarity for Peace in East Timor).[66] The work of these organizations was critical in increasing the political costs of the occupation for Indonesian authorities, and by the late 1990s had contributed to what one scholar has called "Timor fatigue" among elements of the political elite.[67]

Though often dismissed as powerless or worse, the United Nations also played a vital role. Indeed, in the United Nations and in the body of human rights and humanitarian law that developed under its auspices, many East Timorese found a basis for hope that their dream of national independence was legitimate and could be achieved. More concretely, the United Nations set in motion various institutional mechanisms that helped to ensure that the East Timor question was not forgotten, and provided both the legal and political framework through which independence was ultimately achieved.[68]

The United Nations' refusal to recognize Indonesian sovereignty, for instance, meant that East Timor remained on the agenda of the UN Special Committee on Decolonization. Through the 1980s and 1990s, that committee's annual hearings provided a forum for critics of Indonesia's political and human rights record to voice their views. The UN Commission on Human Rights that met annually in Geneva eventually became another important forum for the expression of criticism, and generating diplomatic pressure on Indonesia and its allies. While the commission had no authority to impose sanctions or initiate military action, it could and did pass resolutions and authorize human rights investigations by a variety of special UN bodies.[69] These investigations, and the reports that resulted from them, often placed Indonesia under a most unwelcome spotlight and constituted a key form of political pressure. And while it is true that the East Timor question was removed from the agenda of the General Assembly in 1982, that was done on the condition that the UN secretary-general would continue to seek an internationally acceptable solution to the problem. It was under this arrangement that tripartite meetings between Portugal, Indonesia, and a succession of UN secretaries-general were held throughout the 1980s and 1990s. And it was in that forum that the three parties finally reached agreement on a mechanism for determining East Timor's future political status in May 1999.

Finally, mention must be made of the vital work undertaken on East Timor's behalf within the UN Secretariat over more than two decades, particularly within the Department of Political Affairs (DPA). During the lean years of the 1980s and early 1990s, the small staff of DPA's Asia and the Pacific Division worked tirelessly, and with considerable success, to keep East Timor on the international political and human rights agenda. Among the most important figures in that effort were Tamrat Samuel, for many years the desk officer responsible for East Timor, and Francesc Vendrell, the head of the Asia and the Pacific Division who in 1999 was appointed Deputy Personal Representative of the Secretary-General for East Timor. It is safe to say that without the efforts of these men, and others within the UN Secretariat, the peaceful resolution of the conflict over East Timor might never have happened.

Another vital ally was the Catholic church. Notwithstanding its colonial origins and long association with authoritarian rule, it is fair to say that by the early 1980s, the Catholic church constituted the moral center of resistance to Indonesian rule. It was telling, for example, that when Indonesian occupation authorities required the population to choose one of the state's five recognized religions after 1975, some 90 percent of East Timorese chose Catholicism. It was therefore uniquely placed to bring together East Timorese of different regions, generations, and political persuasions.

One reason that the church became a focus of East Timorese cultural identity and a center of resistance to Indonesian rule was that for several years after the invasion of 1975, it was completely cut off from the universal church. In the process, it developed a view and practice rooted in the ideals of social justice and service to the people. Those ideals were articulated in a remarkable document written from East Timor in 1981:

> The people are aware that their faith comes from God whose Word takes the form of social justice. This justice derives from the justice of God in His relations with His people. This justice must be built by the people themselves based on faith and co-operation with God and with one's fellow men who are still the sacrifices of oppression. For us, living the faith without serious endeavors for the building of social justice is the same as making faith merely foreign and mystical. Creating justice together with the present Indonesian government is not possible, or not yet, although the people desire justice greatly.[70]

A key figure in the transformation of the church was Monsignor Martinho da Costa Lopes, vicar general and then apostolic administrator of the diocese of Dili in the crucial first decade of the occupation. A fearless and outspoken critic of Indonesian rule, he was removed from his position by the Vatican in 1983, after which he lived in Lisbon until his death.[71] Although his efforts to influence international opinion after 1983 did not bear immediate fruit, they contributed to a growing awareness of the problem outside of East Timor and helped to lay the foundation for future work.[72] His successor, Monsignor (later bishop) Carlos Filipe Ximenes Belo, played an equally significant role over the next fifteen years of the occupation.[73] A member of the Salesian order who had been abroad at the time of the Indonesian invasion and for several years thereafter, Belo was appointed in 1983 amid doubts that he would have the strength to stand up to the Indonesians. Within a few years, he had proven his critics wrong, and had emerged as a powerful defender of not only the church but also the cultural and political rights of East Timorese.

While Bishop Belo and other church leaders did not necessarily or openly support East Timorese independence, they sought consistently to defend their people from abuse by Indonesian security forces, and demanded that they be given an opportunity to decide their own political future. In a letter written on February 11, 1989 to UN Secretary-General Perez de Cuellar, Bishop Belo maintained that

> the people of East Timor must be allowed to express their views on their future through a plebiscite. Hitherto the people have not

FIGURE 4.3. Bishop Carlos Filipe Ximenes Belo and U.S. President Bill Clinton meet in the office of U.S. national security adviser Sandy Berger in June 1997. A powerful defender of the cultural and political rights of the East Timorese people, Bishop Belo used his position in the Catholic church to inform and influence world opinion. In 1989, he famously called for a plebiscite to resolve East Timor's status, and declared that "we continue to die as a people and as a nation." Together with José Ramos-Horta, he was awarded the Nobel Prize for Peace in 1996. (White House)

been consulted. Others speak in the name of the people. Indonesia says that the people of East Timor have already chosen integration, but the people of East Timor themselves have never said this. Portugal wants time to solve the problem. And we continue to die as a people and as a nation.[74]

Beyond the principled positions taken by its clergy, the unique advantage of the Catholic church in East Timor lay in the fact that it was administered directly from Rome (via the papal nuncio in Jakarta) and not as part of the Indonesian church. While that did not prevent Indonesian authorities from trying to co-opt, threaten, and otherwise interfere in its work, it gave East Timor's church an unusual and vital measure of autonomy. One practical consequence of that arrangement, with profound symbolic implications, was the Vatican decision in 1981 to make Tetum—and not Indonesian—the language of the liturgy in East Timor. Pope John Paul II's visit to East Timor in 1989 was also of enormous significance because it offered hope to East Timorese that they had not been forgotten and were recognized by the universal church. As one person who demonstrated in favor of independence on that occasion later said, "We felt very proud. If he'd only come to Indonesia, it would have meant he accepted East Timor as part of Indonesia, but he singled us out. It gave us a lot of hope."[75] More generally, the arrangement eventually provided the local church with an extraordinarily wide network of international support that Indonesian authorities were powerless to obstruct.[76]

Paradoxically, international linkages of various kinds were further strengthened after the capture of Gusmão in late 1992. Given his unusual stature with all different elements of the resistance, Gusmão's removal from the field of battle seemed to some to signal the beginning of the end of East Timor's hopes.[77] Remarkably, however, in the years of his imprisonment in Jakarta, Gusmão's stature only grew, particularly in international circles. Gusmão began to emerge, Mandela-like, as an internationally respected statesperson. On visits to Jakarta, foreign dignitaries would make a point of meeting him, and virtually all would later comment on his intelligence and sincerity. Gusmão also took advantage of his time in prison to develop his ties with a range of international organizations, such as A Paz é Possível em Timor-Leste, Tapol, and Amnesty International, and individuals whom he knew to be sympathetic to the cause of independence. Through these interactions, he deepened his understanding of international affairs and, on that basis, adjusted his approach to the resistance.

The growing importance of these international linkages in Gusmão's thinking and in the strategy of the resistance was revealed soon after his incarceration. In June 1993, he authorized several young East Timorese to enter the embassies of Finland and Sweden in Jakarta to seek political asylum. The action was carefully planned to have the maximum possible international impact. The letter that the group presented to the embassy officials in support of their asylum claim made careful use of the language of international human rights, citing relevant treaties and covenants.[78] The timing coincided exactly with the UN World Conference on Human Rights in Vienna, where Indonesia was playing a central role in efforts to weaken international human rights standards. Moreover, with the help of Gusmão's future wife, Kirsty Sword, essential information about the asylum seekers—including their names, photos, and biographical details—was communicated in advance to select individuals and organizations outside of Indonesia.[79] As a consequence, when the young people entered the embassies on June 23, an international network was poised to act. Amnesty International's first report on the action was released within twenty-four hours, in fact, prompting Alatas to accuse the organization of orchestrating the action to embarrass the Indonesian government.[80] The same tactic was employed again in November 1994, on the third anniversary of the Santa Cruz massacre. With U.S. president Bill Clinton and thousands of journalists in Jakarta for an economic summit, twenty-nine East Timorese students leaped over the walls of the U.S. Embassy and remained there for more than a week, demanding the release of Gusmão and his inclusion in peace talks, once again successfully forcing East Timor to the center of the international agenda.[81]

A further international development that served to undermine Indonesia's position, both at home and abroad, came in 1996 when Ramos-Horta and Bishop Belo were jointly awarded the Nobel Peace Prize. In bestowing the prize, the Nobel Committee said explicitly that it hoped the award would "spur efforts to find a diplomatic solution to the conflict in East Timor based on the people's right to self-determination."[82] Indonesian officials were incensed by the choice of Ramos-Horta, whom they regarded not as a peacemaker but rather a partisan, and they spared no effort to besmirch his reputation in the media. As for Bishop Belo, there was little that could be said against him, which may explain why President Suharto refused to offer him any word of congratulations—but also refrained from criticizing him—during a visit to East Timor shortly after the prize was announced.

The Nobel Prize raised East Timorese hopes for independence to unprecedented levels. When Bishop Belo returned to Dili in December 1996, hundreds of thousands of people lined the streets to greet him. The prize also increased international awareness of the East Timor issue, and gave a new status and credibility to all advocates of independence. When he visited Jakarta in July 1997, President Nelson Mandela made a point of meeting Gusmão in prison. Two months later, a group of Nobel Prize laureates and other prominent figures wrote an open letter to President Suharto calling on him to work with Mandela and UN Secretary-General Kofi Annan to find a lasting solution to the East Timor problem.[83]

Buoyed by such indications of international support and predictions that Suharto's New Order was on its last legs, in early 1998 Gusmão, still in prison, lent his support to another strategic adjustment of the resistance: the formation of a truly nonpartisan, national coalition, called the CNRT (Conselho Nacional de Resistência Timorense, or National Council of Timorese Resistance). For the first time since the Fretilin-UDT coalition of early 1975, the CNRT brought together the two principal political parties in a formal alliance, based on a broad nationalist agenda, with the common goal of independence.[84] Significantly, it also invited former collaborators, including Apodeti leaders and members, to join. Led by Gusmão and represented abroad by Ramos-Horta, the CNRT did a good deal to enhance the credibility of the resistance, both at home and internationally. Most importantly, it helped to undermine suggestions that East Timorese were too deeply divided to become an independent nation. In view of the fact that such arguments were seriously entertained within the United States and other key governments, this was a great achievement.

Viewed in retrospect or through the eyes of nationalist historians, these developments may seem to point naturally and inexorably to East Timor's eventual independence. From the perspective of early 1998, however, that was hardly the case. In spite of the widespread sympathy for the victims of human rights abuse, the courage of the young activists and the church, the international legitimacy bestowed by the Nobel Prize, and the new unity of the political leadership, the prospects for East Timor still looked grim. Indonesian authorities remained adamant that East Timor was an integral part of Indonesia and refused to entertain any change in its status. To make matters worse, Indonesia and its allies began to argue that if East Timor were given the right to secede, Indonesia would be in danger of breaking apart like Yugoslavia. With the trauma of the violence and ethnic cleansing in the Balkans still fresh, this was an ominous threat, and it seemed likely to inhibit any serious action by any of the states that really mattered.

CHAPTER FIVE

MOBILIZING THE MILITIAS

THE BEGINNING OF THE END of this impasse came in May 1998 when, faced with economic crisis, widespread demands for democratization, and unprecedented rioting in Jakarta and other cities, President Suharto finally stepped down. Following his resignation, events moved quickly. In a series of moves that surprised many observers, Suharto's successor, Habibie first proposed that East Timor might be offered greater political autonomy, and later that the people of the territory should be permitted to express their views on that offer in a referendum. By May 1999, Indonesia and Portugal had signed a set of UN-sponsored agreements that spelled out plans for a popular consultation on the question of East Timor's political status, and the UN Security Council had begun to set up UNAMET to oversee that process.

These were dramatic changes. For the first time since 1975, there was the real possibility of a peaceful and internationally acceptable solution to the conflict in East Timor. But the agreements that opened up that exciting prospect also created the opportunity for the process to be subverted by its opponents. Chief among those opponents were high-ranking officers of the TNI, and a fair number of East Timorese who had thrown in their lot with Indonesia. The latter group included some, though certainly not all, who had done well economically and politically under Indonesian rule. It also included a good many of the poor and the unemployed who were linked by patronage or family networks either to the pro-Indonesian elites or directly to the TNI.

From the time that Habibie proposed the idea of special autonomy for East Timor in mid-1998, and especially after January 1999 when he suggested that there should be a vote on the question, these groups began to set in motion a strategy designed to ensure victory for the pro-

Indonesian side or, failing that, to derail or discredit the process altogether. That strategy entailed, above all, the selective use of violence and terror against likely supporters of independence. Three decades of experience with rigged elections in Indonesia had given TNI planners reason to believe that the targeted use of violence, together with a campaign of disinformation and material inducement, would ensure a favorable vote. However, in anticipation of the fact that the process would be closely monitored both by the United Nations and hundreds of independent observers, the strategy called for most of the violence to be carried out by local militia groups, while the TNI and the police would maintain an outward posture of neutrality. That approach not only provided the TNI and the Indonesian government with a measure of plausible deniability for the acts of violence that would inevitably occur but also allowed the TNI to portray itself as the essential peacemaker in what it would pretend was a conflict among East Timorese. This strategy was facilitated in great measure by the feebleness of key states—especially the United States, Australia, and even Portugal—in the course of the UN-brokered negotiations over the referendum. Still eager not to offend Indonesian authorities, those states and UN negotiators agreed to deeply flawed security arrangements that left the TNI free to orchestrate a campaign of terror, while also leaving the UN mission utterly powerless to stop it.

The May 5 Agreements

When Suharto named his vice president, Habibie, as his successor in late May 1998, many expected that little would change. Nothing could have been further from the truth. Indeed, it was Habibie, the Suharto "crony," who took the decisions that would ultimately bring an end to the twenty-four-year Indonesian occupation of East Timor. The first step came in June 1998, when Habibie's administration announced that it would be prepared to offer East Timor "wide-ranging autonomy" in exchange for an end to demands for independence.[1] Emboldened by the new climate of political openness and believing that the opportunity had finally come to end Indonesian rule, thousands of East Timorese took to the streets of Dili to demonstrate against the "autonomy" proposal and in favor of complete independence. For the first time in twenty-three years, proindependence banners, posters, and flags were openly displayed, without any immediate response from military and police authorities. At public meetings, under the very noses of the Indonesian authorities, dozens of speakers expressed their anger and impatience with Indonesian rule. Remarkably, the speakers sometimes included Indonesians. In an emotionally charged gathering in August 1998, for instance, three Indonesian human rights activists—Yenny Rosa Damayanti, Coki Naipospos, and the Catholic priest Romo Mangun—shared the podium with East Timorese, each declaring their unconditional support for an independent East Timor. As they did so, the packed hall filled with cries of "Viva!" and "Viva Timor Leste Independente!"[2]

Meanwhile, at a meeting with the UN secretary-general in August, the Indonesian and Portuguese foreign ministers—Alatas and Gama—commenced in-depth discussions of the autonomy option. They agreed for the moment to differ on whether autonomy should be the final arrangement, as Indonesia preferred, or as Portugal insisted, an interim solution pending a further exercise of self-determination by the people of East Timor.[3] On that basis, and with input from the different parties, the United Nations began drafting a plan for East Timor's wide-ranging autonomy. At that stage in the negotiations, there was no talk of a referendum, and no serious discussion of immediate independence—at least among those who were party to the negotiations.[4]

Then, in an astonishing break with past government policy, in late January 1999 Habibie announced that the people of East Timor should be given a chance to express their views on the political future of the territory. Clarifying the policy, Foreign Minister Alatas told journalists that East Timorese would be asked whether they accepted or rejected the UN plan to grant the territory autonomy within Indonesia. If they rejected it, he explained, Indonesia would withdraw and East Timor would be on its own.[5]

Both his detractors and supporters suggested that Habibie's proposal was a bid to win the support of the international community, whose backing Indonesia badly needed if it was to rebound from the financial crisis. That is undoubtedly true. In late 1998, for example, the Australian government suggested that Indonesia might defuse the crisis by promising a referendum on the question of independence at some point in the future. That idea was spelled out in a letter dated December 19, 1998, from Prime Minister John Howard to President Habibie. Habibie was initially angered by the letter, but he gave Howard's proposal his attention, and it formed the basis for internal discussions over the next few weeks.[6] Australia was not alone in urging Indonesia to do more to resolve the East Timor problem. The U.S. and Portuguese governments and UN Secretary-General Annan had also been pushing, albeit gently, in the same direction.

Nevertheless, the boldness of Habibie's proposal seems to have surprised even those urging change. Certainly none of the major powers involved had proposed anything as drastic as Habibie's offer of an immediate consultation on autonomy or independence.[7] In fact, as late as February 1999, the U.S. government was still hoping to avoid a direct popular ballot in East Timor. I became aware of this surprising position in February 1999 during a working dinner on Indonesia policy with Secretary of State Madeleine Albright. There, to my amazement, I learned that State Department officials were still searching for alternatives to a referendum.[8] When I asked why the administration was reluctant to support such a course, an official explained that it was because both Alatas and the Indonesian army opposed it.[9] Paul Wolfowitz, who had previously served as ambassador to Indonesia and was present at the dinner, added misleadingly that the Indonesian army had been the only guarantor of peace and order in the territory, and that a referendum would likely give rise to renewed violence among East Timorese. In seeking to avoid a popular vote, then, U.S. officials were taking their cues from the Indonesian foreign minister and the army, not from President Habibie or East Timor's political leaders.

At least as important in Habibie's decision to call for a referendum was the mounting pressure from international human rights and solidarity groups. While Indonesia's state allies were seeking gentle ways to help Indonesia out of its bind over East Timor, these groups were stepping up the pressure for an immediate withdrawal or at least a credible referendum on the issue. Through public demonstrations, critical media attention, and persistent pressure on their own political leaders, they were threatening to undermine relations with key creditor countries at precisely the moment when Indonesia needed their assistance more than ever. It is not an exaggeration to say that in the final years of the Suharto period and the months after Habibie assumed power, the international solidarity movement dramatically increased the costs of the Indonesian occupation of East Timor. As Alatas acknowledged, "East Timor is still a nuisance internationally, leading to many misunderstandings, even among our allies, and creating difficulties in our diplomatic work."[10] To Habibie and his circle of "modernist Muslims," East Timor must have appeared to be far more trouble than it was worth. In that light, the offer to hold a referendum to settle the matter once and for all made sense.

Habibie's initiative was not only a response to such international pressures, however, but also an attempt to resolve the matter swiftly for domestic political reasons. By the late 1990s East Timor had become a central concern of Indonesian human rights advocates and anti–Suharto activists, and it was held up as a symbol of all they believed was wrong with the New Order. Habibie and his advisers were only too aware that against that backdrop—and in the context of insistent demands for democratization, demilitarization, and the protection of human rights that preceded and followed Suharto's resignation—the continued occupation of East Timor would do little to improve his administration's fragile political legitimacy. By contrast, a bold move that captured the prevailing spirit of "reformasi" might improve his administration's credibility with its staunchest critics, while also satisfying the international community's demand for some kind of action. So when it began to appear that even with the granting of autonomy, the issue might yet drag on for several more years, Habibie decided that it was time to bring an end to the problem once and for all.[11]

Finally and crucially, Habibie and most of his cabinet agreed to a referendum because they were confident that the vote could be won, and that with victory, the East Timor issue would be settled permanently in Indonesia's favor. Their confidence stemmed from two considerations. First, with some three decades of experience in orchestrating electoral victories, they assumed that the same methods could be used again to similar effect in East Timor. More specifically, the case of the "Act of Free Choice" in Irian Jaya in 1969—in which the population had been intimidated and cajoled into voting for integration with Indonesia, and the result endorsed by the United Nations—gave them reason to believe that they knew precisely how to assure victory, even under the nose of international observers. The fact that the victory in Irian Jaya had been orchestrated by retired general Feisal Tanjung, who now held the powerful post of coordinating minister for political and security affairs, must have reinforced that belief considerably. Second, like so many colonial powers and authoritarian regimes, they appear genuinely to have believed their own propaganda and internal intelligence reports.[12] For years, the reports generated by army intelligence had described the supporters of independence as a small band of disgruntled troublemakers and guerrilla fighters whose influence over the general population was sketchy. With a combination of material inducement and targeted intimidation, they believed, the vast majority of the population could easily be convinced to vote for continued Indonesian rule. Needless to say, these calculations proved to be disastrously off the mark, but they were likely the basis on which the decision to proceed with the vote was made and on which the strategy for victory was based.

Whatever his motives in proposing it, Habibie's idea of a popular consultation on autonomy dramatically altered the focus of UN-sponsored negotiations. When the parties met the secretary-general in March 1999, they quickly agreed to the idea of a direct UN-administered ballot for or against the autonomy proposal. Further negotiations in April paved the way for a set of accords, signed on May 5, 1999, and thereafter known as the May 5 Agreements.[13] The main agreement, between Indonesia and Portugal, stipulated that East Timorese would be asked to accept or reject the offer of a special autonomy package whose terms had been agreed to by the parties in earlier negotiations. A second agreement, on the modalities for the popular consultation, made it clear that the rejection of the proposed autonomy framework would set East Timor on the path toward independence. The question posed on the ballot (in Tetum, Portuguese, Indonesian, and English) would read as follows:

Do you accept the proposed special autonomy for East Timor within the unitary State of the Republic of Indonesia?

OR

Do you reject the proposed special autonomy for East Timor, leading to East Timor's separation from Indonesia?

If these elements of the May 5 Agreements appeared too good to be true, there was another piece that from the outset was tragically flawed. That was the Agreement on Security. Hammered out in the final stages of negotiations in April 1999, the agreement placed sole responsibility for maintaining law and order during and after the referendum in the hands of Indonesian security forces. The United Nations itself, including its police and military contingents, would be completely unarmed. The danger of that arrangement was not lost on outside observers, or even on those who had helped to negotiate it. UN Secretary-General Annan was evidently so concerned about it that in a separate memorandum to the Indonesian and Portuguese foreign ministers, dated May 4, 1999, he set out several criteria by which he would judge whether the security situation was conducive to a free and fair ballot. These included bringing armed civilian groups under firm control, an immediate ban on rallies by armed groups, the prompt arrest and prosecution of those inciting or

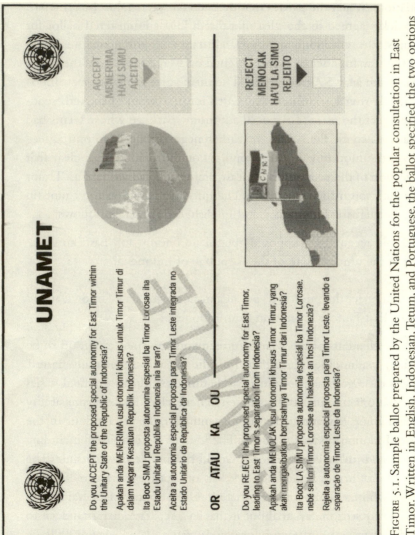

UNAMET

Do you ACCEPT the proposed special autonomy for East Timor within the Unitary State of the Republic of Indonesia?

Apakah anda MENERIMA usul otonomi khusus untuk Timor Timur di dalam Negara Kesatuan Republik Indonesia?

Ita Boot SIMU proposta autonomia espesiál ba Timor Lorosae iha Estadu Unitariu Repúblika Indonézia nia laran?

Aceita a autonomia especial proposta para Timor Leste integrada no Estado Unitário da República da Indonésia?

OR   ATAU   KA   OU

Do you REJECT the proposed special autonomy for East Timor, leading to East Timor's separation from Indonesia?

Apakah anda MENOLAK usul otonomi khusus Timor Timur, yang akan mengakibatkan berpisahnya Timor Timur dari Indonesia?

Ita Boot LA SIMU proposta autonomia espesiál ba Timor Lorosae, nebé sei tori Timor Lorosae atu haketak an hosi Indonézia?

Rejeita a autonomia especial proposta para Timor Leste, levando a separação de Timor Leste da Indonésia?

ACCEPT
MENERIMA
HA'U SIMU
ACEITO

REJECT
MENOLAK
HA'U LA SIMU
REJEITO

FIGURE 5.1. Sample ballot prepared by the United Nations for the popular consultation in East Timor. Written in English, Indonesian, Tetum, and Portuguese, the ballot specified the two options open to voters: to accept the proposed special autonomy for East Timor within Indonesia or to reject it, leading to East Timor's independence. To assist voters with limited literacy, the ballot also displayed the symbols of the proautonomy and proindependence options. (Geoffrey Robinson)

threatening violence, the assumption of the Indonesian police of sole responsibility for law and order, the redeployment of Indonesian military forces, and the immediate commencement of a process of laying down arms, to be completed well before the ballot. He also made it clear that in accordance with the terms of the security agreement, he would stop the process should he find that these criteria were not being met.[14] The memo pointed accurately to the main sources of trouble and became a basis for later UN assessments that the security situation was not in fact acceptable. Nevertheless, because it was not formally part of the May 5 Agreements, and because its provisions were completely at odds with Indonesian plans for the referendum, there was little prospect that its provisions would be implemented.

Some of those who were privy to the negotiations of early 1999 have suggested that the agreement on security was a necessary compromise—that insistence on an armed international force was simply not politically "realistic" in light of Indonesia's strident opposition to the idea.[15] Like most arguments about realism in politics, this is a dubious one. So many things happened in 1999 that had not previously been considered possible, that one simply cannot say with confidence whether, if vigorously advocated, the idea of an international security force might have been accepted. And it seems clear that the argument for such a force was abandoned without being seriously tried. In a press conference in New York announcing the agreement, Alatas told reporters that "throughout our discussions, UN peacekeeping forces have not been an issue that has been raised."[16] Once again, old habits and assumptions ruled. As a Jakarta-based diplomat later admitted, in the course of those negotiations "everybody conceded too much."[17]

Militia Mobilization

By all accounts, there was no opposition to Habibie's proposal when it was presented to the Indonesian cabinet in January 1999, but that did not mean that everyone welcomed it. Opposition was especially pronounced within the TNI, whose officers worried that a popular consultation would raise questions about the legality of the 1975 takeover of East Timor and create a dangerous precedent for other areas seeking independence, especially Aceh and West Papua. Despite the challenges to its authority that had attended President Suharto's fall, moreover, in 1999 the TNI remained the most powerful political institution in the country, and its influence was especially great in East Timor. Largely for these reasons, the TNI took the lead in devising a strategy to ensure that the referendum would produce the desired outcome.

As in previous years, the unique power of the TNI along with certain aspects of its doctrine, structure, and standard operating procedure shaped its strategy, and so also the violence in 1999. Among the most conspicuous elements of that strategy was the mobilization of armed militia groups dedicated to maintaining the tie with Indonesia. Although as we have seen these groups had deep historical roots, the mobilization of the militias began with a new vigor in mid-1998, shortly after President Habibie first floated the autonomy option for East Timor.[18] By March 1999, more than two dozen militia groups were active, and they quickly became the main conduits for pressuring the population to vote for autonomy and the main perpetrators of violence. In that month, Australian intelligence concluded that the Indonesian army was "clearly protecting, and in some cases operating with, pro-Jakarta militias in attacks in East Timor."[19]

Some of the groups that came to light at this time had existed for many years, such as Halilintar in the district of Bobonaro, Team Saka and Team Sera in Baucau, Makikit in Viqueque, and Team Alfa in Lautem. But others were new, including Besi Merah Putih, based in Liquiçá, Aitarak in the district of Dili, Dadurus Merah Putih in Bobonaro, Mahidi in Ainaro, Laksaur in Covalima, Darah Merah in Ermera, Ahi in Aileu, and Ablai in Manufahi.[20] Reflecting their close ties to the TNI, the militia groups adopted military rhetoric and modes of organization. They were organized into companies and platoons, and their members were described as soldiers or freedom fighters. By early 1999 the different militia groups had been drawn together under a single military-style structure, called the PPI. The PPI was led by a longtime pro-Indonesia figure, João Tavares, who was given the military title of *Panglima* or "commander." In a further imitation of military organization, the PPI was made up of three sectoral commands, each of which was under the control of a deputy PPI commander.[21]

Militia members were a varied group and became involved for many different reasons. Some joined more or less willingly. They included men who had fought on the Indonesian side at some stage since 1975, who had relatives who had been killed by the proindependence party, Fretilin, or patrons who had done relatively well under Indonesian rule. Others were recruited directly from criminal gangs involved in gambling rings, protection rackets, and so on, or they were what one observer has

FIGURE 5.2. Eurico Guterres in Dili, 1999. A trusted ally of the Indonesian military, in 1999 Guterres was named commander of the notorious prointegration militia group Aitarak and deputy commander of the overall militia organization, the PPI. In this photograph, taken in front of the governor's office, he is set to lead prointegration militias on a rally through Dili. (Eddy Hasby)

called "pathetic nobodies," easily seduced by money, alcohol, drugs, and the possibility of wielding a gun and exercising raw power over others. A good many, perhaps the majority, were poor, uneducated, and unemployed.[22] As such, they were dependent on the patronage of TNI officers, particularly those from Kopassus, or those East Timorese elites who had opted to side with Indonesia. Having failed at school, with few employment prospects, their only option was to follow the lead of their patrons, in the hope that they would prevail and be rewarded for their loyalty. That was certainly the profile of the notorious militia leader, Eurico Guterres.

A considerable number, however, joined the militias under duress. In each district, a target was established by government and military authorities for the number of militiamen to be recruited. The target was typically about ten men per village. It was the responsibility of the respective village heads and subdistrict heads to ensure that the target was met, but TNI officers were invariably involved. Speaking to journalists in early 1999, the Korem chief of staff, Lieutenant Colonel Supardi, said that the military had already recruited roughly twelve hundred militiamen, and that recruitment was scheduled to continue until March.[23] The former pro-Indonesian figure, Tomás Gonçalves—who fled the country to Macau in early 1999 out of disgust with the TNI militia strategy—alleged that officers of the Kopassus unit Satgas Tribuana played an especially important role in recruitment efforts. Speaking in early 1999, he said, "It's these people who are recruiting the militias—they force them. If they don't, they are picked up at night and killed. [Those who join] are given military training, arms, and indoctrinated."[24]

Although it was not the case that all those who refused to join were killed, coercion and threats were common elements of the recruitment effort. At public meetings and in house-to-house campaigns conducted in early 1999, members of existing militias and TNI soldiers pressured men to join. Those who refused or resisted for whatever reasons were typically accused of harboring proindependence sentiments, and were subjected to reprisals. Many had their homes burned and their families threatened, and some were killed. Where village heads or subdistrict heads were themselves unenthusiastic about forming militia groups, they were subjected to threats and reprisals by militia groups, and TNI soldiers, from neighboring communities. As one former militiaman testified, "They called us, took our names and said, 'you've got to join this group.' We said, 'what are we joining it for?' They said, 'If you refuse to join, you'll see what happens.' So we were scared and we joined."[25] Similarly, as the wife of a man who had fled his village after refusing to join the militias testified, "They came to our village and destroyed everything. They killed our chickens, they took what they could carry and sold it. And they said, if [they couldn't] find [my] husband they would come back and beat me and my children to death."[26]

In addition to those who were recruited under duress and those who joined willingly, there were some militiamen who were not East Timorese civilians at all but Indonesian army soldiers dressed up as local militias. Particularly in the pre-UNAMET and postballot periods, there were frequent reports that the militiamen were in fact TNI soldiers in civilian clothing. Drawing on the testimony of rape survivors from 1999, the UN Special Rapporteurs reported in late 1999 that "on many occasions no distinction could be made between members of the militia and members of the TNI, as often they were one and the same person in different uniforms."[27] Film footage, shot in 1999, that shows a TNI soldier changing into militia costume and donning a long-haired militia wig, lent support to allegations that at least some of the militia were not what they appeared. Those allegations were later confirmed with the discovery of several internal military documents, discussed in more detail below, showing that some militiamen were in fact TNI soldiers, and some militia groups were designated as TNI units.

Not surprisingly, the stated aims of the militias reflected a preoccupation with the outcome of the popular consultation, and an approach that was both dogmatic and bellicose. In a letter to his post commander, dated March 30, 1999, for example, an Aitarak member spelled out his vision for the coming months:

> Aitarak, which now has 400 men, is going to answer and destroy all threats from the pro-independence side.... If in spite of that there are still those who insist on asking for independence, they are welcome to it but they should beware that independence will, without a doubt, end with the spilling of blood.... This is the foundation on which Aitarak has been created, under the leadership of Eurico Guterres.[28]

Indonesian authorities insisted that these groups were spontaneous reflections of local support for integration, and that the violence was the unavoidable result of conflict among proindependence and prointegration East Timorese.[29] Accordingly, they argued, the TNI and police were more than ever needed to preserve the peace. That claim was no doubt intended to disguise the central role of the TNI in creating and supporting the militias responsible for the violence. But evidence soon emerged demonstrating a close link between the TNI and the militias.

The early evidence included a memorandum dated March 11, 1999, addressed to East Timor's supreme militia commander, Tavares, and other militia leaders. Issued by the commander of the Darah Merah militia, Lafaek Saburai, the memo announced plans for the start of Operation Clean Sweep (Operasi Pembersihan) at 00:00 hours on May 1, 1999.[30] According to the document, the operation would "capture and eliminate" key proindependence supporters, by first moving the entire pro-Indonesian population of Dili to the district of Bobonaro, and then killing all those who remained in Dili as of a certain date. Although the Clean Sweep document did not prove definitively that there was a high-level plan for violence by Indonesian military intelligence, as some observers have claimed, it did provide compelling evidence of the nature of the relationship between the militias and the Indonesian authorities. It showed, for instance, that militia groups aspired to broad coordination with the TNI. It also revealed the extent to which the rhetoric of terror, a hallmark of the TNI's own counterinsurgency strategy, had become a standard feature of the militia style by early 1999.[31]

Among the clearest indications of the TNI link to the militias was the evidence that military officials were supplying them with modern firearms and permitting them to carry other weapons in contravention of the law.[32] Much of that evidence came from the public statements of high-ranking TNI officers and militia leaders. In February 1999, for example, the deputy commander for East Timor, Colonel Mudjiono, told a journalist that firearms had been distributed to prointegration groups to allow them to resist Falintil forces.[33] The regional military commander, Major General Adam Damiri, also told the media that the TNI had supplied arms to the militias, though he denied that the intention was to support the prointegration side.[34] In Jakarta, the army chief of staff, General Subagyo Hadisiswoyo, acknowledged that the army was supplying weapons to East Timorese auxiliaries to help in the effort to secure East Timor.[35] The armed forces spokesperson, General Sudradjat, likewise confirmed that guns had been distributed to the militias, but helpfully clarified that "we only give weapons to those we trust."[36]

At about the same time, the leader of the Mahidi militia, Cancio Carvalho, told journalists that the TNI had given his group twenty Chinese-made SKS automatic weapons in late December 1998, which had then been used to carry out a number of deadly attacks on nearby villages.[37] The attacks reportedly included one in Galitas village, in Zumalai, on January 25, 1999, in which several people were killed, including a pregnant woman and a fifteen-year-old boy.[38] Speaking to journalists shortly after these events, Carvalho admitted to his personal involvement in the killings while commanding a militia unit: "I was leading them and we attacked in two lines. I ordered them to fire in a scissor action, like this. The woman was torn apart." He also sought to explain why the pregnant woman and other victims had been targeted: "This woman was the wife of a Falintil commander. I'm not sure if the old man was a troublemaker or not."[39] The Aitarak militia leader, Guterres, likewise confirmed that weapons had been distributed at this time, but insisted that "I was given guns not just to protect myself and the other integrationists but to protect opponents of integration as well."[40]

This evidence, which was widely known in 1999, was further substantiated by a number of secret military documents that came to light somewhat later. One of these, from the Kodim in Baucau, dated February 3, 1999, lists ninety-one members of the Pusaka Special Company, also known as the Saka militia. Titled "List of Members of the Pusaka Special Company, Kodim 1628/Baucau," the document records the type and registration number of the weapon assigned to all but one member of the group. The document is signed by the well-known militia leader Joanico C. Belo, who is identified as a first sergeant and commander of the Pusaka Special Company.[41] A second document, from the Kodim in Viqueque, lists more than forty-nine members of the Makikit militia authorized to carry weapons, and specifies the type and registration number of the weapon assigned to each member.[42] A third document is a secret telegram, dated February 2, 1999, from the commander for East Timor to all Dandim and the commander of the Kopassus Task Force, Satgas Tribuana V. The document, issued in anticipation of a visit to East Timor by a UN delegation later that month, makes it clear that the TNI had temporarily withdrawn weapons from the militias only to return them later. The telegram orders all Dandim and the commander of Satgas Tribuana V to prepare reports on acts of violence committed against militias by the proindependence side, and instructs them to focus on the "period after weapons were withdrawn from the Ratih and Surwan until the weapons were returned to them."[43]

It is worth noting that apart from demonstrating direct TNI involvement in arming the militias—and confirming that some militiamen were in fact TNI soldiers—this documentary evidence also confirms that the militias were not given unrestricted access to modern firearms. Rather, the weapons were stored—usually at a military command post—and distributed to militias in advance of particular military operations. Speaking to Indonesian investigators in late 1999, General Wiranto made precisely this point: "Sometimes weapons were provided," he said, "but this does not mean that [militias] carried weapons wherever they went. The weapons were stored at Sub-District military headquarters."[44] This pattern of TNI control over militia access to weapons, often mentioned in witness testimony, is confirmed by other military documents as well. One of these is a secret telegram, dated January 28, 1999, from Colonel Suratman to all thirteen Dandim in the territory. The telegram orders the Dandim to "collect all weapons held by Wanra and Ratih members when they are not conducting special tasks or combat operations in their respective areas."[45] Taken together, this evidence confirms that TNI officers exercised a significant measure of control over militia access to weapons, and that military authorities were directly involved in planning and coordinating militia operations.

The deadly consequences of such official support for the militias were brought home in a series of violent incidents in March and April 1999, as the UN negotiations entered a critical stage. Across the territory, but especially where the CNRT had begun to organize openly, militia groups backed by the TNI and police forces began to assault and detain known advocates of independence, and to burn down the houses of those thought to be supporting them. Dozens of civilians were killed in these operations, and several thousands more fled for what seemed to be the relative safety of nearby towns. These brazen attacks coincided with a visit to East Timor by a UN assessment team and may even have been intended to derail the negotiations for a popular consultation that were then reaching a critical stage in New York. They very nearly did so. On its return to New York in early April, the team reported ominously that it had found "a very dangerous level of tension and political violence, which, if not quickly curbed, could easily spiral out of control."

Indeed, unless ABRI [as the TNI was known until April 1] adopts a neutral stand and disarms or otherwise neutralizes the militias, the situation risks becoming unmanageable in the period prior to and after the consultation, particularly if the result is in favor of East

Timor's separation from Indonesia. . . . It is abundantly clear that a free and fair poll could not be held under the prevailing circumstances.[46]

From his prison cell in Jakarta, Gusmão—who had earlier ordered Falintil forces to observe a policy of restraint—lashed out angrily against the mounting attacks and the apparent indifference of the international community to them. In a statement issued on April 5, he announced that he had authorized proindependence forces to "take all necessary action" to protect the population and called for a "general popular insurrection" against the militias.[47] Indonesian officials immediately portrayed his call as an act of provocation, and said that it proved the need for continued Indonesian rule to prevent further "clashes" among East Timorese. Fearing that a Falintil mobilization at that delicate stage would provide Indonesia with an easy pretext for a crackdown and for the cancellation of the referendum, Gusmão's closest advisers—as well as UN officials and some Jakarta-based ambassadors—urged him to retract his statement. He did, and from that point onward, he maintained the earlier policy of restraint. That decision helped to ensure that the negotiations could continue, and won the resistance a considerable measure of international credibility and sympathy in the months ahead.

It did nothing, however, to stop the militia violence. Indeed, the days after Gusmão's statement and retraction saw a further escalation of militia attacks, and continued official support for them. On April 6, for example, members of the Besi Merah Putih militia attacked a group of people who had taken refuge in the Catholic church compound in the town of Liquiçá, killing at least fifty, and probably many more.[48] Standing by throughout the attack were well-armed TNI, police, and paramilitary Mobile Brigade (Brimob) troops. Not only did those troops do nothing to prevent the attack, by most accounts they helped to organize and carry it out. Pastor Rafael dos Santos, the parish priest, gave this account of the opening moments of the massacre:

> I heard shooting by the Besi Merah Putih (BMP) and Brimob group in front of the Parish house. They were firing into the air. After this the Besi Merah Putih and Kodim members entered and surrounded the community in the Church complex. They started to shoot everyone. Men whom they found outside the Parish house were hacked down. . . . The militia members were accompanied by Kodim troops and the Brimob elements. They entered the

residence of the church and they started to kill people with machetes and shoot people in the house. At the time there were still women, children and men in the complex. They started to kill the men first because they were closer to the door. The men had pushed the women and children to the back.[49]

Against this backdrop, Indonesian officials continued to take part in public ceremonies officially legitimizing the proautonomy militia groups, and spurring them to take action against proindependence forces. On April 17, 1999, for instance, top officials gathered in front of the provincial governor's office in Dili for a proautonomy rally, attended by hundreds of militiamen from all over the territory. In the course of the rally, the notorious militia leader, Guterres, reportedly urged those present to "conduct a cleansing of all those who have betrayed integration. Capture and kill them if you need to."[50] A secret TNI report on the events of April 17 provided a fuller account of Guterres's remarks. According to that document, Guterres said:

> Aitarak forces are going to carry out a cleansing operation [*operasi sisir*] against civil servants who have used official facilities while being traitors to the integration struggle. Aitarak forces are going to crush [*memberantas*] anyone—be they government officials, community leaders or businessmen—who has assisted the anti-integration camp. Aitarak forces will not hesitate to kill [*menghabisi*] Mário Viegas Carrascalão and his circle, who have been traitors.[51]

The rally was attended by some of the most senior government officials in the territory, including the governor, Abílio Osório Soares, and the East Timor military commander, Colonel Tono Suratman. Video footage obtained by UN investigators, moreover, showed Suratman standing on the first-floor balcony of the governor's office, together with Major General Kiki Syahnakri (assistant for operations to the army chief of staff) and four other senior military officers.[52] None of those officials expressed any public opposition to or concern about Guterres's remarks, or about the presence of armed militias. Nor did any military or police authority seek to disarm them.

Later that afternoon, an estimated fifteen hundred of these militias went on a rampage through Dili, firing their weapons, attacking the homes of known proindependence leaders, and killing more than a dozen people. Most of those killed were among some 150 people who had sought refuge in the Carrascalão home in Dili.[53] As in many other cases of serious militia violence in 1999, Indonesian military and police authorities sought to portray the attack and killings as a clash between prointegration and proindependence groups. But there was no evidence that the refugees in the house had engaged in any violence whatsoever. By contrast, there was substantial evidence of direct TNI involvement in the attack, and also of culpable acquiescence in the violence by high-ranking TNI and police authorities.[54] As if to reward him for his role in fomenting the violence, two days later Guterres was officially sworn in as the commander of the Aitarak militia by the Bupati of Dili.

The attacks in Liquiçá and Dili prompted unusually strong rebukes from the United Nations and the states principally involved in the negotiations, including Australia, the United States, and Portugal. At that point, Indonesian authorities began to deny that weapons had ever been given to the militias, and efforts were made to conceal any further distributions.[55] These efforts notwithstanding, weapons continued to be made available to the militias after April. In another attempt to meet international criticism, on April 21 Wiranto came to Dili to oversee the signing of a "peace agreement" between proindependence and proautonomy East Timorese.[56] By portraying the problem as one of conflict between pro- and anti–Indonesian East Timorese, Wiranto's peace deal once again obscured the central role of the TNI in fomenting that violence, and suggested that the TNI was an indispensable arbiter of peace and order. Whatever value it may have had as a public relations exercise, the peace agreement did absolutely nothing to weaken official support for the militias or to bring an end to the violence. In that respect, it ominously foreshadowed the position that Indonesian officials would adopt toward the militias and militia violence throughout the popular consultation.

"Socialization" and Other Strategies

Another key component of Indonesian strategy in early 1999 was a campaign to socialize the proposed autonomy package. As depicted by government authorities, socialization was a community education effort aimed at explaining the advantages of the autonomy option to the people of East Timor. In practice, it was a concerted propaganda offensive involving a combination of inducements, threats, and acts of violence designed to pressure civil servants and ordinary citizens to support continued Indonesian rule.

From early 1999, public socialization meetings and rallies were organized throughout the country, at which civilian and military authorities spoke at length about the benefits of autonomy. Official speakers underlined their case by distributing T-shirts, rice, and other goods, and by promising more of the same to those who supported Indonesian rule. Such inducements were supplemented by open and veiled threats of violence should the autonomy option fail. Threats were reinforced by the public statements of proautonomy leaders, and further underscored by the menacing presence of armed proautonomy militiamen. Indeed, the militias effectively served as enforcers of the socialization campaign—ensuring that people came to meetings, and threatening or physically abusing those who refused.

Under the auspices of the socialization campaign, government officials also used the authority of their office to pressure civil servants and others to support the autonomy option, and persecute those who favored independence. In some cases, the names of independence supporters were recorded and submitted to military intelligence authorities. The governor of East Timor, Abílio Osório Soares, had started to issue such demands and threats against disloyal civil servants as early as mid-1998. A secret Indonesian military intelligence report dated June 23, 1998 on his remarks to a meeting of the prointegration group, Garda Paksi, quotes him saying, "I am going to call together all government servants of Echelon IV and above, and tell them that if they do not support integration, they must resign immediately."[57]

Such measures were explicitly ordered by the governor in a circular, dated May 28, 1999, distributed to the heads of all government bodies in East Timor, and copied to the Indonesian minister for home affairs.[58] The circular stated that any civil servant who supported independence would be "terminated." It further stipulated that civil servants suspected of harboring proindependence sympathies would be made to sign oaths of loyalty to the government, and would be threatened with dismissal should they later engage in proindependence activities. These were not idle threats. Known or suspected supporters of independence were indeed forced from their jobs and homes under the auspices of the socialization campaign. The agents of enforcement, more often than not, were the militias. Indeed, the letter from an Aitarak militia member cited earlier confirms that the militias regarded this as one of their main purposes:

> We members of Aitarak are going to take a tough stance in investigating and rooting out civil servants who support independence. We will oust them from their positions, we will strip them of the official uniforms they are wearing, and we will confiscate from them any official vehicle they may be using. This is the concept behind the operations we plan to undertake in April 1999.[59]

The socialization campaign was also a mechanism through which many young men were press-ganged into joining militia groups. As described above, those who refused to join would quickly be labeled as proindependence and subject to reprisals.

In keeping with its status as an element of government policy, the socialization campaign was amply funded by the Indonesian treasury.[60] Indonesian government documents uncovered since 1999 suggest that roughly Rp.3 billion ($400,000) was channeled to *each* of the thirteen districts to support the campaign in 1999, for a total of at least Rp.39 billion ($5.2 million).[61] Although the amount varied somewhat from one district to the next, in every case some part of that total was allocated to pay for the militias. The clearest piece of evidence in support of these conclusions is a May 1999 letter from the governor of East Timor to all Bupatis. In it, the governor instructed each Bupati to prepare a budget proposal, in accordance with an outline that included expenditures for socialization and "Pamswakarsa" (i.e., militias).[62] A few weeks later, the governor wrote to the Bupatis of Lautem and Occussi granting official approval for proposals requesting roughly Rp.3 billion for the socialization campaign in each district. "We are pleased to inform you," the governor wrote, "that in principle your proposal and funds totaling Rp.3,000,000,000, have been approved."[63]

Government documents and the testimony of former civil servants also provide information about the sources of this government funding. They show that funds were diverted, with official approval, from the budget lines of various government departments (including education and culture, public works, transmigration, and foreign affairs) to the socialization budget. In a May 1999 letter sent to all provincial heads of departments (*Kakanwil*) in East Timor and copied to key ministers in Jakarta, the governor explicitly instructed that a portion of departmental budgets should be diverted to fund the socialization campaign. "All available resources in the province," he wrote, "should be mobilized in an optimal fashion to ensure the success of the autonomy option. All departments are therefore asked to contribute between 10 percent and 20 percent of their 1999/2000 budgetary allocations for the socialization of autonomy."[64] There is also good evidence that much of the roughly Rp.3 billion made available to each district administration was drawn from a World Bank–mandated "Social Safety Net" welfare project (Proyek Dukungan Jaringan Pengamanan Sosial, or JPS). The May 1999 letter from the governor to all Bupatis, noted earlier, referred explicitly to the Social Safety Net project as the source from which funds would be drawn:

> Further to my letter Number: 915/712/II.BIPRAM/V/1999 of May 5, 1999 concerning the implementation of the Regional and District Development Program, Social Safety Net Project (JPS) in each District, you are hereby requested to prepare a draft outline for the use of these funds, in accordance with the following proposal.[65]

This evidence might appear to suggest that the funding of the socialization campaign and the militias was organized exclusively at the district and provincial levels, and that the parties ultimately responsible were the governor and the thirteen Bupatis. Yet the reality is that given the highly centralized structure of the Indonesian bureaucracy at the time, these funding arrangements could not have been made without the approval of central government officials in Jakarta.

A related element of the government's strategy was the encouragement and funding of a number of new prointegration political organizations, led and staffed by East Timorese. The two principal organizations were the FPDK (Forum Persatuan, Demokrasi dan Keadilan, or Forum for Unity, Democracy, and Justice) and the BRTT (Barisan Rakyat Timor Timur, or East Timor People's Front), both of which were established in the first half of 1999.[66] The FPDK was more closely linked to the militia groups—with which it claimed an "advisory" relationship—than was the BRTT, some of whose leaders were concerned that militia violence was counterproductive. Despite these differences, the FPDK and the BRTT both represented the East Timorese face of the Indonesian government position.

Like the mobilization of the militias—and in an echo of Indonesia's strategy in 1975—the formation and encouragement of these political organizations was intended, in part, to substantiate the official claim that the conflict was among East Timorese, with the Indonesian government and military serving as neutral arbiters. That claim was weakened, however, by the fact that the FPDK and BRTT leaders were overwhelmingly Indonesian government officials. The leader of the BRTT, for example, was none other than the Indonesian government's ambassador-at-large for East Timor—and former leader of the UDT's pro-Indonesian faction—Francisco Lopes da Cruz.[67] In addition to their overt political goals, there is some evidence that these proautonomy political organizations also served a more covert purpose—as a conduit for the disbursement of funds and materials to the militias.[68]

A final vital element of the government's strategy was the creation of a number of specialized political bodies in East Timor. These bodies—most notably the KPS (Komisi Pengamanan dan Stabilitas, or Commission on Peace and Stability) and Satgas P3TT (Satuan Tugas Pengamanan Penentuan Pendapat mengenai Timor Timur, or Task Force for the Implementation of the Popular Consultation in East Timor)—served primarily as purveyors of disinformation.[69] The latter also served as a cover for the coordination of covert Indonesian government and military strategy.

The KPS was a product of Wiranto's peace agreement of April 21, 1999. Ostensibly established to facilitate dialogue among the different parties in East Timor, in practice the KPS almost invariably served as a mouthpiece for the Indonesian government position. This was partly the consequence of its composition, which was heavily weighted toward the Indonesian and proautonomy side.[70] It also stemmed from the deeply partisan position adopted by representatives of Indonesia's Komnas HAM (Komisi Hak Asasi Manusia, or Human Rights Commission), which had been drawn in to convene the KPS. The public relations antics of the KPS were part of a broader government effort to present its version of events and preferred option to East Timorese and Indonesian audiences. It was assisted in this effort by a generally compliant domestic media.

The Task Force for the Implementation of the Popular Consultation in East Timor, commonly known as the Task Force, represented a national ministerial group (TP4 OKTT) headed by the powerful coordinating minister for political and security affairs, Tanjung.[71] The task force itself was headed by a former Indonesian permanent representative to the United Nations in Geneva, Ambassador Agus Tarmizi, and like its parent body, included representatives from several central government ministries. Formally, the task force represented Indonesian government interests in East Timor, and served as a direct point of contact with UNAMET, in the context of the popular consultation. Because it reported directly to the coordinating minister for political and security affairs in Jakarta, however, the task force also constituted a crucial channel of authority directly under the control of the minister. Moreover, the task force leadership included a number of high-ranking military officers, active and retired, with long experience in East Timor, and backgrounds in military intelligence or Kopassus, or both.[72]

The key figure on the task force was Makarim. A career military intelligence officer, Makarim had served until January 1999 as head of the BIA (Badan Intelijen ABRI, or Armed Forces Intelligence Agency).[73] Officially appointed to his post in East Timor in early June, he had been involved in military and political operations there for some time before that.[74] In the early 1990s, he had been a military intelligence officer in Aceh, at the height of a counterinsurgency campaign in which the army mobilized armed local militia groups to assist in their effort to crush a local independence movement. The most senior military officer in East Timor until the declaration of martial law in September 1999, Makarim was the most likely candidate for the role of overall field coordinator of military and government strategy in East Timor. To the extent that this strategy entailed the mobilization of armed militia groups and the commission of systematic acts of violence against the civilian population, he was also a chief suspect among those later accused of crimes against humanity.[75]

By the time the May 5 Agreements were signed, most of these elements of the Indonesian strategy for the popular consultation were already in place. Indeed, by that date the most important component of the strategy—the mobilization of local militia groups to terrorize proindependence populations—had been up and running for almost a year, while the socialization campaign had been under way for several months. When the first wave of UNAMET staff began to arrive in Dili in late May and early June, then, they were stepping into a political situation already marked by serious violence and a distinctly uneven political playing field. Under these circumstances, the already difficult task of making arrangements for a vote just three months away was fraught with peril. The flawed security agreement, which ensured that Indonesia's strategy could be carried out without hindrance, compounded the problem, leading those who knew something about the history of East Timor and Indonesia seriously to doubt that it could be done.

CHAPTER SIX

BEARING WITNESS—TEMPTING FATE

THE DEVASTATION THAT FOLLOWED the August 30 vote has made it easy to forget much of what preceded it. It has been especially easy to lose sight of the fact that the May 5 Agreements represented an extraordinary political breakthrough, and the arrival of the United Nations in East Timor an emotional and historic turning point. However quaint or misguided the idea might have seemed to Americans—so convinced that the United Nations is capable only of blunders—for East Timorese and many others, the United Nations' arrival in East Timor generated considerable excitement and optimism. The optimism of those early days, though, stood in marked contrast to the unsettling reality on the ground. As UN staff and independent observers spread out across East Timor in June, they began to notice distinctive patterns in the behavior of the militias, the TNI, and the police. Those patterns further reinforced earlier reports that the violence against supporters of independence was being fomented, or at the very least condoned, by senior TNI and civilian authorities.

In light of these observations and what was already known about Indonesian strategy in East Timor, the question naturally arose whether it was wise to proceed with the popular consultation as planned or instead to postpone it pending a significant improvement in the security situation. The decision that was ultimately taken—to proceed despite the warning signs—has in turn raised legitimate questions about what UNAMET knew of the dangers, what it recommended to the United Nations in New York, and how those decisions were finally made. The simple answer is that UNAMET staff in East Timor knew a great deal about the dangers and for a time argued strongly against proceeding. That recommendation, however, was openly opposed by Indonesia and by the most influential states involved in the process, notably the United

States and Australia. Importantly, the idea of postponing the vote until the security situation had improved was also opposed by the CNRT leadership and many East Timorese, who feared that such a course might derail the process forever. The considerable political pressure brought to bear by this constellation of actors necessarily shaped the decisions made within the UN Secretariat and the Security Council, and made it difficult for any contrary position to be heard.

Patterns of Violence

When the first UNAMET staff members began to arrive in Dili in May and June—an odd mix of career UN bureaucrats, police officers, academics, soldiers, computer technicians, journalists, and NGO workers from all over the world—they were welcomed like heroes. Though they had done nothing to deserve it, those who ventured out of Dili into the surrounding towns and villages in the early weeks were frequently mobbed by excited residents, who greeted them with shouts and tears. In some places, dance and musical performances were put on to celebrate their arrival. The scene was emotional, too, when the first UN vehicles rolled off ships in Dili harbor and the UN flag was raised above the UNAMET headquarters in Dili on June 9. These were experiences that few UN workers would forget, and that inevitably colored all that they thought and did in the following weeks and months.

Having spent the better part of my professional life working with East Timorese to achieve some recognition of their basic human rights, I found these days to be especially moving. When I first arrived at the UNAMET headquarters in Dili in mid-June, the sight of the UN flag flying overhead quite unexpectedly raised a lump in my throat. Here, in a place that had been so vigorously closed off from the world community— and whose occupying authorities had so routinely scoffed at UN criticism and international law—the United Nations had finally established a meaningful presence. It was a transformation that few people could have predicted or imagined even a year before. I was not alone in feeling that there was now some real hope that even without weapons, the United Nations would be able to help resolve East Timor's problems.

In light of what was already known about TNI and militia activities, and what happened later, this faith in the United Nations sounds naive. But it was not wholly without foundation. Within just a few weeks of the United Nations' arrival in Dili, there were unmistakable signs that militia violence had begun to diminish, apparently as a result of the international presence. Some CNRT leaders who had been forced into hiding or protective police custody as a result of militia violence earlier in the year began to return to their homes and play an active role in negotiations related to the referendum. Also encouraging, in June several hundred internally displaced persons in the district of Covalima were able to return to the town of Suai, where most found temporary sanctuary inside the compound of the half-built Catholic cathedral.[1] These developments gave reason to hope that by bearing witness, even a completely unarmed UN mission could have a positive effect.

So in those early weeks, when East Timorese and foreigners asked skeptically how the United Nations would manage to carry out the vote without an armed presence, UN staff pointed to the evidence of declining violence and expressed the belief that the trend would likely continue as UNAMET—and hundreds of accredited observers and journalists—moved out into the countryside. The positive change had after all begun with the arrival of just a handful of UN staff, so it was not unreasonable to think that as the presence grew, the trend would continue.

And the presence did grow. At full deployment UNAMET had some eight hundred international staff and volunteers on the ground. Fewer than one hundred of those were based at the main headquarters in Dili, with the remainder serving in nine district offices, and frequently traveling to the remotest corners of the territory.[2] The vast majority of UN staff and volunteers were working with the electoral unit—conducting voter education campaigns, organizing registration, and staffing the polling centers on election day. Smaller contingents worked in several other units: as UN civilian police (Civpol), military liaison officers (MLO), political affairs officers, public information officers, and security officers, and in a variety of administrative and technical support positions. The UN staff was eventually joined by several hundred journalists and election observers from around the world. As this small army spread throughout the territory, the positive trend appeared to continue. For the first time in almost twenty-five years, the TNI, the militias, and the civilian authorities in East Timor were confronted with an extensive network of outside observers, and it seemed to be putting a crimp in their operations. The pattern lifted spirits and made us optimistic about a further decline in violence.

Our optimism was tempered somewhat by what we began to see and hear within days of arriving on the ground. In addition to the joyous welcomes, many of us also had direct personal encounters of a less encouraging sort—with pro-Indonesian militias, and with police, TNI soldiers, and Indonesian government officials. In mid-June, for example, several UNAMET staff witnessed the TNI and militias forcibly displacing the population from villages in Liquiçá district, and burning the contents of their houses.[3] Later the same month, a fellow political affairs officer, Colin Stewart, and I observed a sweeping operation in a neighborhood not far from the UNAMET headquarters in Dili. We watched, dumbfounded, as three men wearing black bodysuits and balaclavas sped off the road and into a field on high-powered trail bikes, scattering residents and onlookers alike. A man in plainclothes, whom we would come to know as a senior military intelligence officer, remained by the side of the road, barking orders into a walkie-talkie.

On the other side, we got to know some of the many people working with or sympathetic to the resistance. One of these was Sister Esmeralda, a diminutive Canossian nun in her mid-thirties, whose broad smile and impish manner gave no hint of her inner strength or political inclinations. After working with the resistance in her youth, Sister Esmeralda had decided to join the Canossian order. In 1999 she worked tirelessly to protect and assist families and children displaced by the violence, and to communicate their needs and concerns to UNAMET officials and whoever else might listen. Never ruffled, her gray and white nun's habit always immaculately cleaned and pressed, she was unstoppable. In my brief time there, I saw her chase armed miltiamen away from a group of displaced children under her care, and I heard her tell the Canossian Mother Superior that she would not be leaving East Timor in early September as ordered.

We also learned about the situation on the ground through frequent interactions with local residents. In the first few weeks after UNAMET's deployment, hundreds of people came to the headquarters in Dili and district offices throughout the territory to recount what had happened to them in the preceding months. Others submitted written statements and documents. Their stories, which were duly noted and stored in a makeshift UNAMET archive, were harrowing, and confirmed what we had learned from our own experience and analysis.

On the basis of these encounters, UN staff began to note certain patterns in the behavior of the TNI, the Indonesian police, and especially the militias. From the time they began to deploy in May, for example,

UNAMET and other observers repeatedly witnessed TNI officers training and conducting joint operations with militia groups. Militias were
commonly seen carrying firearms and operating sophisticated two-way
radio equipment usually available only to the armed forces, and wearing
new or nearly new TNI uniforms. UNAMET officials attending militia
ceremonial events were invited to sit on chairs and under green tents
marked "ABRI" (as the TNI was known until April 1999), and the ceremonies—which imitated TNI events in most respects—were always attended by local military figures. Militias were also observed, even photo-
graphed, riding in TNI and police vehicles, and gathering or taking
refuge in TNI and police installations. These patterns tended to confirm
what we had heard and read about the links between the TNI and the
militias.

A second pattern we observed was the routine failure of the Indonesian police to respond to acts of violence by militia groups while they
occurred, or to take adequate measures to investigate or punish them
after the fact. The problem was not one of legal ambiguity. Even in East
Timor, Indonesian law unequivocally prohibited murder, kidnapping,
property destruction, and the carrying of weapons without a license, so
there was ample legal foundation for police action against the militias.
Nor was it really a matter of inadequate training or expertise. On occasion the police did act assertively and professionally, although this was
usually in pursuit of an alleged criminal from the proindependence side.
The real problem was that the Indonesian police were politically and
operationally subordinate to the TNI, even after they were given formal
autonomy in April 1999. To the extent that East Timor's militias were
backed by the TNI—and the police were under no illusions on that
score—the chances were extremely slim that the police would dare to
interfere with them.[4] Indeed, senior Indonesian police officers told UN
Civpol officers quite explicitly that they were constrained by the TNI.[5]
This was not only a matter of following TNI demands or orders. It was
also the result of a general perception that some of the militias were actually TNI, perhaps even Kopassus, soldiers. Under the circumstances, the
police were understandably afraid to intervene in any meaningful way.

Over time, we also observed clear patterns in the behavior of the militias themselves. Although the different militia groups had distinct geographic bases from which their leaders and members were drawn, and
there was some geographic variation in the intensity of their activities,

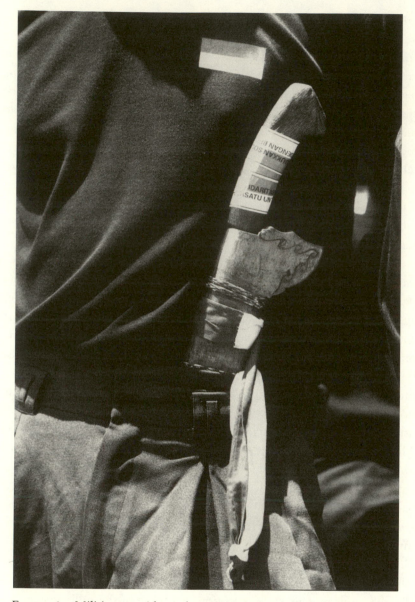

FIGURE 6.1. Militiaman with machete, 1999. Indonesian authorities mobilized more than two dozen armed proindependence militia groups in
an effort to influence the outcome of the referendum. While some were
provided with modern firearms, many carried traditional weapons, such
as machetes, spears, knives, and homemade guns. Like the militiaman in
this photo, most also donned insignia or bandanas of red and white, the
color of the Indonesian flag. With their army patrons, the militias engaged in a systematic campaign of violence before and after the ballot,
killing hundreds of supporters of independence, and forcibly displacing
some four hundred thousand others. (Eddy Hasby)

there were unmistakable similarities in the technology and language used by all militias and in what I call their "repertoire of violence." In keeping with earlier reports, we observed that some militias did indeed have access to advanced weapons of the sort used by the TNI and the police. This pattern suggested not only a close relationship between the militia and the TNI but also a degree of planning and coordination on the part of the latter, at least at the Kodim level and more likely at the Korem.

On the whole, however, the firearms carried by the average militia-man were so-called homemade weapons (*senjata rakitan*). Fashioned from two or more tubes of steel attached to a wooden grip, these weapons were fired by holding a match or cigarette lighter to a fuse on top of the weapon at the base of the steel tubes. The resulting explosion sent a ball or cluster of metal shot down the tubes and more or less in the direction of the target. To the untrained eye, they resembled seventeenth- or eigh-teenth-century firearms, and by all accounts they were just as unreliable. Although these weapons were almost as likely to injure their owners as their intended targets, they could inflict serious wounds, and they had a terrifying effect. The same was true of the other weapons commonly used by the militias, such as machetes, knives, spears, swords, and rocks.

The militia's reliance on such basic low-tech weapons did not seem at first to accord with the claim that they were officially backed by the powerful TNI or that the violence was carefully planned. If they were serious about using the militias to intimidate the opposition and create mayhem, surely the TNI would simply have given them all access to so-phisticated weapons and let them loose. Yet, on closer analysis, the use of such basic weapons technology appears to have been part of the strategy. From the point of view of TNI strategists, homemade guns, machetes, spears, and knives had at least three advantages. First, they made it easier to sustain the illusion that the militias had grown spontaneously from the community. Second, there was much less danger that such weapons would be turned against the well-armed TNI or police in the event of a mutiny, or of the weapons' loss or sale to the other side—problems with which the TNI had had bitter experience in the course of the occupa-tion. Finally, these simple weapons were extremely effective in spreading terror by creating the *impression* of anarchy. Thus, while the use of low-tech weapons seemed to indicate an element of autonomy and sponta-neity among the militias, it did not in any sense rule out the possibility of TNI control and planning.

The public language or discourse of the militias was also common throughout the territory. With only minor variations, all militias employed the same slogans: "Live and Die for Integration!" "With autonomy the blood will trickle. With independence, the blood will flow!" These slogans and threats were shouted at rallies and public ceremonies, and printed on the T-shirts and uniforms sported by militias and other supporters of Indonesian rule. Like the common technologies of violence, the marked similarity in the vocabulary of the militias suggested a degree of coordination above the local or district level. Moreover, the fact that so much of the sloganeering was in Indonesian—and not in the local lingua franca, Tetum, or any of the roughly one dozen other local languages—suggested that the direction came from Indonesian officers or officials.

Like their technology and language, the militias' repertoire of violence was virtually the same everywhere in the territory. The militia modus operandi seemed deliberately designed to terrorize and intimidate with a view to winning the compliance of the members of a community. Significantly perhaps, none of the methods used was unique to East Timor. Like the very idea of using civilian militia forces, they appeared rather to be drawn from the repertoire developed by TNI forces in counterinsurgency and anticrime operations conducted elsewhere in Indonesia over more than thirty years.[6] The most common methods included beatings, house burning, public death threats, the brandishing and firing of weapons, and in the case of women, rape and other forms of sexual violence.[7] Killing was also part of the repertoire, and again following standard TNI counterinsurgency practice, it was evidently intended to be exemplary—to send a message to others in the community of what would happen to those who did not heed the militias' or TNI's warnings. Accordingly, the bodies of victims were often mutilated in some way—decapitated or disemboweled—and then left in full public view.[8] Likewise, when militias staged an attack, they did not do so with the cool precision of professional hit men. Rather, they created the impression—perhaps intentionally—of men in a state of frenzy, shouting and slashing the air with their weapons. In other words, they behaved as one imagines a man "running amok."

Finally, there were significant geographic variations in the pattern of violence before the ballot. The worst areas by far were the western districts of Bobonaro, Covalima, Ermera, and Liquiçá, with the central districts of Dili and Ainaro occasionally reaching similar levels of insecurity.[9] Likewise, the most feared and violent of the militia groups—Besi

Merah Putih, Aitarak, Mahidi, Laksaur, Darah Integrasi, Dadurus Merah Putih, and Halilintar—were all concentrated in the western and central districts. By contrast the six easternmost districts of Aileu, Manufahi, Manatuto, Baucau, Lautem, and Viqueque were relatively calm, and their militias somewhat smaller and less effective.[10] Although we did not fully understand the logic of that variation at the time, subsequent examination of the pattern suggested that the violence was systematic, and that it rested in some measure on the relationship between militia forces and Indonesian authorities. More precisely, the concentration of violence in the western and central districts appears to have been related to three main factors: the geographic proximity to Indonesia; the attitude and background of individual military and civilian authorities at the local level; and the historically conditioned location of pro-Indonesian bosses and networks.

These distinctive patterns and variations of TNI, police, and militia behavior, together with the documentary evidence then available, pointed strongly to the conclusion that the militias were trained and their actions orchestrated by the TNI, with the acquiescence of the police and civilian authorities. The fact that markedly similar behavior was evident in different parts of the territory suggested that coordination was happening at least on the provincial level and possibly higher up. Even if the patterns were not entirely the result of direct TNI coordination, it was abundantly clear that the militias could not have behaved as they did without the acquiescence and encouragement of the TNI, and to a lesser extent, the police and civilian authorities.

Given this mounting evidence, we were under no illusion about the difficulties that UNAMET would face in carrying out the registration and the vote. But through May and June most UN staff remained cautiously optimistic that by bearing witness, and providing accurate information to those in a position to influence Indonesian authorities, it would be possible to contain the violence and carry out the referendum as planned. That cautious optimism gave way to despair in late June and early July when pro-Indonesian militia groups suddenly turned their fury on UNAMET staff and humanitarian workers, first in the town of Maliana on June 29, and a few days later in the town of Liquiçá. Both incidents were captured on film and were the subject of detailed internal UNAMET investigations.[11] The film footage and investigations highlighted many of the patterns that we had already begun to discern, and they sent a chill up the spine of most UN workers.

In Maliana, about a hundred members of the Dadurus Merah Putih militia attacked the regional UNAMET headquarters, injuring several people and causing considerable property damage. A UNAMET investigation found incontrovertible evidence that the attack had been coordinated and planned by the district military commander, Lieutenant Colonel Baharuddin Siagian, and the head of military intelligence in the district, First Lieutenant Sutrisno. It also found that the two had actually been at the scene of the incident as it unfolded, alongside a number of militia leaders who were either active or retired TNI soldiers. In the second incident, in Liquiçá on July 4, members of the armed militia group Besi Merah Putih used machetes and firearms to attack a convoy of vehicles returning from a successful humanitarian mission to assist internally displaced persons. One UNAMET staff member was directly targeted, many NGO personnel were assaulted, and one was hospitalized with a serious head injury. An internal UNAMET report on the incident provided the following graphic account:

> About five minutes after the convoy stopped in Liquica, a blue-green mini-van with the word "Miramar" on the side sped down the hill from the south, and came to a sudden stop near the middle of the line of parked vehicles. As the van stopped, some 20 young men jumped out and began to approach the NGO and UNAMET staff, shouting "kill them!" Most were carrying machetes, knives or home-made guns. At least one member of the group was carrying an automatic weapon. Without warning or provocation the militia members began to attack, waving their machetes and knives menacingly, pointing their guns at members of the convoy, and smashing the windows of most of the vehicles. The attack continued as people tried to flee on foot and in vehicles.[12]

In response to the increasingly unsafe situation, it was decided to evacuate all UNAMET personnel from the Liquiçá area the same day, and a helicopter was sent from Dili for this purpose. The evacuation plan had to be aborted, however, when another group of armed militias, probably Besi Merah Putih, attacked the helicopter with stones and homemade guns.

The incidents in Maliana and Liquiçá were by no means as bloody as the April 1999 massacres in Liquiçá and Dili. Nor were they as deadly as many of the attacks on local people that would eventually follow. But because UNAMET staff had witnessed them firsthand, and because we were able to gather reliable evidence about them, they tended to lend additional credence to other reports suggesting similar patterns. They also had a deep political significance. By targeting the United Nations and international NGOs, these attacks indicated a shift in the focus of militia violence and greatly upped the political ante. The pro-Indonesian side had effectively declared that the United Nations was the enemy. That trend developed further over the next two months, leading to malicious legal and political charges, physical assaults, death threats, and ultimately to the murder of more than a dozen UN staff.

Decision to Proceed

In light of this clear pattern of violence and intimidation, the question naturally arose whether it would be better to proceed with the registration and vote, or postpone it pending a substantial improvement in the security situation. Indeed, this was one of the central issues on which UNAMET's head of mission was expected to advise the UN secretary-general. The Political Affairs Office where I worked, was responsible in turn for providing advice to the head of mission on that question.[13] It was only one of many units offering advice, and events would prove that its influence was limited. But we took our responsibility seriously, and it cannot be said that the decision to proceed was taken lightly. In considering what advice to offer, we were acutely aware that the future of East Timor and to some extent the credibility of the United Nations hung in the balance. We knew that the wrong decision could lead not only to bloodshed but also to a result that did not reflect the wishes or interests of the population. While we viewed the threat of violence seriously, I think it is fair to say we were primarily concerned about its possible effect on the fairness of the consultation. If the United Nations moved ahead under less than ideal conditions, for example, we were worried that the pro-Indonesian side might win—a result that in our judgment would be most unlikely in a free vote. And while a majority of East Timorese would almost certainly reject such an outcome, the United Nations would forever have given it an aura of credibility and legality that would be difficult to remove. On the other hand, if we chose to postpone the process we risked throwing away a unique opportunity for the resolution of East Timor's political status. As the weeks passed, these considerations framed all of the advice we offered.

The question of whether to proceed first arose shortly after the head of mission, Ian Martin, arrived in Dili in early June, and several weeks before UNAMET's local and international staff were fully deployed. On June 14, Martin recommended that the entire process should be postponed by a minimum of three weeks.[14] Although there was some debate in New York about whether to attribute the delay to logistical difficulties, there was no serious objection to a three-week postponement. Accordingly, on June 22 Annan announced in his report to the Security Council that voter registration would not begin until mid-July and that voting day would be moved to the end of August. Following Martin's recommendation, he cited both logistical and security reasons for the decision.[15]

In early July, with the new registration date drawing near, the question of whether to proceed gained a new urgency. The security situation remained extremely poor. International and media attention naturally focused on the frightening militia attacks on UNAMET and humanitarian personnel in Maliana and Liquiçá. But in the assessment of the Political Affairs Office these were merely symptoms of a much more serious security problem that had already forced some fifty thousand East Timorese from their homes, and that made it most unlikely that registration or balloting could be carried out safely and fairly. Accordingly, we strongly advised that UNAMET should *not* proceed with the process as scheduled and that the threat of postponement should be used to pressure the Indonesian government into fulfilling its commitments to establish conditions for a fair process. This strategy was hardly a sure bet. Indonesia could easily have refused to make any significant changes, leaving the United Nations with nothing to do but cancel the referendum. But many of us in Political Affairs believed that the threat of postponement at that stage was the only credible leverage UNAMET had at its disposal.

More to the point, we could not in good conscience recommend a determination that the conditions existed for a free and fair ballot. As noted earlier, the criteria for making such a determination had been spelled out quite clearly in a May 4, 1999, memorandum from the secretary-general to the governments of Indonesia and Portugal. If we were going to do our jobs properly and provide impartial advice on the basis of the secretary-general's own orders, we really had no choice but to advise against proceeding. At this stage, the head of mission—and all the unit heads within UNAMET—took the same view. Martin wrote to New York to recommend the postponement of registration until there was clear evidence of an improvement in the security situation.[16] He wrote again on July 8 with the same advice: "It remains our collective judgment that it is impossible to conclude that the necessary security conditions exist for the commencement of the operational phase of the popular consultation. . . . My recommendation is that a negative determination be made."[17] In other words, in early July UNAMET's unambiguous advice to New York was that the referendum should *not* go ahead, and the principal reason given was the unacceptable security climate. In the end, however, that position did not prevail. Although there was one further three-day postponement in the start of registration (to July 16), and a series of declarations and démarches by UNAMET and the secretary-general that Indonesia would need to do more to guarantee security, the process went ahead without significant interruption.

The decision to proceed was strongly influenced by political pressures emanating from the United Nations in New York and from the capitals of major powers. At the political level, the United Nations' position on East Timor was constrained by the interests of the permanent members of the Security Council. It was also guided by a group of five states specially convened for this purpose, the United States, the United Kingdom, Australia, New Zealand, and Japan, together known as the Core Group. As far as we could tell from Dili, the Permanent Five and the Core Group were anxious to move ahead with the consultation—despite warnings of danger—and reluctant to do anything that might unduly upset the Indonesian government and military. As one official of the UN Secretariat later told me, there were simply no advocates of a delay at headquarters.[18]

Within the UN Secretariat, the lead agency was the Department of Political Affairs (DPA), although several other units were involved, including the Office of the Secretary-General, Electoral Affairs, and the Department of Peace Keeping Operations (DPKO). These units did not always work easily together. Most notably, there was tension between DPA and DPKO, with the latter apparently resentful of DPA's lead role and unhappy with its own lack of resources. For much of the summer DPKO responded by paying little attention to the East Timor operation; for example, its officials seldom showed up for consultations with the Security Council. The tension would surface only later, especially over the question of whether to support a peacekeeping force. In the early stages, though, all units within the Secretariat tended to share, or to be strongly influenced by, the concerns expressed by the Core Group and the Permanent Five. In any case it was taken as given that little could happen without the agreement of those two groupings. It was also understood that any statement or resolution that did not have the support of Indonesia would be rejected by China and Russia, and as a consequence such initiatives were simply avoided. The lowest common denominator ruled. And so while UNAMET's head of mission was mandated to advise the secretary-general on whether the conditions existed for a free and fair ballot, his recommendations were not automatically adopted as policy.

Thus, despite UNAMET's early July advice, in New York there was strong pressure to move ahead. DPA and DPKO officials wished to proceed according to schedule because they feared that a delay might lead to a decline in international support for the mission, especially among powerful states within the Security Council and the Core Group. In Dili, we were never told exactly which states were threatening to withdraw their backing, or why they would so quickly do so. We surmised, however, that resistance to a delay was coming primarily from the United States, the United Kingdom, and Australia. We knew that the U.S. Department of Defense and Department of State had never been keen on the idea of a UN-sponsored referendum in the first place, and that they were anxious not to offend Indonesia or upset long-established ties to the Indonesian military. And while the United Kingdom and Australia had initially supported UN involvement, we understood that they shared the U.S. concern not to disturb relations with Indonesia.

There was also genuine concern at UN headquarters that any serious delay might provide Indonesia with an excuse to back out of the agreement. Indonesian government officials in New York and Jakarta played on these anxieties, suggesting at critical junctures that delays might lead to a domestic political backlash and an end of official cooperation. They added to the pressure by stating that the voting could not possibly take place after August 29, when Indonesia's People's Consultative Assembly was due to meet to select a new president. These kinds of political pressures and threats shaped the thinking of those making decisions in New York and, inevitably, Dili as well.

The decision to proceed with registration—like the disastrous decision to leave security in Indonesian hands—was also influenced by the personal representative of the secretary-general for East Timor, Ambassador Jamsheed Marker of Pakistan. A diplomat of the old school, Ambassador Marker was a firm believer in the value of cordial face-to-face

discussion. In keeping with that philosophy and because of his friendship with Indonesian foreign minister Alatas, he was more inclined than
many others in the United Nations to accept assurances of good faith
offered by Indonesian officials. From our perspective in Political Affairs
he also had a tendency to understate, often quite grossly, the seriousness
of the security situation and to let the Indonesians off the hook far too
easily.[19] Insofar as this approach was expressed in public, it also gave a
rather skewed impression of what UNAMET actually knew and thought
about the political and security situation. After hearing Marker's reassuring statements, journalists and East Timorese would frequently express to
us their concern that the United Nations simply didn't understand what
was going on. This was deeply frustrating. More to the point, it sent dan-
gerously misleading signals to New York and major governments.

Though initially the Political Affairs Office took a stand against them,
and some remained skeptical, it must be said that the arguments in favor
of proceeding with the registration had some merit. Perhaps most important, they coincided with the views of many East Timorese, including
Gusmão, Ramos-Horta, and other CNRT leaders, with whom we had
regular contact. In spite of the known dangers, many of them took the
view that registration should proceed without delay. They pointed out
that any delay would only benefit the side that was responsible for the
violence and that did not wish to see a free expression of the popular
will. This is where some critics get it wrong or tell only part of the story.
The fact is that despite the terrible violence that followed the vote, it is
far from clear that it would have been preferable, morally or politically,
to postpone the process.

The arguments against postponement also gained force as a result of a
shift in the political situation on the ground, after the militia attacks on
UNAMET in late June and early July. Although not widely covered in
the world media, the attacks in Liquiçá and Maliana stimulated an unusual chorus of condemnation by the international community and
UNAMET itself. Shortly after the July 4 attack in Liquiçá, Martin flew
to Jakarta to speak directly with TNI commander Wiranto and national
police commander Roesmanhadi, and to demand that the militias be
brought under control.[20] He took with him and passed to Wiranto an
internal UNAMET report that spelled out clearly the available evidence
of TNI and police complicity in the Maliana incident.[21] At the same
time, the Security Council and the secretary-general expressed their serious concern, and pressed the Indonesian authorities to take concrete

measures to improve the situation.[22] Perhaps because they came just as the United Nations was set to determine whether the process should proceed, such démarches seemed to have an impact in Jakarta. On July 12, just a few days before registration was due to start, several senior government officials, including Alatas, Wiranto, and Tanjung, visited East Timor. During that visit, Wiranto reportedly impressed on East Timor's military commander, Suratman, that the TNI was to cooperate fully with UNAMET and help it fulfill its mandate.[23] Similarly, in a meeting on July 12, Alatas sought to reassure Martin and Francesc Vendrell—the deputy personal representative of the secretary-general for East Timor—of the government's commitment to the process and to the improvement of security conditions.[24]

These unusual gestures by high-ranking Indonesian officials made it possible to believe that the government and the TNI had decided to make a sincere effort to improve the security situation. That impression was reinforced by evidence of a marked decline in militia activity in the days and weeks immediately following Martin's visit to Jakarta and the official Indonesian visit to Dili. While cautioning that the level of militia threat to the local population remained high and that there was a danger of a militia backlash against their declining influence, Martin and others took the view that the political pressure appeared to be working. Reporting to New York about two weeks after his trip to Jakarta and a week after the high-level Indonesian visit to Dili, he noted that "the TNI and the militia appear more subdued following the recent démarches made to the Indonesian Government and the visit to East Timor of General Feisal Tanjung, General Wiranto, F[oreign] M[inister] Alatas and other Cabinet Ministers."[25]

That perception, together with continued urgings from New York to avoid delay, encouraged a gradual adjustment in the UNAMET position over the course of several days in mid-July. In a memorandum to New York on July 14, Martin reiterated UNAMET's collective view that "it is impossible for the Secretary-General to conclude that the necessary security situation now exists for the peaceful implementation of the consultation process.... If he appeared to reach this conclusion, the credibility of UNAMET would be fatally undermined with all objective observers of the situation here (and with UNAMET's own staff)."[26] Nevertheless, recognizing that there were strong arguments for moving ahead, he proposed that registration could proceed as scheduled, on July 16, on two conditions. First, in announcing the decision, the secretary-general should make it absolutely clear that the security situation remained unsatisfactory and that the Indonesian government would be expected to make substantial improvements. Second, the security situation should be reviewed at the halfway point of the twenty-day registration period, with the understanding that the process would be halted if measurable improvements had not been achieved.

These proposals were readily accepted in New York and quickly spelled out in a letter from the secretary-general to the Security Council.[27] Two days later, on July 16, voter registration began. At the time, Martin fully expected that it would be necessary to halt the process at the halfway point. Notwithstanding the government's renewed assurances, it seemed most unlikely that the security situation would improve sufficiently in ten days to permit UNAMET to recommend a positive determination. Once again, however, the momentum of events on the ground in East Timor and continued pressure from New York led to some surprises, and resulted in another significant shift away from the earlier recommendation to postpone.

Turning the Faucet Off—and On

One of the pleasant surprises of the first several days of voter registration was the relative absence of militia activity. While there were instances of violence—including some that forced the temporary closure of registration centers in four or five locations—the many threats of major, coordinated militia attacks on UNAMET staff and local people simply did not materialize.[28] More general indicators of militia activity—roadblocks, shooting incidents, house burnings, and beatings—also appeared to decline slightly during this period. Moreover, the TNI, the police, and some Indonesian civilian authorities seemed to be making an effort to behave in accordance with the May 5 Agreements.

But if there was relief within UNAMET that the level of violence had declined during this period, there were differences in interpretation of the causes and significance of that decline. The Political Affairs Office in particular, remained skeptical. The metaphor we began to use was that of a water faucet that could be turned on and off at will. What we were witnessing, we argued, was an example of the violence being turned off, in a carefully calibrated official effort to avoid a negative determination at the halfway point of the registration. If the violence could be turned off, we reasoned, it could just as easily be turned back on. The essence of our contention was that notwithstanding government assurances and a temporary lull in militia activity, the underlying security situation had not changed. We had always been somewhat skeptical that the official visits and gestures in early July constituted a meaningful change in the government's posture. Indeed, we took the view that they were primarily an effort by the government to defuse international criticism without actually addressing the problem. In a security assessment completed and sent to New York on July 9, we had concluded that the deep-seated pattern of official complicity in the violence remained unchanged and that not a single one of the criteria stipulated by the secretary-general in his memo of May 4 had been satisfied.[29] That position was spelled out again in our situation report for the week ending July 18, which noted that "the fundamental causes of insecurity have not changed, and it would be premature to conclude that the conditions are conducive to a free and fair consultation."[30]

Others within UNAMET and in New York took a less pessimistic view. Although they largely accepted the notion that the violence could be controlled by Indonesian authorities, they did not agree that this was necessarily a bad thing. It was possible, they argued, that concerted international political pressure at the beginning of July had brought a genuine change in government and TNI policy. Viewed in this light, the lull in violence in the first half of registration was a hopeful sign that the rest of the consultation might go smoothly. This more optimistic perspective encouraged New York to proceed without further delay.

That decision might well have proven disastrous. The fact that it did not is attributable in large part to the courage of East Timor's people. As the registration process got under way, they walked or rode for miles, stood in long lines in the hot sun, and braved the threatened militia attacks—all for the chance to register. In spite of dire warnings that the registration requirements were too onerous and complicated, virtually everyone showed up with the correct documents. Ten days into the process, it was clear that they were registering at rates far exceeding the expectations of the United Nations' electoral experts.[31] In other words, despite our fears, the poor security situation—the intimidation, the threats, and the killings—was not interfering with the delicate and difficult process of registration. That realization rightly or wrongly gave UNAMET the courage to move ahead with the second half of the registration process. Accordingly, on July 26 the head of mission recommended the continuation of registration for another ten days, and that advice was duly endorsed by New York.

Events in the second half of the registration period provided a sobering reminder of just how volatile the political situation remained—and some unwelcome support for the Political Affairs Office's more pessimistic interpretation of the decline in violence in mid-July. The first day of the second half of registration, July 26, was marred by a major militia incident in Dili that left several casualties, and revealed once again that the police were either unwilling or unable to control the situation. Further acts of violence followed, including a shocking politically motivated murder in front of UNAMET's Dili regional headquarters on August 1. And as the end of the registration period neared in early August, there were serious militia attacks on UNAMET staff in Bobonaro and Ainaro, and then a sudden spasm of violence in Dili on the final day of campaigning in which at least eight people were killed.[32] The spike in militia violence prompted UNAMET to seek a number of meetings with high-ranking TNI and police authorities.[33]

The problem was not simply a resurgence of militia activity, though, but what seemed to be a coordinated strategy to sow doubts about the fairness and credibility of the entire registration process, and perhaps even to scuttle the consultation altogether. Fears that the violence was being deliberately orchestrated at the highest levels were heightened by two documents that surfaced at about this time. The first, which began to circulate in Dili in the third week of July, was a confidential report, dated July 3, 1999, and titled "General Assessment If Option I Fails." ("Option I" referred to the government's offer of special autonomy.) The report offered a candid assessment of Indonesian government strategy toward the popular consultation process as of early July. The author, Major General (retired) H. R. Garnadi, was special assistant I to the powerful coordinating minister for political and security affairs, General Tanjung. The fact that the report had been written by an important government official, and sent to a senior minister and ex-TNI general, gave it a singular significance.

There were a number of passages that gave rise to particular concern. The document spoke of the government's duty to protect and support the militias, whom it described as "heroes of integration." The relevant passage read as follows: "We cannot ignore the attitude of the East Timorese militias that were recruited from the pro-integration groups. They are the heroes of integration."[34] More explosively, the document appeared to speak of a central government plan to destroy East Timor in the event of a proindependence victory at the polls. The relevant passage stated that "evacuation routes must be planned and secured, possibly by destroying facilities and other key assets."[35]

The fact that East Timor was utterly destroyed after the ballot has lent credence to claims that the Garnadi report had spelled out a "scorched earth" plan, but a closer look at the document reveals that it did not actually do so. In fact, Garnadi's main point in the report was that in its confidence of victory, the government had failed to plan for the possibility of defeat, and that it had better start doing so without delay. He wrote, for example:

> We have another six weeks to ensure that Special Autonomy wins. But if it fails, then six weeks is a very short time to prepare an evacuation plan for the pro-integration personnel and their property. Therefore a contingency plan in case of independence must be developed as quickly as possible. The government must allocate a budget to finance such a plan.[36]

His comment that vital infrastructure might be destroyed by departing Indonesian troops in the event of the defeat of special autonomy was offered as one of several suggestions in the direction of developing such a contingency plan. But it was not an expression of agreed policy at that stage. Indeed, what the Garnadi report indicated most clearly was that as of early July, contingency and operational planning for a proindependence victory had not really begun.

In short, the Garnadi document itself did not reveal the degree of official involvement in the planning of violence that some have since claimed that it did. At the same time, it did highlight important aspects of the relationship between Indonesian authorities and the militias, and official attitudes toward the latter. It confirmed official government support for and solidarity with pro-Indonesian militias, and suggested that they should be taken care of in the event of a proindependence victory. It also made clear that high-ranking officials in Dili and Jakarta were at least considering the destruction of East Timor in the event of a defeat for the autonomy option as early as July. Finally, it suggested that the powerful coordinating minister for political and security affairs, Tanjung—who, it may be recalled, was also the head of the ministerial team overseeing government strategy in East Timor—was probably very much involved in those discussions as they developed after July 3, 1999.

The second document to make waves in East Timor at this time was an instruction, dated July 17, 1999, purportedly signed by João Tavares, East Timor's supreme militia boss, formally known as commander of the Integration Fighters Force. The two-page instruction was addressed to the principal militia commanders in East Timor, and copied to various senior military and police officials, including the armed forces commander (General Wiranto) and the regional military commander for Kodam IX (Major General Damiri). With shocking bluntness, the Tavares instruction directed all militia commanders to "continue your terror and intimidation campaign against those who are influencing the public to reject Special Autonomy," and urged them to "pressure and threaten the public not to participate in the campaign being conducted by the pro-independence leaders."[37] The instruction also promised that the Indonesian authorities would provide the militias with substantial material support. "Before the results of the Popular Consultation are announced," it said,

> weapons will be distributed—1500 modern weapons that have been made available by ABRI [*sic*]. You will be supported by TNI elite troops and backed by heavy artillery/tanks and 50 modern fighter jets.... When the results of the Popular Consultation are announced, if the pro-Autonomy forces are defeated then Operation Clean-up [*Operasi Pembersihan*] will be simultaneously launched in full strength against the pro-independence forces beginning with those 15 years and older, both males and females, without exception.[38]

The document first appeared in early August 1999 and was immediately seized on by observers as proof of TNI-militia cooperation in orchestrating violence across the territory.[39] In view of its potential significance, UNAMET's head of mission asked his staff for their opinion of the document. Civpol consulted with its Indonesian police counterpart, which quickly concluded on technical grounds that the document was a fake. Political Affairs also had doubts about the authenticity of the document, but these were rooted in political and textual, rather than forensic, analysis. For one thing, the language in the instruction presented altogether too tidy a package of outrageous threats and claims to be wholly credible. Tavares was certainly powerful, and he may have been utterly ruthless, but he was not stupid. Even if at some stage he had issued some or all of the orders and promises cited in the document, it seemed unlikely that he would have put them in writing above his signature.

The manner in which the document surfaced contributed to our skepticism. We noted that several copies of the document had been delivered to UNAMET in a matter of just a few days. This was unusual, especially for so sensitive a document, and it made us suspicious of its provenance. How and why had so many copies of such a document become so quickly available? Two possibilities came to mind. The first was that the document had been a psywar fabrication designed by the pro-Indonesian side to discourage and sow fear among proindependence supporters. Another possibility was that it had been created by the pro-independence side in order to discredit the TNI and the militias with one satisfying documentary blow, and at a critical moment in the process. Based on these considerations, we concluded that the Tavares document was probably not authentic. But that did not mean that we dismissed its importance. So many people believed it to be real that its political and psychological effects were profound. If it was, in fact, part of a psywar campaign devised by Indonesian intelligence to spread terror, it had served its purpose to perfection.

Against the backdrop of the rising political tensions generated by these documents, Indonesian government officials in East Timor and elsewhere as well as pro-Indonesian figures and militia leaders joined in accusing UNAMET of bias in the formulation and implementation of registration procedures. The allegations were so consistent and the campaign of misinformation so concerted that it looked very much like an intelligence operation designed to lay the basis for later Indonesian challenges to the legitimacy of the vote, should it go the wrong way. A central element of the Indonesian subterfuge was the dubious claim that UNAMET had not made sufficient provision for the registration of East Timorese residing in West Timor and other parts of Indonesia, and that this failing would seriously skew the vote against the Indonesian side. At one stage Indonesian government officials claimed that several thousand qualified voters might be disenfranchised as a result of UNAMET's unfairness. The fact was that the government had been given ample opportunity to identify suitable registration sites inside Indonesia back in May, but had failed to designate any at all in West Timor.[40]

Despite the flimsiness of the charge of UNAMET unfairness, as the final day of registration approached, Indonesian authorities pressed on with their demand for registration in West Timor. UNAMET initially declined on logistical grounds, but realizing that the issue might easily become the focus for later political challenges, eventually agreed to establish additional registration centers in the border area.[41] While these arrangements were still being negotiated, bus- and truckloads of people suddenly began to appear at registration sites along the border, especially in Bobonaro. Many of them were carrying bogus identity documents. Local UNAMET authorities managed to resist their demands to register, but it was clear that the issue had the potential, and may even have been intended, to escalate into violence and chaos. In the end, only a few hundred came across the border to register—a far cry from the ninety-two hundred the government had promised.

A second element of the Indonesian strategy was the claim that the twenty-day registration period was too short, and that it would disenfranchise a large percentage of the population. Again, it was a dubious claim. With a few days still remaining, the number of voters registered already exceeded the expected total for East Timor.[42] Accordingly, UNAMET initially resisted the idea of an extension, pointing out that it was unnecessary and would inevitably lead to a delay in the vote—something the Indonesian government itself strongly opposed. Nevertheless, Indonesian authorities continued to insist on an extension, and the call was taken up by the Indonesian media and Indonesian politicians of all stripes. Even the future president, Abdurrahman Wahid, who was less antagonistic toward the United Nations than many, spoke out in favor of an extension following a visit to East Timor in early August. At times it seemed that the issue might spiral into a serious confrontation between the United Nations and the government of Indonesia.

The danger was especially acute in the western district of Bobonaro, where the Bupati, Guilherme dos Santos—an influential figure who from the outset had adopted a bellicose posture toward UNAMET—had joined forces with local militia chiefs to threaten violence if an extension were not granted. The threats became so open and so provocative that Martin decided to fly there on August 3 to resolve the matter. A meeting was arranged in the Bupati's office, the ostensible purpose of which was to clarify misunderstandings and resolve outstanding differences. The Bupati, dressed in a rose-colored safari suit, sour faced, his eyes concealed behind gold-rimmed dark glasses, presided over the meeting. Martin, the picture of an English gentleman, also in a safari suit, sat immediately to his left. From the opposite end of the table, I had a good view of both men. After a brief exchange of pleasantries, the Bupati launched into a tirade against UNAMET and laid out his demand for an extension of registration. Among other things, he declared that if one single resident of Bobonaro were unable to register, he would order a blockade of the entire district and take all UNAMET staff hostage until registration centers were reopened. As the Bupati railed on, rising occasionally to fever pitch, Martin's face reddened, and his eyes opened slightly wider than usual. When he was finally permitted to speak, Martin responded with a vehemence that I had never before witnessed. Banging the table with his hand, he said that he had come to Bobonaro to resolve difficulties peacefully, not to hear threats of unlawful action by a government official. The Bupati retorted disingenuously that he had not issued a threat but had merely been expressing "the people's desire for justice." Later that day we returned to Dili, secretly pleased with Martin's show of strength, yet anxious about the prospects for peace in Bobonaro and the rest of the country.[43]

In spite of those concerns, the process moved ahead without interruption. Indeed, in view of the unexpected success of registration and the concerted pressure from all sides to move ahead, the decision to proceed with the vote could scarcely have been avoided. And so, in the first week of August, attention turned to finalizing arrangements for the campaign period and the ballot itself, which was now scheduled for August 30.

CHAPTER SEVEN

THE VOTE

IF THE DECISION TO PROCEED with the vote was logically sound or inevitable, events in the days shortly before and immediately after the ballot were a sobering reminder of the awful fragility of the political experiment on which the United Nations and East Timor had embarked. In these few days, every moment seemed pregnant with meaning and danger. On the one hand, there was a sense that even the smallest decisions or missteps had the potential to undermine the process and to change the course of East Timor's history. At the same time, there was a powerful impulse to assist those caught up in the violence, regardless of the consequences—perhaps to make good on the often repeated promise that UNAMET would not leave after the vote or abandon East Timor in its hour of need. Thus, while some analysts have accused the United Nations of a reckless disregard for human life by proceeding in the face of widely predicted violence, a careful account of those days reveals a far more complicated picture, in which UN officials and East Timorese struggled with difficult moral and political questions to which there were in fact no simple answers. It demonstrates, for example, how the controversial decision to surrender an independence leader to Indonesian authorities on the eve of the vote, which was highly problematic from a human rights perspective, might well have averted widespread violence on voting day. More generally, it highlights the morally ambiguous and contingent quality of the events and decisions that preceded the worst of the violence.

Campaigning

By early August, preparations for the campaign and the ballot itself had been under way for some time. Decisions had already been taken about the number and location of polling stations, and the wording and appearance of the ballot. The contending parties had also agreed to a campaign schedule, which spelled out a precise calendar for campaigning activity by each side. The campaign period was to last from August 14 to 26, with the final few days before the ballot designated as a "cooling off" period. In accordance with a mandate spelled out in the May 5 Agreements, UNAMET drafted a Campaign Code of Conduct, which was signed by all parties and launched in a public ceremony on August 9.[1] Among other things, the code required parties to refrain from inciting or committing acts of violence.

Despite these achievements, there was still the pressing question of how campaigning should be organized to ensure the greatest possible fairness and minimize the likelihood of violence. One of the key conditions for the conduct of a fair ballot, spelled out in the May 5 Agreements, was the establishment of a level playing field between the two sides.[2] In reality, this was still far from being achieved as the campaign period got under way. CNRT offices had been forced to close in many districts in early 1999 in the face of attacks and threats by pro-Indonesian militias. While a handful of offices had reopened in July and early August, most were still closed. In fact, just three weeks before the vote, CNRT had offices in only five of the thirteen districts.[3] And while some CNRT leaders had begun to appear in public and to play a role in political life, many more remained in hiding. That was especially true in the western districts, where official support for Indonesia had been strongest and most aggressive. Even where CNRT offices had managed to open, the party was unable to campaign openly due to continued threats and violence from the pro-Indonesia camp. When they did attempt to speak or hold rallies, they were generally answered by acts of violence by pro-Indonesian militias. Perhaps most seriously the principal CNRT leader, Gusmão, remained in detention in Jakarta. Meanwhile, proautonomy parties faced no obstacles to their political activity. In fact, they made abundant use of Indonesian government resources and the power of office, in defiance of the May 5 Agreements and the Campaign Code of Conduct. In one of the more obvious examples of that pattern, in early August the Indonesian government official Francisco Lopes da Cruz made a whirlwind proautonomy speaking tour of the territory, using a TNI helicopter.[4]

This situation might well have proven disastrous—and there were some outside observers who predicted that it would mean defeat for the

CNRT at the polls. But in the end, the absence of a level playing field did not appear to matter. The most obvious reason—though this was only evident in retrospect—was that most East Timorese knew very well which way they were going to vote and did not require a campaign to convince them. As CNRT and Falintil leaders frequently noted, a formal campaign was hardly necessary because the resistance had been campaigning for independence for twenty-three years. An additional reason, not without importance, was that the CNRT adapted its campaign strategy to the contingencies of the situation. That strategy was spelled out in a July 7 directive from Gusmão establishing the formation of the CNRT Campaign Planning and Coordination Commission. According to the directive, the proindependence campaign should seek to create a climate of stability, reconciliation, and nonviolence as a prerequisite for the successful realization of the popular consultation. That meant using language that "will not offend the other side," "refraining from triumphalism and arrogance," and in general reducing "the possibilities of rupture" with the supporters of autonomy. Substantively, the campaign should simply clarify two key points: first, that "autonomy amounts to integration" with Indonesia, and second, that "we are fighting for independence. Liberation will allow the exit of the Indonesian occupant. We want freedom, peace and progress, harmony between all East Timorese, and security."[5]

To a remarkable extent, the proindependence side adhered to this strategic vision. Rather than organizing large rallies, parades, or motorized convoys, as their opponents did, throughout the campaign period the CNRT generally stayed out of sight, campaigning by word of mouth, through extended families and other networks. As Fretilin had done in 1974–75—and as the resistance had done for more than a decade—the CNRT also relied on a network of students and young people, a mobile radio station, and clandestine and semiclandestine bulletins to spread information, while leaving scarcely a trace. [6] This light-footed, low-profile approach was in keeping with the CNRT's broader strategy for the popular consultation, articulated in early 1999, which emphasized nonconfrontation and nonviolence.

On the whole, the strategy worked well, and together with the Campaign Code of Conduct, it helped to avoid an escalation of violence during the campaign period. But there were notable exceptions. One of these came on August 26, the last official day of campaigning by the pro-Indonesian side, which saw some of the worst violence in months. As it

FIGURES 7.1 AND 7.2. Unarmed independence supporter Bernadino Joaquim Afonso Guterres is shot dead by Indonesian troops in Dili, August 26, 1999. An East Timorese university student, Guterres was urging Indonesian police to stop an attack by armed prointegration militias when troops surrounded him and shot him in the neck. With help from UNAMET officials, his body was retrieved from the morgue at the military hospital in Dili later that night. (Eddy Hasby)

happened, I found myself caught up in the aftermath of that violence. The call came just after dusk. "Our son's body is at the military hospital. We have to retrieve it but we can't go alone. Please help us." Even under normal circumstances, it would have been unusual to head out after dark to retrieve a dead body in Dili. Although there had been fewer acts of violence since the United Nations arrived in May, armed pro-Indonesian militias were still active, especially at night. And the circumstances on this night were hardly normal. In Dili alone, at least six people had been killed in a single day. One of them was Bernadino Joaquim Afonso Guterres, a twenty-four-year-old university student, whose father was now on the telephone. Bernadino's father understood only too well how dangerous the situation was, and how little one could trust the militias or the Indonesian military and police who were responsible for keeping the peace. That was precisely why he wanted UNAMET to accompany the family to the military hospital without delay—and why he refused to take no for an answer.

It took some work to gather allies for this mission, but eventually two Civpols, a New Zealander, Peter Burt, and an Englishman, Rob Walker, agreed to go along. At about 9:00 p.m. the three of us headed out in a single UN Land Rover, armed only with a two-way radio, to meet the family in the Bemori district at the eastern edge of Dili. The streets of the city were deserted and dark, and we wondered aloud whether this

had been a wise move. Suddenly, a group of about ten men, some holding machetes, appeared from the shadows by the side of the road. Militias. Burt hit the accelerator, and we sped past. Rattled and realizing that
we were lost, we stopped at a small police post about a kilometer up the
road. Seven or eight officers were gathered inside watching television.
When they told us Bemori was back the way we had come, we asked
whether they would accompany us past the militias. They declined but
agreed to escort us, by a different route, part of the way to Bemori.

At the office of the village head in Bemori, we were greeted by a
large group of Bernadino's family and friends. They seemed relieved that
we had finally arrived, but anxious to get moving. After some discussion,
we set out in two vehicles toward the military hospital, reaching it without incident about fifteen minutes later. Someone in Bernadino's family
knew exactly where to look for the body—a small concrete building,
known as the "corpse room," not far from the main hospital.

I stepped out of the car and walked toward the building behind the
family. The attendant had already opened the door, and he watched im-
passively as the family moved inside. A bare lightbulb hung crookedly
from a wire in the ceiling. Beneath it, on a concrete slab, lay Bernadino.
His feet were bare and dusty, and his T-shirt was caked with blood from
a gaping wound in his neck. His eyes were open, staring. Some of the
women and the men caressed him, uttered prayers barely audible, and
cried. A few minutes later they carried him from the room and loaded
him into the open back of the family's pickup truck. As we headed back
down the winding road to Bemori, our headlights played on the scene
in the back of the truck—Bernadino, surrounded on all sides by family
and friends, his bare feet visible, bouncing stiffly.

It was a few days before I learned how he had died. The story helped
to explain why the family had been so anxious to retrieve his body and
spoke volumes about the political situation in East Timor in the final
days before the vote. It turned out that Bernadino had been gunned
down by an Indonesian police officer as he tried to run away.[7] The incident had begun as an angry confrontation between proindependence
and pro-Indonesian youths in the Kuluhun district of Dili, not far from
Bernadino's home in Bemori. According to one report, the conflict was
ignited when pro-Indonesian youths tore down and burned a poster of
resistance leader Gusmão, and also burned a house and a taxi in the
neighborhood. Among the pro-Indonesian supporters, bystanders said,
were members of the local militia, Aitarak—identifiable by their black

shirts and insignia—some of whom were armed with automatic weapons. The proindependence side was armed with rocks, which they used to counter the periodic volleys of militia gunfire. Indonesian police eventually arrived at the scene, but to the dismay of the proindependence side and bystanders, they did nothing to stop the militias from shooting. In a sworn statement before the UN Electoral Commission, an accredited observer described what happened next:

> The crowd shouted to the police to stop the militias who were shooting. One of them . . . remonstrated with the police, directing their attention to the militias. A policeman who was not wearing a beret like his comrades . . . told [the youth] that he could shoot him because he was exciting the people. [The youth] turned and ran. The policeman thereupon shot him at a range of about three paces. I subsequently saw a gunshot wound in the middle of his back and one behind the neck. He died there. When the ambulance attendants lifted the body later I saw a large gaping wound to the throat.[8]

A local resident who called UNAMET later the same day claimed that Indonesian police had been observed handing weapons to militia members before and during the incident. Other bystanders alleged that the Aitarak militiamen were in fact TNI soldiers. These claims were never independently verified, but they were consistent with the well-established pattern of official support for the militia and the other events of that day.

Peace and Reconciliation?

The events of late August made it more obvious than ever just how easily the referendum process and East Timor's future could be derailed by violence. They also added a degree of urgency to various efforts at peace and reconciliation that had been under way for some time. At least since June, UNAMET had been directly involved in various initiatives to broker a peace deal between the proindependence and pro-Indonesia groups. At a minimum, it was hoped that the two sides could reach some sort of understanding on how to conduct themselves during the consultation and what the rules would be in the postballot period. The hope was that both sides would agree to avoid violence during the process and to accept the results once they were announced. It was also hoped that the losing side would avoid violence in exchange for the promise of its involvement in the new political setup.

These were among the central goals of the peace talks that took place in late June in Jakarta. Known as the Dare II Peace and Reconciliation Talks, after the site of the seminary just south of Dili where a first round of talks was held in September 1998, these negotiations brought together representatives of the proautonomy and proindependence sides along with the Indonesian government. UNAMET's role was primarily as a facilitator. Regrettably, but not surprisingly, the talks failed to have any meaningful effect on the situation on the ground.[9] A somewhat more promising meeting was held between pro-Indonesian and proindependence leaders on June 18. That meeting produced an agreement stipulating, among other things, that both sides had an obligation to appeal to their followers to surrender all types of weapons to the authorities, and cease all forms of hostile attitudes and acts of violence.[10]

That noble objective was consistent with one of the stipulations in the secretary-general's memorandum of May 4 and with the security agreement of May 5. Unfortunately, it was never achieved, largely because the Indonesian side and its East Timorese proxies refused to carry it out. A major sticking point was the Indonesian refusal to contemplate the CNRT/Falintil demand that the TNI—and not just the militias—be required to disarm or at a minimum withdraw to their barracks. Repeating its contention that the conflict was among East Timorese and that Falintil in particular was responsible for fomenting the violence, Indonesian authorities insisted that the TNI was a neutral force whose presence was essential to maintaining security and order.

In an effort to break the impasse, in late July Gusmão ordered the unilateral cantonment of all Falintil forces. In ordering the cantonment, Gusmão was seeking to demonstrate that Falintil was not the source of the violence, as Indonesian officials claimed, and to put pressure on the militias and the TNI to reciprocate with their own disarmament.[11] By August 12, some 670 Falintil guerrillas had been grouped at four cantonment sites—at Uai Mori in Viqueque (July 26), Atalari in Baucau (August 9), Poetete in Ermera (August 10), and Aiassa in Bobonaro (August 12)—and both Gusmão and Falintil's deputy commander, Taur Matan Ruak, had given a firm commitment that they would not move out of those sites with their weapons. Senior UN military liaison officers visited each of these sites, and came away impressed not only by Falintil's evident logistical capabilities in establishing these camps but also its ap-

FIGURE 7.3. Falintil forces at Uai Mori, Viqueque, August 1999. Formed in 1975 and decimated by Indonesian forces four years later, Falintil continued to carry out guerrilla resistance against Indonesian forces until 1999. Nevertheless, Falintil's importance began to diminish in the mid-1980s, as the strategy of the resistance shifted away from direct armed confrontation, and toward diplomacy and nonviolent demonstrations. In late July 1999, Xanana Gusmão ordered all Falintil units to assemble in four cantonment sites, including this one at Uai Mori, to demonstrate that proindependence forces were not responsible for the violence, as Indonesian officials claimed. (Eddy Hasby)

parent professionalism. Indeed, the cantonment process confirmed what many UN military officers had already come to believe: that Falintil was a more professional military force than the TNI.

Just over a week later, the Indonesian side responded with a series of public cantonment "ceremonies" of its own, at which militias handed over a small number of older weapons—certainly no more than a small fraction of those to which they had been given access—to Indonesian authorities amid much marching and patriotic fanfare. UNAMET officials who attended these ceremonies listened with discomfort as militia commanders used the occasion to threaten further violence should people vote "the wrong way" on August 30. At the ceremony in the village of Cassa on August 18, for example, the notorious militia leader Cancio Carvalho repeatedly warned those assembled that "those who choose wrongly will suffer the consequences," and "if you choose wrongly there will be war"[12] Immediately after the public ceremonies, moreover, the militias dispersed; a few days later they were back in action, fully armed.

As voting day neared, and as the threats and portents of violence mounted, the efforts to secure some kind of peace between the parties went into high gear. As part of that effort, starting in mid-August, UNAMET organized a series of low-profile reconciliation meetings between the two sides. At UN-sponsored meetings in Jakarta on August 11 and 22, pro-Indonesian and proindependence leaders agreed to the establishment of a twenty-five member East Timorese Consultative Commission, to be launched on the day after the vote, that would seek to foster reconciliation and cooperation regardless of the outcome.[13] A few days later, Gusmão issued a public message that reiterated his own and the CNRT's commitment to a peaceful process and transition. "The birth of the Timorese Nation," he wrote,

> cannot take place in the midst of division and marred by discord and rancour. Regardless of past political positions, all citizens are called upon to embrace the need for harmony, and to show forgiveness and tolerance for their brothers for the sake of our national interests. The difficulties endured to this day cannot remain a permanent shadow obstructing our future. Our Nation will be greater if each and every one of us is able to forgive, including those who have committed the most reprehensible acts. In such an exacting time, each of us is called upon to overcome differences and bury hatred. . . . The State of Timor Lorosae will welcome into its bosom all the East Timorese, regardless of the positions they assumed in the past. I particularly refer to those who are part of the pro-integration paramilitary forces.[14]

Finally, on the morning of August 29, just one day before the ballot, the two sides came together in a remarkable public ceremony at UNAMET headquarters to announce an agreement reached only the previous day. The agreement, which was read out by Martin, declared that Falintil and the militias had promised to refrain from recourse to violence, and abide by the outcome of the vote. In their own words, representatives of the two East Timorese parties as well as senior police and TNI officers spoke of their commitment to peace and reconciliation.[15]

While these agreements were being announced, local peace and reconciliation initiatives were taking place in other parts of the country. Among the most poignant was a reconciliation ceremony at the Catholic church in Suai. Presided over by the parish priest, the ceremony brought together proautonomy and proindependence leaders, and closed with what appeared to be a sincere commitment on both sides to avoid violence in the coming days. Those in attendance could not have imagined that just over one week later, the church in Suai would be the scene of some of the most terrible violence anywhere in the country, and that its victims would include three Catholic priests. Some analysts have suggested that the reconciliation ceremony in Suai failed to achieve its desired end because those who conducted it did not take sufficient account of East Timor's traditions of peacemaking.[16] It seems far more likely that the failure stemmed from the fact that the violence had already been planned in advance, and that those involved in the ceremony either had no power to stop it or no genuine interest in doing so.

A Gamble

In the view of most fair-minded observers, the greatest threat to the popular consultation came from pro-Indonesian militias. Ironically, it was a rare act of violence by the proindependence side that almost brought the whole delicate house of cards crashing down. That act also drew UNAMET into an agonizing moral quagmire, which those involved would probably prefer to forget.

The first sign of brewing trouble came at about 1:30 p.m. on August 29, when a Civpol officer, Wayne Sievers, radioed from the Dili police station to report an encounter with the volatile leader of the Aitarak militia, Eurico Guterres, who had spoken on behalf of the PPI at the reconciliation ceremony earlier that morning. Guterres, he said, had come to the station to report that an Aitarak member, Placido Meneses, had been abducted by proindependence youths earlier in the day. An entry in UNAMET's Joint Operations Center daily log gave a taste of what was to come: "Guterres is very agitated and threatened not to follow the peace agreement signed this AM at UNAMET HQ and to start violence this evening if P. Meneses is not found/returned."[17]

In fact, as we discovered later, Meneses—who was a relative of Guterres—had not only been abducted, he had been killed, and his assailants were in all likelihood proindependence youths. A critical part of the story was captured on film by a television camera crew and broadcast on CNN later that day. The footage showed a crowd of youths beating and kicking a man as he lay on the ground. Before long, a tall, strongly built man entered the scene, ordered the youths away, and dragged the victim into a nearby taxicab that then drove off. What the film footage did not show was that the man in the taxi was eventually taken to a spot along the road just outside Dili and thrown into a deep ravine, where his dead body was discovered several hours later. Television and media coverage also missed the political drama that unfolded over the next twelve hours.

Anxious to avert Guterres's promised campaign of violence on the eve of the vote, a UNAMET delegation went to his Dili headquarters at about 4:00 p.m. on the afternoon of August 29 to discuss the alleged abduction. The delegation included two senior MLOs, the assistant to the head of mission, and me. The aim of the meeting was to assure Guterres that the case would be properly investigated and to urge him not to resort to violence. Guterres' headquarters was in an old hotel, the Tropical, located not far from the Dili military command (Kodim Dili). As we navigated the roadblock that controlled access to the street we saw scores of Aitarak militiamen, some of them armed, loitering menacingly outside the hotel. After a minute or two, Guterres approached. He thanked us for coming and then, swinging wildly from calm to fury, accused UNAMET of paying no attention to abuses by the proindependence side. Ignoring our assurances that the case was indeed being taken seriously, he spelled out his ultimatum. UNAMET must locate Meneses and arrest the alleged perpetrator, or he would unleash a storm of violence and derail the referendum. The man responsible, he said, was João da Silva, a well-known proindependence leader in the Becora district of Dili.

About half an hour later we left, with little confidence that we would be able to meet Guterres's demands and uncertain whether it was even wise to try. Nevertheless, making use of our network of contacts in the proindependence movement, a few of us in the Political Affairs Office worked hard to discover what had happened and to contact da Silva. By about 8:00 p.m., still on the eve of the vote, that work paid off. Accompanied by a number of his friends, da Silva arrived at UNAMET headquarters to tell us his version of events. He admitted that he had witnessed the assault on Meneses that morning, but denied responsibility for the beating and for the subsequent murder and dumping of the body. As the conversation unfolded, it became clear that he was in fact the man in the television footage who had stopped the beating and shoved Meneses into a taxicab. In a sworn statement made at UNAMET that evening, he gave the following account:

About five of our group set on him. They did not do so on my orders. Many in the group had come from other places, such as Kuluhun, Bemori and Bidau, and were strangers. They accepted me as their commander, but the five were acting on their own initiative. They attacked him because he was wearing a pro-autonomy t-shirt and because he reached for something in his pocket.

First, they searched him for a weapon. Then they kicked him and hit him, and one of them threatened him with a machete [*parang*]. He was wounded on the back of the head. It was a moderately serious injury, neither heavy nor light. He was not unconscious and could stand. The others in the group [who had not attacked him] were hurling insults at him and shouting "Kill him." I stopped them. I was aware at the time that we were being filmed by a foreign television cameraman. I dragged him about 10 meters and put him in a taxi. . . . Then I told the taxi driver to take him to Bidau hospital. . . .

About one hour after the incident I was told by a friend that he had been thrown into a ravine from the top of Fatuahi mountain between Hera and Dili, so I thought he must be dead. . . . I was shocked because the victim should have been taken to the hospital.[18]

This account made it clear that da Silva bore some responsibility for the assault on Meneses. As the acknowledged commander of the proindependence group in Becora, he could have done more to prevent the attack from occurring and to stop it sooner. His testimony also suggested that he might not have intervened at all had there been no foreign television crew. At the same time, there was no definitive evidence that da Silva was personally responsible for Meneses's murder.

The matter came to a head later the same day when a group of Indonesian police officers arrived at the UNAMET compound to arrest da Silva. Under the terms of the May 5 Agreements, UNAMET was bound to cooperate with the Indonesian police, so we had little basis on which to resist handing him over. On the other hand, we had serious concerns for da Silva's safety if he were surrendered to the police. Just as important, we were dismayed by the obvious political bias of the police in handling this case. Time and again over the previous four months we had observed the police fail utterly to take action to stop pro-Indonesian militia groups from committing serious crimes, including murder, or to investigate and prosecute such cases after the fact. Now, faced with a rare instance of criminality by the proindependence side, the police were pursuing the case with unprecedented vigor. Worse still, acting primarily on the basis of allegations by a notorious militia leader, Guterres, who had himself been implicated in serious crimes, there was a good chance that they were about to arrest the wrong man.

With these concerns in mind and Guterres's ultimatum hanging over us, a small UNAMET group discussed how best to proceed. Also involved in the conversation were two senior leaders of the resistance, including the deputy commander of Falintil, Taur Matan Ruak. During these deliberations, a decision was taken to place a telephone call to Gusmão, then still under house arrest in Jakarta. Somewhat to our surprise, after much discussion Gusmão ordered da Silva to give himself up to the police in the interest of ensuring that the popular consultation would go ahead according to plan the following day. That decision was in fact entirely in keeping with Gusmão's insistence that proindependence forces should refrain from any acts of violence, regardless of the circumstances.[19] Da Silva himself appeared to accept this order as a necessary sacrifice. In the statement already cited, he said, "What is important is that the popular consultation takes place. It does not matter to me whether I am dead or alive. After the vote I believe I will be free."[20]

Before acting on this decision, we laid down a number of conditions designed to ensure da Silva's safety and fair treatment. He would not be taken into police custody that evening but would instead remain under UNAMET supervision until the following day. Once he was transferred to police custody, he would be visited regularly by a Civpol officer, he would be guaranteed access to a lawyer, and UNAMET would ensure that any legal process met acceptable standards of fairness. These provisions were better than nothing, but we knew that they offered no real guarantee of da Silva's safety. The risk became increasingly obvious as violence descended in the days after the August 30 vote. In Dili, armed Aitarak members moved freely in and out of the regional police headquarters in search of their enemies, unimpeded by police. On one occasion shortly after the vote, a militiaman reportedly entered the police cell block where da Silva was being held and threatened to kill him.

Ultimately, UNAMET was unable to monitor da Silva's safety properly, and after the evacuation of September 14 there was simply no way to know what had become of him. When the Civpol chief, Commissioner Alan Mills, returned to Dili in late September, he asked the Indonesian police chief, Colonel Timbul Silaen, about da Silva. With a shrug, Silaen said he didn't know. At that point, we assumed the worst: we had gambled with a man's life, and lost. It was not until November, when Colin Stewart and I happened to meet da Silva in Dili, that we learned what had actually happened. As the situation in Dili had deteriorated after the vote, da Silva had been transferred from the police station to the main prison, known as LP Becora. Shortly after he had arrived there, a group of militias had stormed into the prison looking for him. By good fortune the militias knew only his name, not his face, so when all the prisoners were lined up they did not notice him, and none of da Silva's fellow prisoners said a word.

More remarkably perhaps, the prison guard then on duty, an Indonesian, did not give him up either. In fact, after the militiamen had left, the prison guard took da Silva aside and offered to take him to safety. Although he had reason to suspect that this was a trap, da Silva decided to place his life in the guard's hands. Soon, they were in a car together, navigating the countless militia roadblocks and checkpoints, as they made their way west toward the border. On the other side, in the town of Atambua in West Timor, the guard took da Silva to a relative's house, where he stayed for almost two months, protected by a circle of Indonesian friends, before finally returning to East Timor in November. It was one of the more striking ironies of the crisis that a proindependence leader was surrendered to the Indonesian police by the United Nations and subsequently rescued from the militias by an Indonesian prison guard.

Ballot Day

Nobody who was there on voting day will ever forget it. East Timorese—many dressed in their Sunday best, and some having left home in the middle of the night to reach the polling station by dawn—defied the militias for the chance to vote on their future. UNAMET electoral officers reported that when the polls opened at 6:30 a.m., roughly half of all registered voters were already in line.[21] And when the figures were tallied at the end of the day, they showed that an extraordinary 98.6 percent of those who had registered had cast their ballots. The 1.4 percent who had not voted included a number who had died or become gravely ill in the days between registering and voting. I had occasion to observe

FIGURE 7.4. Ballot day, August 30, 1999. East Timorese, including the elderly and the infirm, defied threats of militia violence for the chance to vote on their future. A remarkable 98.6 percent of those who had registered to vote cast their ballots, and of that number 78.5 percent opted for independence. Local UNAMET staff members who had assisted in the registration and polling process were later targeted by prointegration militias, and more than a dozen were killed. (Patrick Burgess and Galuh Wandita)

firsthand just how seriously East Timorese took this unique opportunity when I visited a polling station in Dili on the afternoon of August 30, together with a fellow Political Affairs officer, Stewart. As we approached the station we noticed that the local UNAMET staff looked somewhat disheartened. When we asked why they were looking morose on such a momentous day, they replied that with less than an hour to go before polling closed, there were still *three* registered voters from the district who had not cast a ballot. At the same polling station, we met a middle-aged man who had not been able to vote because of a problem with his registration documents. He pleaded with us to allow him to vote—something we were regrettably unable to do—and he cried openly when 4:00 p.m. came and the poll finally closed.

A handful of polling stations had to be closed down temporarily during the day as a result of threats or acts of violence. But on the whole, voting proceeded much more smoothly than anticipated. The same was true of the ballot count that took place in the government-run museum next door to the regional police headquarters in Dili a few days later. Both of these occasions—the vote and the ballot count—offered ample opportunity for pro-Indonesian militias to completely derail the process, but they did not do so.

The only plausible explanation for the sudden lull in violence at these critical junctures was that the militias and their Indonesian patrons still believed their side was likely to win. Indeed, in comments to the media after the vote, key Indonesian officials—including Foreign Minister Alatas and the highest-ranking army officer in East Timor, Major General Makarim—indicated that they had expected the vote to be won or lost by a narrow margin.[22] If they had believed otherwise, the days of the vote and the ballot count would have been the ideal times to step up the intimidation and violence, rather than stopping it. The fact that the same pattern occurred across the territory seemed to indicate that the decision not to attack on these days must have been made at a high level. Moreover, despite their concerted efforts to influence the outcome through violence and intimidation, those who favored continued ties with Indonesia recognized the critical importance of the August 30 referendum.

It was not only East Timorese and Indonesians who took the vote seriously. In a few short months, the vast majority of international UNAMET staff had become so deeply committed to the process that they were prepared to work exceptionally long hours and, quite literally, to place their lives on the line to ensure its success. The Civpols who helped to guarantee the security and integrity of the ballot boxes on voting day were a case in point. Within just a few hours of the close of voting, all ballot boxes had to be transported from polling centers to concentration points around the country, and then trucked or airlifted by helicopter to Dili, where the counting would take place. Officially, the Indonesian police were responsible for maintaining the security of the ballot boxes, and in many cases they did their job adequately. In a number of instances, however, and particularly where militias were active, they failed utterly to do what was required, leaving the Civpols to pick up the pieces.

In Ermera, for instance, Indonesian police failed to secure the field where the UN helicopter was due to land and pick up several dozen sealed ballot boxes. When a group of armed militiamen rushed on to the field toward the landing site, the Indonesian police contingent did nothing to prevent them; indeed, most ran for cover. The only thing standing between the armed militia and the blue plastic boxes were four Civpols—all of them unarmed. As the militiamen ran toward them, shouting and brandishing their weapons, the Civpols reached down to grab whatever they could find—a rock perhaps or a stick—and then stood together, defending those precious boxes. And this they did, long enough to get the boxes in the helicopter and fly them to safety.

Many old UN hands and journalists commented during those days that they had seldom seen such displays of selflessness and purpose in a UN mission. I do not know if that is true, but I can testify that the work in East Timor inspired a remarkable sense of mission in even the most jaded and apolitical UN technicians, police officers, soldiers, and electoral workers. That sense of mission was partly driven, I think, by the consistently disgraceful behavior of the pro-Indonesian side and by its open hostility to the United Nations. It was primarily for this reason and not because UN staff had any preexisting bias in favor of independence that there was such a determination to see that the process was successfully carried out. And so, when we realized that virtually every registered voter had cast a ballot and that contrary to predictions, the voting had not been disrupted by major acts of violence as widely predicted, there was an overwhelming sense of joy and relief. While it had not been the course we Political Affairs officers had advised, the decision to proceed with the vote appeared to have been vindicated.

Backlash

Almost immediately, however, the wisdom of that decision was thrown into question. Within hours of the end of voting, pro-Indonesian militia groups began a rampage of violence against those they perceived as enemies. Among the first victims was a local UNAMET staff member, João Lopes Gomes. A fifty-year-old schoolteacher and family man, Gomes was stabbed in the back and killed by militiamen as he helped to load the ballot boxes into a UN vehicle near Atsabe village in Ermera, just after the polls had closed. The news came to us in Dili in a garbled radio message from one of our outlying posts that one of our own people had been murdered.[23]

Early the next morning, August 31, I went with a small UN group to investigate the killing and retrieve Gomes's body.[24] From our helicopter, the scene was one of extraordinary beauty. The village of Atsabe was tucked in the mountains, treetops just visible above the morning mist.

But as we walked toward the building where we were told Gomes's body lay we could hear anguished cries. As we approached the building, we saw that it was surrounded by about fifty militiamen—quite possibly the very men who had killed Gomes—armed with machetes, handguns, and rifles, wearing their characteristic red and white bandanas. Mingling among them were members of the Indonesian army and police. As soon as we arrived, the militia began to make demands: they were not going to allow the local UNAMET staff to leave the village or allow the ballot boxes to be taken until we made certain concessions. Specifically, they demanded that we nullify all the votes from the district because in their view the polling had been unfair.

Hours by road from Dili, with no phone communication and no radio link, we had no choice but to negotiate with them, and so we found ourselves in conversation with the militia leader—who explained that Gomes had been killed because the militias believed UNAMET had acted unfairly—and with local police and TNI authorities, who effectively defended the actions of the militias. Lengthy discussions with a nervous local police chief (Kapolsek) and an Indonesian police liaison officer based in Ermera produced assurances that the militias would be dispersed and restrained. But no action was ever taken, and the armed militias remained in the immediate vicinity—angry and with weapons in hand. In response to our protests, the Kapolsek explained that he did not dare to order the militias to do anything.

Our discussions with the local military commander (Danramil) were similarly unproductive, although they revealed a good deal about the ties between the TNI and the militias. The Danramil told us, for example, that he had been forewarned of the planned attack on UNAMET the previous night. When we asked why he had not sought to prevent the attack, he explained that had he interfered, the militias might have turned against him. Apparently believing that we would be impressed, however, he hastened to add that he had instructed the militia not to injure any UN international staff; only local staff were to be targeted. Like the police chief, he refused to provide any guarantee that the militias would be restrained, let alone arrested.

After a few hours of discussion, we were no closer to leaving with the ballot boxes or conducting investigations, so we decided to return to Dili to collect a higher-level delegation. That delegation, which included Civpol commissioner Mills along with several senior Indonesian police and TNI officers, returned to Atsabe at about noon. After several more hours of tense negotiations, we were finally able to leave with the local staff and the ballot boxes. Yet the threats of militia violence and the unwillingness of Indonesian authorities to stop them ensured that no proper investigation could be conducted. It was not until November, when both the militias and the Indonesians were gone, that the inquiries resumed, and it was discovered that one more person and possibly others had been killed that day with the acquiescence of TNI authorities.

The postballot murders in Ermera were not isolated events. In the hours and days immediately after the vote, violence seemed to spread like wildfire through most of the territory. The first signs of serious trouble came from Maliana.[25] Relations between UNAMET and Indonesian officials had deteriorated badly in the weeks before the ballot, and the Political Affairs officer there, Peter Bartu, had warned that serious postballot violence was a virtual certainty.[26] Local residents had been preparing for it. Some had even carried their belongings to the polling stations so that they could flee to the hills immediately after casting their ballot. And as predicted, within hours of the end of voting, the violence began. Militias and TNI solders began to roam the streets, firing their weapons, setting fire to houses and offices, and killing their presumed enemies. As in Ermera, local UNAMET staff were among the first victims. On the evening of September 2, the Indonesian police confirmed that two local UNAMET staff members, Domingos Pereira and Ruben Soares, had been killed, and the home of one of the two had been burned to the ground. At least five other local staff were reported missing. These events and the general insecurity in the district led to the evacuation to Dili of all remaining UNAMET Maliana staff, local and international, on the morning of September 3.

The situation grew even more volatile after the announcement on September 4 that an overwhelming majority (78.5 percent) had voted for independence. At about 2:30 p.m. that day militias shot up and then burned Dili's "luxury" hotel, the Mahkota—where Martin had earlier announced the result of the ballot—while police and army officers stood by. At almost exactly the same time, militias began to fire weapons in the immediate vicinity of UNAMET's Dili regional office, prompting the staff to relocate to the main headquarters. About fifteen minutes later, militias surrounded the house of the Portuguese government delegation, where some sixty to seventy refugees were also sheltering. Again the Indonesian police failed to intervene, leaving the refugees and the delegation with no choice but to flee to the UNAMET compound. As evening fell, we began to receive reports that Indonesian police were ordering people onto trucks heading for West Timor.

Indonesian officials and some outside observers gave the impression that the postballot violence was erupting spontaneously—that the militias and a small number of East Timorese soldiers were simply running out of control in an emotional response to the outcome of the vote. At the time, Indonesian foreign minister Alatas alluded to "rogue elements" within the TNI.[27] A few months later, as previously noted, Major General Makarim told journalists that the violence had been part of an Indonesian cultural pattern of running amok. From the perspective of those on the ground these explanations seemed at first to make some sense. The militias did indeed appear angry, and a number of UNAMET personnel reported that the police seemed nervous and to have no clear plan of action. Yet as we began to piece together testimony and information from different parts of the country, we saw evidence that far from being spontaneous, the violence and confusion were being carefully organized—and that the Indonesian army and police were the principal organizers.

Some of the most powerful evidence that the violence was being orchestrated came from the testimony of UNAMET staff posted in the different district offices at the time of their evacuation. Although they did not know it at the time, the events leading to their evacuation bore remarkable, indeed chilling similarities. A Political Affairs Office report about the five separate evacuations of September 3 and 4 concluded that the violence had been part of a "deliberate strategy to force UNAMET to withdraw from certain regions back to Dili"[28]

In every instance, the sequence of events began with militias roaming freely through the main town, more heavily armed than usual, shooting, setting fire to buildings, and killing. In every case, the Indonesian police and army either made no attempt to restrain the militias, or actively assisted them. Within a matter of hours, the police in every affected district warned that they could no longer control the situation and recommended that all UNAMET staff relocate to the district police station. Once they had gathered UN staff in their stations, the police suddenly announced that they would be leaving and advised UNAMET to follow. Having no means of guaranteeing their own security and cut off from all independent sources of information, district UNAMET officials had little choice but to go along. And so in each case, they joined the police convoy out of town and back to Dili.

Another striking feature of the postballot evacuation operations was that in spite of the apparent chaos, not a single member of the United Nations' international staff was killed.[29] While some considered this to be simply a matter of good fortune, it reinforced our suspicions that the descent into violence was carefully planned. An essential part of the plan, it appeared, was to create an *impression* of lawlessness calculated to terrify—but not to kill—UNAMET and all international observers and journalists. A similar approach had been used in the assaults on UNAMET in late June and early July, and in Atsabe on August 30. The strategy, it may be surmised, was based on the recognition that the death of a foreigner was likely to stimulate a strong international response. By contrast, the creation of an appearance of lawlessness and even the death of some East Timorese would provide a perfect pretext to remove all international observers from the countryside, and to call on the Indonesian army to "restore order." The strategy appeared for a time to have worked. With most international observers confined to the UNAMET compound in Dili by the end of the day on September 4, Indonesian authorities and the militias were free to take their revenge against East Timorese who had voted for independence. Over the next three weeks, that is precisely what they did.

CHAPTER EIGHT

A CAMPAIGN OF VIOLENCE

IN THE DAYS immediately after the announcement of the ballot result, militias and TNI soldiers sought out and killed supporters of independence, forcibly displaced more than half of the population from their homes, and systematically burned or destroyed much of the physical infrastructure in the country. Shockingly, many of those killed were people who had sought refuge in churches and other places that they assumed would be secure, and some of the victims were priests and nuns. During the same period, the UNAMET compound in Dili came under siege, rendering UN staff powerless to stop or even witness the violence, and placing in grave danger both several hundred staff and some fifteen hundred East Timorese who had taken refuge there.

The rapid escalation of violence in those few days confirmed what many critics and most East Timorese had predicted: that an unarmed UN mission would be no match for the TNI and its militia proxies. It also raised troubling moral questions and serious disagreements about the nature of the United Nations' responsibility to the people of East Timor, and in particular to those who had served with it or had sought its protection. In scenes reminiscent of Rwanda in 1994 and Srebrenica in 1995 where, in similar circumstances, the United Nations had effectively abandoned local people to their fate, officials in New York and Dili gave orders for a full evacuation, without the East Timorese. That order was openly and successfully challenged by other UNAMET staff who insisted that the United Nations should remain in Dili alongside those who had sought its protection. Thus, while the mounting violence dramatically highlighted the inherent flaw in the effort to resolve the conflict in East Timor through a peaceful electoral process, the drama and debate of those days inside the compound complicate the simple view that the United Nations as a whole acted with callous disregard for human life.

Siege

A surge of violence had been expected on the day of the announcement, September 4, so nobody was especially surprised when it began. UNAMET officials appreciated its seriousness, and so ordered all staff to remain at the compound that night, but many nevertheless believed that the trouble would be short-lived. When we woke the next morning, September 5, the city was quiet, and it seemed that after the previous day's violence, life might soon return to normal. We were sufficiently confident of this that around midday, a number of us from the Political Affairs Office ventured out in two UN vehicles to pick up a few things at our hotels and houses, and survey the situation in the city. We stopped first at the residence of East Timor's Bishop Belo. Gathered in the compound we found some two thousand people who had taken refuge there. We listened to the stories of a number of people who had been threatened or ill-treated by the militias, and urged them to begin documenting these stories with a view to future human rights prosecutions. When we left about an hour later, we had no sense that they were in imminent danger. After all, we reasoned, what place could be safer than a bishop's house in a predominantly Catholic country?

From the bishop's residence we headed to the Hotel Turismo, just next door. Built during the Portuguese era, facing Dili's pleasant waterfront, the Turismo had long been a favorite with visiting journalists and travelers. I had been living there happily since June, and in recent weeks I had been joined by a lively contingent of journalists and international observers. It was a pleasant place, and despite the occasional army or police spy, it was considered safe. As we drew up to the hotel, however, we noticed something out of place—a large TNI troop-transport vehicle stood idling on the road, with several heavily armed soldiers standing by. In the back of the truck, with all their gear, were dozens of foreigners, whom we recognized as journalists. Others were rushing out the front door of the hotel or scrambling to get onto the truck. Within a minute or two, and before we had been able to discover what was happening, the truck was gone. We later learned that it was taking the journalists to the airport, where planes were waiting to evacuate them. In this way, within a day or two, the number of journalists in East Timor declined from about five hundred to perhaps a dozen.

In spite of this rather unsettling scene, it was far from clear that Dili was about to descend once again into violence. By the time we left the Turismo, though, we did have a feeling that it would be wise to return to the UNAMET compound as soon as possible. And as we drove back across town those feelings were reinforced in dramatic fashion. Turning a corner in what was normally a busy part of town, but was now empty, we saw before us in the road two militiamen, both with red and white bandanas wrapped around their heads, and one of them carrying a long-barreled weapon. The first vehicle, in which I was riding, passed too quickly for the men to react. But as the second vehicle passed, they managed to fire at least one weapon. Something hit the rear window, shattering it, but causing no injuries.

Shortly after we returned to the compound, we heard that two other colleagues from Political Affairs, Elodie Cantier-Aristide and John Bevan, had also come under fire by militiamen. Seeing the militias standing squarely in their path, Cantier-Aristide—who had previously worked with the United Nations in Haiti and Sarajevo—pulled a quick U-turn on the narrow street, and squeezed between a telephone pole and a metal pylon, before speeding away in the opposite direction. The militiamen fired from behind and blew out the rear window of their vehicle. The same afternoon, still on September 5, militias attacked and set fire to the office of the Catholic diocese of Dili in the center of town, killing several people and wounding many more. At about the same time militias surrounded the office of the international medical relief organization, Médecins Sans Frontières. As evening fell, gunfire could be heard across the city, especially in the immediate vicinity of the UNAMET compound. Around midnight, militias surrounded the offices of the main local human rights organization, Yayasan HAK, forcing its staff to flee to the regional police headquarters before being evacuated by air.[1]

It was becoming abundantly clear that our predictions of a return to normal life had been too optimistic. In fact, from the afternoon of September 5 until the predawn evacuation of September 14, the UNAMET compound in Dili effectively came under siege. UNAMET personnel who ventured out on emergency patrols came under attack by militias while the Indonesian army and police stood by. Huddled inside the walls of the compound, we slept on sheets of scrap cardboard, and got used to the constant clatter of automatic and homemade weapons fire outside. From behind the walls we could see plumes of black smoke rising from the burning city. We worried that the militia might come over the wall at any time. And even if they did not, we had no way of knowing how long the ordeal might last. Worst of all, the siege rendered us powerless to assist East Timorese who needed protection—a fraction of whom called us in desperation when telephone lines were still functioning. We could only guess how many were being killed or forced to flee their homes.

As the violence descended in Dili, hundreds of people fled to the school yard adjoining the UNAMET compound. At about 8:00 p.m. on the evening of September 5 a barrage of automatic and homemade weapons fire erupted nearby. Terrified and not realizing that the side entrance to the compound had been opened to let them in, the refugees began to throw their children over the high fence topped with razor wire. In less than an hour roughly one thousand people had joined the five hundred already inside the compound. Remarkably, the only injuries suffered that evening were to the refugees and UNAMET staff who had held back the razor wire with their hands to allow people over the fence.

The refugees, many of them carrying children, food, and a few belongings, were ushered into the compound's large auditorium. Some food and water was distributed, but the adults were distressed, and many of the children were crying. Their distress mounted when a UNAMET security official announced through a translator that they would not be able to stay inside the compound. The crying of the children was now joined by screams and shouts of disbelief from the adults. To the relief of many UNAMET staff, the decision was soon overturned, but the anxiety of the refugees was not easily allayed. Later that evening I noticed that the crying and wailing had suddenly stopped. As I approached the auditorium to find out what was going on I heard two voices, sweet and pure, singing in Tetum. Looking in through the open door I saw two young women, who until then I had known only as local staff assistants in the Political Affairs Office. Now, Tata and Elisa stood before almost a thousand people, most of them women and children, soothing them through the power of their young voices.

There was uncertainty and disagreement about how to deal with this unexpected influx of people. The UNAMET compound had previously been a high school campus, with about a dozen buildings of assorted size scattered over one or two acres of land. Although it had its own water well and a generator, it was not designed as living quarters, certainly not for fifteen hundred people. For example, it had only eight or ten rather unreliable toilets, and the bathing facilities consisted of half a dozen large basins filled with water that was sloshed over the body with a plastic saucepan. We had a supply of army rations provided by France and Australia, and bottled water, but only enough to feed UN staff for a few days. The compound had no functioning kitchen and no supply of fresh food.

In order to minimize the danger to UNAMET staff, and preserve limited supplies of food, water, and fuel, Martin had already recommended on September 4 that "nonessential staff" be evacuated to Darwin as soon as possible. The recommendation to move to "Security Phase III" was approved by New York, and led to the first major evacuation of UN personnel on the morning of September 6. On the way to the airport, a UN vehicle was struck by a projectile that shattered one of its windows. In the end, however, some 250 people were safely loaded onto three C-130 aircraft bound for Darwin.[2]

It was a rare piece of good news on what would turn out to be an extremely bad day. At 11:00 a.m. we heard that Bishop Belo's residence in Dili, which we had visited less than twenty-four hours before, was under militia attack.[3] A Political Affairs officer, Anthony Goldstone, who knew the bishop well, immediately called him on his direct line. The bishop answered and confirmed that dozens of militias had stormed into the compound, and were at that moment firing their weapons and threatening the refugees. He then hung up. An elderly Canossian nun, Sister Margarida, who was at the bishop's residence when the attack took place, later said that the militias shot at the crowd of refugees, that many of them fell to the ground, and that there was blood everywhere.[4] According to others who were on the scene, the bishop came out of his residence and tried to calm the situation by speaking to the militiamen as well as the police and army officers present. A short time later, he was escorted away by the police and flown by helicopter to the town of Baucau.[5] With the bishop out of the way, the militias began to round up the refugees onto trucks and buses, threatening those who resisted.

About half an hour later, at 11:30 a.m., we heard that the militias had attacked the office of the ICRC, next door to the bishop's residence, where a few hundred more refugees had taken shelter. As in the attack on the bishop's residence, the militias rounded up the refugees, marching some of them out to the nearby beach, and loading others onto trucks and buses. In the midst of the attack, the police reportedly escorted six expatriate ICRC staff to the airport, but the fate of some forty local staff and hundreds of refugees was not known. In the face of these brazen attacks on places that had been assumed to be safe havens, most of what was left of Dili's population fled the city. Some fifteen thousand of those, including several leading CNRT figures, made their way to Dare, situated in the hills about ten kilometers south of Dili.[6] The site of the Jesuit seminary attended by several resistance leaders and the peace talks of late 1998, Dare was also well defended by Falintil forces and offered some measure of security to those who fled there. Several thousand more were said to have taken refuge in the wooded hills between Dare and Ermera to the west, where Falintil had established one of its four cantonment sites.

Mass Killing

With UNAMET staff trapped inside its compound, and with most journalists gone, further details of the situation outside were almost impossible to ascertain. But it was clear that a systematic campaign of forced displacement of the population was under way, and that it was being aided and abetted by the Indonesian police and army. It was later learned that many of the displaced were being transported to the regional police headquarters and assembly points on the Dili waterfront. At those sites, refugees were again systematically loaded onto trucks or ships, and transported to West Timor and neighboring islands.[7] Meanwhile, a similar campaign of violence and forcible displacement was unfolding in other towns and villages across the country, especially in the western districts.[8] TNI and police officials, with the support of the militias, were warning local people that they would be killed—or that their safety could not be guaranteed—if they did not board the trucks and buses that had been readied for them. Faced with such threats and conscious of the uncontrolled violence, many felt they had no option but to comply, and so allowed themselves to be transported. By September 13, less than two weeks after the ballot, there were an estimated 115,000 people in the Indonesian camps, and by the end of the month that figure had jumped to some 250,000.[9]

One the earliest and most shocking acts of violence in this period was the massacre at the Ave Maria Church in the town of Suai on September 6, 1999, in which at least forty but possibly as many as two hundred people were killed.[10] Of the forty who could be identified, three were Catholic priests, ten were under the age of eighteen, and more than a dozen were women. The dead were among some fifteen hundred to two thousand people who had taken refuge at the church compound because of mounting violence and intimidation by militias and security forces. Witnesses and prosecutors said that several high-ranking officials were at the scene throughout the massacre and participated in the attack. They included the Bupati, Colonel (retired) Herman Sedyono; the Dandim, Lieutenant Colonel Liliek Koeshadianto; the district chief of police, Lieutenant Colonel (police) Gatot Subiaktoro; and the Danramil, Lieutenant Sugito.[11]

The attack began shortly after 2:30 p.m. According to witnesses, two grenades were thrown, and then the militia and the TNI started to fire their weapons into the church compound. The first to enter the church were scores of Laksaur and Mahidi militiamen, armed with machetes, swords, knives, and homemade firearms. Immediately behind them were a mixed group of TNI soldiers and militias. According to witnesses, the militias headed first toward the priests' and nuns' quarters, adjacent to the old church. As they proceeded they hacked, stabbed, and shot many people in their path. Outside the compound, witnesses said, TNI and Brimob units maintained a perimeter from which they shot at those fleeing the mayhem.

Among the first to be killed were the three priests, Father Hilario Madeira, Father Francisco Soares, both Timorese, and Father Tarsisius Dewanto, an Indonesian. Father Hilario was shot and stabbed by a Laksaur militiaman as he emerged from his room in the priests' quarters. Father Francisco is also said to have been stabbed and hacked to death by a Laksaur militiaman near his quarters. Father Dewanto was reportedly killed by gunfire in or near the old church. A witness said that as Dewanto was about to be killed, one of the attackers shouted, "Don't kill him! He is one of us!" But the warning came too late.

By about 5:00 p.m. the killing had finally stopped. A number of survivors were led out of the compound by militiamen and TNI soldiers. As they walked they were told not to look around them, but they could not help seeing corpses strewn about the compound. One witness said that blood was flowing like a long stream from inside the church, across the compound and all the way to the street outside. From the church, the survivors were taken to the Kodim headquarters and to a nearby

FIGURE 8.1. Massacre in Maliana, September 8, 1999. One of several mass killings carried out by pro-Indonesian forces after the August 30 ballot, the massacre at the Maliana police station left at least fourteen people dead. This paint-
ing by fourteen-year-old Efren Natalino de Jesus da Cruz, who witnessed the
killings, depicts Halilintar and Dadurus Merah Putih militiamen dressed as
Ninjas killing two proindependence youths with machetes on the instruction
of their commanders, who are carrying firearms. (UNICEF East Timor,
Through the Eyes of Children, 2002)

primary school, where they were interrogated. Several of them were
held for about eight days, and at least one woman was reported to have
been sexually assaulted by a militiaman while in detention.

Early the following morning, September 7, TNI and militia leaders
set about disposing of the bodies and destroying as much evidence as
possible. At least twenty-seven bodies, and probably more, were placed
onto trucks and driven out of town, across the border to West Timor. In
late November 1999, Indonesian investigators went to the site indicated
by witnesses and discovered three mass graves. From these graves they
exhumed the remains of twenty-seven people, including sixteen men,
eight women, and three others whose gender could not be determined.
Among those exhumed were the remains of a child of about five years, a
young man whose lower limbs and pelvis were missing, and a teenage

woman who was naked, and whose body had been burned. In addition to those buried in West Timor and others allegedly thrown into the sea, an undetermined number of bodies were reportedly gathered together at the Suai church and burned beyond recognition. Investigators who visited the site in late 1999 found what appeared to be charred human bones and skulls.

A second massacre occurred just two days later, on September 8, in the town of Maliana in Bobonaro district.[12] The victims were among many hundreds of residents who had sought refuge at the district police station as the town erupted in violence after the August 30 vote. As many as fourteen people, some of them children, were killed in the attack.[13] Witness testimonies concur that the massacre at the police station was conducted jointly by TNI soldiers of Kodim 1636 and members of the Dadurus Merah Putih militia, under the apparent supervision of TNI and SGI officers. They also agree that Indonesian police and Brimob forces took no action to prevent the attack, to stop it once it was under way, or to apprehend the perpetrators when it was over.

The attack began at about 5:30 p.m. Two trucks pulled up in front of the police station, and three others stopped on a road running alongside the compound. The vehicles were filled with TNI soldiers and militiamen, armed with machetes, knives, and swords. Many of the militiamen were dressed in black and wearing "Ninja" type hoods or Indonesian flags to cover their faces. The TNI soldiers, most of them wearing combat trousers and black T-shirts, were carrying automatic weapons and side arms. When the vehicles stopped, the soldiers and militiamen jumped down, and took up positions in and around the compound. Meanwhile, dozens of militiamen and TNI soldiers entered the compound from the side entrance, and ran into the area where the refugees were gathered. One witness described the initial moments of the attack: "I saw the militias running in all directions, chasing men and boys to kill them. . . . The refugees were screaming in fear but they could not escape as militias and TNI were all around guarding the place."[14] In panic, many refugees ran to the security post at the front entrance of the compound, but Brimob soldiers there told them to return to their tents. Not all did so, but those who did then witnessed the attack unfold. Among the first victims was a thirteen-year-old boy, José Barros Soares, who was hacked to death by militiamen while his younger sister looked on.[15] But the violence was not as random as that scene suggested. The attackers were clearly singling out well-known proindependence figures for execution.

The victims included a number of CNRT leaders as well as a subdistrict head, two village heads, and several civil servants with proindependence sympathies.[16] The militias also targeted the families of such figures. According to one report, for example, the militias who killed the young boy José Barros Soares told his sister that they were killing him because they could not find his father, a known independence figure. Also singled out were members of the TNI and police who were considered to be independence sympathizers.[17]

In some instances, the attackers asked for their intended victims by name. One witness said that the attackers had a list of names to which they referred as they made their way through the compound. "I was cooking and suddenly the militias came in cars and people started running from one side to the other. Then when people calmed down they divided into sections and entered the tents seeking people on lists to kill."[18] Among those targeted in this way was the prominent Maliana proindependence figure Manuel Barros, who had taken refuge at the police station with his family on September 2. At least four people witnessed his killing, including one man who was just a few feet away when it happened. According to his testimony, shortly after the attack on the compound began, three militiamen walked straight up to Barros and began to speak to him in an aggressive manner. First they ordered him to stand, then to sit, and then to extend his hand. As he extended his hand, one of the three militiamen lunged forward and stabbed him in the chest with a knife. Barros immediately fell to the ground and died soon after. His body was then dragged away by the three militiamen.[19]

The attack continued until about 9:00 p.m., and the disposal of the bodies began shortly thereafter. As in the case of the Suai church massacre, the process of disposal was methodical, and supervised by TNI officers, strongly suggesting that it had been planned in advance. The electricity to the area was cut, and the corpses were loaded onto two or more trucks under the cover of darkness. According to a man who was ordered to assist in loading the bodies onto the trucks, a TNI officer kept track of the identities and the number of dead.[20] The trucks were then driven out of town to Batugade, a proautonomy stronghold near the Indonesian border. The TNI had made arrangements with local militia leaders Rubén Tavares (João Tavares's nephew) and Rubén Gonçalves to receive the corpses and dispose of them. According to prosecutors, the militiamen filled large rice sacks with sand and attached them to the bodies. Weighted down by the sand-filled sacks, the bodies were then taken out to sea on fishing boats and dumped overboard.

The mounting violence also forced the last UNAMET staff to evacuate from the few regional offices that were still functioning. On the evening of September 6, a haggard group of local and international UNAMET staff arrived at the headquarters in Dili having departed from Ermera by road that morning. Militias had prevented them from leaving Ermera for hours, and they had passed through numerous militia roadblocks along the way. UNAMET staff were evacuated from Oecussi to Dili the same afternoon by helicopter, after watching the security situation deteriorate dramatically in the preceding twenty-four hours. The next day, September 7, all remaining staff from the offices in Lospalos, Manatuto, Viqueque, and Baucau were evacuated by helicopter after the Baucau office where they had gathered came under armed attack.[21] And so by the end of the day on September 7, there were no UNAMET staff anywhere outside the compound in Dili.

Outside of East Timor, news of the dramatic escalation of violence after September 4 and the evidence of official complicity in the violence was reaching unprecedented levels of intensity—creating what one close observer called "news with gale force."[22] Already quite intense after the announcement of the ballot on September 4, television and newspaper coverage reached a crescendo after the attacks on Bishop Belo's compound and the ICRC. Much of the coverage spoke of the betrayal of the brave people who had dared to vote in the face of threats and violence. It also highlighted the growing fear that there was a new genocide in the making, and made frequent reference to the possibility of a repeat of the atrocities in Rwanda and Bosnia. Meanwhile, editorial pages around the world thundered that United Nations and international credibility would be severely harmed if Indonesian forces or those under their effective control could be allowed to overturn the election, and thus effectively reconquer the territory and wreak havoc. Through this unprecedented media reporting, ordinary people who had never heard of East Timor became aware of it, while church, human rights, and activist groups pointed to it as definitive evidence that something must be done.

These developments contributed significantly to a mounting international outcry not only in the press but also through official channels.[23] In the face of this pressure—or by some accounts using the pressure to do what he had wished to do earlier—on September 6 President Habibie ordered the release of Gusmão and declared martial law in East Timor, with effect from the following day, September 7. An old East Timor hand, Major General Kiki Syahnakri, was appointed martial law commander, and two battalions of elite Kostrad troops were deployed, ostensibly to restore order. At least two full companies of those troops (from Battalion 507) were tasked to defend the UNAMET compound.[24] The battalion commander, Lieutenant Colonel Wawang, told UNAMET officials, "I will die defending this compound."[25] There was some hope, naive in retrospect, that martial law might turn the situation around.

Far from improving, however, the security situation worsened further in the following days. For example, September 8 was the day of the massacre at the Maliana police station, described above, and it was only one of many atrocities that occurred in the martial law period. UNAMET staff experienced the problem firsthand. To obtain essential supplies—water, rations, and fuel—on September 8 a UN patrol set out for a warehouse outside the compound, with a TNI escort. But near the warehouse, the group was confronted by a group of about fifty Besi Merah Putih militiamen, who surrounded their vehicles, shouting and waving their guns menacingly. One militiaman approached a member of the UN group, pointed his gun at his face, and said, "I could kill you." He held the gun there and began to squeeze the trigger, before raising it and firing into the air. As this scene unfolded, the TNI patrol stood by and did nothing. The UN personnel returned to the compound almost empty-handed, but with a clear message for the rest of us: we were in danger not only from the militias but also from the Indonesian army forces that were ostensibly protecting us.

The question that arose then, and has remained a puzzle ever since, is why those who ordered and carried out this violence did so. What precisely did they expect to gain through a scorched-earth policy, conducted under the noses of the United Nations and the media, and in open defiance of Indonesia's stated commitment to its international obligations?[26] There was undoubtedly an element of bitterness and revenge involved. As the slogans and graffiti of those days suggested, Indonesian soldiers and their supporters were determined that their proindependence opponents would have to start from nothing, and would not enjoy any of the fruits of Indonesian rule. "If you want independence," one scrawled message declared, "six months from now you will be eating rocks."[27] The mass violence and displacement were evidently also part of a broader strategy to discredit the ballot process, with a view to overturning the result, or at a minimum creating so much chaos that a transition to independence would be rendered impossible. Not expecting a swift international intervention—indeed, quite possibly confident that there would be no intervention at all—Indonesian officials appear to have believed that they could create a situation on the ground that would lend credence to their claim that a substantial percentage of East Timorese feared independence and preferred to remain with Indonesia. Finally, there were some who hoped that even after the decisive vote for independence, East Timor might be partitioned, with the eastern part granted independence, and the wealthier and more populous western districts remaining with Indonesia. That option was proposed on a number of occasions both before and after the ballot, most notably by the governor of East Timor, Abílio Osório Soares, who continued to advocate that solution at least until East Timor's formal independence in 2002. The concentration of the violence in the western districts, the forced displacement of some 250,000 people across the border into West Timor, and the efforts made to prevent their return over the next few years were almost certainly designed to lend credence to that option.

Refugees

Despite the mounting violence across the country, life inside the compound gradually took on an air of routine. Families set up makeshift kitchens and households on any flat space they could find. Two or three families with small children lived in the sheltered passageway just outside the office where I worked and slept with several colleagues. We woke early each morning to the sound of children playing, and we often heard the adults talking and playing cards late into the night. Other families established themselves on the few grassy spots in the compound or inside the large auditorium once used for staff meetings. Wherever they were, people went about their daily business of cooking and cleaning, and caring for their babies. And there were plenty of babies, including at least three born inside the compound in the space of twenty-four hours. The first of the three was baptized Pedro Unamet Rodrigues.

There were some among the UNAMET staff who felt that the refugees were making life quite intolerable, and that it had been a serious mistake to allow them to remain in the compound. On one occasion a senior MLO complained to me that the refugees were "shitting all over the place" and generally making a mess of things. In fact, the refugees kept themselves and the compound remarkably clean. More to the point, I think it would have been nearly impossible to go through what we did without them. With gunfire and explosions erupting constantly in the vicinity of the compound, it was oddly reassuring to see children playing and mothers nursing.

The refugees also provided us with invaluable information about life outside the compound. They did so in a number of ways. As new groups arrived over the course of the siege, they brought with them stories about military and militia activities in their own areas, and testimony of particular incidents that helped us to piece together a picture of what was going on. In addition, quite beyond UNAMET's capacity to control, there were refugees who moved into and out of the compound on a fairly regular basis, usually through the back fence that bordered a hilly, wooded area to the south. One, a young man named Rogerio, went regularly to Dare. When he returned every day or so, he was in a position to provide us with detailed information about the situation there and also to convey messages from the CNRT leadership. In venturing out in this way, Rogerio and others risked being captured or killed by the TNI and militia units that patrolled the perimeter of the compound. At the same time, they formed a vital channel of communication without which UNAMET would often have been operating in the dark.

As the days passed, the situation inside the compound grew critical. Although many of the refugees had brought some food with them, basic necessities—rations, drinking water, and fuel—began to run low, and the logistical problems of housing fifteen hundred to two thousand people were becoming serious. Complicating these problems, another five hundred refugees had gathered in the school yard adjoining the compound. On September 7, the day martial law began, our radio and telephone communications networks began to break down.[28] Apart from severely limiting our contact with the outside world, that meant that anyone who ventured out of the compound was essentially on their own. Later the same afternoon, we learned that the city electric supply was now reaching only half the compound, so that the other half had to be supplied by a generator, which was in turn dependent on a dwindling supply of diesel fuel. The next morning, September 8, power and water supplies were completely cut throughout the city, and we were wholly dependent on the generators. With fuel supplies low, there was a real possibility that we would soon be without power. And without power,

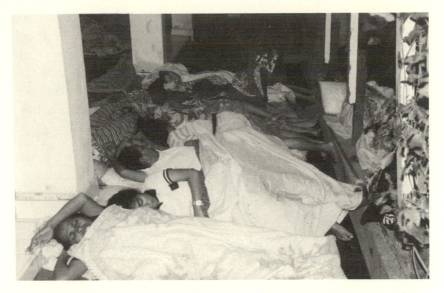

FIGURE 8.2. Refugees inside the UNAMET compound, Dili, early September 1999. As violence escalated following the announcement of the ballot result, some fifteen hundred East Timorese sought refuge in the compound, alongside several hundred UN staff. On September 8, UN officials ordered an immediate evacuation without the refugees, but following protests inside the compound and discussions with Indonesian and UN authorities, that order was postponed. In the early morning of September 14, all of those still in the compound were safely evacuated to Darwin. (Patrick Burgess and Galuh Wandita)

we would not only be operating without light, computers, and other essential equipment, we would also be unable to pump water from our own well.

In this context, a troubling question arose: Would the United Nations evacuate its international staff, leaving behind roughly four hundred local staff and more than fifteen hundred East Timorese who had taken refuge in the compound? From the perspective of those responsible for UN security both in Dili and New York, the answer was clear. The security situation was untenable, and the standard UN procedure in such circumstances was to evacuate international staff—but not refugees, and perhaps not even local staff—as soon as possible.

The news that local UN staff might be left behind in a general evacuation was met with incredulity, particularly among those unfamiliar with UN procedures and rules. To outsiders, it seemed that the United Nations was drawing an invidious distinction among its employees, based solely on their race or national origin. Not only did such a demarcation seem to run counter to all that the United Nations stood for, and to the promises that UNAMET had made to stand by the population through thick or thin, it also placed in harm's way those UN employees—the local staff—who were in the greatest danger. After all, several local UN staff had already been killed in the days after the vote, and there was every reason to believe that they would continue to be targeted. By contrast, although one Civpol officer had been seriously wounded, no international staff had been killed.

After strong representations from UNAMET, the decision was taken in New York to evacuate local staff alongside all nonessential international staff. Credit for that unusual decision rests with a number of parties. According to Martin, it was ultimately secured by the newly arrived chief of UNAMET security, who made the case to his superiors in New York. But credit is also due to those within UNAMET who first pointed out the obvious problems with the standard operating procedures in this case, and advanced sound arguments for an exception to them. One of those was Martin himself, who on September 6 recommended to headquarters the evacuation of all UN staff, international and local.[29] A second was the head of UNAMET's Humanitarian Affairs Office, Patrick Burgess. While others seemed resigned to follow the procedures, Burgess sat down and examined the UN rules. He discovered that those rules permitted the evacuation of local staff under certain conditions, and in a memo he argued that those conditions obtained in this case. That memo, and the oral arguments that others made in the same spirit, provided an important stimulus without which the security officials in Dili and New York might not have sought an exception to the normal procedures.

UN rules, however, were not the only obstacle to the safe departure of local staff. For some time, Indonesian officials did their best to prevent it. More surprisingly perhaps, some Australian government officials also argued against, and for a short time actually obstructed, the evacuation of UN local staff. The issue arose on September 7 in the context of the UN evacuation from the town of Baucau, where the international and local staff from four different regional offices (Baucau, Manatuto, Lospalos, and Viqueque) had gathered in the preceding days. According to plan, on the afternoon of September 7, an Australian Airforce plane arrived in Baucau to airlift the UN personnel to Darwin. International staff were allowed to board, but armed militia groups and Indonesian officials prevented local UN staff from doing so. After negotiation, the militias agreed to allow the local staff to fly by helicopter to Dili, but no farther. In Dili, UNAMET made plans to place the local staff onto another Australian Airforce plane bound for Darwin. At that point, however, personnel from the Australian Consulate intervened to prevent their departure, citing the agreement with the militia and Indonesian officials in Baucau, and a fear of retaliation if that agreement were broken.[30] The Australian Consulate evidently took the view that it was more important to honor an agreement with Indonesian officials and their militia accomplices than to protect hundreds of people who had already risked their lives as local UN staff. Happily, Australian opposition was eventually overcome, and all local UNAMET staff were permitted to depart on September 10.

Evacuation Order

The question of what to do with the refugees inside the compound was not so easily resolved. The issue came to a head in a dramatic way on the evening of September 8, when Martin announced that all remaining international staff would be evacuating to Darwin later that night, leaving the fifteen hundred refugees behind. Issued from headquarters in New York, the evacuation order had been recommended by Martin on advice from UNAMET Security officers as well as the heads of the Civpol and MLO contingents. The decision provoked a storm of protest within the compound, and brought to a head fundamental questions about the United Nations' priorities and its responsibilities to the people of East Timor.

Although we had not been party to the decision to evacuate, four of us from Political Affairs and Humanitarian Affairs were given the unwelcome task of conveying the news to the community leaders in the compound.[31] Sitting on wooden chairs in our drab office, surrounded by people like the courageous Sister Esmeralda and others whom we had come to know and respect in the preceding months, we could scarcely find the strength to speak. We knew that when we left, all those inside would be in mortal danger. Worse, we were asking fifteen hundred people to decide in a matter of just a few hours whether to stay and await their fate, or flee through the night into the hands of waiting militia and TNI soldiers.

Sister Esmeralda waited patiently for us to finish. And when we had, she spoke. "Whatever else may happen," she said, "this referendum has removed any doubt that East Timorese wish to be free. For conducting it, we will always be grateful to UNAMET." Wiping tears from her eyes, she went on: "We knew there would be violence after the vote and we hoped that you would stay. And yet, we are not surprised that you plan to leave us now. We are used to being abandoned in our times of greatest need." Finally, indicating that she and the others had no more time for talk, she added: "Before you leave, please consider whether in the years to come you will be able to sleep soundly knowing what you have done." Overcome with shame, we delegated Burgess to approach Martin and convey our view that the decision to evacuate was wrong. Martin did not disagree, but explained that the heads of Security, Civpol, and MLO had all strongly advised evacuation. The heads of those units, he said, had given the impression that the majority of their staff were seriously demoralized and anxious to leave.

While that discussion was going on upstairs, two of us headed across the compound to the Joint Operations Center to begin packing up the valuable archive that the Political Affairs Office had been amassing over the preceding months. Among other things, the archive contained hundreds of detailed, handwritten accounts, from every district of the territory, of human rights violations committed by militias, TNI soldiers, and police. It also contained documents—letters, instructions, and memorandums—strongly indicating official complicity in the acts of violence and intimidation committed prior to the ballot. Because of their sensitivity and value, these materials had been kept in the Joint Operations Center, which was staffed twenty-four hours a day, seven days a week, and was therefore assumed to be the safest possible place for them.

When I entered the Joint Operations Center, I noticed that the doors to the metal cabinet in which these documents had been stored were open. Inside the cabinet were two or three empty ring binders, and a few more lay scattered on the floor. As I stared trying to make sense of the scene, a British MLO strode past carrying an armful of empty binders that I immediately recognized as part of the Political Affairs archive. I asked him where the rest of the binders were. Stopping just long enough to turn and stare at me, he replied simply, "Burnt." A moment later the deputy chief MLO, Colonel Neville Riley, a New Zealander, arrived on the scene. When I told him what had happened, he was livid and demanded to know why his soldiers had not consulted Political Affairs before destroying the archive. The British MLO who had been burning the files said he had received his order from the Joint Operations Center duty officer. The duty officer in turn claimed that he had received the order from a Security officer. With that reply, Riley's attitude changed abruptly. It was deeply regrettable, he said, but if the burning order came from Security, there was nothing more that could be done about it.

Later that evening, I asked one of the two Security officers whether he or his colleague had given the order. He declined to say, but he did volunteer that the destruction of sensitive materials was standard operating procedure in the event of evacuation. That may have been true. But the truth is that it would have been quite easy to select the most important or sensitive documents, and bring them out by hand in the course of evacuation. In fact, that is precisely what happened. Every Political Affairs officer who evacuated after September 8 carried a bag or small box of the few documents that had been rescued. These were later reassembled and organized at the UN headquarters in Darwin, and became the basis for later UN investigations into possible crimes against humanity committed in 1999.

Meanwhile, a sense of outrage had begun to grip other UN staff and the handful of journalists and observers who had taken refuge in the compound. Those feelings fueled a rebellion of sorts. A group of journalists demanded to speak to Martin, and when they did get in to see him, they threatened to denounce the decision publicly. Outside I was confronted by a journalist from the *Sunday Times* who demanded that I make an exception to get an East Timorese friend and his family onto the UN evacuation flight, and likewise threatened media exposure should I fail to do so. As it happened the man in question, José Antonio Belo, was also an old friend of mine, whose safety I would have done almost anything to secure. I told José and the journalist this, although I was deeply pessimistic at the time that he or anybody else would be able to leave.

Notwithstanding the earlier claims by Security, Civpol, and MLO chiefs that most of their staff were anxious to evacuate, by about 9:00 p.m. there was a strong sentiment that international UN staff should *not* leave before the safety of the refugees had been secured. More precisely, a quick straw poll conducted at Martin's request had revealed that at least eighty of the hundred or so international staff in the compound were prepared to stay on even if the evacuation were to proceed. Surprised but I believe also heartened by this show of resolve, Martin conveyed the news by telephone to UN officials in New York, where it was still the morning of September 8. At the same time, he informed them that General Wiranto had urged UNAMET to stay, and that the TNI commanders on the ground in East Timor had concurred. By the end of the evening the decision to evacuate UN staff had been postponed by twenty-four hours.[32] And it was clear that while some UNAMET staff would then evacuate, a significant number would not be leaving.

The news of the postponement of the evacuation spread quickly through the compound, and there was jubilation. In retrospect, it may seem odd that a twenty-four-hour reprieve would be the cause for re-joicing. But the reality was that against the backdrop of the original plan for a total evacuation that very night, twenty-four hours seemed an eter-nity. More important, there was confidence that a critical turning point had been reached. UNAMET, it seemed, would not abandon the East Timorese in their darkest hour. That understanding was underscored by a message sent to UNAMET by Kofi Annan on September 9. The mes-sage made it clear that the secretary-general was fully committed to finding a solution to the crisis and suggested that he was most unlikely to order a second precipitous evacuation.[33] "I wish to express my com-mendation," he wrote,

> to you and to all UNAMET staff who remain in Dili in the ser-vice of the United Nations and to help the people of East Timor. In a challenging moment for the Organization, your courage in perilous conditions has been a source of inspiration and renewed determination for all who labour for a just and peaceful outcome to the crisis in East Timor. We are facing an extremely difficult sit-uation whose outcome will have lasting consequences for the peo-ple of East Timor and for the United Nations. We at headquarters are making every effort to obtain an outcome that will fulfill the obligations of our agreements and the wishes of the people of East Timor. I wish to express my gratitude to you and to those who volunteered to stay on in the face of dangerous circumstances. You will all be in our thoughts and prayers in the coming days and weeks, as we seek to return the people of East Timor to a path of peace and prosperity.[34]

No Relief

As the days passed, we waited anxiously for news of the international intervention that we felt sure was now inevitable. It was encouraging to hear that France had dispatched a naval vessel to the area, that Canada's prime minister had said the international community would have to step in if the violence continued, that NATO's secretary-general had called for urgent international intervention, that Japan's prime minister had said that the world "cannot just stand by," and that Australia's defense minister had said its forces could be ready to move within days.[35] But it was deeply distressing to read in the press that Ambassador Marker, a member of our own team, had "refused to lend credence to reports of [Indonesian] military support for the militia" when for months we had carefully documented and argued precisely that case.[36] And we learned with disbelief that the most important state of all, the United States, was still equivocating. When asked why the United States had not taken the lead in resolving the mess in East Timor, National Security Adviser Sandy Berger reportedly said, "You know, my daughter has a very messy apartment up in college; maybe I shouldn't intervene to have that cleaned up. I don't think anybody ever articulated a doctrine which said we ought to intervene wherever there is a humanitarian problem."[37] The sheer stupidity of that comment aside, it signaled that the United States was still insisting that responsibility for restoring order rested with the Indonesian Armed Forces. Passed by word of mouth through the compound, this piece of news was greeted with groans of disbelief. Everyone understood that it was precisely those forces that were orchestrating the violence. It was preposterous to insist that they be entrusted to stop it.

The next few days brought more unpleasant surprises, including a succession of brazen militia attacks and renewed calls by some senior UNAMET officials for an immediate evacuation without the refugees. On the afternoon of September 9, a UNAMET convoy with a TNI escort tried once again to reach the warehouse at the port to obtain essential supplies. Near the port, but not yet at the warehouse, the two TNI escort trucks stopped, leaving the five UN vehicles sandwiched between them with no way out. Almost immediately some thirty to forty Aitarak and Besi Merah Putih militiamen, wearing red berets, surrounded the UN vehicles. They were armed with a variety of weapons including machetes, swords, homemade pistols, and semiautomatic rifles, and some wore grenades on their belts. Shouting abuse they struck the sides of the UN vehicles with their weapons, and pointed them through the windows. Some fired shots just above the vehicles and into the air. The TNI soldiers made no attempt to stop the attack, nor to disarm or arrest the militia.[38] Unable to leave their vehicles or reach the warehouse, and worried by the lack of TNI action, the convoy headed back

FIGURE 8.3. Evacuation from the UN compound in Dili, early September 1999. In the face of mounting violence, and rapidly diminishing supplies of water, food, and fuel inside the compound, UN officials ordered the phased evacuation of nonessential staff. This photo, taken on the morning of September 10, shows a convoy of Indonesian military vehicles, each staffed by several Indonesian soldiers, preparing to transport UN personnel to the Dili airport. UNAMET's head of mission, Ian Martin, wearing a flak jacket and holding a piece of paper, stands in the left foreground with other UN officials. (Patrick Burgess and Galuh Wandita)

to headquarters. On the way they were followed by militiamen on motorbikes who pointed their weapons and shouted abuse. They also passed five police trucks, each carrying militiamen armed with automatic weapons. The TNI escort again took no action. On their return, UN staff who had been in the convoy said it seemed that the TNI had actually been in control of the situation throughout. By the end of the day, there was serious tension in the compound, and many looked forward to their evacuation early the following morning.

Carefully planned and executed by MLOs and Security officers, the evacuation of September 10 went smoothly. By midday, 444 international and local UN staff had been airlifted to safety in Darwin, leaving 81 international staff inside the Dili compound.[39] Almost immediately after the last convoy had set off for the airport, however, about a dozen armed militiamen entered the school yard adjoining the UNAMET compound where several hundred people had taken refuge. The first news of the assault came from Sister Esmeralda, who was with the refugees in the yard when it began. For more than an hour, the militias looted vehicles parked in the yard and fired their weapons in the air, before eventually melting away just minutes before the head of mission returned from the airport. At the time of their assault, the yard was ostensibly being protected by two companies of Kostrad soldiers, but those troops did nothing to impede the militias. Indeed, according to a note written by the Political Affairs Office a few hours after the incident, TNI soldiers actually assisted the militias throughout:

> TNI soldiers made little or no effort to protect the IDPs [internally displaced persons] in the yard. That task was left to unarmed UNAMET personnel who rushed to the scene after hearing shouts and screams and learning of the incursion from the Canossian Sisters living with the IDPs. Nor did TNI soldiers make any serious effort to impede the militia members once they were in the yard.... As in several similar incidents in the past, TNI soldiers were observed guardedly shepherding the militias, but neither leveling nor firing their weapons at them even as they brandished their weapons and rushed at UNAMET personnel and IDPs. When a UNAMET staff member asked a soldier why the TNI had failed to use their weapons, the reply came that they had not received orders to do so. Given the fact that the territory is currently under martial law, this was an extraordinary response.[40]

MLOs and Security officers concluded that there was a serious threat that the militias might now come over the wall and kill UNAMET personnel. They also concluded that should the militias do so, the TNI would not provide any meaningful resistance. The latter concern was compounded by information suggesting that the TNI itself might be preparing to pull out of East Timor very soon. At 12:15 p.m. on September 10, while the militias were marauding in the yard, an MLO stationed at the TNI regional headquarters in Dili radioed to report that the TNI had begun to shred its files. According to a memorandum of his call, the MLO strongly advised that "a decision to execute an orderly withdrawal be made without delay." A comment on the memo added: "This action indicates TNI plan to withdraw from Dili and will probably hand over to militias. The question is will TNI protect UNAMET personnel or will they abrogate their responsibility as they are now doing in the parking compound."[41]

On the basis of these considerations, an emergency meeting was convened. After a few preliminaries, the MLO representatives recommended an immediate evacuation of the eighty-one remaining international staff. It was unfortunate, they said, but the refugees would have to be left behind. Senior Civpol and Security officers concurred, while representatives from Humanitarian Affairs, Political Affairs and the UN High Commissioner for Refugees registered their dissent.[42] At about this point, Martin returned from the airport and joined the meeting. After a good deal of discussion and weighing up the arguments, Martin decided against an immediate evacuation.

The commitment to ensure the safety of the refugees had been reaffirmed, at least for now, but there was little optimism that it could be achieved. Of the various options proposed—which included transportation to the regional police headquarters or to Dare—the only acceptable one was a complete evacuation to Darwin. When that idea was floated, however, it was more or less dismissed as impossible. The Indonesians would never allow it, the Australians were not keen on it, and it would present almost insuperable logistical obstacles. That view prevailed at least until September 12, less than two days before the massive evacuation of some fifteen hundred refugees to Darwin actually happened. The shift in attitude was driven partly by the realization that the plans for relocation within East Timor simply would not work. More important, it was the result of dramatic developments on the international scene, and in particular the surprising decision taken by major powers and the UN Security Council to support armed intervention to stop the violence.

CHAPTER NINE

INTERVENTION

FROM THE MOMENT the May 5 Agreements were signed, critics had highlighted the extreme danger of leaving security in Indonesian hands and had called for the early deployment of an armed international peacekeeping force to forestall widely predicted violence in the postballot period. As East Timor was engulfed in violence in early September, those calls were reiterated with increasing urgency, and there was anger and disbelief when powerful states continued to insist that the restoration of order was Indonesia's responsibility. The foot-dragging of the United States was especially hard to accept.

In retrospect, however, what is most striking about this period is just how quickly key states and institutions changed their posture, and began to exert unprecedented pressure on the Indonesian authorities. So formidable was that pressure, in fact, that by September 12, just over a week after the ballot result was announced, Indonesia had dropped its strident opposition to the deployment of an international military force. While it is certainly true that the violence might have been prevented entirely by the deployment of an international force *before* the ballot, by any reasonable standard this was an unusually quick and effective intervention. Perhaps most obviously, it stands in stark contrast to the complete absence of international action in the face of the mass violence of the late 1970s. The obvious question is why powerful states and institutions changed their posture so dramatically in these days, and why they advocated armed intervention, as opposed to any number of softer options like boycotts or diplomatic isolation.

There is no simple answer to that question. Indeed, a close examination of the events of late 1999 reveals their highly contingent quality and

FIGURE 9.1. International intervention, late September 1999. Just over a week after UNAMET's evacuation from Dili, the UN-authorized International Force for East Timor (Interfet) began to deploy. Led by Australia, but comprised of units from several other states, it met little resistance from either militias or the TNI. By late September 1999, the violence had largely ended, except in those areas where Interfet had yet to arrive. (Eddy Hasby)

indicates how easily things might have turned out differently. It reveals that among the most powerful states, notably the United States, resistance to intervention persisted for several days after the violence had begun to spiral out of control, and that the eventual decision to intervene was the consequence of an unusual conjuncture of events and conditions, including dramatic media coverage, the existence of a long-standing network of NGO and church organizations, and the surprisingly effective diplomacy of the UN Security Council and the secretary-general himself. More than anything else, though, it shows that the actions of a relatively small number of people, some but not all of them powerful, profoundly influenced the course of events, mainly by preventing an early withdrawal of UN staff, by keeping the spotlight of media attention on East Timor, and by making a compelling moral case for intervention. Without this unique confluence of events and acts of conscience, in all likelihood we would now be speaking not of fifteen hundred dead but rather tens of thousands.

Early Calls for Peacekeepers

As the portents of future violence mounted in July and August, many East Timorese and some UNAMET staff took the view that an armed international peacekeeping force ought to be deployed *before* the vote. As one East Timorese health worker commented to a foreign journalist, "If there is trouble, the UN will send in peace-keepers right? Because there will be trouble."[1] CNRT and Falintil leaders were even more direct. Noting that militia and TNI officials were openly mocking UNAMET's lack of arms, in July the secretary for CNRT's region 3 called for the immediate deployment of armed peacekeepers:"In spite of the UNAMET presence, the population is still scared because people have been killed like animals along all these 24 years. UNAMET should intervene directly so that people can vote freely and without fear on the ballot day."[2] Although UNAMET's Political Affairs Office was never formally asked for advice on this issue, as early as July some of us began informally to convey the same view to UN officials in New York and any visitors who would listen. Among those who did listen, and who reached similar conclusions, was a delegation from Canada. At the end of their visit, on August 12, the delegation's spokesperson said, "Unless Indonesia is going to live up to its obligation, we believe it is critical for a peacekeeping force to be sent to the territory immediately."[3] Members of a U.S. congressional delegation made similar statements following a visit to East Timor in late August.[4]

But however obvious the need for peacekeepers seemed to those who had been in East Timor, the idea never got off the ground. The reason was simple: in the course of negotiations in April 1999 and the months leading up to the ballot, it was either ignored or actively opposed by elements within the UN Secretariat and key powers on the Security Council, most notably the United States. This is not to say that these powers remained silent in the face of the mounting violence. There was plenty of criticism, and even some veiled threats, for example, at a donors meeting for Indonesia in Paris in late July and again as voting day approached.[5] In the final week of August, for instance, President Clinton wrote to President Habibie warning that relations with the United States would be seriously damaged if mass violence occurred during or after the ballot.[6] But peacekeepers were never mentioned. Instead, the concerned states stuck steadfastly, one might even say pigheadedly, to the position that security was the responsibility of the Indonesian authorities.

When UN staff or outside observers asked about or urged the possible deployment of peacekeeping forces, the answer was more or less the same: that it would be impossible to deploy peacekeepers without Indonesian approval or by invoking Chapter VII of the UN Charter.[7] And because it was assumed that neither of these things would happen, we were told it was "unrealistic" to expect peacekeepers. We were also told as early as July that it would take too long—three months at least—to mobilize such a force, so there was no point in discussing a preballot deployment in any case. The more practical and cost-effective approach, a series of policy and planning memorandums from New York explained, was to insist that the Indonesian authorities live up to their obligations for maintaining peace and security.

Significantly, when the Security Council finally lent its unanimous support to the multinational force in mid-September 1999, its resolution invoked Chapter VII of the UN Charter, and gave that force, the International Force for East Timor (known as Interfet), the authority to use all necessary means to restore security. Moreover, notwithstanding the earlier claim that a force would take at least three months to deploy, the first Interfet troops were on the ground within a week of the Security Council resolution. This was possible, it turned out, because Australia had begun to mobilize troops as early as March 1999, and by late June had a contingent of some six thousand troops ready to go. The United States had also been drawing up contingency plans and would certainly have been in a position to deploy troops had the command been given. In other words, all that was said in July and August about the impossibility of deploying peacekeepers was simply untrue. What prevented it from happening in the preballot period was not "political reality" and certainly not logistical difficulties but rather an acute lack of political courage and leadership.

Some measure of the lack of support for the peacekeeping option may be found in the various planning documents for the postballot period developed within the UN Secretariat starting in mid-July 1999. None of the many plans discussed the matter of peacekeepers at all. Instead, they repeated the mantra that regardless of the outcome, in the immediate postballot period the Indonesian authorities would continue to be responsible for maintaining security. It was as though by mere repetition, this pipe dream would come true. The only concession made to the likelihood of violence was a proposal to increase the number of *unarmed* UN Civpol and MLOs in the postballot period.[8]

Within the UN Secretariat, the argument against a preballot deployment of armed peacekeepers was put most stridently by the Department of Peace Keeping Operations (DPKO), and its objections effectively torpedoed an idea that did have some support in other departments, notably in the Department of Political Affairs (DPA). When DPA drafted a postballot planning document in July and circulated it to the relevant units, DPKO insisted on the deletion of all references to peacekeepers. It maintained that a force would take three to five months to deploy, that it could not be done against Indonesian objections, and that in any case DPKO had neither the mandate nor the resources to plan such an operation.[9] In some respects, this was an honest assessment. The problems of mandate and resources were shortcomings highlighted in the report on UN peace operations issued in 2000, and the reports on Srebrenica and Rwanda.[10]

But these were not the only reasons for resistance to the idea. The DPKO position, especially the concern not to do anything without Indonesian approval, also reflected the views of powerful states within the UN Security Council and particularly the United States. As the *New York Times* reported in early September 1999, "no major country on the Council urged the creation of an armed peacekeeping force. Diplomats said the U.S., in particular, remained opposed to such action."[11] U.S. opposition stemmed in part from concerns that it would have to foot a large part of the bill. More important, it was the legacy of the death of U.S. soldiers in Somalia in 1993 and the presidential directive that followed from that incident (PDD 25) that imposed strict conditions on U.S. support for any future UN peacekeeping mission.[12]

Within the United States, the strongest opposition to the peacekeeping option appears to have come from the Pentagon, whose officials had adopted a decidedly sympathetic posture toward the TNI throughout the popular consultation.[13] The White House also resisted the idea. On the eve of the vote, a Clinton administration official told a journalist bluntly that peacekeepers were not an option: "Some people would like us to be making more specific threats about what we are prepared to do if the situation gets worse, but that's not where we are right now."[14] There was somewhat more support for the idea within the State Department. Leaked Australian documents reveal that as early as July, the U.S. assistant secretary of state for Asia and the Pacific, Stanley Roth, was arguing that a peacekeeping force would have to be deployed in order to avoid a major disaster.[15] At the same time, the State Department scrupulously avoided mentioning peacekeepers in its public statements.[16] In early August, high-ranking State Department officers told DPA officials that it would not be "remotely possible" to get even additional *unarmed* personnel to East Timor before September. At the United Nations, the U.S. ambassador Richard Holbrooke—who would later criticize Congress for slashing peacekeeping budgets—gave no hint of support for peacekeepers in East Timor until well after the referendum.[17] Nor was there much support for the idea in Congress until very late in the game. A congressional letter to Secretary of State Madeleine Albright, written on the eve of the mass killings of April 1999, called for concrete measures to improve security, including closing down the militias, but made no mention of peacekeepers.[18] It was only in late August, as noted earlier, that some Congresspeople called publicly for the deployment of a peacekeeping force.

From the outset, the Australian government was somewhat more open to the idea. In April 1999 the foreign minister, Alexander Downer, said that Australia hoped that the process could be managed peacefully, "but if that does not eventuate, and if the UN makes the call, Australia will respond appropriately."[19] That position was repeated by Australia's army chief, and serious preparations for such a deployment were set in motion in March.[20] On the other hand, in an effort to avoid offending Indonesia, the government refrained from advocating for a peacekeeping force. Speaking in the wake of the mounting violence in late August 1999, Downer said: "the Indonesians have made it very clear all along whenever this has been discussed that they absolutely will not have foreign troops on their ground in Indonesia. . . . It doesn't matter how many people write letters to the editor or make claims that peace keepers should be there. . . . At the end of the day the responsibility for security is going to rest with the Indonesians."[21] In short, the opposition to the deployment of international peacekeepers prevailed in all major capitals and at the United Nations throughout the preballot period. And so it was that the United Nations found itself utterly helpless to do anything as the violence descended.

The Tide Turns

In the days following the announcement of the ballot result, international pressure to end the violence was considerable, but uneven. Powerful representations were made by the Catholic church, particularly as it emerged that violence was being directed against church leaders and places of worship. A key stimulus came from Bishop Belo, who traveled to Australia, Portugal, the United Kingdom, and the Vatican in the days after his evacuation from Dili on September 6. On September 9, Vatican foreign minister Archbishop Jean-Louis Tauran said publicly, "We are facing another genocide, a genocide that does not spare the Catholic Church."[22] NGOs, which had warned of the likelihood of violence, also spoke out strongly and mobilized well-established networks of supporters to press for the immediate deployment of peacekeepers. Among states, the greatest pressure came initially from Portugal and Australia, which by no coincidence also had among the most vocal and best organized church and NGO networks, and which were experiencing some of the largest mass demonstrations in their recent histories.[23] Portugal called almost immediately for the earliest possible dispatch of international peacekeepers, and on September 4 Australia announced that it had troops on standby and was prepared to lead a "coalition of the willing" acting under a UN mandate.[24]

The main problem was that Indonesia and especially its military remained adamantly opposed to the deployment of international forces. The presence of such forces, they said, would represent an unacceptable violation of Indonesian sovereignty, and if foreign troops tried to land without prior Indonesian agreement, they would have to fight their way ashore. Notwithstanding the dubious legal basis for Indonesia's claim to sovereignty in East Timor, most major powers, including Australia and the United States, made it clear they would not move ahead without Indonesian approval.

In the face of these obstacles, Kofi Annan adopted an unusually active role. Late at night on September 5, he called Habibie and urged him to accept an international force. Habibie acknowledged that international assistance might be required, but asked whether it would be acceptable if he first declared martial law, to take effect on September 7. Annan agreed, with the caveat that martial law would have to show positive results soon. He added pressure to that caveat by declaring publicly that if the situation had not improved significantly in forty-eight to seventy-two hours, Indonesia would have to accept international assistance.

At the same time, Annan was undertaking an extraordinary campaign of personal diplomacy, urging world leaders to contribute to an international force and exert pressure on Indonesia to accept it.[25] In the words of one official at the UN Secretariat, in this period Annan became "the desk officer for East Timor."[26] That fact was reflected in his telephone call log. On September 5 and 6, for example, he spoke repeatedly with U.S. president Clinton and Australian prime minister Howard as well as the president of Portugal, the president of Mozambique, the prime minister of New Zealand, the foreign minister of the Philippines, and Xanana Gusmão, who was then still under house arrest in Jakarta.[27] Annan's direct and forceful diplomacy at this point stood in marked contrast to his cautious, even passive stance as head of the UN Department of Peace Keeping Operations during the Rwanda and Srebrenica crises, and it may well have been a crucial factor in stimulating a more serious response from other leaders. Still, it was several days before these efforts began to bear any fruit in the changed posture of key states.[28]

The most resistant to the idea of international intervention in these early days (apart from Russia, China, and Bahrain) was the United States. For several days after the ballot, the Clinton administration's response to the crisis, both in public and behind closed doors, was to intensify calls on Indonesian leaders to control the violence.[29] That message was reportedly delivered in personal messages and phone calls to Indonesian leaders by Clinton, Albright, and the chairman of the Joint Chiefs of Staff, General Henry Shelton. But if that is true, their message was seriously weakened by the public statements of senior administration officials—most notably National Security Adviser Sandy Berger, who it will be recalled flippantly compared the crisis in East Timor to the mess in his daughter's dorm room. As one observer has noted, that comment, made on September 7, "indicated that even at that stage top White House policy makers still had no coherent plan or desire" to address the dire situation in East Timor.[30]

U.S. efforts to convince Indonesia to control the violence were also undermined by the administration's marked reluctance to participate in an international peacekeeping force. Such reluctance was especially evident within the U.S. military, which it will be recalled had stood in the way of earlier U.S. support for intervention. On September 7, for example, a Pentagon official said that the United States still believed that the Indonesian military could restore order, and that there were no plans for the United States to help an evacuation or contribute troops to a peacekeeping force.[31] The next day, September 8, Secretary of Defense William Cohen confirmed that "the U.S. is not planning an insertion of any peacekeeping forces," and insisted that "the U.S. cannot be, and should not be viewed as, the policeman of the world."[32] On the same day, September 8, the commander in chief of the U.S. Pacific Command, Admiral Dennis Blair, flew to Jakarta to meet General Wiranto.[33] Blair declined to reveal the substance of his discussions with Wiranto.[34] But given the views expressed by other Pentagon officials at this time—and given Blair's reported failure to convey a clear message to Wiranto to close down the militias at an earlier meeting in April—legitimate questions were raised about whether he and the U.S. government had delivered a sufficiently strong message.[35] Among those raising questions was Australian foreign minister Downer. In a series of private conversations and public comments, he expressed impatience with the cautious U.S. position and called on the administration to reciprocate Australian support for past U.S. military operations. Portugal sent a similar message, threatening that it could not continue to support the NATO operation in Kosovo if the United States refused to lend its support for a similar operation in East Timor.[36]

The first signs of a significant shift in U.S. thinking came on September 9, just one day after UN staff had refused to evacuate from the compound in Dili. Speaking to journalists on the eve of his departure for the Asia–Pacific Economic Cooperation (APEC) summit in New Zealand, President Clinton said: "If Indonesia does not end the violence, it must invite—it must invite—the international community to assist in restoring security."[37] He also announced that he had ordered the suspension of military cooperation with Indonesia and warned that U.S. support for future economic assistance hung in the balance. Clinton and other U.S. officials stopped short of cutting arms sales and economic assistance to Indonesia, and stressed that intervention would only be possible if Indonesia agreed to it. Nevertheless, the president's statement signaled a dramatic about-face in the U.S. position that by some accounts, changed the political dynamic both in Jakarta and at the United Nations in New York.[38]

The following day, September 10, Annan issued a public statement about the crisis that raised the stakes even higher. Speaking more than seventy-two hours after the imposition of martial law in East Timor and just twelve hours after the militia invasion of the UN compound in Dili, he said that "the time has clearly come for Indonesia to seek the help of the international community in fulfilling its responsibility to bring order and security to the people of East Timor." He urged Indonesia to accept this help, and warned that "if it refuses to do so, it cannot escape responsibility for what could amount, according to reports reaching us, to crimes against humanity."[39] The allusion to crimes against humanity was the first made by any world leader with respect to the violence in East Timor and reflected Annan's strong belief that claims of national sovereignty must not be allowed to stand in the way of effective international action in defense of human rights. The statement also highlighted Annan's view that the United Nations bore a special responsibility in this instance because it had supervised the process that had now culminated in violence, and because that violence was being directed in part against UN personnel. Finally, his remarks pointed to the powerful influence of mounting public outrage on his deliberations. "I know," he stated, "not least because of thousands of messages I have received from all over the world in the past few days, that many people believe the United Nations is abandoning the people of East Timor in their hour of greatest need. Let me assure you emphatically that that is not the case."[40]

Annan's September 10 statement was echoed by increasingly forceful threats and actions by other world leaders, including some who had been resisting intervention only days earlier. On his way to the APEC summit in New Zealand, President Clinton openly accused the TNI of responsibility for the violence and said, "The Indonesian government and military must reverse this course—to do everything possible to stop the violence—and allow an international force to make possible the restoration of security" in East Timor.[41] Then, in his address to U.S. and Asian business leaders at the APEC meeting on September 12, Clinton declared that the United States was ready to support an international armed force and announced the suspension of all military ties to Indonesia, while threatening to withhold U.S. support for future International Monetary Fund and World Bank assistance. His speech revealed that the decision to support international intervention was not based solely on humanitarian considerations but also on the view that Indonesia had offended widely accepted international norms and specific obligations to the United Nations. "Now it is clear," he noted,

> that the Indonesian military has aided and abetted militia violence in East Timor, *in violation of the commitment of its leaders to the international community*. This has allowed the militias to murder innocent people, to send thousands fleeing for their lives, to attack the UN compound. The U.S. has suspended all military cooperation, assistance, and sales to Indonesia, I have made [it] clear that my willingness to support future economic assistance from the inter-

national community will depend on how Indonesia handles the situation from today forward. . . . The Indonesian government and military must not only stop what they are doing but reverse the course. They must halt the violence not just in Dili but throughout the nation. They must permit humanitarian assistance and let the UN mission do its job. They must allow the East Timorese who have been pushed from their homes to return safely. They must implement the results of the balloting, and they must allow an international force to help restore security. We are ready to support an effort led by Australia to mobilize a multinational force to help bring security to East Timor under UN auspices. . . . *And because the UN helped organize the vote in East Timor, we have a special responsibility to help to see it through, to stand up to those who now break their promises to the international community.*"[42]

Significantly, the argument that Indonesia had broken its promises to the international community and had offended widely accepted international norms was among the contentions made in the preceding days by the *Washington Post*, the U.S. Catholic Bishops Conference, and a number of Congresspeople, including prominent Republicans.[43] Particularly after Berger's statement on September 7, the administration had faced a firestorm of protest from all of these quarters. Under the circumstances, it is difficult to escape the conclusion that whatever else may have motivated it, Clinton's about-face on East Timor on September 9 reflected an assessment that the political costs of inaction had become too great and that some policy shift was essential to defuse the crisis.

Whatever the reasons for the U.S. administration's change of heart, the APEC summit where Clinton spoke provided a unique opportunity for world leaders to discuss the problem and coordinate strategy.[44] It was also critical in forging something close to a consensus among Western and Asian leaders on the need for intervention. On September 11, the British foreign secretary announced the suspension of British sales of Hawk fighter aircraft to Indonesia, and on September 13, the European Union agreed to a general arms boycott against Indonesia.[45] Perhaps even more surprisingly, the Philippines and Malaysia, regional powers that had traditionally refrained from involvement in Indonesia's "internal affairs," indicated their willingness to contribute troops to a UN-sanctioned force.

The APEC meeting and Clinton's threat to withhold U.S. support for international economic assistance also increased pressure that had already begun to be exerted by powerful financial institutions. Indeed, even before the APEC meeting, both the World Bank and the International Monetary Fund had warned that they would be suspending or postponing the disbursement of new funds, pending a satisfactory resolution of the East Timor crisis. In a letter to Habibie, dated September 8, World Bank president James Wolfensohn had written that "for the international financial community to be able to continue its full support, it is critical that you act swiftly to restore order, and that your government follow through on its commitment to honor the referendum outcome."[46] The World Bank later announced that it had frozen $300 million that had been scheduled for disbursement the following week. Similarly, on September 9, the International Monetary Fund announced that it had postponed a mission to Indonesia for discussions on its economic recovery program, citing the problems in East Timor.[47] That decision meant in effect that the International Monetary Fund would not disburse some $460 million as planned in mid-September.[48]

These unprecedented statements and actions were underscored, and likely influenced by, the forceful diplomacy of the UN Security Council delegation that had arrived in Jakarta on the morning of September 8. The first of its kind since 1994, the mission had been set up at the urging of the Portuguese and the UN under-secretary-general, and was organized in record time. Its presence on the ground in Jakarta and Dili at the height of the crisis, and the stinging report it prepared on its return, unquestionably influenced opinion within the Security Council and the United Nations more generally.[49] Just as important, the delegation's tough posture in meetings with Habibie, Alatas, and Wiranto would appear to have affected the political calculus inside Indonesia.

The Security Council's toughness and its impact on the political balance in Jakarta was partly the consequence of a fortuitous coincidence of events on the ground. Quite by chance, the delegation was in a meeting with Wiranto and several of his staff when the September 10 militia incursion into the UNAMET compound began to unfold. News of the attack was flashed by satellite telephone to a UN official at the meeting in Jakarta, who passed it on to the delegates, who then asked Wiranto for an explanation. After a few nervous moments and some telephone consultations of his own, Wiranto sought to downplay the seriousness of the event. But armed with what it considered to be incontrovertible evidence of TNI complicity in an attack on the United Nations, the delegation was in no mood to listen to his assurances. By the end of the meeting, they had made it clear that they simply did not believe him, and that they expected a significant change on the ground or a prompt request for international assistance.[50]

The following day, September 11, the delegates visited Dili, where they joined Wiranto who had flown out earlier that morning at their suggestion. The day was marked by an almost total absence of violence, prompting the British delegate, Sir Jeremy Greenstock, to comment that those responsible appeared capable of switching the violence on and off at will.[51] Nevertheless, any lingering doubts that the delegation or Wiranto might have had about the severity of the violence and destruction must surely have been laid to rest in the course of the day. As they drove into town from the airport, they saw with their own eyes the utter devastation that the militia had wrought with TNI assistance. Dili was a flattened, smoking ruin, and with the exception of militias, soldiers, a few stray pigs, and some refugees huddled anxiously near the waterfront, all of its inhabitants had fled. Because several journalists were accompanying the delegation, these images soon made their way around the world and helped to fuel the already furious protests that had begun a few days earlier. Even Wiranto appeared to have been shocked by the extent of the destruction. In the course of the day, he conceded to the delegation that the situation was much worse than he had earlier claimed and appeared to soften his opposition to the early deployment of international peacekeepers.[52]

Following a series of meetings with Indonesian military authorities in Dili, the delegation came to the UNAMET compound. There, crammed two or three deep in Martin's office, they were first briefed on different dimensions of the crisis. Political Affairs outlined what was then known about the systematic nature of the destruction that had taken place since the ballot and offered an assessment of the degree of official responsibility for the violence.[53] The delegation also heard the views of Civpol, MLO, Security, and the head of mission himself. Whatever differences of perspective the different UNAMET offices might have had, the message delivered to the delegation was unambiguous: Indonesian assurances had become meaningless, and swift international intervention was essential.

The most powerful message, however, did not come from UNAMET officials but from East Timorese refugees. The opportunity came when the delegation went on a brief tour of the compound, guided by Sister Esmeralda. As we walked among the hundreds of residents, so many of them children, it was impossible not to be moved. And the delegation was obviously touched when introduced to Pedro Unamet Rodrigues, now three days old. But the critical moment was completely unexpected. Out of nowhere, a youngish woman rushed up to the chair of the delegation, the Namibian permanent representative to the United Nations, Martin Andjaba. Seizing his hands, she said, "Please do not leave us here. We are so afraid." Andjaba, a former South West Africa People's Organization freedom fighter, first answered somewhat stiffly that the United Nations would do everything possible to ensure their safety. But the woman interrupted and still holding his hands, said: "No, you don't understand. If you leave us here, we will die. You must promise." At that moment, Andjaba's countenance changed. Looking straight into the woman's eyes and then wrapping his arms around her, he said: "We will not leave you. I give you my word." Outside the UN compound, beyond Dili, in the capital cities of powerful states, on the streets and on front pages, over telephone lines to the offices of Indonesia's president and armed forces commander, the pressure had begun to build—indeed, the crucial decisions may already have been made. But as far as I was concerned at the time, the tide of fortune had turned with those words.

Later the same day, in New York, there was an unusual open debate about East Timor in the UN Security Council.[54] Organized against the advice of the Security Council mission, but with information about its experiences well-known to all present, the debate highlighted and further solidified the emerging consensus on the need for action in East Timor. Following an opening statement by the secretary-general, in which he reiterated his view that the violence might amount to crimes against humanity, the representatives of some fifty states addressed the council. With only a few exceptions, every delegation spoke in favor of urgent international intervention, and many echoed the stance that the violence was an affront to the United Nations itself, which required a firm response. Even China and Russia refrained from expressing opposition to that course, arguing only that intervention should be contingent on Indonesian approval.

On September 12, against this backdrop, President Habibie met with his top military officers and cabinet to discuss the crisis. With Wiranto's support, he proposed that Indonesia should now permit an international force to assist in restoring order in East Timor. Despite resistance from a handful of officers and cabinet members—notably General Tanjung, the minister who had coordinated Indonesian strategy for the referendum—

the proposal was accepted. After the meeting, Habibie called Annan, then met the Security Council delegation one last time, and finally made the public announcement that effectively brought an end to the crisis.

Gathered around a radio inside the UN compound with several East Timorese friends, we listened as Habibie declared, first in English and then in Indonesian, that he had decided to invite an international peacekeeping force to assist in restoring security. "Too many people have lost their lives since the beginning of the unrest, lost their homes and security," he said, "We cannot wait any longer."[55] With that announcement, the last obstacle to the deployment of an international force had been removed. So too had Indonesia's will and ability to obstruct the evacuation of the refugees to Darwin. In a meeting the following morning, September 13, Martin confirmed that the Indonesian government had agreed to allow the refugees to leave and that the Australian government had agreed in principle to receive them. Almost immediately, full evacuation plans were set in motion.

At about 11:00 p.m. that night, September 13, we called together the main community leaders in the compound and explained that all who wished to do so would be leaving for Darwin within two hours. We hoped that they would be ready to go, with no more than fifteen kilograms of luggage, by 12:00 midnight. In the event, some fifteen hundred people were standing in orderly lines, bags packed, within a half hour. Just after midnight, in the early hours of September 14, a convoy of military trucks began rolling out of the compound carrying refugees and UN staff toward the airfield several miles out of town. From my vantage point in the back of the lead truck, I could see the flattened, burning remnants of the city, and through the darkness and smoke, the headlights of the ten or more trucks behind us. Once at the airport—where the trashed files of Indonesian airlines mingled on the floor with the excrement of marauding militiamen—we waited together for the planes to arrive. As the morning sun nosed above the horizon, we heard the rumbling engines of the first C-130 Hercules as it landed. We cheered, and then watched in wonder as the first hundred or so refugees clambered on board.

By noon, the last of the giant planes had been loaded and was ready to go. Haggard and exhausted, I walked toward the open hatch at the rear of the plane, together with an elderly man and woman. Confronted with the hot blast from the plane's propellers and the terrible noise of its engines, it seemed for a moment that we would not make it onto the plane. I reached out and held them by the shoulders, and they did the same to me. Together, with heads down, we made our way through the hatch. Inside, where 120 people sat dazed on slings of nylon webbing, there was relief that so many had made it to safety. But there was anguish for the hundreds of thousands who had been left behind, and serious doubt that those responsible for the violence would ever be held to account.

The Logic of Intervention

What, then, can be concluded about the reasons for the international armed intervention of mid-September? One of the essential ingredients in prompting that course was undoubtedly the dense media coverage of the violence, which included graphic television and still images of the events of early September. Those images, together with the growing realization that the violence was being abetted by the Indonesian military, generated widespread outrage among ordinary citizens, and provided the basis for mobilizing protests and demands for international action. A senior Western diplomat involved in the East Timor issue later told me that his country's policy "was not driven by realpolitik but by reactions to images on the television."[56] The impact of media reporting was accentuated by the presence of international UN staff along with a handful of foreign journalists and observers in Dili as the violence spiraled out of control. Terrible as it may seem, without the possibility that their own citizens would die, it appears likely that key governments might never have felt compelled to act. Their presence on the ground probably forced key member states to act to avoid sharing responsibility for a political and humanitarian fiasco. In pressing for UN intervention in early September, for example, New Zealand's foreign minister said, "What one hopes comes out of the Security Council of course is that you can somehow cordon off those UN-related people over there and give some kind of protection for them."[57]

Still, it is unlikely that media images and reporting alone would have translated into a change in policy had there not already been a sophisticated worldwide network of grassroots organizations with expert knowledge of East Timor in place long before the crisis. When I asked a Canadian diplomat what it was that had finally convinced his government that it must support intervention, the answer was unequivocal: it was the NGOs. "The media was not as important as the NGOs' long-term ac-

FIGURE 9.2. Kofi Annan. During his tenure as UN secretary-general, Annan played a pivotal role in the search for a political solution to the conflict in East Timor. A powerful advocate of "humanitarian intervention," with direct experience of past UN failures in preventing genocide, he was also instrumental in bringing an end to the postballot violence in September 1999. Crucially, he undertook an intense campaign of personal and public diplomacy, urging world leaders to contribute to an international force and exert pressure on Indonesia to accept it. (Dreamstime)

cess to [Foreign Minister] Axworthy. . . . That access multiplied our interest in East Timor."[58] And Canada was not alone in this. Over the years,
an international network of religious and secular NGOs had built up an
unusually rich portrait of the human rights problem in East Timor, and
had established channels of access and influence not only to the media
but also to government and legislative decision makers and to various
UN bodies. That essential groundwork—for years considered a rather
hopeless task carried out by naive idealists—meant that when the crisis
came, the lobbying effort did not have to begin at square one. In retrospect, many diplomats still marvel at the success of that effort in keeping
East Timor on the international agenda, against all odds.

An additional factor was the openness toward the idea of international
humanitarian intervention that existed, if only briefly, at the turn of the
millennium.[59] The principle that state sovereignty might legitimately be
infringed by the international community in order to protect a people
from gross human rights abuse or humanitarian catastrophe was being
forcefully articulated, above all by Annan, and somewhat belatedly by
Clinton, among others.[60] As Annan would write in his "Millennium Report" a few months later, "If humanitarian intervention is indeed an unacceptable assault on sovereignty, how should we respond to a Rwanda,
to a Srebrenica—to gross and systematic violations of human rights that
offend every precept of our common humanity?"[61] Indeed, while the
Security Council had resisted it, precisely that argument had been used
to justify the NATO bombing of Kosovo just a few months earlier. That
precedent and the near consensus that the Kosovo campaign had been a
success made a similar response in East Timor far more likely than it
would otherwise have been. At the very least, it gave those who favored
armed intervention a strong argument.[62]

Equally important was the sense that in East Timor, the principles and
integrity of the United Nations were being openly attacked by Indonesia. In their statements on behalf of intervention, UN officials and member states referred repeatedly, often angrily, to the fact that Indonesia had
broken its promises to and solemn agreements with the United Nations—to maintain security and honor the result of the ballot. Under
the circumstances, they said, the United Nations had a unique obligation
to take action. If it did not, they asked rhetorically, who would ever believe the United Nations again?[63] This sense that the postballot violence
was a brazen attack on the United Nations itself was reinforced by the
fact that local and international UN personnel were themselves the tar-

get of some of the violence. In the same way that states felt compelled to respond to threats against their citizens, the United Nations felt a special obligation to act forcefully in defense of its own people.

The notion that the United Nations itself was being attacked stimulated an unusual consensus among its member states and the Secretariat staff on the need for action. That consensus, in turn, paved the way for the swift and forceful diplomacy of the Security Council on the issue. Of particular importance was the Security Council's visit to Jakarta and Dili from September 8 through 12, in the course of which international pressure on Indonesia mounted to unprecedented levels. Through their personal experience of the violence and of the mendacity of Indonesian officials, the Security Council delegation was effectively transformed into a powerful advocate for international action.[64] Likewise, Annan's personal commitment and his energetic diplomacy at the height of the crisis were critical in bringing about a change within the United Nations and among key powers, including the United States.

Historical memory unquestionably played a part as well. From the start of the UN mission in East Timor, the 1994 genocide in Rwanda and the 1995 massacre in Srebrenica were on the minds of UN officials in Dili and New York, and they must have played a role in the deliberations of various states.[65] The parallels were difficult to ignore, especially for those with some direct involvement in the earlier debacles. That group included Clinton, Albright, Annan, and Annan's chef de cabinet, Iqbal Riza. Partly for the sake of the United Nations' reputation, but also for much more profound moral reasons, some of these people seemed determined that civilians would not be abandoned in East Timor. Annan offered a clear glimpse of the effect of those events in late 1999, when he received the UN report on the genocide in Rwanda. "Of all my aims as Secretary-General," he wrote, "there is none to which I feel more deeply committed than that of enabling the United Nations never again to fail in protecting a civilian population from genocide or mass slaughter."[66]

Finally, a case can be made that the intervention in East Timor was driven by the decisions and actions of a handful of individuals, some of them powerful, and others scarcely known. Gusmão's decision to adopt a policy of restraint in the face of the mounting violence, and the ability of the CNRT and Falintil leadership to make that decision stick, helped to ensure that the postballot violence was properly understood by international observers to be one-sided and wholly unjustifiable. Had the CNRT and Falintil opted instead to respond to the violence in kind, as they certainly could have done, the international consensus on the need for swift intervention on humanitarian grounds would quickly have evaporated. Less obviously, the extraordinary physical and moral courage of many ordinary East Timorese, like Sister Esmeralda, left an indelible impression on all those who encountered it, and made it much more likely that they would do everything in their power to bring an end to the violence.

CHAPTER TEN

JUSTICE AND RECONCILIATION

JUST TWO DAYS after the United Nations' early morning evacuation from Dili, the Security Council passed resolution 1264 authorizing the establishment of a multinational force under Chapter VII of the UN Charter. That force had begun to deploy in East Timor within another week. Led by Australia, but comprised of units from several other states, including Malaysia, Thailand, the Philippines, and New Zealand, it immediately set to work rounding up militias, and in some cases killing them. Despite protests from some in Indonesia about its behavior, Interfet met little resistance from either militias or the TNI, and by late September, the violence had largely ended. The pivotal role of the multinational force in halting the violence was highlighted by the fact that where Interfet troops were slow to deploy, serious violence continued. In Lospalos, for example, a group of four Catholic clergy and five laypeople were ambushed and executed by a gang of militiamen on September 25, just days before Interfet deployed there. And in Oecussi at least twelve people were killed in the village of Maquelab on October 20, just two days before Interfet troops finally arrived in the district.[1] Interfet also facilitated the timely delivery of humanitarian assistance to the many tens of thousands of people who had been displaced. In striking contrast to the almost total absence of international humanitarian assistance in the late 1970s, emergency relief began to be delivered within a few weeks of the onset of the humanitarian crisis. The speed and efficiency with which that assistance was delivered almost certainly averted a major humanitarian crisis.

In all of these ways, Interfet helped to prevent killing and death on a massive scale. At the same time, there were problems that it could not solve, and that no military intervention could reasonably have been expected to address. Nor, as it turned out, could they be solved by the UN Transitional Administration in East Timor (UNTAET) that governed the territory between October 1999 and May 2002, or by the fledgling government of Timor-Leste that followed it. Chief among these problems was the question of justice.[2] There was an early consensus, both inside East Timor and internationally, on the need to investigate thoroughly the crimes that had been committed and to bring the perpetrators to justice, if necessary before an international criminal tribunal. Before long, however, that consensus began to fray. Some ten years later, not a single Indonesian officer or official had been convicted of a crime, and support for an international tribunal had largely dissipated. In place of the urgent calls for justice, there was now talk of reconciliation, or at least of the need to balance demands for justice against the ostensibly greater need for peace and reconciliation.[3]

While East Timor's experience has in some respects been unique, the way in which the tension between justice and reconciliation has played out there arguably holds lessons for other places emerging from years of violent conflict.[4] One point that has become clear is that in the absence of justice, there is little possibility of securing any genuine or meaningful reconciliation between the perpetrators of violence and its victims.

Early Investigations

The events of September stimulated strong international pressures to investigate, at a minimum, the violence of 1999 and to bring those responsible to justice. Two separate Security Council resolutions in September and October demanded precisely that, as did a resolution of the UN Commission on Human Rights at a special session in late September.[5] Accordingly, in early November a team of three UN Special Rapporteurs came to East Timor to conduct a joint investigation.[6] About a week later a delegation from Indonesia's Human Rights Commission visited to conduct its own investigation. Later in the month a UN Commission of Inquiry visited the country to conduct an inquiry called for by the Human Rights Commission in its resolution of September 27.[7]

Notwithstanding the enormous logistical obstacles and some resistance from Indonesia, the UN Special Rapporteurs and the UN Commission of Inquiry conducted serious and credible investigations. And despite some understandable initial suspicion among East Timorese about its intentions, the same was true of the investigation conducted by Indonesia's Human Rights Commission.[8] Significantly, all three investigations reached similar conclusions: that the violence of 1999 amounted to crimes against humanity, that the Indonesian state and in particular the TNI bore responsibility for those crimes, and that if Indonesia failed to bring the perpetrators promptly to justice, an international criminal tribunal should be established to do so.

The two UN reports were especially emphatic on one point: that the United Nations as an institution had a responsibility to ensure that the crimes committed in 1999 would not go unpunished. Ensuring that the perpetrators of crimes against international human rights and humanitarian law are brought to justice is, of course, a general concern of the United Nations. Yet in the case of East Timor in 1999, that general principle applied with special force, for three reasons. First, as mentioned earlier, the crimes committed in 1999 occurred in the context of a process overseen by the United Nations under an explicit mandate from the Security Council.[9] Second, those crimes constituted direct breaches of Security Council resolutions and the May 5 Agreements.[10] Third, resolutions adopted by the Security Council and the Commission on Human Rights after September 1999 explicitly committed the United Nations to bringing the perpetrators of the crimes in question to justice.[11]

The special responsibilities of the United Nations were highlighted by the International Commission of Inquiry. In its January 2000 report, the commission stressed that

> the actions violating human rights and international humanitarian law in East Timor were directed against a decision of the United Nations Security Council acting under Chapter VII of the Charter and were contrary to agreements reached by Indonesia with the United Nations to carry out that Security Council decision. Under Article 25 of the Charter, Member States agree to accept and carry out the decisions of the Security Council. The organized opposition in East Timor to the Security Council decision requires specific international attention and response. The United Nations, as an organization, has a vested interest in participating in the entire process of investigations, establishing responsibility and punishing those responsible and in promoting reconciliation.[12]

Significantly, the commission's view was endorsed by the secretary-general. Annan, furthermore, stressed his commitment to cooperate with and monitor progress on the matter. In his January 2000 letter to the president of the Security Council, introducing the commission's report, he wrote, "I wish to assure Member states of my firm commitment to cooperate with the intergovernmental process in this important matter. I will closely monitor progress towards a credible response in accordance with international human rights principles."[13]

On the question of what exactly should be done to give effect to these commitments, the Commission of Inquiry was also clear. It recommended that the Security Council should establish an international criminal tribunal, along the lines of those created for Rwanda and the former Yugoslavia. More specifically, it recommended that

> the United Nations should establish an international human rights tribunal consisting of judges appointed by the United Nations, preferably with the participation of members from East Timor and Indonesia. The tribunal would sit in Indonesia, East Timor, and any other relevant territory to receive the complaints and to try and sentence those accused by the independent investigation body of serious violations of fundamental human rights and international humanitarian law which took place in East Timor since January 1999 regardless of the nationality of the individual or where that person was when the violations were committed.[14]

The three UN Special Rapporteurs who conducted investigations in East Timor in late 1999 made essentially the same recommendation. In their report of December 1999, they argued that in keeping with accepted norms of international law, primary responsibility for investigating the crimes in East Timor and bringing the perpetrators to justice lay with the Indonesian government. Accordingly, they argued that the Indonesian authorities should be given an opportunity to conduct such investigations and prosecutions before any further action was contemplated. They noted, however, that in the event that the Indonesian authorities failed to make satisfactory progress in that work, it would be appropriate to establish an international criminal tribunal. More specifically, the Special Rapporteurs recommended that

> unless, *in a matter of months*, the steps taken by the Government of Indonesia to investigate TNI involvement in the past year's atrocities bear fruit, both in the way of credible clarification of the facts and the bringing to justice of the perpetrators—both directly and by virtue of command responsibility—the Security Council should

consider the establishment of an international criminal tribunal for the purpose. This should preferably be done with the consent of the Government, but such consent should not be a prerequisite. Such a tribunal should then have jurisdiction over all crimes under international law committed by any party in the Territory [of East Timor] since the departure of the colonial Power [Portugal].[15]

The Special Rapporteurs made it clear, then, that the need for an international criminal tribunal was contingent on both the adequacy and the timeliness of any measures taken by the Indonesian authorities.

The broad consensus expressed in these reports helped to generate some hope that an international tribunal might soon be established to bring those responsible to account. For a variety of reasons, that did not happen. The most important reason was a marked lack of enthusiasm for the idea among powerful states, most notably the United States, and therefore also within the UN Security Council. Eager to mend its relations with Indonesia and in particular with the TNI, the Bush administration sought to restore military ties, including International Military Education and Training programs that had been cut in mid-September 1999. While the U.S. Congress repeatedly resisted these efforts, by early 2000 the United States and other major powers had begun to soften demands for an international inquiry, suggesting that an Indonesian judicial process might suffice. That position was rooted in a general reluctance to support international criminal tribunals, partly for ideological reasons and partly out of a concern that U.S. personnel might easily be brought before them.

Whatever the reasons for it, the folly of the velvet glove approach became apparent before a year had passed. In September 2000, Indonesian security forces stood by and watched as militiamen killed three UN High Commissioner for Refugees staff members at their office in West Timor, and then burned their bodies beyond recognition. The victims were among the humanitarian workers assisting the estimated 250,000 East Timorese who had fled their homes in 1999, and the perpetrators were the very militiamen who had forced them to flee. The murders were met by a storm of international condemnation—from the United States, which announced a full suspension of military assistance, and the UN Security Council, which condemned "this outrageous and contemptible act." But the underlying resistance to an international tribunal did not change, and the matter was left in the hands of Indonesian authorities.[16] Several months later, the Indonesian prosecutor in the case announced that the six alleged perpetrators would only be charged with assault—a decision described by a diplomat as a "despicable whitewash"—and in May 2001 they received sentences of between ten and twenty months.[17]

Against this background, in July 2001 the Bush administration announced its intention to seek the resumption of military sales to Indonesia and a further restoration of direct military ties.[18] Pentagon and other officials claimed that the resumption of military ties and sales were appropriate "rewards" for Indonesian advances in the areas of democratization and civilian control of the armed forces. But while it was true that there had been some progress in these areas since Suharto's resignation in 1998, that progress had not been achieved by the TNI alone, but rather against the resistance of all but a handful of its most powerful officers and units. Moreover, there had been virtually no progress in the prosecution of human rights violations in East Timor—an explicit condition of the congressional legislation prohibiting military sales.[19] As the director of Human Rights Watch-Asia said at the time, the decision to restore ties in this context sent "exactly the wrong signal."[20]

The priority of restoring good relations with the TNI was given added impetus after September 11, 2001, and the declaration of Southeast Asia, including Indonesia, as a "second front" in the "war on terror."[21] Pentagon officials sought to justify the resumption of military ties on the grounds that these were the best way to ensure continued U.S. influence on the TNI and in Indonesia generally, and therefore the best way to guarantee respect for human rights and civilian rule. Such arguments conveniently overlooked the fact that close ties with the TNI had done nothing to end the pattern of gross violations of human rights in Indonesia and East Timor for more than thirty years. Nor did they do anything at all to prevent the widely anticipated violence in 1999, or to stop it once it had begun. Indeed, it was only when the United States and other states acted by *cutting* military ties and arms sales that the wanton violence was finally brought to an end.

In spite of all this, some observers genuinely believed that it was better to have Indonesia take the lead in the investigation and prosecution of the perpetrators of the violence in East Timor, on the grounds that this would help to build human rights institutions and norms inside Indonesia. As East Timorese knew only too well, and as legal experts concurred, Indonesia's judicial process was seriously flawed.[22] Under the circumstances, it was naive and irresponsible to expect that these institutions could suddenly be made to meet international standards of fairness. It was also unfair that East Timor's interests should, yet again, be made secondary to the presumed needs of Indonesia.

Needless to say, the lack of support for an international tribunal among key states and on the Security Council emboldened Indonesian resistance to the idea. Instead, Indonesian authorities set about, usually without resort to evidence, to challenge the most basic conclusions reached by all previous investigations and to deflect demands for an international judicial process. That effort took various forms. A number of high-ranking TNI officers, including Major General Makarim, and the two former East Timor commanders, Colonel Suratman and Colonel Nur Muis, wrote memoirs or papers in which they sought to lay the blame for the violence of 1999 on UNAMET.[23] The violence, they claimed, was the regrettable but unavoidable consequence of UNAMET's proindependence bias and cheating, fueled by a local cultural pattern of running amok. More important, Indonesia sought to deflect lingering demands for an international tribunal by setting in motion what it claimed to be serious domestic mechanisms to investigate the violence and bring those responsible to justice.

Trials in Jakarta and Dili

Against this backdrop, in 2001 Indonesia established the Ad Hoc Human Rights Court to try cases arising from the events in East Timor.[24] After considerable delay, in January 2002 indictments were finally issued against eighteen individuals for crimes against humanity allegedly committed in 1999. The accused included several high-ranking Indonesian TNI and police officers, including Major General Adam Damiri, Brigadier General Nur Muis, and Police Colonel Timbul Silaen. Of the eighteen people charged, twelve were acquitted in first instance trials, and six were later acquitted on appeal, including the notorious militia leader Eurico Guterres. No Indonesian officers or officials were ever jailed, and some were actually promoted and appointed to highly sensitive command positions.[25]

This is not the place for an exhaustive analysis of the trials or the Ad Hoc Human Rights Court that heard them. Yet a few general points can be made by way of judging their effectiveness in clarifying the facts and bringing the perpetrators to justice.[26] First, there were fatal problems with the mandate of the court. Most glaringly, the presidential decree through which it was established limited its jurisdiction to violations that had occurred in only two months of 1999 (April and September), and in just three of East Timor's thirteen districts (Dili, Liquiçá, and Covalima). That decision effectively guaranteed that a majority of crimes would never be investigated or tried, and that the widespread and systematic nature of the crimes would not be established. Second, the attorney general decided to prosecute only four cases, thereby further limiting the likelihood of establishing that the violence was widespread and systematic. Key suspects—including many of the high-ranking officers identified in the report of Indonesia's own Human Rights Commission—were not named as defendants. Among the most glaring omissions were General Wiranto, Major General Makarim, and Major General Syahnakri. Third, the prosecutions were poorly prepared and weakly argued. The prosecutors generally failed to take advantage of the abundant documentary and testimonial evidence available to them. Most also appeared reluctant to argue their cases vigorously, especially against high-ranking TNI officers. The call for the acquittal of Major General Damiri, *by the prosecution*, in mid-2003 was a case in point.[27] In some cases, moreover, the judges appeared more diligent and energetic than the prosecutors in uncovering evidence against the accused. Finally, the conduct of the trials, and the comments of some government and judicial authorities, indicated that the Ad Hoc Court was established and the trials carried out primarily to deflect demands for an international criminal tribunal, rather than as a genuine effort to see that justice was done.

For these and other reasons, respected international human rights organizations characterized the process as fundamentally flawed and a travesty of justice. In early 2003, for example, Amnesty International wrote that "the process in Indonesia has been extremely limited in scope and has, despite some convictions, to a large extent failed in the objectives of delivering truth and justice."[28] Credible national human rights organizations and bodies, both in Indonesia and East Timor, reached similar conclusions. In a letter to the UN High Commissioner for Human Rights, the National Alliance for an International Tribunal for East Timor, a coalition of some twenty NGOs in East Timor, referred to the trials as "a disgrace and a sham."[29] Religious groups also joined the call. In May 2003, for example, a group of ninety-two religious leaders and organizations from across the United States issued a statement condemning the

Indonesian trials, and calling for the establishment of an international tribunal.[30]

Notwithstanding their interest in maintaining cordial relations with Indonesia, the trials were so obviously and egregiously flawed that key governments had little choice but to express their concern. In late 2002, for instance, the U.S. Department of State said it was disappointed with the acquittals recently handed down by the Ad Hoc Court, and noted that the prosecutors had "consistently failed to use the resources and evidence available to them from the UN and elsewhere in documenting the East Timorese atrocities."[31] Similarly, in June 2003 the U.S. ambassador to Indonesia expressed concern about the prosecutor's request for the acquittal of Major General Damiri. "While reserving judgement until the final verdict is reached," he said, "we find it particularly disappointing that it was the prosecution that sought a not-guilty verdict in this case."[32] In short, it is fair to conclude that by late 2004, Indonesia's national judicial process had not borne fruit, either in the way of credible clarification of the facts or in bringing the perpetrators to justice. On the contrary, the trials before the Ad Hoc Court had served effectively, and no doubt intentionally, to slow or derail altogether the momentum for an international process.

While Indonesia was staging show trials that were designed to fail, East Timor's fledgling judiciary, with UN assistance, was conducting something close to a serious investigative and judicial process, in accordance with accepted international standards. In 2000, pursuant to UN Security Council resolution 1272 (1999), UNTAET enacted a statute establishing Special Panels for Serious Crimes within the Dili District Court to try serious crimes, including crimes against humanity.[33] Under the same statute, the norms of international law were adopted as the basis on which such crimes would be prosecuted and tried. UNTAET also established a Serious Crimes Unit with a mandate to investigate serious crimes that had occurred between January 1 and October 25, 1999, and prosecute those responsible for such crimes.[34]

After a series of false starts and delays, in 2002 these mechanisms began to achieve some notable successes. By late 2004, indictments had been filed against a total of 391 individuals, most of whom were charged with crimes against humanity.[35] Those indictments accounted for roughly half of all the killings reported to have been committed in 1999. Notably, those indicted included General Wiranto, 6 other high-ranking

TNI officers, and the former governor of East Timor. Of the 391 individuals indicted, some 50 had been convicted and sentenced to jail terms
by late 2004, and 2 had been acquitted. Given the fact that East Timor
had no functioning judiciary in 2000, and few qualified lawyers, prosecutors, or judges, this was a remarkable achievement—an example of
effective and meaningful international cooperation and assistance.

Yet the picture was not all rosy. For one thing, as the Serious Crimes
Unit mandate expired in 2005, the vast majority of those indicted remained at large in Indonesia, effectively beyond the court's jurisdiction.[36]
And there was virtually no chance that any of the senior officials and officers who had been indicted—that is to say, the managers and planners
of the violence—would ever be tried through East Timor's judicial process. The main reason was that the government of Indonesia categorically refused to extradite any suspects to East Timor or even to recognize
the competence of East Timor's courts to try them. In response to the
indictment of General Wiranto et al., issued in February 2003, for example, Indonesia's foreign minister was quoted as saying, "[The Timor-
Leste court] is not at all an international tribunal. . . . [T]hey don't have
international jurisdiction and for that matter legally they don't have the
capacity to reach non-East Timorese."[37] As a consequence, the only cases
that had actually been tried by late 2004 were those of low-ranking
local militiamen.

This situation led to growing frustration among East Timorese, who
noted with dismay that it was only local people of lowly means who
were being caught up in the judicial net, while the big fish went free. I
heard that view expressed on many occasions in East Timor after 1999,
most memorably at the national public hearing on massacres held by the
CAVR in November 2003, and in a well-attended public forum on the
subject of justice and reconciliation at the University of Dili. It is wrong,
said one speaker to enthusiastic applause, for the courts to try and punish
only low-level East Timorese militiamen, when it is well understood
that the crimes they committed were part of a plan conceived and coordinated by Indonesian authorities. The same sentiment was captured by
an East Timorese judge on the Special Panel for Serious Crimes. "Speaking as an East Timorese and not as a judge," he said, "I think this system
is not fair. Is it fair to prosecute the small East Timorese and not the big
ones, the Indonesians, who gave the orders?"[38]

The problem was not simply one of legal jurisdiction. It was first and
foremost a political problem, with at least three dimensions: First, there

was the unhelpful posture of the Indonesian government. Although the Serious Crimes Unit issued indictments against some of these figures— and the court issued arrest warrants—Indonesia simply refused to accept their authority. Under the dubious guise of seeking reconciliation between the two countries, moreover, Indonesia placed pressure on East Timor's leaders not to support or comply with the judicial process. Following a meeting with Xanana Gusmão shortly after the Serious Crimes Unit had issued an indictment of General Wiranto and others, the TNI commander General Endriartono Sutarto told reporters: "We sought an understanding from Xanana that if the case continues it will not be good for the situation ahead of the [Indonesian] presidential elections. . . . We need reconciliation and to look to the future of our countries' relationship, rather than resurrect the past . . . and Xanana welcomed the initiative."[39]

Second, there was the problem that East Timor's government was reluctant to take primary responsibility for prosecuting high-ranking Indonesian officials.[40] That reluctance was understandable. A tiny, fledgling state, impoverished and decimated by long years of occupation and war, and still sharing a vulnerable border with Indonesia, it could not reasonably be expected to take the lead in the costly and complex process of bringing to justice some of Indonesia's most powerful officials. Furthermore, even if the government had wished to take on this task, it would have been seriously hampered by the lack of resources, capacity, and expertise in the country's new judiciary.[41]

Finally, there was the failure of key states and the Security Council itself to accept responsibility in the matter. Notwithstanding early expressions of outrage and demands that those responsible be brought to justice, after September 1999 there was no serious support for the one mechanism through which that goal might be achieved: an international tribunal. Instead, powerful governments claimed that it would be wrong to act against the will of the government of East Timor. But that was a disingenuous argument. It was precisely because East Timor could not undertake this monumental and sensitive task alone that the United Nations and others ought to have done so.

The net result of these developments was that by late 2004, none of the principal Indonesian perpetrators of the crimes of 1999 had been arrested or tried. As a result, pressure began gradually to grow again on the United Nations to do something about it—particularly in light of the Security Council resolutions and statements by the secretary-general indicating that the United Nations had much at stake and would follow the situation closely. The pressure came in the first instance from a broad coalition of international NGOs—including Human Rights Watch, Amnesty International, the East Timor Action Network, and the International Center for Transitional Justice—but it was reinforced by impatience for progress within the U.S. Congress.[42] Rather than taking the logical next step of establishing an international criminal tribunal for East Timor, however, in January 2005 the secretary-general decided to appoint a Commission of Experts to assess the progress made by the judicial processes in Jakarta and Dili, and recommend measures to ensure that the perpetrators would be held accountable and justice secured for the people of East Timor.[43] That approach was dictated, to a great extent, by the posture of powerful members of the Security Council—most notably the United States—which while recognizing that the Jakarta trials were an embarrassing sham, had lost any appetite they might once have had for bringing Indonesian military authorities to account.[44] The appointment of a Commission of Experts was a compromise that permitted the United Nations to postpone any decision for at least another year while giving the appearance of taking action.

Nevertheless, in its report of May 2005, the Commission of Experts reached the only reasonable conclusion it could. While praising the Serious Crimes Unit and Special Panels in Dili for their professionalism, it found that this process had "not yet achieved full accountability for those who bear the greatest responsibility for serious violations of human rights committed in East Timor in 1999."[45] The commission's findings on the Ad Hoc Court in Jakarta were more damning. It concluded that

> the prosecutions before the Ad Hoc Court were manifestly inadequate, primarily owing to a lack of commitment on the part of the prosecution, as well as to lack of expertise, experience and training in the subject matter, deficient investigations and inadequate presentation of inculpatory material at trial. The failure of the Jakarta process to investigate and prosecute the defendants in a credible manner has not achieved accountability for those who bear the greatest responsibility for serious violations. Many aspects of the ad hoc judicial process reveal scant respect for or conformity to international standards.[46]

On the basis of these findings, the Commission of Experts recommended that Indonesia, with assistance from a team of experts in relevant international law, should substantially strengthen its judicial and prosecutorial capacity, and then reopen the prosecutions that had been brought before the Ad Hoc Court. Should Indonesia fail to implement these recommendations within a time frame of six months, the commission recommended that "the Security Council adopt a resolution under Chapter VII of the Charter of the United Nations to create an ad hoc international criminal tribunal for Timor-Leste, to be located in a third State."[47]

These conclusions and recommendations found further support in two detailed investigations published in 2006. The first was a report commissioned by the UN Office of the High Commissioner for Human Rights that focused on the violence committed in 1999.[48] Completed in July 2003, but not published until 2006, it drew on a large number of documents, witness statements, and interviews that had not been available to earlier investigators. It named more than eighty senior Indonesian military officers and officials who appeared to be responsible for crimes against humanity committed in 1999, and recommended that they should be further investigated and tried. Noting that Indonesian and East Timorese judicial procedures had failed utterly to bring to justice any of those officers or officials, the report recommended that the United Nations should establish without further delay an international criminal tribunal to do so.[49]

By far the most comprehensive investigation of the problem of violence and the question of justice in East Timor was conducted by East Timor's CAVR. Established in 2001 on the initiative of the CNRT, in consultation with local communities and experts, the CAVR was given a broad mandate to establish the truth about the pattern of human rights abuse and violence that had occurred during the period 1974 to 1999, to write a comprehensive report of its findings, to assist victims of the violence, to promote human rights, and to foster reconciliation among East Timorese.[50] In carrying out this mandate, between 2002 and 2005 the CAVR held 52 public hearings in East Timor's districts and 8 national public hearings in Dili, gathered and analyzed 7,824 victim statements, conducted several workshops for the worst-affected victims of violence, and processed 1,403 depositions from individuals requesting adjudication through a Community Reconciliation Process (CRP) established and implemented by the CAVR. In the course of that work, it amassed what is arguably the most comprehensive body of material on East Timor's modern history, comprising tens of thousands of pages of testimony, thousands of pages of documents, and many hundreds of hours of audio- and videotape. Based on a careful analysis of that material, the CAVR concluded in 2006 that both Indonesia and other states bore responsibility for the crimes committed in East Timor, and called for the establishment of an international criminal tribunal.

By 2006, then, no fewer than six independent investigations—including one by an official Indonesian body, the Komnas HAM—had concluded that crimes against humanity had been committed in East Timor in 1999, and urged the establishment of an international criminal tribunal to bring the perpetrators of those crimes to justice. Despite that broad consensus, none of those believed most responsible had been convicted, and an international tribunal seemed no closer to being formed. Those who had once advocated accountability and justice now spoke instead of the need for reconciliation.

Among the more surprising advocates of that path were East Timor's leaders, President Gusmão and Foreign Minister Ramos-Horta. In March 2005, they agreed in principle to establish with Indonesia a joint Commission on Truth and Friendship (CTF), ostensibly to establish the "conclusive truth" about the events of 1999 and bring about reconciliation between the two countries. The timing of that initiative was no coincidence. Coming just a few weeks after the appointment of the Commission of Experts by the secretary-general, the CTF was self-evidently an effort to deflect demands for justice and in particular an international criminal tribunal.[51] Predictably, when the Commission of Experts' report was completed in May 2005, the two governments expressed strong reservations about it, especially its call for justice and an international tribunal.[52] In July, the two governments reiterated their misgivings about the commission's report, and announced their intention to move ahead with the CTF, which formally began its work in August 2005.[53]

It was against this backdrop that the UN secretary-general and his staff prepared a report for the Security Council on the question of justice and reconciliation in East Timor. The report, submitted in July 2006, noted the views of the two governments—particularly their preference for reconciliation over "punitive" justice—but stressed the need to ensure that there would be "credible accountability" for the crimes of 1999.[54]

While I am encouraged by the efforts of the two Governments to seek truth and achieve reconciliation, they also have a responsibility to ensure credible accountability and an end to impunity. Crimes against humanity, gross violations of human rights and

FIGURE 10.1. José Ramos-Horta. A founding member of Fretilin, Ramos-Horta served for more than twenty years as the international representative of the resistance. With East Timor's Bishop Belo, he was awarded the Nobel Prize for Peace in 1996. After Indonesia's withdrawal from East Timor in late 1999, he served, in succession, as foreign minister, prime minister, and president. Once in power, he and Xanana Gusmão surprised many supporters by advocating reconciliation with Indonesia rather than insisting on accountability and justice for past crimes. (Humberto Salgado)

grave breaches of humanitarian law were committed in East Timor in 1999. There can and should be no impunity regarding such acts. Those who committed such crimes must be held accountable and brought to justice.... I hold out hope that justice can be achieved ... in a timely manner.... It would be deeply regrettable . . . if the reconciliation process foreclosed the possibility of achieving accountability for serious violations of human rights and international humanitarian law."[55]

Despite these noble sentiments, the secretary-general's report bore the imprint of the efforts by the governments of Indonesia and Timor-Leste to emphasize reconciliation over justice. Indeed, notwithstanding his apparent misgivings about the two governments' preference for reconciliation over justice, in his recommendations the secretary-general steered clear of any mention of an international criminal tribunal. He proposed instead a series of half measures, the most substantive of which was the establishment of a "community restoration programme" and a "justice programme" aimed at strengthening justice and the rule of law, and permitting the resumption of serious crimes investigations, but not prosecutions, in Timor-Leste.[56] Not surprisingly, when it met in August 2006, the Security Council adopted a similar line. While it reaffirmed "the need for credible accountability for the serious human rights violations committed in East Timor in 1999" and took note of the findings of the Commission of Experts, it said nothing whatsoever about an international tribunal.[57] The CTF initiative had achieved its purpose.

It is fair to ask why East Timor's leaders went along with such a dubious arrangement. Why, having relied with such success for twenty-four years on the principles and mechanisms of international human rights law, did they suddenly become ardent practitioners of realpolitik? And why did they allow the goal of good relations with Indonesia to trump a widespread popular desire for justice? In one sense, their decision is easy to understand. Apart from an apparently sincere belief in the importance of reconciliation with Indonesia and other former enemies, as noted above Gusmão and Ramos-Horta had no desire to antagonize their powerful and dangerous neighbor, or risk losing the benefits of good economic relations. At the same time, those goals might easily have been achieved by simply remaining neutral or even lukewarm on the issue of an international tribunal. Yet both Gusmão and Ramos-Horta campaigned actively against a tribunal, against what they termed punitive justice, and in favor of a vaguely defined reconciliation in the form of the CTF.[58] Whatever their reasons for doing so, in adopting those positions East Timor's leaders undermined profoundly the arguments for an international criminal tribunal, and placed an almost insurmountable obstacle in the path to securing justice for the crimes of 1999 and the quarter century of Indonesian rule.[59]

Reconciliation?

The ideal of reconciliation was not new in East Timor. In the final years of Indonesia's occupation, it had been one of the central tenets of the advocates of independence and the basis on which the nationalist coalitions (the CNRM and the CNRT) had been formed. Even as proautonomy militias mounted their campaign of violence in 1999, Gusmão had insisted that the proindependence camp should do nothing to alienate the supporters of Indonesian rule and should instead look forward to the future collaboration of both sides in an independent East Timor. Some of the reconciliation initiatives undertaken after 1999 honestly reflected that spirit and intent, and produced surprisingly positive results. Other initiatives, by contrast, seemed designed mainly to deflect demands for justice rather than achieving genuine reconciliation. More to the point perhaps, in the absence of justice, the goal of reconciliation—no matter how sincere or well intended—remained elusive.

By far the most impressive and successful of the initiatives aimed at reconciliation were those undertaken by the CAVR. As its name suggests, the mandate of the Commission for Reception, Truth, and Reconciliation extended well beyond the determination of truth to encompass the reception of supporters of Indonesian rule who had fled the country, and their reconciliation with the advocates of independence. A central component of that effort—and among the most innovative aspects of the CAVR's work—was the Community Reconciliation Process (CRP).[60] Designed primarily to facilitate the reintegration of proautonomy activists and militiamen into their communities, the CRP also served as a complement to a still young and seriously overstretched judicial system.

The reconciliation process drew creatively from aspects of local customary law and lessons learned in other postconflict situations, including South Africa. The CRP hearings, which were convened by the CAVR but entailed the active participation of local communities, did not have a mandate to handle cases of serious crimes, such as genocide, crimes against humanity, murder, torture, or rape; such cases were referred to the Special Panels. They did hear and pass judgment on a wide

range of lesser crimes, such as arson, theft, and beatings. Still, the punishment meted out through the CRP was in most cases restorative rather
than retributive—designed to permit perpetrators to make amends for
their crimes by repaying victims for their loss, contributing to the reconstruction of a burned house, and so on. The underlying aim was to
provide a basis through which perpetrators might be reintegrated into
the community, rather than live in fear or remain pariahs, and for the
community to regain a measure of social cohesion.

Under the procedures established for the CRP, an individual would
make a statement to the local office of the CAVR. In most cases, those
who submitted depositions were former militiamen who had experienced difficulty returning to their home communities, or had been accused of committing one or more crimes in 1999. They understood that
the CRP might offer an alternative to a full judicial proceeding and to
the possibility of imprisonment. Their statements were reviewed by the
national office of the CAVR, with a view to determining if a serious
crime had been committed. The CAVR then conveyed the deposition
to the national Office of the General Prosecutor. If there was any evidence that the deponent had committed a serious crime, the file would
be held by that office with a view to bringing criminal charges. If there
was no evidence of a serious crime, the CAVR would convene a CRP
hearing, usually in the community in which the deponent lived. Following the public hearing, the community would devise a Community
Reconciliation Agreement, spelling out what was required of the defen-
dant, and that agreement would be filed with the district court, giving it
the force of law.

A CRP hearing I attended in Cananain, Manatuto, in November 2003
was typical in most respects. The village was located high in the mountains, at least four hours by winding dirt road from the coastal plain. In
the center of the village, a large temporary shelter had been constructed
of bamboo to serve as the meeting place. Perhaps a hundred people, including men and women of all ages, had gathered inside. Seated at the
front on woven mats was a representative of the local CAVR (wearing a
tie), and two or three village leaders. To one side, next to the leaders,
were the four "accused," all of them young men. Also present were individuals and family members who claimed to have suffered harm at the
hands of the accused. Following some introductory remarks by the
CAVR representative, the proceedings were taken over by the village
head. He began with a ceremonial "rolling out of the mat" (*nahe biti bot*),

which signified the commencement of an important process of community deliberation. After some additional preliminary remarks, the deponents were invited to offer their statements. Some gave simple confessions of wrongdoing and asked for forgiveness, while others sought to explain (and justify) their actions, often on the grounds that they had been forced to join the militias under duress. The floor was then opened to the aggrieved families and the community at large, which used the opportunity to pepper the defendants with questions, and in two cases to accuse them of lying about the extent or nature of their guilt. This public grilling continued for several hours. Eventually, the defendants admitted to virtually all of the allegations made against them and agreed to do whatever the community had asked by way of compensation. The village head finally declared that it was time to put the question. Pointing to each of the accused in turn, he called out, "Shall we accept him back into our community?" Then, in a chorus of voices, the answer came: "Accept!" And with that the village head declared that the hearing was over, and that it was time to roll up the mat and celebrate. Within a few minutes, the shelter was transformed into a banquet hall, the scene of feasting and dancing that continued well into the night.

On the whole, the process was extraordinarily successful—indeed, far more successful than many critics ever expected when it was first established. Some fourteen hundred depositions in all were made—a figure 50 percent higher than the CAVR's most optimistic projections. In that respect, they provided a quick, just alternative to handling thousands of cases through a weak and overstretched judicial system. Community participation was also unexpectedly high; all told, between thirty and forty thousand villagers took part in the hearings. Among those who did, moreover, some 90 percent later said that the process had been positive and that it had improved the situation in their community. The emphasis on restorative rather than retributive justice, it seems, was useful to victims and went some way to relieving tensions at the local level. For example, some victims said that they had gained an understanding of why perpetrators had acted as they did, and often forgave them. Most perpetrators felt that they could finally be part of the community. The sense of restored community and hope was captured by a village elder who concluded a CRP in November 2003 with the following words:

Today is the end of 24 years of suffering, violence and division for our community. In 1999 we saw the Indonesian soldiers and militia leave. On May 20, 2002, we celebrated our independence as a nation. But it is only today that as a community we can be released from our suffering from this terrible past. Let us roll up the mat, and this will symbolize the end of all of these issues for us. From today we will look only forward.[61]

Nevertheless, the CRPs did have significant shortcomings. The victims of violence were not always satisfied with the outcome, in particular with what they viewed as the light punishment meted out to the perpetrators. The process also made it far less likely that perpetrators would admit to serious crimes, because they knew that if they did so, they would likely be brought before a real court and be subject to serious punishment. In that way, the process served as a disincentive to truth telling, and may actually have left serious crimes unpunished, and the victims of those crimes bitter and unsatisfied. A related problem was that in focusing on community reconciliation, the CRP scarcely touched the problem of justice for the most serious crimes and their perpetrators. As the CAVR's chief legal adviser wrote in 2004:

> In almost every CRP hearing there were expressions of serious discontent because those involved in the planning and execution of the programs of violence—the Indonesian military commanders and militia leaders—remained free and prosperous in Indonesia. This was the major block for deep healing in the communities.[62]

The problem was summed up neatly by a participant in a CRP in Viqueque who said, "I still have doubts about reconciliation. My father was murdered. Do you think I can reconcile with the person who killed him? I suggest that the offender be punished."[63]

More odious still in the eyes of many East Timorese were the reconciliation initiatives between East Timor and Indonesia promoted by political leaders on both sides. The chief object of derision was the joint Indonesia–East Timor CTF—more commonly known in East Timor as the TFC or "Timor Fried Chicken." As discussed above, the CTF was established in mid-2005 primarily to deflect calls for an international tribunal. Under the circumstances, it was hardly surprising that its terms of reference were poorly framed. It had the controversial mandate, for example, to offer amnesty to real or alleged perpetrators of the violence who testified before it.[64] This was the dubious bargain that had been struck in South Africa, and was explicitly rejected by the United Nations in 2000 and as a model for the CAVR in East Timor precisely because of the serious problems that had arisen in the South Africa case.[65] Moreover, the public proceedings of the CTF did not come close to those in South Africa in their seriousness. In the view of most independent observers they were, in fact, little more than a forum for the articulation of official lies and a mechanism to provide additional cover from demands for meaningful judicial proceedings.

While some of the East Timorese members of the CTF apparently did their best to keep the proceedings honest, most independent observers saw it as a dangerous whitewash and refused to have anything to do with it.[66] In its May 2005 report, for instance, the UN Commission of Experts noted with concern that there were provisions in the CTF's terms of reference that "contradict international standards on denial of impunity for serious crimes" and that there was no mechanism "for compelling witnesses to tell the truth." Largely on those grounds, the United Nations refused to participate in the CTF's public hearings, as did several individuals with firsthand or expert knowledge of the events of 1999. The most scathing condemnation, however, came from a wide range of civil society groups in East Timor, Indonesia, and around the world.[67]

In light of the CTF's many shortcomings and the evident political machinations that drove its creation, the commission's final report, completed in March 2008, came as something of a surprise.[68] In important respects, the report was far stronger than any of its critics had imagined it would be. It concluded, for example, that crimes against humanity had indeed been committed in 1999, and that these included "murder, rape and other forms of sexual violence, torture, illegal detention, and forcible transfer and deportation carried out against the civilian population."[69] Noting that most of the violence had been committed by pro-Indonesian forces, it concluded that the militias, the TNI, and Indonesian police and civilian authorities bore "institutional responsibility" for those crimes. Significantly, the CTF also decided not to grant amnesty to any individuals or groups. Apart from its curious reference to the concept of "institutional responsibility"—a vague and legally meaningless term—these conclusions supported in most respects the conclusions of all previous reports about 1999, including those of the CAVR, Komnas HAM, and various UN bodies.[70]

Those directly involved in or close to the CTF process attributed the unexpected strength of these conclusions to a number of different factors. First, they noted that the Indonesian commissioners—like the TNI and the Foreign Ministry that had devised the plan—saw the CTF as a way to divert or definitively end demands for justice, and especially an international tribunal.[71] Particularly those with some knowledge of international diplomacy understood that the only way to achieve that objective was to ensure that the CTF's conclusions appeared credible.[72] Given the weight of the evidence already available, a report that denied that crimes against humanity had occurred simply would not meet that test. That message was underlined by key foreign embassies—especially the United States—which sent clear messages to the Indonesian Foreign Ministry and directly to the commission that the report would have to tell the truth to be credible.[73] Also important was the fact that the Indonesian side of the commission included some members who were known to be reformers and had axes to grind with those chiefly responsible for the crimes of 1999. The most notable among them was retired general Agus Widjojo, a respected military reformer and critic of General Wiranto, the TNI commander in 1999. The informal leader of the Indonesian CTF team, General Widjojo was apparently insistent that the report should tell the truth about the violence, and that there should be no amnesty granted for any person or institution involved.[74] Finally, most observers concur that the report's conclusions and the quality of its analysis owed a great deal to the work of international legal scholar David Cohen of the University of California at Berkeley.[75] Brought on board halfway through the process to provide advice to the commission on critical questions of international law, Cohen was also instrumental in reconciling the contending drafts prepared by the Indonesian and East Timorese staffs. Having been nominated by the Indonesian side and backed by the political pressures on the commission to appear credible, Cohen was in a strong position to craft a report that accurately reflected the facts of the violence.

Whatever its merits, however, the final report was unusually weak—indeed, virtually silent—on the question of justice. Despite its conclusion that crimes against humanity had been committed, it made no findings about individual criminal or command responsibility. Its recommendations, moreover, also included none about the pursuit of judicial remedies for the crimes committed. In keeping with the commission's mandate, the only sort of justice referred to positively was restorative justice. The odd disjuncture between the report's strong conclusions and its weak recommendations stemmed primarily from the essentially political nature of the CTF's purpose: to facilitate friendly relations between Indonesia and East Timor on the basis of reconciliation, not justice. That "gentlemen's agreement" ensured that the commission had no mandate to pass judgment or make recommendations on the question of individual criminal responsibility.[76]

The one piece of good news in all of this was that in spite of its silence on the question of justice, the CTF did not preclude the possibility that its findings—together with those of the CAVR and other bodies—might be used as the basis for future prosecutions, whether in Indonesia, East Timor, or before an international tribunal. Indeed, some of those close to the process suggested that at least some of the commissioners understood very well that the report "left the door ajar" for future prosecutions.[77] For that reason, they were content with the CTF's strategic silence on the issue.[78] On the other hand, in the months after its release, there was considerable pessimism among the advocates of justice that such prosecutions would begin any time soon. It appeared for the time being that the CTF had served its purpose well.

What, then, can be concluded about the search for justice and reconciliation in East Timor? On the positive side, through the work of the CAVR, there has been some real progress in reconciliation at the village level. That is important, and there may be lessons there about how to achieve a suitable balance between reconciliation and justice in other post-conflict situations. One such lesson is that there may be advantages in a quasi-judicial process that entails the involvement of local communities, stresses restorative rather than retributive justice, and draws on local norms and custom, provided these are not inconsistent with internationally recognized principles of justice and human rights. East Timor's experience suggests that such an approach can supply a meaningful remedy where formal judicial systems are ill equipped to handle the sheer volume of cases. On the other hand, it is clear that the success of reconciliation efforts at the local level in East Timor has not been matched by successes in the field of justice, especially for the perpetrators and organizers of the most serious crimes. In fact, it is fair to say that the search for justice in that more conventional sense has effectively been sacrificed to the dubious and politically expedient reconciliation of states, as epitomized by the CTF, and by the failure of the United Nations and its most powerful member states to give substance to their commitments and responsibilities.

The consequences of those political compromises and that failure are likely to be far-reaching. For while East Timorese have gone a long way in seeking truth and working toward reconciliation, that work can easily be undone if the sense of justice is left unsatisfied. Indeed, the failure to prosecute those who authorized and organized the violence of 1999 has already given rise to growing frustration and anger in East Timor, to a lack of trust in the judiciary, to vigilante justice, and to genuine threats to the peace. The failure may also have serious consequences for Indonesia. By perpetuating the invidious cycle of impunity there, it is likely to encourage future abuses, pave the way for a return of the TNI to power, and undermine the prospects of punishing those responsible for the many acts of violence committed by Indonesian forces during the Suharto years. Finally, the failure in East Timor sends a message to others in positions of authority, wherever they may be, that they have no reason to fear prosecution for even the most egregious and well-documented crimes against humanity. That will serve ultimately to further undermine the system of norms and institutions so painstakingly established since World War II to prevent such outrages against the most fundamental rights of all peoples.

What then should be done? My answer is straightforward: the UN Security Council should establish without further delay an international criminal tribunal to try those responsible for the crimes committed in East Timor between 1974 and 1999. That has been the recommendation of every serious investigation into those crimes conducted since 1999, and it is the solution that both the Security Council and the High Commissioner for Human Rights are on record as supporting. That does not mean that a criminal tribunal or a system of retributive justice can ever be the whole answer in postconflict societies. On the contrary, it is clear that such judicial mechanisms must be part of a broader process, of which reconciliation is an integral part. But reconciliation efforts on their own will never be enough.

CHAPTER ELEVEN

CONCLUSIONS

As this brief history suggests, the violence of 1999 in East Timor was emphatically *not* the result of immutable ethnic, religious, or socioeconomic tensions among East Timorese, or between them and Indonesians. Nor was it the result of age-old traditions or predispositions toward violence. Indeed, what is most striking about the violence in East Timor is the almost complete absence of underlying ethnic or religious tensions prior to or even after 1975. As we have seen, in fact, Indonesia justified its invasion and occupation of East Timor, at least in part, on the grounds that its peoples were "brothers" who had been cruelly separated by centuries of European colonialism. Even the marked religious difference between predominantly Catholic East Timor and largely Muslim Indonesia never really became the focus of conflict or violence. Overwhelmingly, the line of tension in 1999, as in the preceding twenty-four years, was a political one—between those who sought East Timor's independence and those who preferred integration with Indonesia. When Catholic clergy and parishioners were murdered in 1999, it was not because of their religious beliefs but rather because of their presumed proindependence political sympathies. For the most part, their assailants were not Muslims but fellow Catholics.

That political conflict, moreover, was without question the *consequence* of the Indonesian invasion and occupation, not its cause. Prior to 1975, there simply was no serious political rift between the people of the two countries. The political enmity between supporters and opponents of Indonesian rule that had developed by the late 1970s, and that was so much in evidence in 1999, was instead the result of the Indonesian invasion and occupation that had left so many dead. The experience and memory of that violence had first created and then hardened identities on both sides, and in that way laid an important foundation for the violence of 1999.

Yet to suggest that the violence of 1999 was somehow the natural or inevitable result of simmering political tensions among East Timorese—as Indonesian authorities and their allies have consistently done—is also misleading. For whatever political animosity may have existed among East Timorese by 1999, the violence of that year did not spring spontaneously from it. For that enmity to take the form of mass violence, I have argued, required a substantial measure of conscious organization and a strategic decision by state authorities to deploy violence to achieve a political objective. The centerpiece of that effort was the remobilization of pro-Indonesian militia groups starting in mid-1998. Also crucial was the aggressive government-run campaign to socialize the pro-Indonesian autonomy option—which entailed open threats of violence against those who hesitated to support the government position. That effort was spearheaded by Indonesian military and political authorities, with the assistance of those East Timorese leaders who supported Indonesian rule.

In other words, the violence in 1999 was the result not of deep-seated hatreds but rather of strategic planning by state officials and agencies. The principal evidence to that effect lies in the scores of internal army and militia documents that reveal that the militias were organized, funded, trained, and armed by the army, and that those efforts were supported by senior civilian officials, both in East Timor and Jakarta. As I have argued here and elsewhere, an equally compelling case that the violence was organized can be made by analyzing the distinctive patterns and variations of the violence observed and reported in 1999. Three patterns were especially revealing. First, across East Timor the militias shared a virtually identical style, discourse, technology, and repertoire of violence. Wherever they were, they dressed and behaved alike, mouthed the same slogans, used the same kinds of homemade weapons, and committed the same kinds of violent acts. Second, across the territory, the violence ebbed and flowed over time in ways that seemed designed to serve Indonesian political interests. By July 1999, the marked temporal variation in the violence was so conspicuous and often so finely calibrated that UN officials and others began to speak in terms of it being turned on and off like a water faucet. And third, the significant geographic variation in the severity of the violence—with the worst occurring in the western border areas—reflected both long-standing ties with Indonesian

military authorities and strategic political calculations about the most effective way to undermine the credibility of the popular consultation
process.

Taken together, this evidence supports the conclusion that the acts of
violence in 1999 were part of an operation planned and carried out by
the Indonesian authorities, and that senior Indonesian officials bear individual criminal and command responsibility for the crimes committed.
More specifically, the evidence points to at least fifty military officers at
or above the rank of lieutenant colonel, and some thirty senior civilian
government and police officials, who may bear responsibility for crimes
against humanity, and should be the subject of further criminal investigation. At the same time, the conclusion that the violence was orchestrated at the highest levels of the Indonesia military has tended to obscure the possibility that there were other historical or political forces at
work.

One reason to doubt that the violence of 1999 was solely the work of
high-level Indonesian planning is the fact that the principal agents of
that violence—the militias—were not new in East Timor. The historical
record outlined here makes it clear that in some form, militias had been
around for centuries, and that the modern variant drew on antecedents
and models from East Timor's past. That was evident in their choice of
low-tech and handmade weapons, their repertoires of violence that included head taking, rock throwing, and house burning, and elements of
their organization, which relied to a great extent on local leaders. Such
historical continuities did *not* mean, however, that the militias of 1999
were simply reenacting immutable, ancient traditions. On the contrary, a
closer look at their history has revealed that the traditions on which East
Timor's modern militias drew were, in crucial respects, the product of
long interaction with a succession of outside powers—Portuguese, Japanese, Australian, and Indonesian. It has highlighted, in particular, the profound influence on those militias of Indonesian military doctrine and
practice, and what I have called a culture of terror within the Indonesian
armed forces that operated in East Timor from 1975 to 1999.

As early as the eighteenth century, Portuguese governors had sought
the assistance of loyal liurai to mobilize local militias, known as moradores and arraias, to fight against recalcitrant or rebellious power holders.
The Japanese likewise made effective use of militia forces during their
brief interregnum during World War II, as did the Australian commandos deployed there to resist them. In all of these cases, the ostensible

traditions of East Timorese warfare were adapted and shaped to the needs of outside powers. The traditions changed quite fundamentally in the process, becoming both more widespread and more deadly. As a consequence, by the time Indonesian forces were preparing to invade the country in 1975, East Timorese were not only familiar with the idea of militia forces, they had centuries of experience serving in them.

Like earlier colonial powers, Indonesia mobilized local people to fight its war in East Timor. Starting in 1975, thousands of ordinary Timorese were conscripted to join counterinsurgency operations against Fretilin and its armed wing, Falintil. By the early 1980s, semipermanent militia units were spread throughout the entire territory, tightly controlled by Indonesian military officers. Those forces were supplemented in the 1990s by a network of army-sponsored thugs, known as Ninja, whose role was to provoke violence, and terrorize or kill alleged supporters of independence. Many of these forces were still active in 1999, and played a critical role in the violence. Thus, the militias that appeared to come from nowhere in 1998–99—and are often described as having been created at a stroke by the Indonesian army—had in fact been around for years. Had this not been the case, it is unlikely that they would have formed as quickly and widely as they did, or that they would have had such a clear understanding of how to carry out their mission.

The singular importance of the longer history of Indonesian rule in explaining the violence of 1999 is also underscored by the fact that essential features of that violence were not unique to East Timor. In fact, they bore marked similarities with violence seen in all areas where the Indonesian armed forces had conducted counterinsurgency operations, at least since 1965—notably in Aceh, Bali, Java, and West Papua. The common pattern of violence in all of these areas reflected standard Indonesian military doctrine and strategy, which in turn stemmed from certain distinctive features of the New Order state that emerged following the anti-Communist military coup and massacres of 1965–66. These included the unquestioned political dominance of the army, the solidification of a state ideology obsessed with security and national unity, the systematic use of terror for maintaining internal security, and the articulation of a military doctrine of total people's defense that entailed the mobilization of the civilian population to wage war on the state's internal enemies. Of course, all of these tendencies had deeper historical roots in Indonesia—some of them traceable at least to the Dutch colonial period and the Japanese occupation. My point is that after 1965, they became institutionalized and part of the army's standard operating procedures for dealing with the regime's political opponents. These patterns, all of them well established by 1975, were instrumental in shaping Indonesian behavior there over the next twenty-four years and giving rise to the violence of 1999.

The systematic use of terror against the civilian population was perhaps the most conspicuous element of Indonesian strategy in East Timor from 1975 to 1999. It was evident in the massive bombardment of civilian populations, the forced relocation of some three hundred thousand people into concentration camps where many died of malnutrition and disease, the use of torture to extract information and secure confessions needed for political show trials, and the disproportionate use of force against civilians, resulting in dozens of massacres. Over time, these tactics became normalized—a process that was facilitated by the near complete autonomy and impunity enjoyed by the army. It was also accelerated and then extended to the civilian population at large by the systematic mobilization of militia forces to assist in the counterinsurgency campaign.

These features of the Indonesian state and counterinsurgency strategy helped to create what I have called an institutional culture of terror within the army and in those institutions most closely associated with it, including the police and the militias. The existence of such an institutional culture arguably meant that no explicit order or plan was necessary in order to trigger the actions that were observed in 1999. It is possible, then, that the behavior of the militias in 1999 was not the product of an army master plan at all but rather the result of a process of historical learning through which a range of technologies and techniques of violence had spread through interaction with the army. Forged during the twenty-four years of Indonesian rule, and shaped by Indonesian military doctrine and practice, the distinctive militia style and repertoire of violence replicated the deliberate brutality that was central to the army's own institutional culture.

It needs to be stressed that this is not an argument against assigning criminal responsibility for the violence of 1999. Rather, as noted above, it is clear that certain individuals bore either individual or command responsibility for that violence, and that they should be held accountable in law for their actions. Nevertheless, because the violence was rooted in a historically conditioned institutional culture, the attribution of responsibility—and the search for meaningful remedies—cannot stop with the criminal prosecution of individual officials. Any serious effort to address the question of responsibility must also uncover the roots of the institutional problems and pathologies that ultimately shaped their unlawful actions.

The problem of responsibility is further compounded by the degree to which the violence of 1999, and in preceding years, was facilitated by international actors, institutions, and norms. As many observers have noted, the violence of 1999 was made possible by the long history of international support for Indonesia in the face of its systematic brutality in East Timor. The most egregious example of that pattern was the substantial political, economic, and military assistance given to Indonesia by major powers—most notably, the United States, Australia, and the United Kingdom—in the course of its 1975 invasion, and through the period of the genocide. Indonesian occupation was also facilitated by a long history of near silence and misrepresentation of the situation of human rights in East Timor by the mainstream media and many foreign scholars. Apparently fearful of losing access to Indonesia, media representatives and scholars alike accepted far too easily the dubious notions that serious human rights violations were a necessary price to pay for development, and that international human rights standards did not necessarily apply in Indonesia, where the so-called Asian values of community, consensus, and duty were said to be more important than civil and political rights.

With this sort of backing, it is hardly surprising that for more than twenty years, Indonesia refused to contemplate any challenge to its claimed sovereignty in East Timor—whatever the UN resolutions may have said. Notwithstanding some significant challenges to Indonesia's position—most notably the fallout from the Santa Cruz massacre of 1991 and the awarding of the Nobel Peace Prize to two East Timorese in 1996—the pattern of international support and acquiescence continued through most of 1999. The clearest example of the problem was the feeble position of key powers on the issue of security for the popular consultation. In spite of the mounting militia violence in the early months of 1999 and credible predictions of worse to come, the most influential states made no serious effort to ensure that there would be effective security arrangements before or after the vote. Instead, the May 5 Agreements placed sole responsibility for maintaining law and order in the hands of Indonesian security forces. Even a brief glimpse at the history of the Indonesian army and its behavior in East Timor would have indicated what a dangerous approach that was. There was, likewise, no serious effort to deploy peacekeeping forces even after it became clear that serious postballot violence was likely. Indeed, opposition to peacekeepers prevailed in the United States and among many of its allies at least until September 9—that is, for ten days after the militias and the army had begun their campaign of violence. As a consequence, UNAMET found itself unable to do anything as violence descended in East Timor. It was in those ten days that much of East Timor was burned to the ground, at least one thousand people were killed, and one-half of the population was forcibly displaced.

In short, a good case can be made that the violence of 1999 and of the previous twenty-four years was facilitated, and in some cases encouraged, by the positions adopted by the most powerful states and by elements of the media and civil society. Through their actions, in the form of economic and military assistance, and through their inaction with regard to systematic human rights abuse, they effectively encouraged the invasion of East Timor, facilitated the institutionalization of state terror in Indonesia, and abetted crimes against humanity in both Indonesia and East Timor. In the absence of such international support, it is quite possible—and indeed probable—that the violence of 1999 and the death of at least a hundred thousand people in the previous twenty-four years would never have happened.

But if the United Nations and the international community were a major part of the problem in 1999, they were also a crucial part of the solution. In fact, as I have argued here, the decisive difference between the late 1970s and 1999—the factor that prevented a second genocide in 1999—was swift and effective armed international intervention. This may sound like an argument for preemptive military action in all cases of mass violence. It is not. International military force should not be the preferred method of resolving humanitarian crises or ending political violence; nor is there any reason to believe that such interventions would often be successful. But the violence in East Timor could be—and arguably had to be—stopped by such means, precisely because it rested critically on the complicity of powerful states. By belatedly breaking that cycle of complicity in mid–September 1999, the international community proved just how important it had been to the sustenance of terror over the preceding twenty-four years.

It is worth noting in this connection that the portrait of UN incompetence and hubris drawn by some critics does not really capture the political and moral complexity of the organization or its role in East

Timor in 1999. While it is undoubtedly true that the United Nations failed to prevent the widely predicted violence in East Timor and chose to move ahead with the vote in spite of dire warnings, there were substantial differences of opinion within the United Nations, and some within the organization acted in ways that saved lives. More to the point perhaps, it is not at all obvious that it would have been preferable for the United Nations to cancel the referendum, as some critics suggested it should. To do so might have prevented the postballot violence, but it also would have deprived East Timorese of a chance to determine their own future and escape finally from a brutal twenty-four-year occupation in which a substantial part of the population had already died. Whatever its failings, it is worth recalling that the United Nations helped to achieve something in August 1999 that had long been considered impossible: a legitimate act of self-determination for the people of East Timor.

Still, in view of the long history of international acquiescence in Indonesian violence in East Timor, it is fair to ask why key states and the United Nations suddenly changed their position in mid-September 1999, and agreed to the deployment of a military force they had for so long resisted—and that they had never even contemplated in 1975. The answer, I have contended, lies in large part in a unique historical conjuncture of events and trends in late 1999 that distinguished that moment from earlier periods—and especially from the late 1970s. First and perhaps most obviously, support for intervention was influenced by the unusual presence of international media and UN staff on the ground in East Timor as the campaign of violence was set in motion. In addition to supplying graphic images and firsthand accounts that fueled popular outrage and protest around the world, the presence of foreigners at the center of the violence significantly increased the potential political costs of *inaction* for national governments. Second, the change in position was shaped by the prior existence of an impressive network of secular and religious NGOs with unusually good access to national and international decision makers. At the moment of crisis, the credibility of those organizations and their access to those in positions of power lent them a singular authority and significance. Third, the decision to intervene was affected by an important, if short-lived, change in prevailing international norms. For a brief period in the late 1990s, there was an unusual openness to the idea of international humanitarian intervention and—particularly after the NATO operation in Kosovo in mid-1999—a sense that such interventions could succeed. Fourth, the move to intervention was driven by the long engagement of the Catholic church and the United Nations with East Timor, and the deep personal commitment to a peaceful outcome of key figures within each institution. The forceful diplomacy of UN Secretary-General Annan and the moral authority of East Timor's Bishop Belo were especially significant. The perception that Indonesia was aiding and abetting the assault on their institutions was also crucial in stimulating a strong response by others within those institutions. Fifth, the shift toward intervention was affected by the workings of historical memory—and specifically the memory of recent UN failures in similar situations. From the start of the mission in East Timor, the 1994 genocide in Rwanda and the 1995 massacre in Srebrenica were on the minds of UN officials in Dili and New York, and they inevitably played a role in the decisions that were made. Equally important was the extraordinary courage displayed by East Timorese throughout the process—a courage that moved many others, both inside East Timor and elsewhere, to do whatever they could to bring an end to the violence.

The decision to intervene was also profoundly influenced by certain actions and decisions that could not have been predicted. Two were especially noteworthy. The first was the decision taken in early April 1999 by the resistance leader Xanana Gusmão to adopt a policy of restraint in response to the concerted campaign of violence by pro-Indonesian forces. The principal rationale for that position was that armed resistance by proindependence East Timorese, even if it might seem justified, would undermine the international sympathy that he deemed essential to an independence victory. As a result of that decision, the period from mid-April to the end of 1999 was notable for the almost complete absence of acts of violence by proindependence forces, even as the militias and the TNI waged a systematic campaign of killing and destruction. While there were some in the resistance who objected strongly to the policy, in retrospect it appears that it was fundamental in bringing a final end to the violence by both sides. Indeed, had the leadership not adopted and successfully implemented that approach, and had it instead responded in kind to acts of provocation by pro-Indonesian forces, the international intervention that ultimately ended the conflict might never have happened, and East Timor might still be at war.

A second decision that could not have been predicted but that arguably helped to bring an end to the violence was the refusal by several dozen UN staff and a handful of journalists at the UN compound in Dili to evacuate to Australia as ordered on the evening of September 8,

1999. Unwilling to abandon to their fate some fifteen hundred East Ti-morese who had sought refuge in the compound, the staff declared sim-ply that they would not leave as ordered and insisted that no evacuation should be conducted until the safety of the refugees had been guaran-teed. That act of defiance was a key factor—though of course not the only one—in the United Nations' decision to remain in Dili for another week. That decision, in turn, placed renewed pressure both on the Secu-rity Council delegation that visited Dili a few days later and on powerful member states that then faced an unprecedented barrage of critical media coverage and political pressure to act. It was in that context that both the Security Council and the major powers began to place serious pressure on Indonesia, leading President Habibie to "welcome" interna-tional assistance in East Timor, and paving the way for the swift deploy-ment of a multinational force. While it is impossible to know what might have happened if the UN evacuation had gone ahead as planned on September 8, it seems more than likely that the media scrutiny would have diminished, the intense pressure for international intervention would have been relieved, and the violence and forced displacement would have accelerated, perhaps to the point of genocide.

In short, it would seem that political leaders in the United States and other powerful states were shamed into action by the media, by their citizens, and by their memories. Quite unusually, they also faced pressure for armed intervention from other members of the UN Security Coun-cil and from the secretary-general himself. All of this pressure, moreover, came at a moment when there was comparatively broad support for the principle of humanitarian intervention. Faced with this unusual and ar-guably unique combination of trends, even the most reluctant of the major powers—and even the most recalcitrant of departments or minis-tries within them—found it virtually impossible *not* to act. It is sobering to think that without such pressures and without that unique conjunc-ture of historical events, they might have done nothing at all.

That point has been underscored by the dismal record of interna-tional action on the question of justice for the victims of the violence. For a few months after the intervention of September 1999, there was consensus on the urgent need to bring the perpetrators promptly to jus-tice, if necessary before an ad hoc international criminal tribunal. With the immediate crisis resolved, however, and the removal of foreigners and UN staff from the line of fire, that consensus quickly dissipated, and powerful states were once again free to act according to more conventional standards of their "national interest." Specifically, that meant the restoration of ties with Indonesia and its military, and the softening of demands for justice. That tendency was further reinforced by the events of September 11, 2001, which simultaneously provided a rationale for the resumption of military ties with Indonesia, while also raising doubts about the wisdom of the doctrine of international humanitarian intervention and the associated idea of universal jurisdiction. The result was that ten years after the violence in East Timor, not a single Indonesian army or other official had been convicted of any crime, and the idea of an international tribunal—which had been urged by no fewer than six independent inquiries—had effectively been abandoned.

Although East Timor may in many ways constitute a unique case, I think its experience does suggest a number of more general conclusions about the dynamics of mass political violence and genocide, and about related questions of humanitarian intervention, responsibility, and justice. Some of these conclusions lend weight to existing approaches, while others either challenge or suggest refinements to the conventional wisdom.

Perhaps most obviously, the evidence from East Timor poses a serious challenge to the view that political violence and genocide are natural by-products of immutable ethnic, religious, or economic tensions, or of certain cultural predispositions to the use of extreme violence. On the contrary, it shows that such identities, traditions, and tensions may in fact emerge from a longer history of violence. It suggests, in other words, that mass violence and genocide must be understood not only or even primarily as outcomes to be explained by reference to a set of exogenous variables, and not as the natural consequence of age-old primordial loyalties, but as a vital part of the process through which identities, loyalties, and enmities are formed, solidified, or broken, and through which both the motivations and models for future violence are forged. In short, violence has its own history or genealogy, with a variety of long-lasting social and political consequences, including future violence.

At the same time, East Timor's experience also highlights the fact that the power of past violence to motivate future violence is seldom, if ever, automatic. Many communities, perhaps most, have such histories and memories, yet few experience mass violence or genocide. Clearly, something else is needed for such histories and memories to become salient in the production of new instances of extreme violence. The most important agents in that process, I have argued, are state officials and political leaders who consciously encourage violence to achieve political goals. In that sense, East Timor's modern history lends support to the contention that mass killing is the result of strategic calculation by state leaders. In the absence of such strategic calculation, underlying tensions and past experiences of violence are seldom transformed into mass violence and genocide.

East Timor's experience indicates that states can influence the incidence and nature of violence in several ways. Most obviously, they may organize and directly carry out a campaign of violence through the deployment of their regular armed forces. Yet even where they are not the principal perpetrators of violence, states can play a critical role in facilitating and provoking it. They can do so, for example, through the production and dissemination of inflammatory propaganda, the use of psychological warfare techniques designed to spread fear and suspicion, the mobilization of citizens' militia groups to carry out their strategic goals, and inaction in the face of violence by their own security forces. Crucially, I have argued here, states can fuel mass violence by permitting the development of institutional cultures of terror within key state agencies, such as the military and police. Such institutional cultures can have an effect on violence that extends well beyond the will or intention of any individual commander or official. Their singular importance stems from the fact that ideas about violence travel easily through time and space, so that the violence of the past readily comes to shape the violence of the future, both within a particular locale and beyond it. Over time, and through the practice of war, institutions like armies, militias, and guerrilla forces develop distinctive styles and repertoires of violence. As these institutions move to new theaters of operation—or as their methods come to be known through training, propaganda, or personal networks—these repertoires are easily transferred, reenacted, and sometimes refined.[1] In this way, states can serve as a vital link in the formation and spread of violent societal norms and modes of political action. Through the power and example of states—and through their unparalleled institutional reach—distinctive forms, repertoires, and discourses of violence can become normalized, ready to be employed by nonstate actors in their own conflicts, even where the state has not played a central role.

East Timor's history also suggests that mass violence and genocide are shaped by the distinctive, historically conditioned *character* of states. More specifically, it points to the possibility that these kinds of violence are more likely to occur where a state is dominated by the military and its

norms. Why should that be? One part of the answer is that military institutions are designed primarily to organize violence, so that where they
control or dominate the state, they are likely to organize it principally
along those lines. Moreover, whatever else they may think, military pro-
fessionals are trained and socialized to believe that violence can be used
to address a wide range of political and social problems, most notably
the problems of disorder and insecurity. It follows that states dominated
by the military tend to resort to violence when such problems arise. The
case of Indonesia and East Timor also suggests that where state formation has occurred under military auspices, the propensity for high levels
of violence may well outlast the period of formal military dominance.
The reason seems to be that over time, the laws, institutions, and norms
of those states, and the societies over which they preside, come to reflect
those of the military—even after a formal transition to democracy. As a
consequence, the use of violence—and particular forms and discourses
of violence—become deeply embedded in the society itself, and so survive long after the military as an institution has been formally removed
from power.

It is worth noting that these observations about the significance of
military dominance of the state run against the tide of conventional wisdom about the political conditions favorable to genocide and mass violence. As noted at the outset, that wisdom suggests that states with utopian or revolutionary ideologies are more likely to commit genocide or
other forms of mass killing than other states. The experiences of Cambodia under the Khmer Rouge, Nazi Germany, China during the Great
Leap Forward, and the Soviet Union under Joseph Stalin, among others,
certainly appear to support the conventional view. On the other hand,
the genocides in East Timor in 1975–79 and the mass killings of 1999—
both of which were committed by a decidedly antirevolutionary Indonesian regime—suggest that the key ingredient may instead be the toxic
combination of extreme nationalism and militarism. That conclusion,
furthermore, is arguably supported by the Cambodian example—and
perhaps others. After all, before it seized power in 1975, the Khmer
Rouge had fought a protracted insurgency for more than a decade, and
was both organized and predisposed to deal with its enemies and solve
the country's problems by resort to violence. If its ideology was Maoist
in inspiration, it was also dogmatically nationalist.[2] In short, it was arguably the quintessential nationalist military regime, and the genocide that
it carried out followed almost inevitably from that fact.

These observations about the role of states are especially important in understanding the mass violence perpetrated by militia and paramilitary forces—an increasingly common phenomenon in the late twentieth and early twenty-first centuries, as the cases of Rwanda, Sierra Leone, Zimbabwe, and Iraq, among others, attest. Contrary to the received wisdom, it would seem *not* to be the case that militias arise only, or even primarily, where state power is weak or contested.[3] Rather, if the historical experience of East Timor is any guide, militias tend to emerge where state actors or agencies decide that they are militarily or politically useful. Militias arise and flourish, for example, where states seek to "subcontract" violence that they are unwilling to entrust to their normal security forces—because of normative and legal constraints, resource considerations, or political calculations.[4] Militias may be encouraged by states, for instance, because they allow state leaders to distance themselves from such violence, creating a veneer of "plausible deniability." States may also encourage the activities of violent militia groups because there is a clear political advantage in creating the appearance of internecine conflict, or even lawlessness, into which the armed forces or some other agency may step to restore order.

The case of East Timor also points to the critical importance of the international political, legal, and normative environment in giving rise to political violence and genocide—and in stopping it. Perhaps most obviously, it suggests that mass violence, especially of the state-sanctioned variety, tends to flourish where the international environment permits it to do so. At the same time, the evidence from East Timor serves as a reminder that one of the few demonstrably successful mechanisms for bringing an end to mass violence, including genocide, is direct military intervention by outside powers. It was, after all, the military assault by Vietnam in 1978–79 that brought an end to the Cambodian genocide, and the NATO bombing of early 1999 that stopped the mass killing and displacement in Kosovo. That is not an argument for "preventive" armed intervention in all cases of political conflict or humanitarian crisis. On the contrary, the events of 1999 in East Timor suggest that armed intervention is likely to be effective in stopping mass violence only under certain unusual historical conditions, specifically: where the violence that is the target of intervention is one-sided, committed overwhelmingly by one group against another that is either unarmed or has foresworn violence; where the principal perpetrators of the violence are constrained by other factors, such as extreme economic vulnerability or political weakness, to accept the intervention; where there is broad international consensus (at least within the Security Council) on the desirability of intervention and its terms; and where the international force is sufficiently robust to defeat the perpetrators swiftly, without being drawn into prolonged combat. Needless to say, it is extremely rare to find all of these conditions together, and that may explain why armed humanitarian interventions, even when they happen, so often fail.

Beyond the issues of whether and under what conditions armed intervention might work to end mass violence, there is the more difficult question of whether such interventions are a good thing. The wisdom and morality of armed intervention have been hotly contested, especially since the 1990s when a number of such actions were actually carried out under NATO or UN auspices, in Bosnia, Kosovo, Sierra Leone, East Timor, Iraq, and Afghanistan. On one side of this debate have been those who take the view that military force is never an appropriate means to achieve humanitarian objectives. Humanitarianism, they contend, must not become bound up with threats or manifestations of military power, because that will necessarily undermine the most fundamental premises of humanitarian work and likely lead to further violence, possibly including crimes against humanity.[5] That argument was especially made with respect to Kosovo (1999) and Afghanistan (2001), where it was felt that humanitarian NGOs had worked far too closely with the military.[6] Opposition to the idea of armed humanitarian intervention has also been expressed by political leaders and scholars worried about the weakening of national sovereignty that has accompanied the expansion of international human rights and humanitarian law since the Second World War. That expansion, they maintain, has served as a cover for a new sort of imperialism, in which relatively weak and powerless states are subjected to intervention by the most powerful acting in the name of the international community under the guise of human rights and humanitarianism.[7]

On the other side of this debate are those who claim that the use of military force may be the only meaningful way to ensure an effective humanitarian response and prevent a government from abusing people under its sovereign control. One reason, they note, is that humanitarian crises are seldom, if ever, solely the result of "natural" disasters, but are to some extent always bound up with questions of political and military power. Under the Genocide Convention and the UN Charter, they argue, the international community has not only a right but also a responsibility to prevent egregious acts of violence by states against their own populations. Just as the critics of armed intervention find support from the defenders of state sovereignty, the proponents of humanitarian intervention tend to be those who see the postwar constraint on state sovereignty as a positive development. They insist that humanitarian intervention—and the whole body of humanitarian and human rights law that underpins it—is *not* simply a means by which powerful states impose their will on the powerless but also a necessary and valuable check on the ability of states to abuse their own citizens.[8]

The East Timor case suggests that the opponents of intervention may be missing the point. For while it is undoubtedly true that the arguments in favor of humanitarian intervention can be easily misused, with disastrous consequences, it does not follow that *all* instances of intervention are morally wrong or examples of neoimperialism. On the contrary, East Timor's experience shows that an absolute or dogmatic opposition to the use of force in the face of egregious violence by a sovereign state can be catastrophic. The point is made most simply by comparing the consequences of international inaction in the late 1970s with the results of intervention in 1999. Was the genocide of the earlier period really preferable to the intervention of 1999? If it tells us anything, then, East Timor's experience indicates that a judgment about the wisdom and morality of intervention needs to be made on the basis of a careful assessment of the conditions in each case.

The evidence from East Timor also underscores the point that while outside states play a crucial role in both facilitating mass violence and stopping it, they do not act alone. International organizations, civil society organizations, and individuals all have the capacity either to subvert or to reinforce such trends. The role of the United Nations warrants special attention in this regard. While it has been widely and justifiably criticized for its failure to act decisively in the face of mass violence and genocide over the years, its role in East Timor suggests the need for a somewhat more nuanced assessment. Perhaps most obviously, the evidence from East Timor serves as a reminder that the United Nations is not a monolithic organization, and even at its highest reaches, its capacity for independent action is always constrained by the views and interests of the most powerful members of the Security Council.[9] At the same time, it shows that when its most powerful member states permit it to do so, the United Nations does in fact have the capacity and authority to act decisively to stop mass violence and impending genocide. Just as important, East Timor's history forces us to accept that whatever the cynics and realists might say, the United Nations as an institution can be a powerful source of inspiration and hope—not to mention a valuable forum for political and legal argument—for people struggling against injustice. It is also a reminder that the whole body of human rights laws, norms, and ideals that emerged in the second half of the twentieth century are not mere empty words—and do not articulate only the values of Western peoples. On the contrary, they have the power to bring about profound historical transformations.

The role of human rights NGOs in this equation is worth noting as well. Some scholars and pundits dismiss them as largely powerless, having an impact only where their concerns and demands happen to coincide with the national interest of powerful liberal states.[10] But others argue that they have served to alter prevailing norms and legal regimes, and to affect the calculus by which states determine their national interests. They point, for example, to the role of NGOs like Amnesty International and Human Rights Watch in stimulating crucial changes in international legal covenants and norms in the direction of greater respect for human rights and acceptance of the idea of universal jurisdiction.[11] The history of East Timor in the last quarter of the twentieth century, and particularly in 1999, tends to confirm the latter view. It also demonstrates that under the right conditions, civil society organizations can indeed play a decisive role in preventing and stopping mass violence and genocide.

The recent history of East Timor also highlights and suggests possible avenues for addressing some of the difficult questions that arise in the pursuit of justice in societies emerging from periods of widespread political violence and human rights abuse. What is the appropriate balance between the demands for truth and justice, and the need for reconciliation and peace? Is it better, for example, to draw a line beneath the abuses of the past in the name of reconciliation or to insist that the perpetrators of violence be brought to justice? These questions have been at the center of a lively debate, particularly since the 1990s. On one side have been the proponents of formal justice who argue that without the attribution of legal responsibility for past violence, the victims of mass violence will remain bitter and the perpetrators will gain a sense of impunity—making future violence much more likely. On those grounds, they have supported the formation of various international ad hoc criminal tribunals—for the former Yugoslavia, Rwanda, Sierra Leone, Cambodia, and East Timor—and the International Criminal Court. An article of faith within the international human rights community, this position has also found considerable support among many ordinary people in societies emerging from conflict and violence—especially those who have suffered grievous harm during the years of violence. Not surprisingly, such arguments have been resisted by political and military leaders seeking to avoid criminal liability for past crimes against humanity committed on their watch, and by some who sincerely believe it would be better turn the page rather than reopen the wounds of the past.

Increasingly since the 1990s, this debate has been played out in the context of national truth commissions formed in the aftermath of periods of extreme conflict and violence.[12] By the early twenty-first century, such commissions had been, or were in the process of being, established in at least two dozen countries, including El Salvador, South Africa, Rwanda, Argentina, Chile, Haiti, Sierra Leone, Peru, East Timor, and Indonesia. Originally inspired by the idea that truth telling and reconciliation were essential foundations for the process of healing and the development of a healthy postconflict society, in the past two decades truth commissions have become the site of wrangling over the relative weight that should be given to justice and reconciliation. Some early experiments such as South Africa's Truth and Reconciliation Commission, while doing an exemplary job of establishing the truth about the nature of the apartheid regime, have been criticized for leaning too heavily in the direction of truth at the expense of justice—mainly by granting amnesty to perpetrators in exchange for their testimony. While learning from such experiences, later commissions have nevertheless found it difficult to move too far in the direction of providing a judicial remedy for past crimes, largely because of resistance from state officials and former perpetrators who fear that they might be implicated.

The experience of East Timor since 1999 suggests that reconciliation and peace, while of course desirable, will remain elusive in the absence of justice. That experience also makes clear, however, that there are serious impediments to the pursuit of justice even in the most egregious cases. The difficulty in seeking justice for past crimes is especially acute in countries that remain dependent on the economic and technical assistance of powerful states, and vulnerable to military threats from their neighbors. Ironically perhaps, the greatest single obstacle to the pursuit of justice in such circumstances is the unwillingness of powerful states to share the substantial political and financial burden that is required to mount credible criminal proceedings. A further obstacle lies in the fact that those states whose support is vital to the successful prosecution of crimes against humanity, including genocide, may themselves be complicit in the crimes that are to be prosecuted. How and under whose jurisdiction shall their responsibility be judged?

Finally, and perhaps most important, East Timor's history highlights the critical role of individuals and of historical contingency in shaping the character and duration of mass violence and genocide, and their aftermath. It shows that notwithstanding the powerful historical forces that structure such violence, the actions and decisions of ordinary people can substantially alter its patterns and character. It is this historically contingent quality of mass violence and genocide that makes any effort to locate their precise historical, social, or political causes such a difficult task, and ultimately dooms any effort to generalize too broadly about the mechanisms by which they might be prevented or brought to an end. But it is also this quality that leaves room for hope that when genocide or mass violence appear inevitable, something might yet be done to stop them.

NOTES

CHAPTER ONE: INTRODUCTION

1. From June to September 1999, I served as a political affairs officer at the UN Mission in East Timor (UNAMET) headquarters in Dili. I returned to East Timor in November 1999 to assist with international human rights investigations.

2. Among those who described the events in East Timor in early September as genocide were Xanana Gusmão, Bishop Belo, José Ramos-Horta, and Vatican foreign minister Archbishop Jean-Louis Tauran.

3. Human rights organizations and others long believed that as many as 200,000 people had died in this period. See, for example, Amnesty International, *East Timor—Violations of Human Rights: Extrajudicial Executions, "Disappearances," Torture, and Political Imprisonment, 1975–1984* (London: Amnesty International, 1985), 6. More recent studies have suggested that the total number of deaths was somewhat lower than these initial estimates. In 2006 East Timor's national Commission for Reception, Truth, and Reconciliation (CAVR) concluded that "at a minimum, during the period 1975–99, 100,000 people died due to hunger and illness in excess of the peacetime baseline," and that an estimated 18,000 more were deliberately killed. The CAVR added that "the total deaths due to hunger and illness in excess of the peacetime baseline could be 103,000, with a possible (but improbable) high-end estimate of 183,300" (CAVR, *Chega!* [Dili: CAVR, 2006], part 6, 13).

4. I am grateful to Samantha Power for this insight (personal communication, March 9, 2007).

5. On the 1965 killings, see Robert Cribb, ed., *The Indonesian Killings, 1965–1966: Studies from Java and Bali*, no. 21 (Clayton, Victoria: Monash Papers on Southeast Asia, 1990); Geoffrey Robinson, *The Dark Side of Paradise: Political Violence in Bali* (Ithaca, NY: Cornell University Press, 1995), esp. chapters 1, 11, 12.

6. For an outline of the growth of the militias and their activities in late 1998 and early 1999, see Amnesty International, "Paramilitary Attacks Jeopardize East Timor's Future" (London: Amnesty International, April 16, 1999); East Timor International Support Center, "Indonesia's Death Squads: Getting Away with Murder," occasional paper no. 2 (Darwin: ETISC, May 1999). On the history of the militias, see Geoffrey Robinson, "People's War: Militias in Indonesia and East Timor," *South East Asia Research* 9, no. 3 (November 2001): 271–318.

7. "Agreement between the Republic of Indonesia and the Portuguese Republic on the Question of East Timor, 5 May 1999," Annex I in United Nations, Secretary-General, "Question of East Timor: Report of the Secretary-General," May 5, 1999.

8. The most sophisticated and complete analysis of the role of the international community in aiding and abetting the violence in 1999, and in the preceding twenty-four years, is Joseph Nevins, *A Not-So-Distant Horror: Mass Violence in East Timor* (Ithaca, NY: Cornell University Press, 2005).

9. In September 1999, Indonesian foreign minister Ali Alatas conceded that some TNI soldiers had joined in the postballot violence, but insisted they were acting alone: "Some rogue elements have been noted. . . . We have had, in the past, difficulties with

rogue elements" (cited in "Island of Death," *Time International* 154, no. 11 [September 20, 1999].)

10. For examples of Indonesian explanations of the violence, see Brigadier General Tono Suratman, *Merah Putih: Pengabdian dan Tanggung Jawab di Timor Timur* (Jakarta: Lembaga Pengkajian Kebudayaan Nusantara, 2000); Zacky Anwar Makarim, Glenny Kairupan, Andreas Sugono, and Ibnu Fatah, *Hari-Hari Terakhir Timor Timur: Sebuah Kesaksian* (Jakarta: PT Sportif Media Informasindo, 2003); Colonel Muh. Nur Muis, "Kecurangan UNAMET Selama Jajak Pendapat di Timor-Timur Pada Tahun 1999" (paper prepared for workshop on Masalah Kecurangan UNAMET, Jakarta, October 6, 2000).

11. Shortly after testifying to the Indonesian Human Rights Commission, Makarim said, "What happened there was part of the culture of people who ran amok, so that was an emotional outburst" (*Jakarta Post*, January 5, 2000).

12. On the history and meaning of the term amok, see John C. Spores, *Running Amok: A Historical Inquiry* (Athens: Ohio University Monograph Series, 1988).

13. A useful summary of these arguments among others, is provided in Helen Fein, "Genocide: A Sociological Perspective," *Current Sociology* 38, no. 1 (Spring 1990): 1–7, 32–50.

14. Robinson, *The Dark Side of Paradise*.

15. See, for example, Alexander L. Hinton, "Why Did You Kill? The Cambodian Genocide and the Dark Side of Face and Honor," *Journal of Asian Studies* 57, no. 1 (February 1998): 93–118.

16. Christopher Browning, *Ordinary Men: Reserve Police Battalion 101 and the Final Solution in Poland* (New York: Harper Perennial, 1998), 159–89. For later elaborations on this argument, see Jan T. Gross, *Neighbors: The Destruction of the Jewish Community in Jedwabne, Poland* (New York: Penguin Books, 2002); Scott Straus, *The Order of Genocide: Race, Power, and War in Rwanda* (Ithaca, NY: Cornell University Press, 2006).

17. Browning, *Ordinary Men*, 189.

18. For variations on this idea, see Paul R. Brass, *Theft of an Idol: Text and Context in the Representation of Collective Violence* (Princeton, NJ: Princeton University Press, 1997); Stanley Tambiah, *Levelling Crowds: Ethnonationalist Conflicts and Collective Violence in South Asia* (Berkeley: University of California Press, 1996).

19. See, for example, Nancy Lee Peluso, "Passing the Red Bowl: Creating Community Identity through Violence in West Kalimantan, 1967–1997," in *Violent Conflicts in Indonesia: Analysis, Representation, Resolution*, ed. Charles Coppel, 106–28 (New York: Routledge, 2006).

20. "The Kopassus-Militia Alliance," *Tapol Bulletin*, November 1999.

21. This claim was made by, among others, Nemesio Lopes de Carvalho against the background of official attempts to arrest the Aitarak militia leader Eurico Guterres and bring charges against other militia members. See "Habibie Perintahkan Sapu Rata," *Tempo*, October 18, 2000.

22. On the evidence and conclusions about criminal responsibility, see below; Geoffrey Robinson, *East Timor 1999: Crimes against Humanity. A Report Commissioned by the UN Office of the High Commissioner for Human Rights* (Jakarta: Elsam and Hak, 2006).

23. Benjamin Valentino, *Final Solutions: Mass Killing and Genocide in the Twentieth Century* (Ithaca, NY: Cornell University Press, 2004).

24. Straus argues, for example, that the nature of state institutions in Rwanda was one of three critical factors that drove the 1994 genocide. In particular, he notes the considerable capacity of the Rwandan state to mobilize civilians to carry out official policy (*The Order of Genocide*, 8).

25. A growing body of literature has stressed the link between war and genocide. See, for example, Straus, *The Order of Genocide*; Browning, *Ordinary Men*; Manus I. Midlarsky, *The Killing Trap: Genocide in the Twentieth Century* (Cambridge: Cambridge University Press, 2005).

26. Some recent scholarship has raised doubt about the link between authoritarianism and genocide. For instance, Straus argues that the "Rwandan state capacity to enforce decisions and mobilize the citizenry was critical to the outcome, but an authoritarian regime was not" (*The Order of Genocide*, 11).

27. See, for example, John T. Sidel, *Riots, Pogroms, and Jihad: Religious Violence in Indonesia* (Ithaca, NY: Cornell University Press, 2006); Gerry van Klinken, *Communal Violence and Democratization in Indonesia: Small Town Wars* (London: Routledge, 2007); Jacques Bertrand, *Nationalism and Ethnic Conflict in Indonesia* (New York: Cambridge University Press, 2004).

28. Referring to the Soviet Union under Vladimir Ilyich Lenin and Joseph Stalin, Nazi Germany, Cambodia under the Khmer Rouge, and Serbia during the Bosnian war, Weitz writes: "If these movements and regimes envisaged distinctive utopias, they shared a common orientation in their determination to remake fundamentally the societies and states they had either inherited or conquered. . . . The effort to transform the very composition of the population required a powerful state that could unleash its security forces and mobilize populations to do the work of exclusions and genocides" (*A Century of Genocide: Utopias of Race and Nation* [Princeton, NJ: Princeton University Press, 2003], 237).

29. Straus has also taken issue with this argument, noting that the leaders who instigated the genocide in Rwanda "did so primarily to win a civil war, not to radically restructure society" (*The Order of Genocide*, 11).

30. That conclusion is broadly consistent with a wider scholarship suggesting a close link between nationalism and mass killing. See, for example, Michael Mann, *The Dark Side of Democracy: Explaining Ethnic Cleansing* (New York: Cambridge University Press, 2004).

31. See, for example, Nevins, *A Not-So-Distant Horror*.

32. On this point see, for instance, Noam Chomsky, "East Timor, the United States, and International Responsibility: 'Green Light' for War Crimes," in *Bitter Flowers, Sweet Flowers: East Timor, Indonesia, and the World Community*, ed. Richard Tanter, Mark Selden, and Stephen Shalom (New York: Rowman and Littlefield, 2001), 127–47.

33. See, for example, Samantha Power, "*A Problem From Hell*": *America and the Age of Genocide* (New York: Basic Books, 2002).

34. See United Nations, *Report of the Independent Inquiry into the Actions of the United Nations during the 1994 Genocide in Rwanda* (New York: United Nations, December 15, 1999); United Nations, Secretary-General, *Report of the Secretary-General Pursuant to General Assembly Resolution 53/55, 1998: The Fall of Srebrenica* (New York: United Nations, November 15, 1999); United Nations, *Report of the Panel on United Nations Peace Operations* (New York: United Nations: August 17, 2000).

35. Gross, *Neighbors*, xxi. Browning makes a similar case in *Ordinary Men*: "The reserve policemen [who killed some fifteen hundred Jews in a Polish village in summer 1942] faced choices, and most of them committed terrible deeds. But those who killed cannot be absolved by the notion that anyone in the same situation would have done as they did. For even among them, some refused to kill and others stopped killing. Human responsibility is ultimately an individual matter" (188).

36. See, for example, David Webster, "Non-State Diplomacy: East Timor, 1975–99," *Portuguese Studies Review* 11, no. 1 (Fall–Winter 2003): 1–28.

37. See, for instance, Geoffrey Robertson, *Crimes against Humanity: The Struggle for Global Justice* (New York: New Press, 2000).

38. Power, *A Problem From Hell*, xviii, xxi; Samantha Power, "Increasing the Cost of Genocide," in *The New Killing Fields: Massacre and the Politics of Intervention*, ed. Nicolaus Mills and Kira Brunner (New York: Basic Books, 2002), 245–64.

CHAPTER TWO: COLONIAL LEGACIES

1. For summaries of those early accounts, see Gonçalo Pimenta de Castro, *Timor: Subsidios Para a Sua História* (Lisbon: Agência Geral das Colónias, 1944), 13–14, 159–60. Also see Hélio A. Esteves Felgas, *Timor Português* (Lisbon: Agência Geral do Ultramar, 1956), 180–82, 211.

2. Alfred Russel Wallace, *The Malay Archipelago: The Land of the Orang-utan and the Bird of Paradise* (London: Macmillan and Co., 1869), 307.

3. C. R. Boxer, *Fidalgos in the Far East, 1550–1770* (London: Oxford University Press, 1968), 189.

4. Even when not preparing for battle, the anthropologist H. O. Forbes wrote, a Timorese "has always a knife or short sword of some description, and is rarely without a gun, flintlock or percussion" ("On Some Tribes of the Island of Timor," *Journal of the Anthropological Institute of Great Britain and Ireland* 13 [1884]: 409).

5. Cited in Jill Jolliffe, *East Timor, Nationalism, and Colonialism* (St Lucia: University of Queensland Press, 1978), 30. See also de Castro, *Timor: Subsidios Para a Sua História*, 13.

6. Captain Francisco Elvaim, cited in Katharine Davidson, "The Portuguese Colonisation of Timor: The Final Stage, 1850–1892" (PhD diss., University of New South Wales, 1994), 196. Forbes's late nineteenth-century description leaves a similar impression: "It is carried on mostly by the offensive army pillaging and ravaging all they can lay their hands on, robbing every undefended dwelling, ruthlessly decapitating helpless men, women, and children, and even infants" ("On Some Tribes," 423).

7. On the history of Portuguese involvement in Timor, see de Castro, *Timor: Subsidios Para a Sua História*; Felgas, *Timor Português*, esp. 215–99; A. Pinto Correia, *Timor de Lés a Lés* (Lisbon: Agência Geral das Colónias, 1944); Boxer, *Fidalgos in the Far East*, 174–98; C. R. Boxer, "Portuguese Timor: A Rough Island History: 1550–1960," *History Today* 10, no. 5 (May 1960): 349–55.

8. Boxer, "Portuguese Timor," 354.

9. Referring to the eighteenth century, Felgas writes, "The wars with the native kingdoms . . . were frequent and destructive, although the Portuguese continued to win the day using the same policy as at the start—personal influence and the support of certain kingdoms against the others" (*Timor Português*, 305). See also de Castro, *Timor: Subsidios Para a Sua História*, 159, 198, 213.

10. The rebellion, led by the liurai of Manufahi, Dom Boaventura, was crushed with the aid of Timorese loyal to the liurai of Lacló, Dom Luis dos Reis de Noronha. For a detailed Portuguese account of the rebellion, see de Castro, *Timor: Subsidios Para a Sua História*, 123–37. See also Davidson, "The Portuguese Colonisation of Timor," chapter 8.

11. For a summary of the Portuguese administrative efforts in this period, see Felgas, *Timor Português*, 307–21; de Castro, *Timor: Subsidios Para a Sua História*, 196–98.

12. United Nations, "Decolonization: Issue on East Timor," August 1976, 7.

13. Wallace, *The Malay Archipelago*, 295, 307.

14. On the coffee plantations, see Felgas, *Timor Português*, 459–66; de Castro, *Timor:*

Subsidios Para a Sua História, 78–79, 173–74. In 1953 the colony had 42 schools, in which 6,292 elementary students and 107 high school students were enrolled (Felgas, *Timor Português*, 377–83); at the same time, it had 1 hospital, 6 district clinics, 47 health posts, and 12 doctors (ibid., 359–74).

15. "Timor suffered severely . . . all the towns and villages were destroyed, the plantations devastated, and many people killed" (Boxer, "Portuguese Timor," 355). For a Portuguese account of the Japanese invasion and occupation, see Felgas, *Timor Português*, 288–97.

16. According to the 1950 census, there were only 568 Europeans in Portuguese Timor at that time. That figure did not change significantly in the next two decades. See Felgas, *Timor Português*, 339.

17. Republic of Indonesia, "East Timor: Building for the Future" (Jakarta: Department of Foreign Affairs, July 1992).

18. United Nations, "Decolonization: Issue on East Timor," 7. For a summary of the changing political arrangements under which Timor was governed, see de Castro, *Timor: Subsidios Para a Sua História*, 84–85.

19. Benedict Anderson has argued that the increasingly aggressive colonialism of the late nineteenth and early twentieth centuries—the "explosive combination of development, education, and repression"—was an important stimulant to the emergence of nationalism in Indonesia and other colonial settings. See Benedict Anderson, "Gravel in Jakarta's Shoes," in *The Spectre of Comparisons: Nationalism, Southeast Asia, and the World* (London: Verso Press, 1998), 131, 134.

20. J. Stephen Hoadley writes that in 1975, the colonial army in Portuguese Timor numbered roughly two thousand soldiers, "mostly conscripts" ("The Future of Portuguese Timor," Occasional Paper no. 27 (Singapore: Institute of Southeast Asian Studies, March 1975), 11. Ken Conboy notes that three full European companies (of 120 men each) were returned to Portugal in early 1975, leaving a colonial force of roughly two thousand regular troops, mostly Timorese (*Kopassus: Inside Indonesia's Special Forces* [Jakarta: Equinox, 2003], 209).

21. The official name of the secret police changed several times, but it was generally known in Timor as the PIDE, or DGS (Direcção Geral de Segurança, or General Security Directorate), the name it assumed in 1969.

22. Bernardina Fernanda Alves, quoted in Peter Carey, "Third World Colonialism, the *Geração Foun*, and the Birth of a New Nation: Indonesia through East Timorese Eyes, 1975–1999," *Indonesia* 76 (October 2003): 31–32.

23. The moradores were a more permanent and better-trained formation than the arraias, but the latter were more numerous. Though officially designated as second-line troops, in fact they formed "the strongest first line of defence for the colonial community and its outlying *posto*" (Davidson, "The Portuguese Colonisation of Timor," 136). On the organization of the moradores and for a selection of photographs, see Felgas, *Timor Português*, 183–85. See also de Castro, *Timor: Subsidios Para a Sua História*, 198, 213.

24. As Davidson writes, "The actual defeat of Manufahi's warriors was effected not just by Portuguese use of superior military technology but also by the enormous force of indigenous auxiliaries who had swelled the government ranks" ("The Portuguese Colonisation of Timor," 20). For a Portuguese account of the Manufahi revolt and its suppression, see de Castro, *Timor: Subsidios Para a Sua História*, 123–37.

25. Davidson recounts dozens of instances of this pattern during the late nineteenth and early twentieth centuries (see "The Portuguese Colonisation of Timor," 60, 143, 145, 147, 155, 156, 165, 171, 182, 184–85, 195, 200, 205, 256, 259). De Castro's heroic ac-

counts of Portuguese pacification campaigns of this period are replete with references to the bravery and skill of indigenous auxiliary forces (see *Timor: Subsidios Para a Sua História*, 91–105, 123–52, 198–200, 213; see also René Pélissier, *Le Crocodile et les Portugais* [Orgeval, France: privately printed, 1996]).

26. Cited in Jolliffe, *East Timor*, 45.

27. Felgas, *Timor Português*, 185.

28. See Davidson, "The Portuguese Colonisation of Timor," 22, 31–32, 51. The general pattern of using native forces to maintain security was even more pronounced in Timor than in other Portuguese colonies. Pélissier, *Le Crocodile et les Portugais*, 313.

29. A government directive of 1870 referred explicitly to the economic motive for using native auxiliaries: "It would, therefore, be better to supply the loyal kings [liurai] with powder and shot and let them pursue the war freely in their own manner. . . . Organisation of expeditions from Portugal or other colonies would involve expenses the Public Treasury cannot afford" (cited in ibid., 150).

30. Ibid., 207.

31. The strategy was not without its dangers, as the Portuguese discovered in 1897 when a group of moradores from Motael, angered by a perceived insult to their liurai, killed the governor (see ibid., 166–69).

32. The reality that East Timorese were mobilized by both sides during the war is captured in a photograph of a young Timorese *criado* or "guide" taken in December 1945 and published in Dunn, *Timor*, 128. The boy is dressed in Australian kit and is carrying a rifle. The caption notes, however, that he "had earlier been speared by pro-Japanese Timorese."

33. On East Timor's early experiences with Catholicism, see Arnold Kohen, *From the Place of the Dead: The Epic Struggles of Bishop Belo of East Timor* (New York: St. Martin's Press, 1999), chapter 2. See also Felgas, *Timor Português*, 153–59, 383–87.

34. The figure is from church records, and is cited in Robert Archer, "The Catholic Church in East Timor," in *East Timor at the Crossroads: The Forging of a Nation*, ed. Peter Carey and G. Carter Bentley (Honolulu: University of Hawaii Press, 1995), 121. In 1956, the figure was just sixty thousand, or fewer than 15 percent of the population at the time (Felgas, *Timor Português*, 384).

35. Of the forty-two schools in Portuguese Timor in 1952, thirty-three were run by the missions (Felgas, *Timor Português*, 381–83). On the role of the Catholic missions in education, see de Castro, *Timor: Subsidios Para a Sua História*, 201–3.

36. Luis Cardoso, who attended the school at Soibada as a teenager, writes that by the 1960s, it "had come to be seen as a privileged place for teachers and taught alike . . . a bastion of Portugal in the very heart of Timor." Nonetheless, a number of prominent nationalists were Soibada students, including Ramos-Horta and Xavier do Amaral, both of Fretilin. Other future political figures who attended the school included Francisco Lopes da Cruz, Domingos de Oliveira, and Paulo Pires, all of the UDT. The seminary at Dare was run by a Timorese Jesuit and was, according to Cardoso, a retreat beyond the reach of the PIDE. See Luis Cardoso, *The Crossing: A Story of East Timor* (London: Granta Books, 2000), 39–40, 58–63.

37. In 1884, for example, Forbes wrote that "the color of skin, form of head, features of face, character and distribution of hair I met with in every variety, and amount of comminglement" ("On Some of the Tribes of the Island of Timor," 406).

38. Felgas, *Timor Português*, 339.

39. See Cardoso, *The Crossing*, 50, 56, 86.

40. For a succinct overview of the genesis of East Timor's political parties, see John

G. Taylor, *Indonesia's Forgotten War: The Hidden History of East Timor* (London: Zed Books, 1991), 25–45.

41. John G. Taylor, "The Emergence of a Nationalist Movement in East Timor," in *East Timor at the Crossroads: The Forging of a Nation*, ed. Peter Carey and G. Carter Bentley (Honolulu: University of Hawaii Press, 1995), 36.

42. According to Ramos-Horta, Mário had been the chair of the ANP in Portuguese Timor (*Funu: The Unfinished Saga of East Timor* [Trenton, NJ: Red Sea Press, 1987], 29).

43. See "Interview with Mário Carrascalão," *Indonesia* 76 (October 2003): 1–22. A second Carrascalão brother, João, who had studied in Angola and Switzerland, and worked as chief of the colonial Geographical and Cadastral Services, emerged as the leader of the UDT forces during the civil war of 1975. He went into exile in Australia shortly after the invasion, but remained as a UDT leader. See Ramos-Horta, *Funu*, 31.

44. With da Cruz in the ministry was another early UDT leader, Domingos de Oliveira. Like da Cruz, de Oliveira had attended the school at Soibada before going to Macau for advanced studies (Cardoso, *The Crossing*, 100, 104).

45. A small group of the party's founders had been meeting secretly before April 1974 to discuss the country's political future. They included Ramos-Horta, Mari Alkatiri, Nicolau Lobato, and Justino Mota. See Ramos-Horta, *Funu*, 34.

46. On Fretilin's origins, see Taylor, "The Emergence of a Nationalist Movement," 33–36; Ramos-Horta, *Funu*, 29–39.

47. Ramos-Horta writes that this group, which included Abílio Araújo and the poet Borja da Costa, "began to influence the movement toward a more radical outlook" (*Funu*, 38).

48. Fretilin, "What Is Fretilin? The Revolutionary Front of Independent East Timor Explains Its Aims in a Question and Answer Format" (Sydney: Campaign for an Independent East Timor, 1974).

49. Ramos-Horta, *Funu*, 36.

50. Gusmão's autobiography provides a rich and surprisingly unvarnished account of Fretilin's early years. See Sarah Niner, ed., *To Resist Is to Win! The Autobiogrgaphy of Xanana Gusmão* (Richmond, Victoria: Aurora Books, 2000).

51. Cardoso writes that Gusmão was "a goal-keeper and ex-seminarian, who was too busy making up sonnets to actually stop any goals" (*The Crossing*, 58).

52. Two other parties were formed at this time, the Klibur Oan Timor Aswain (KOTA) and Partido Trabalhista, but neither had any significant support.

53. Hoadley, who interviewed Apodeti leaders in late 1974, says that they acknowledged receiving such funds ("The Future of Portuguese Timor," 5).

54. Helen Hill, *The Timor Story*, 2nd ed. (Fitzroy, Victoria: Timor Information Service, 1976), 5.

55. Cardoso, *The Crossing*, 102.

56. For a useful summary of Abílio Soares's role in the Indonesian invasion and occupation, and the 1999 violence, see Richard Tanter, Gerry van Klinken, and Desmond Ball, eds., *Masters of Terror: Indonesia's Military and Violence in East Timor* (New York: Rowman and Littlefield, 2006), 122–25.

57. Ramos-Horta, *Funu*, 33.

58. By one estimate, some 90 percent of the elected liurai were members or supporters of Fretilin. Helen Hill, "Fretilin: The Origins, Ideologies, and Strategies of a Nationalist Movement in East Timor" (MA thesis, Monash University, 1978), 122–23.

59. This argument is developed in some depth in Taylor, *Indonesia's Forgotten War*. For

a succinct summary of Fretilin's programs, see "Program of the Revolutionary Front of Independent East Timor," in Fretilin, "What Is Fretilin?"

60. Hill, *The Timor Story,* 5.

61. The coalition was formally agreed to on January 21, 1975. Ramos-Horta claims to have been the main Fretilin advocate of the coalition. On the UDT side, Ramos-Horta says that the principal supporters of the coalition were the Carrascalão brothers, while Lopes da Cruz opposed it. Ramos-Horta, *Funu,* 52.

62. On the August coup, see Taylor, *Indonesia's Forgotten War,* 50–54.

63. Indonesian press reports provided a predictably enthusiastic portrait of these developments, while making no mention of official involvement in orchestrating them. See, for example: *Suara Karya,* September 11, 1975.

64. Following a meeting in May 1974, Indonesian foreign minister Adam Malik wrote to Ramos-Horta giving his assurance that Indonesia had no territorial ambitions in East Timor and that it would respect East Timor's right to self-determination. For an account of the meeting and excerpts from Malik's letter, see Ramos-Horta, *Funu,* 41–44. Indonesian authorities, including President Suharto, reiterated that position frequently over the next year. See, for example, official statements reported in the Indonesian press: *Kompas,* February 26 and September 11, 1975; *Pelita,* February 28 and March 19, 1975; *Angkatan Bersenjata,* April 7, 1975; *Suara Karya,* June 18, 1975.

65. Benny Murdani's biographer claims that Operasi Komodo was not established until January 1975, but by most accounts it was set up some time in the third quarter of 1974. See Julius Pour, *Moerdani: Profil Prajurit Negarawan* (Jakarta: Yayasan Kejuangan Panglima Besar Soedirman, 1993), 381; Conboy, *Kopassus,* 197.

66. Conboy, *Kopassus,* 196.

67. Conboy writes that part of Murtopo's operation involved "helping underwrite Apodeti and channeling limited financial incentives to key UDT leaders" (ibid., 198). In September 1974, Radio Kupang began to broadcast reports into East Timor portraying Fretilin as communist. In October, stories of a similar kind began to appear in the Indonesian army newspaper, *Berita Yudha,* and other papers. See Hill, *The Timor Story,* 5–6.

68. Grant Evans, "Portuguese Timor," *New Left Review* 91 (May–June 1975): 78. The headline of an October 2, 1974, story in the paper *Sinar Harapan,* for example, declared "Fretilin Movement Supported and Financed by Communist Chinese."

69. Conboy, *Kopassus,* 198; United Nations, "Decolonization: Issue on East Timor," 15–16.

70. Conboy, *Kopassus,* 205–6.

71. For details of the links between the UDT and the Indonesian military, see Dunn, *Timor,* chapter 8.

72. Hill, *The Timor Story,* 10.

73. Conboy and others argue that the UDT coup was most likely the result of the Jakarta talks (see Conboy, *Kopassus,* 208).

74. The Kopassandha (Komando Pasukan Sandi Yudha, or Special Warfare Force Command) was the forerunner of the notorious Kopassus (Komando Pasukan Khusus, or Special Forces Command).

75. Murdani was appointed assistant for intelligence on February 17, 1975. For his own account of these covert operations, see Pour, *Moerdani,* 387–89. For a fuller account, told from the perspective of those directly involved in combat, see Conboy, *Kopassus,* 198–221.

76. Conboy, *Kopassus,* 199.

77. Ibid., 207.

78. These operations were coordinated under the Joint Task Force Command (Komando Tugas Gabungan, or Kogasgab) established on August 31, 1975 (ibid., 223).

79. The fullest account of the killings and the subsequent controversy is Jill Jolliffe, *Cover-up: The Inside Story of the Balibo Five* (Melbourne: Scribe Publications, 2001). See also CAVR, *Chega!* chapter 7, 31–34.

80. Pour, *Moerdani*, 388.

81. Conboy, *Kopassus*, 211.

82. See, for example, the official statements reported in the Indonesian press: *Berita Yudha*, October 23 and 31, 1975; *Kompas*, November 12, 1975.

83. See Tanter, van Klinken, and Ball, *Masters of Terror*, 151–52.

84. Robert Lawless, "The Indonesian Takeover of East Timor," *Asian Survey* 16, no. 10 (October 1976): 952. The army members' decision to join Fretilin may have been influenced by the fact that one of the most senior Timorese officers among them, Lieutenant Rogerio Lobato, was the brother of leading Fretilin figure Nicolao Lobato.

85. For some sense of the tone and substance of this criticism, see official Indonesian statements reported in *Sinar Harapan*, August 30, 1975; *Berita Yudha*, September 17 and 29, 1975.

86. Republic of Indonesia, "East Timor: Building for the Future," ii.

87. The best account of the role played by Western powers at this time is Brad Simpson, "'Illegally and Beautifully': The United States, the Indonesian Invasion of East Timor, and the International Community, 1974–1976," *Cold War History* 5, no. 3 (August 2005): 281–315.

88. See, for example, ibid., 286–87, 292–94. A July 1975 cable from the British Embassy in Jakarta to Whitehall concluded that "it is in Britain's interests that Indonesia should absorb the territory as quickly as possible, and that if it comes to the crunch in the UN we should keep our heads down" (cited in ibid., 290n47).

89. The words are those of an Australian foreign affairs official who briefed journalists after the meeting (cited in Peter Hastings, "Whitlam Treads Dangerous Ground in Timor," *Sydney Morning Herald*, September 16, 1974). Hoadley notes that this agreement "seems to have been read in Indonesia as a blanket pledge of non-interference in the Timor-Indonesia relationship" ("The Future of Portuguese Timor," 22).

90. Cited in Hill, *The Timor Story*, 12. Other Western states—including the United States, the United Kingdom, and New Zealand—likewise took the position that an independent East Timor would not be "viable" and might therefore cause regional instability (Simpson, "Illegally and Beautifully," 288).

91. In November 2007, an Australian coroner found that the five had been deliberately killed by Indonesian Special Forces on orders from then Captain Yunus Yosfiah and that the killings could constitute war crimes. Associated Press, "Australian Coroner Recommends War Crime Probe in Death of Five Journalists," November 16, 2007.

92. Donald Greenlees, "Complicity Shown in Timor Takeover," *International Herald Tribune*, December 1, 2005.

93. In fact, as early as mid-1974, the Ford administration took the view that relations with Indonesia were the priority, an Indonesian takeover of East Timor was more or less inevitable, and the United States should do nothing to stand in the way (Simpson, "Illegally and Beautifully").

94. "The problem," Suharto explained to Ford, "is that those who want independence are those who are Communist-influenced" (United States, White House, Memorandum of Conversation between President Ford and President Suharto, July 5, 1975, National Security Archive, "East Timor Revisited: Ford, Kissinger, and the Indonesian

Invasion, 1975–76," document 1, available at http://www.gwu.edu/~nsarchiv/NSAEBB/NSAEBB62/).

95. Cited in Ramos-Horta, *Funu*, 79. Even after July, Suharto remained cautious, and in August he twice vetoed an invasion. According to Central Intelligence Agency briefs from August 1975, his caution reflected his concern over U.S. and international reaction to an invasion (Simpson, "Illegally and Beautifully," 291n55).

96. As Simpson writes, "The President's response was doubtless encouraging to the hawks in Jakarta seeking to convince Suharto to agree to an open invasion of East Timor" ("Illegally and Beautifully," 290).

97. Hoadley, who interviewed Fretilin and UDT leaders (do Amaral and de Oliveira) in December 1974, said that he "found their positions virtually identical" ("The Future of Portuguese Timor," 13).

98. Ramos-Horta, *Funu*, 55.

99. There were, of course, exceptions to this rule. For reasons discussed in later chapters, by 1999 a number of early advocates of Indonesian rule, especially from the UDT but also from Apodeti, had decided to throw in their lot with the proindependence movement.

100. See, for example, the testimonies of Ilidio Maria de Jesus, Florentino de Jesus Martins, Mateus Soares, Alexander da Costa Araújo, and António Amado J. R. Guterres in CAVR, "Massacres: National Public Hearing, 19–21 November 2003" (Dili: CAVR, 2005), 14–24.

Chapter Three: Invasion and Genocide

1. In fact, some estimates placed the number of dead at two hundred thousand. See Amnesty International, *East Timor—Violations of Human Rights: Extrajudicial Executions, "Disappearances," Torture, and Political Imprisonment, 1975–1984* (London: Amnesty International, 1985), 6. As noted earlier, however, more recent studies have suggested that the number of deaths in this period was closer to a hundred thousand. See CAVR, *Chega!* (Dili: CAVR, 2006), part 6, 13.

2. The army's changing role in this period is carefully examined in Ruth McVey, "The Post-Revolutionary Transformation of the Indonesian Army, Part I," *Indonesia* 11 (April 1971): 131–76; Ruth McVey, "The Post-Revolutionary Transformation of the Indonesian Army, Part II," *Indonesia* 13 (April 1972): 147–81. See also Harold Crouch, *The Army and Politics in Indonesia* (Ithaca, NY: Cornell University Press, 1978), chapters 1–3.

3. The best summary of the military role in the 1965 coup and its aftermath is Crouch, *The Army and Politics in Indonesia*, chapters 4–8.

4. On the 1965 killings, see Robert Cribb, ed., *The Indonesian Killings, 1965–1966: Studies from Java and Bali*, no. 21 (Clayton, Victoria: Monash Papers on Southeast Asia, 1990); Geoffrey Robinson, *The Dark Side of Paradise: Political Violence in Bali* (Ithaca, NY: Cornell University Press, 1995), esp. chapters 1, 11, 12.

5. See Robinson, *The Dark Side of Paradise*, 282–86; Bradley R. Simpson, *Economists with Guns: Authoritarian Development and U.S.-Indonesian Relations, 1960–1968* (Stanford, CA: Stanford University Press, 2008). For a sampling of the documentary record, see National Security Archive, "CIA Stalling State Department Histories on Indonesia," available at http://www.gwu.edu/~nsarchiv/NSAEBB/NSAEBB52/#FRUS.

6. On the origins and implications of the territorial command structure, see Bob

Lowry, *Indonesian Defence Policy and the Indonesian Armed Forces* (Canberra: Strategic and Defence Studies Centre, Australian National University, 1993), 37, 74–78.

7. For much of the New Order period, the country was divided into ten Regional Military Commands (Kodam). Each Kodam was further divided into a series of successively smaller geographically defined command units known as Resort Military Commands (Korem), District Military Commands (Kodim), and Subdistrict Military Commands (Koramil). At the village level, the armed forces were represented by a noncommissioned officer known as a Babinsa.

8. For details of the history, size, and mission of Kopassus and Kostrad , see Lowry, *Indonesian Defence Policy*, 40, 81–84, 93.

9. The best study of Indonesia's military intelligence system is Richard Tanter, "Intelligence Agencies and Third World Militarization: A Case Study of Indonesia, 1966–1989" (PhD diss., Monash University, 1991).

10. This doctrine is outlined in Departemen Pertahanan-Keamanan Republik Indonesia, *Doktrin Pertahanan Keamanan Negara* (Jakarta, 1991). On the history and political implications of the doctrine, see Geoffrey Robinson, "Indonesia: On a New Course?" in *Coercion and Governance: The Declining Political Role of the Military in Asia*, ed. Muthiah Alagappa (Stanford, CA: Stanford University Press, 2001), 226–56. See also Abdul Haris Nasution, *Fundamentals of Guerrilla Warfare* (New York: Praeger, 1965).

11. On that history, see Geoffrey Robinson, "People's War: Militias in East Timor and Indonesia," *South East Asia Research* 9, no. 3 (November 2001): 271–318.

12. As Benedict Anderson writes, "An apparatus of repression was created which, because it was shielded from the view not merely of the outside world, but of most Indonesians, soon stood above the law. Anything went: systematic torture, disappearances, timeless imprisonments, and so forth" ("Gravel in Jakarta's Shoes," in *The Spectre of Comparisons: Nationalism, Southeast Asia, and the World* [London: Verso Press, 1998], 134).

13. Kepolisian Negara Republik Indonesia, "Tinjauan Strategis Pembangunan Kekuatan dan Kemampuan Komando Antar Resort Kepolisian 15.3 Timor Timur, Tahun 1978–1983" (Dili, March 1978), 6.

14. Soeharto, *Pikiran, Ucapan, dan Tindakan Saya* (Jakarta: PT Citra Lamtoro Gung Persada, 1988), 297–98. Suharto made a similar pitch during his meeting with U.S. president Ford on July 5, 1975. See United States, White House, Memorandum of Conversation between President Ford and President Suharto, July 5, 1975, National Security Archive, "East Timor Revisited: Ford, Kissinger, and the Indonesian Invasion, 1975–76," document 1, available at http://www.gwu.edu/~nsarchiv/NSAEBB/NSAEBB62/).

15. See, for example, *Kompas*, February 26, September 11, November 12, and December 8, 1975; *Pelita*, February 28 and March 19, 1975; *Angkatan Bersenjata*, April 7, 1975; *Suara Karya*, June 18, 1975. The story about the invasion printed in *Kompas* on December 8, 1975, reportedly reproduced the official press release verbatim. Julius Pour, *Moerdani: Profil Prajurit Negarawan* (Jakarta: Yayasan Kejuangan Panglima Besar Soedirman, 1993), 397.

16. I am grateful to an anonymous reader of the manuscript for this suggestion. On the unusual power of Catholic officers and intellectuals under the New Order, see John T. Sidel, *Riots, Pogroms, and Jihad: Religious Violence in Indonesia* (Ithaca, NY: Cornell University Press, 2006).

17. In his memoirs, Suharto alluded to the threat of instability in his justification for the invasion. "Indonesia," he wrote, "could not possibly remain a passive onlooker in the middle of the turmoil in the area, which had disrupted and could pose a threat to our

territorial integrity" (Soeharto, *Pikiran, Ucapan, dan Tindakan Saya*, 298). The same theme runs through virtually all public statements by senior Indonesian officials, from early 1975. See, for example, the statement of Foreign Minister Adam Malik reported in *Pelita*, March 19, 1975. See also the statements of the Indonesian ambassador to the United Nations in 1975, Anwar Sani, recorded in United Nations, "Decolonization: Issue on East Timor," August 1976, 48.

18. Anderson, "Gravel in Jakarta's Shoes," 133.

19. Ibid., 132–33.

20. Grant Evans, "Portuguese Timor," *New Left Review* 91 (May–June 1975): 79. According to an Indonesian press report, a senior Portuguese army officer based in Dili told an Australian journalist in March 1975 that "the troops of Portuguese Timor could put up a little guerrilla resistance in the central mountainous region, but . . . Indonesia could obtain full control in the period of a week" (*Pelita*, March 11, 1975).

21. Asked about Jakarta's East Timor policy by Benedict Anderson in fall 1975, Liem Bian Kie reportedly said with a loud laugh, "Don't you worry. Everything is under control. The whole business will be settled within three weeks" ("East Timor: Some Implications," in *East Timor at the Crossroads: The Forging of a Nation*, ed. Peter Carey and G. Carter Bentley [Honolulu: University of Hawaii Press, 1995], 137).

22. Ken Conboy, *Kopassus: Inside Indonesia's Special Forces* (Jakarta: Equinox, 2003), 246.

23. Pour, *Moerdani*, 400. Murdani sought to distance himself from responsibility for the disaster, saying that it stemmed from the army's decision not to adopt his advice that the invasion should be a small, commando-style operation (ibid., 389–96).

24. The assembly's petition and Law 7/76 are reprinted in Machmuddin Noor et al., *Lahirnya Propinsi Timor Timur* (Jakarta: Badan Penerbit Almanak Republik Indonesia, 1977), 61, 235–37.

25. Citing senior Indonesian army sources, Western intelligence reports confirmed that Fretilin controlled much of the interior during this period. In 1976, for example, Murdani told the U.S. Embassy in Jakarta that the army still controlled less than half, and perhaps as little as 20 percent, of East Timor's territory and population. Brad Simpson, "'Illegally and Beautifully': The United States, the Indonesian Invasion of East Timor, and the International Community, 1974–1976," *Cold War History* 5, no. 3 (August 2005): 301.

26. According to a report prepared by Indonesian relief workers in December 1976, "The total population of villages and towns occupied by the Indonesian forces amounts to 150,000 people" ("Indonesian Relief Workers in Timor," *Tribune* [Australia], December 1, 1976).

27. A secret military document from May 1976 outlined plans to reduce troop levels from twenty-five combat battalions in June 1976, to five to six battalions in October (Departemen Pertahanan-Keamanan Republik Indonesia, "Petunjuk-Pelaksanaan, Nomor: Juklak/06/V/1976, tentang Kegiatan di Bidang Operasi Tempur, Tahun 1976–1977," May 17, 1976, 935).

28. See Departemen Pertahanan-Keamanan Republik Indonesia, "Petunjuk-Pelaksanaan, Nomor: Juklak/02/V/1979, tentang Kegiatan Operasi di Daerah Timor Timur Dalam Tahun 1979–1980," May 11, 1979, 799–800.

29. Departemen Pertahanan-Keamanan Republik Indonesia, "Petunjuk-Pelaksanaan, Nomor: Juklak/06/V/1976," 934.

30. Departemen Pertahanan-Keamanan Republik Indonesia, "Keputusan Menteri Pertahanan-Keamanan/Panglima Angkatan Bersenjata, Nomor: Kep/23/X/1978, tentang Normalisasi Penyelenggaraan Pertahanan-Keamanan di Daerah Timor-Timur dan Pembubaran Kodahankam Tim-Tim," October 12, 1978, 218. Similarly, a military plan-

ning document from May 1979 stated that a key operational objective was "the complete destruction of all remaining armed terrorist elements, so that they will have no chance to rebuild in the future" (Departemen Pertahanan-Keamanan Republik Indonesia, "Petunjuk-Pelaksanaan, Nomor: Juklak/02/V/1979," 802).

31. The precise number of troops involved is difficult to establish, but an internal military document from October 1978 lists twenty-nine combat battalions and twenty-six additional combat units of varying sizes. Those figures do not include so-called territorial units and armed auxiliaries, of which there were many thousands at this stage. See Departemen Pertahanan-Keamanan Republik Indonesia, "Keputusan Menteri Pertahanan-Keamanan/Panglima Angkatan Bersenjata, Nomor: Kep/23/X/1978," 222.

32. For a description of the encirclement campaign, see Amnesty International, *East Timor—Violations of Human Rights*, 29. See also CAVR, *Chega!* part 3, 75–82, and chapter 7.3, 37–49.

33. CAVR, *Chega!* part 3, 83–88, and chapter 7.3, 37–49; John G. Taylor, *Indonesia's Forgotten War: The Hidden History of East Timor* (London: Zed Books, 1991), 82–88; Constancio Pinto and Matthew Jardine, *East Timor's Unfinished Struggle: Inside the Timorese Resistance* (Boston: South End Press, 1997), 60–78; Paulino Gama, "The War in the Hills, 1975–1985: A Fretilin Commander Remembers," in *East Timor at the Crossroads: The Forging of a Nation*, ed. Peter Carey and G. Carter Bentley (Honolulu: University of Hawaii Press, 1995), 97–105.

34. Testimony of Edinha, in Michele Turner, *Telling East Timor: Personal Testimonies, 1942–1992* (Kensington: New South Wales University Press, 1992), 109–12.

35. CAVR, *Chega!* chapter 7.3, 42, 49. Resistance leader Gusmão later wrote that: "I regretted moving all those people to Matebian where it was impossible to cater for them" (cited in ibid., chapter 7.3, 42).

36. Ibid., chapter 7.3, 50–51.

37. This figure was given by the U.S. Agency for International Development in late 1979, on the basis of information provided by Indonesian military officials. See United States, Agency for International Development, "Situation Report No. 1, October 19 1979: East Timor, Indonesia—Displaced Persons." Taylor cites an official Indonesian figure of 372,921 people living in resettlement areas as of December 1978 (*Indonesia's Forgotten War*, 90).

38. CAVR, *Chega!* part 3, 83, and chapter 7.3, 52, 54–60.

39. The CAVR provides a list of 139 camps, but says that the real number was probably higher (ibid., chapter 7.3, 61–64).

40. The acronym GPK was widely used during the New Order as a label for groups considered a threat to national security. While often translated as Security Disruptors' Movement, the rhetorical meaning of the term GPK is closer to the English "terrorist." Departemen Pertahanan-Keamanan Republik Indonesia, "Petunjuk-Pelaksanaan, Nomor: Juklak/02/V/1979," 803.

41. Korem 164/Wira Dharma, Seksi Intel, "Petunjuk Teknis tentang Cara Babinsa/ Team Pembina Desa Dalam Memobongkar Jaringan Pendukung GPK," Dili, 1982.

42. Ibid.

43. David Jenkins, "Timor's Arithmetic of Despair," *Far Eastern Economic Review*, September 29, 1978.

44. The Catholic Relief Services program provided humanitarian relief to some 240,000 people, while the ICRC focused on 60,000 people whose condition was considered most grave (CAVR, *Chega!* chapter 7.3, 71, 74; Amnesty International, *East Timor—Violations of Human Rights*, 15).

45. A secret military document from May 1979 boasts of the success of the operations in East Timor, concluding that they had "achieved the objectives that were spelled out by the leadership of the Department of Defense and Security." The document also notes that the "liquidation" of the main resistance leaders in late 1978 and early 1979 had had "a very positive influence on efforts to restore order in East Timor." See Departemen Pertahanan-Keamanan Republik Indonesia, "Petunjuk-Pelaksanaan, Nomor: Juklak/ 02/V/1979," 799.

46. See, for example, Jill Jolliffe, "Starvation Drive against Timor," *Guardian* (London), November 12, 1979; Paul Zach, "Timorese Battle Famine; Relief Officials Compare It to Biafra, Cambodia," *Washington Post*, November 15, 1979; Daniel Southerland, "East Timor's Agony Rivals That of Cambodia," *Christian Science Monitor*, December 17, 1979.

47. See, for example, "East Timor—The Other Famine," *Christian Science Monitor*, December 18, 1979; An Unjust War in East Timor," *New York Times*, December 24, 1979; "No Bleep on the Moral Radar," *Washington Post*, February 2, 1980.

48. In Australia, this work was led by the Australian Council for Overseas Aid and a number of smaller groups. In the United Kingdom, it was undertaken by Tapol, the Catholic Institute for International Relations and Amnesty International. And in the United States, it was spearheaded by the fledgling East Timor Research Project, founded in Ithaca, New York, in 1976, and the East Timor Human Rights Committee, a grassroots network affiliated with Clergy and Laity Concerned. The East Timor Research Project moved to Washington, DC, in 1979, where it later changed its name to the Humanitarian Project. Arnold Kohen, personal communication, August 15, 2008.

49. The hearings were held in December 1979, February 1980, and June 1980. One of those directly involved in the NGO lobbying efforts at the time recalls Richard Holbrooke, who was then U.S. assistant secretary of state for Asia and the Pacific, emerging from a congressional hearing in June 1980 "cursing his staff about the level of Congressional anger that existed on the issue" (Arnold Kohen, personal communication, August 15, 2008).

50. Arnold Kohen, Testimony before the Commission on Reception, Truth, and Reconciliation in East Timor (CAVR), Dili, March 15, 2004, 8–9.

51. Testimony of Jorge, in Turner, *Telling East Timor*, 172.

52. Report by Taylor, May 21, 1976, document 450, in Wendy Way, ed., *Documents on Australian Foreign Policy: Australia and the Incorporation of Portuguese Timor, 1974–1976* (Canberra: Department of Foreign Affairs and Trade, 2000).

53. See the testimonies in Turner, *Telling East Timor*, esp. part 3.

54. Cited in Taylor, *Indonesia's Forgotten War*, 117.

55. Departemen Pertahanan-Keamanan Republik Indonesia, "Petunjuk-Pelaksanaan, Nomor: Juklak/02/V/1979," 803, 805.

56. CAVR, *Chega!* part 3, 91.

57. The exact number killed is not known. The apostolic administrator of the Diocese of Dili, Monsignor da Costa Lopes, claimed that 500 had died, while Indonesian authorities said the figure was 70. See ibid., part 3, 92, and chapter 7.2, 160–63.

58. Cited in ibid., chapter 7.2, 162.

59. The eight documents in question were prepared by the Intelligence Section of the Resort Military Command (Korem) for East Timor, and signed by the Korem commander, Colonel Rajagukguk, or the chief of intelligence for East Timor, Major Williem da Costa.

60. After referring explicitly to this doctrine, one document declares grandly, "Thus,

at root, it is the whole populace that serves as resisters of the enemy" (Korem 164/Wira Dharma, Seksi Intel, "Rencana Penyusunan Kembali Rakyat Terlatih," Dili, 1982, 2.

61. The presence of SGI and Battalion 745 soldiers is mentioned in Korem 164/Wira Dharma, Seksi Intel, "Petunjuk Tehnis tentang Desa," Juknis/01-A/IV/1982, Dili, 1982, 6–7.

62. Korem 164/Wira Dharma, Seksi Intel, "Petunjuk Tehnis tentang Sistem Keamanan Kota dan Daerah Pemukiman," Juknis/05/I/1982, Dili, July 1982, 4.

63. On TBOs, see Korem 164/Wira Dharma, Seksi Intel, "Petunjuk Tehnis tentang Kegiatan Babinsa," Juknis /06/IV/1982, Dili, July 1982, 9.

64. The procedures to be followed in the event of the death of or injury to an auxiliary member are spelled out in extraordinary detail in ibid.

65. The danger was surely compounded by the army's practice of recruiting former Falintil guerrillas and political detainees to serve in these auxiliaries (see Korem 164/Wira Dharma, Seksi Intel, "Petunjuk Tehnis tentang Cara Mengamankan Masyarakat Dari Pengaruh Propaganda GPK," Juknis/04-B/IV/1982, Dili, 1982, 3–4).

66. "In general [the auxiliary forces] carry arms and so constitute a real armed force. In order to ensure that this force is truly directed at the intended target . . . constant guidance is essential. Without such guidance, the weapons in question could well be misused . . . [and] could even boomerang and be used against the People and ABRI" (Korem 164/Wira Dharma, Seksi Intel, "Petunjuk Tehnis tentang Kegiatan Babinsa," 7–8).

67. On the Kraras massacre, see CAVR, Chega! chapter 7.2, 168–73; Jill Jolliffe, Cover-up: The Inside Story of the Balibo Five (Melbourne: Scribe Publications, 2001), 286–301.

68. Among the best accounts of international complicity in the invasion and genocide—and of the illegal occupation that followed—is Joseph Nevins, A Not-So-Distant Horror: Mass Violence in East Timor (Ithaca, NY: Cornell University Press, 2005), 43–77.

69. UN Security Council, Resolution no. 384 (1975), December 22, 1975. In a resolution adopted on December 12, 1975, the UN General Assembly had said it "strongly deplores the military intervention of the armed forces of Indonesia in Portuguese Timor," and called on Indonesia "to desist from further violation of the territorial integrity of Portuguese Timor and to withdraw without delay its armed forces from the territory in order to enable the people of the territory freely to exercise their right to self-determination and independence" (UN General Assembly, Resolution no. 3485 [December 12, 1975]). For a summary of the discussion and voting on these and other resolutions on East Timor, see United Nations, "Decolonization: Issue on East Timor," 50–64.

70. Agence France-Presse, "US Endorsed Indonesia's East Timor Invasion: Secret Documents," December 8, 2001.

71. The use of U.S.-supplied weapons for offensive purposes was explicitly forbidden under the Foreign Assistance Act of 1961 and the U.S.-Indonesia Mutual Defense Agreement of 1958.

72. U.S. arms sales to Indonesia increased from $12 million in 1974 to more than $65 million in 1975 (William D. Hartung, "U.S. Arms Transfers to Indonesia, 1975–1997: Who's Influencing Whom?" [New York: Arms Trade Resources Center, March 1997], 3). Indonesia's General Murdani testified to the U.S. House Committee on International Relations in June 1977 that "Indonesian armed forces are equipped 90 percent with U.S. equipment" (cited in Helen Chauncey, Jane Clayton, and Rachael Grossman, "Showcase Garrison," Southeast Asia Chronicle 58–59 (December 1977): 11). Declassified U.S. government documents from 1975 and 1977 cite the same figure (see Simpson, "Illegally and Beautifully," 300n111).

73. United States, Department of State, Telegram 1579 from U.S. Embassy Jakarta to Secretary of State, on "Ford-Suharto Meeting," December 6, 1975, "East Timor Revisited: Ford, Kissinger, and the Indonesian Invasion, 1975-76," document 4, National Security Archive, available at http://www.gwu.edu/~nsarchiv/NSAEBB/NSAEBB62/.

74. Indeed, it seems quite possible that Suharto was still considering his options as late as December 3, 1975, when he gathered key military advisers, including Murdani and Sugama, at his home for a special meeting about East Timor (see Conboy, *Kopassus*, 240, 393). Simpson writes that "while Ford and Kissinger were in Beijing on 4 December, the State Department and the CIA both reported that President Suharto had apparently authorized a full-scale invasion of East Timor to begin shortly after Air Force One departed from Jakarta" ("Illegally and Beautifully," 296).

75. In September 1975, the British Embassy in Jakarta reported to London that Suharto "does not want to take any action that might prejudice his hopes of arms supplies from the Americans and Australians" (cited in Simpson, "Illegally and Beautifully," 292n57).

76. Institute for Policy Studies, "Background Information on Indonesia, the Invasion of East Timor, and U.S. Military Assistance" (Washington, DC: Institute for Policy Studies, May 1982). The bulk of this assistance was in the form of transfers of military equipment. For a detailed breakdown of such transfers from 1975 to 1995, see Hartung, "U.S. Arms Transfers to Indonesia," 4–5.

77. Anderson notes that the Carter administration supplied these systems secretly, while telling Congress that no such transfers were taking place ("Gravel in Jakarta's Shoes," 133).

78. On the capabilities of the OV-10, a Rockwell International advertisement from 1978 boasted that in two years, the Royal Thai Air Force fleet of sixteen OV-10s had flown over five thousand hours of counterinsurgency missions, which included "suppression attacks on terrorist camps and mountain fortified positions, escorting ground troops through terrorist territory" ("The Bronco Workhorse: Ask Thailand about It," reprinted in *Southeast Asia Chronicle* 63 [July–August 1978], 25).

79. Hartung, "U.S. Arms Transfers to Indonesia," 4.

80. In testimony to the U.S. House Appropriations Subcommittee on Foreign Operations, Rear Admiral Gene R. La Rocque concluded that "U.S. weapons enabled Indonesia to launch its two major offensives of the year in 1977 and 1978. Deliveries of the Rockwell OV-10 Bronco aircraft changed the entire nature of the war" ("Our Interests Are Not at Stake," *Southeast Asia Chronicle* 74 [August 1980]: 10).

81. Daniel Patrick Moynihan, *A Dangerous Place* (Boston: Little, Brown, 1978), 247. Moynihan later expressed regret over his role in that effort. In a private note to the retired Episcopal bishop of New York, Reverend Paul Moore, Moynihan described U.S. support for the Indonesian position at the United Nations as "the original sin" (Kohen, Testimony before the CAVR).

82. Robert B. Oakley, deputy assistant secretary for East Asian and Pacific Affairs, cited in Ramos-Horta, *Funu: The Unfinished Saga of East Timor*, (Trenton, NJ: Red Sea Press, 1997), 91.

83. See "Declassified British Documents Reveal U.K. Support for Indonesian Invasion and Occupation of East Timor, Recognition of Denial of Self-Determination, 1975–1976," National Security Archive, available at http://www.gwu.edu/~nsarchiv/NSAEBB/NSAEBB174/indexuk.htm.

84. The most complete account of Australia's role in the invasion and its posture thereafter is James Dunn, *Timor: A People Betrayed* (Sydney: ABC Books, 2001). For offi-

cial documents related to Australian policy on East Timor, see Way, *Documents on Australian Foreign Policy*.

85. The Fraser government granted de facto recognition of Indonesia's claim to East Timor in early 1978 (James Dunn, "The East Timor Affair in International Perspective," in *East Timor at the Crossroads: The Forging of a Nation*, ed. Peter Carey and G. Carter Bentley [Honolulu: University of Hawaii Press, 1995], 67).

86. Gareth Evans, "Indonesia: My Mistake," *International Herald Tribune*, July 26, 2001.

87. Taylor, *Indonesia's Forgotten War*, 97.

88. Benedict Anderson, "Testimony for the Subcommittee on International Organizations and the Subcommittee on Asian and Pacific Affairs of the Committee on International Relations of the U.S. House of Representatives," Washington, DC, February 6, 1980.

89. Graham Hovey, "House Panel Hears of Starvation Confronting East Timor in Asia," *New York Times*, December 5, 1979; Arnold Kohen and Roberta A. Quance, "The Politics of Starvation," *Inquiry*, February 18, 1980.

90. Cited in Joel Rocamora, "The Uses of Hunger," *Southeast Asia Chronicle* 74 (1980): 12.

Chapter Four: Occupation and Resistance

1. For a contemporary account and analysis of the massacre and its immediate aftermath, see Amnesty International, "East Timor: The Santa Cruz Massacre" (London: Amnesty International, November 14, 1991), and "East Timor: After the Massacre" (London: Amnesty International, November 21, 1991). For a later account, from the East Timorese governor at the time, see "Interview with Mário Carrascalão," *Indonesia* 76 (October 2003): 1–22.

2. The filmmaker was Max Stahl, who happened to be in East Timor making a documentary film, *In Cold Blood*, when the massacre took place.

3. See, for example, the testimonies of Simplicio Celestino de Deus and Max Stahl at the CAVR national public hearing on massacres. CAVR, "Massacres. National Public Hearing, 19–1 November 2003" (Dili: CAVR, 2005), 50–51, 58–61.

4. See Amnesty International, "Indonesia/East Timor: East Timor Human Rights Protesters Charged with Subversion" (London: Amnesty International, March 27, 1992), and "Indonesia/East Timor: Fernando de Araújo—Prisoner of Conscience" (London: Amnesty International, May 1992).

5. Cited in Amnesty International, "East Timor: After the Massacre," 8.

6. Interview with Major General Mantiri, *Editor* (Jakarta), July 4, 1992.

7. CAVR, *Chega!* (Dili: CAVR, 2006), part 6, 1–47.

8. The Editors, "Current Data on the Indonesia Military Elite," *Indonesia* 53 (April 1992): 99.

9. A similar pattern emerged in Aceh in the 1990s, after several years of combat operations against a rebel movement. There, too, Kopassus units were able to enrich themselves by serving as enforcers, debt collectors, security guards, and extortionists. See *Far Eastern Economic Review*, November 19, 1998, 18, 25; *Gatra*, August 15, 1998, 38.

10. For a summary of Prabowo's career, see Richard Tanter, Gerry van Klinken, and Desmond Ball, eds., *Masters of Terror: Indonesia's Military Violence in East Timor* (Rowman and Littlefield, 2006), 89–90.

11. See Amnesty International, *East Timor—Violations of Human Rights: Extrajudicial Executions, "Disappearances," Torture, and Political Imprisonment, 1975–1984* (London: Am-

nesty International, 1985), "East Timor: Short-term Detention and Ill-treatment" (London: Amnesty International, January 1990), "Indonesia & East Timor: A New Order? Human Rights in 1992" (London: Amnesty International, 1993).

12. Korem 164/Wira Dharma, Seksi Intel, "Prosedur Tetap tentang Cara Interogasi Tawanan," Protap/01-B/VII/1982, Dili, July 1982.

13. Most of the trials (232) were held between 1983 and 1985, and a further 70 were held in 1986. For a description and assessment of the trials, see CAVR, *Chega!* chapter 7.6, 7–26. A nearly complete set of trial documents is held in the CAVR archives in Dili.

14. Ibid., chapter 7.6, 3–4, 9, 25–26.

15. Cited in Robert Archer, "The Catholic Church in East Timor," in *East Timor at the Crossroads: The Forging of a Nation*, ed. Peter Carey and G. Carter Bentley (Honolulu: University of Hawaii Press, 1995), 131.

16. See, for example, Amnesty International, "East Timor: Amnesty International Statement to the UN Special Committee on Decolonization" (London: Amnesty International, August 1990), and "East Timor: Amnesty International Statement to the UN Special Committee on Decolonization" (London: Amnesty International, August 1991).

17. See Amnesty International, "Indonesia/East Timor: Fernando de Araújo," and "East Timor: 'In Accordance with the Law.' Statement before the UN Special Committee on Decolonization" (London: Amnesty International, July 1992).

18. This appears to have been the case for Eurico Guterres, a young independence activist detained by the military in the late 1980s. He later reappeared as the leader of a pro-Indonesian youth organization, and in 1999 led one of East Timor's militia groups, Aitarak. See Tanter, van Klinken, and Ball, *Masters of Terror*, 95.

19. See, for example, the personal account of Donaciano Gomes, who was detained and tortured by Indonesian authorities following a proindependence demonstration in 1989 ("The East Timor Intifada: Testimony of a Student Activist," in *East Timor at the Crossroads: The Forging of a Nation*, ed. Peter Carey and G. Carter Bentley [Honolulu: University of Hawaii Press, 1995], 106–8). See also the memoir of a young leader of East Timor's clandestine front, Constancio Pinto (*East Timor's Unfinished Struggle: Inside the Timorese Resistance* [Boston: South End Press, 1997].)

20. According to the government, it "devoted six times as much of its economic development budget to East Timor on a per capita basis than [sic] to any other province"; in 1991 it provided East Timor with roughly $170 million in government grants (Republic of Indonesia, "East Timor: Building for the Future" [Jakarta: Department of Foreign Affairs, July 1992], 12).

21. Darmosutanto Budiman, deputy chief of mission, Embassy of the Republic of Indonesia, letter to the *Washington Post*, November 1, 1996, A26.

22. Cited in Archer, "The Catholic Church in East Timor," 124.

23. On the formation of these elite paramilitary units, see Ken Conboy, *Kopassus: Inside Indonesia's Special Forces* (Jakarta: Equinox, 2003), 290–91, 310–11.

24. Circumstantial evidence suggests that they emerged in the late 1980s when Abílio Osório Soares, the Apodeti leader and future governor, was the mayor of Dili.

25. On the Petrus killings, see David Bourchier, "Crime, Law, and Authority in Indonesia," in *State and Civil Society in Indonesia*, ed. Arief Budiman, Papers on Southeast Asia 22 (Clayton, Victoria: Monash University, 1990), 177–211; Robert Cribb, "From Petrus to Ninja: Death Squads in Indonesia," in *Death Squads in Global Perspective: Murder with Deniability*, ed. Bruce B. Campbell and Arthur D. Brenner (New York: St. Martin's Press, 2000).

26. Soeharto, *Pikiran, Ucapan, dan Tindakan Saya* (Jakarta: PT Citra Lamtoro Gung Persada, 1988), 364–65.

27. The Editors, "Current Data on the Indonesia Military Elite," 99. This local mafia is said to have included members of Apodeti and its military allies (confidential interview with former Fretilin guerrilla, Lisbon, June 1989).

28. The evidence includes the testimony of at least one East Timorese youth who claims to have been hired by the military to carry a grenade into the procession and provoke just such an incident (confidential communication from East Timor clandestine movement, January 1993). See also "Interview with Mário Carrascalão," 15.

29. "Troop Reduction in East Timor, a Propaganda Trick," *Tapol* 120 (December 1993): 20–21.

30. A few months after the official announcement, the Associated Press obligingly adopted the new line, identifying the victim of a Fretilin attack as an East Timorese who had "led a local spear platoon against pro-independence fighters" (January 24, 1994).

31. Amnesty International, Urgent Action 33/95 (London: Amnesty International, February 13, 1995).

32. George J. Aditjondro writes of "East Timorese military-trained vigilante groups, initially known as ninjas but lately renamed and restructured as Garda Paksi" ("Ninjas, Nanggalas, Monuments, and Mossad Manuals: An Anthropology of Indonesian State Terror in East Timor," in *Death Squad: The Anthropology of State Terror*, ed. Jeffrey A. Sluka [Philadelphia: University of Pennsylvania Press, 1998], 171).

33. As early as 1992 dozens of unemployed East Timorese youth had been sent to Java for job training programs. Some were then forced to undergo military training at the Kopassus-run training complex in Cijantung, West Java, while others were simply left to their own devices. Many fell under the influence of the prominent East Timorese underworld figure, Hercules, and became preman in Jakarta. See Loren Ryter, "Pemuda Pancasila: The Last Loyalists of Suharto's New Order?" *Indonesia* 66 (October 1998): 69; Asia Watch, "Deception and Harassment of East Timorese Workers," May 15, 1992.

34. *Jawa Pos*, December 1, 1994.

35. Cited in "Xanana and Belo Interviewed," *Tapol* 136 (August 1996): 13.

36. For a brief biography of Guterres and an account of his role in 1999, see Tanter, van Klinken, and Ball, *Masters of Terror*, 91–96.

37. The group's nominal leader was Marcal de Almedia, but it is generally recognized that Guterres was effectively in charge (Dionisio Babo Soares, interview, Dili, September 24, 2008).

38. Anonymous manuscript reader, September 2008.

39. The meeting was called the First National Conference for the Reorganization of the Resistance (see Sarah Niner, "A Long Journey of Resistance," in *Bitter Flowers, Sweet Flowers: East Timor, Indonesia, and the World Community*, ed. Richard Tanter, Mark Seldon, and Stephen Shalom [New York: Rowman and Littlefield, 2001], 20).

40. At the Lacluta meeting, Gusmão was elected president of the CRRN and commander in chief of Falintil (ibid., 20).

41. As early as 1981, Gusmão declared that the important thing was not affiliation with any particular political party or ideology but rather "that everyone is moved by a common feeling—that of national identity" (cited in ibid., 20).

42. Among those critical of the new line was Paulino Gama (aka Mauk Muruk), who served from 1975 to 1985 as an operational commander of Falintil, and from 1980 as commander of Falintil's Red Brigade Command. Gama surrendered to Indonesian authorities in 1985. See Paulino Gama, "The War in the Hills, 1975–1985: A Fretilin Com-

mander Remembers," in *East Timor at the Cross-Roads: The Forging of a Nation*, ed. Peter Carey and G. Carter Bentley (Honolulu: University of Hawaii Press, 1995), 97–105.

43. Niner, "A Long Journey of Resistance," 22.

44. At a meeting in Lisbon in 1986, Fretilin and the UDT formed a "Nationalist Convergence" in an effort to garner international support and, more specifically, to win the backing of Portugal, which was set to join the European Union in 1987 (David Webster, "Non-State Diplomacy: East Timor, 1975–99," *Portuguese Studies Review* 11, no. 1 (Fall–Winter 2003): 13.

45. I learned about this discussion firsthand shortly after taking up my position as a researcher for Indonesia and East Timor at Amnesty International's Research Department in early 1989.

46. After describing his early experiences with Indonesian violence against close friends and family members, Donaciano Gomes wrote: "Naturally, I was influenced by these events. Who could not have been?" ("The East Timor Intifada," 107).

47. One of these was José Luís de Oliveira, whose uncle had been killed by Falintil in 1975 when de Oliveira was only seven years old. After witnessing the brutality of Indonesian troops, the seeds of opposition began to grow. Years later, while studying at a university in Indonesia, de Oliveira joined the clandestine student movement and later became a leading figure in East Timor's main human rights organization, Yayasan Hak. José Luís de Oliveira, interview, Dili, September 23, 2008.

48. They became avid readers of neo-Marxist scholarship as well as the publications of Amnesty International and other human rights organizations (Nug Kacasungkana, interview, Dili, September 25, 2008).

49. José Luís de Oliveira, interview, Dili, September 25, 2008; Aniceto Guterres, interview, Dili, September 25, 2008; Elias P. Moniz, interview, Dili, September 25, 2008.

50. Gomes, "The East Timor Intifada," 108.

51. Fernando de Araújo, conversation, Dili, September 23, 2008.

52. The experience of studying in Indonesia and working with Indonesian NGOs also served as the inspiration and model for the formation in Dili of Yayasan Hak. The leading figure in Hak's creation was Aniceto Guterres, who studied law in Indonesia, where he became acquainted with Indonesian human rights lawyers and activists. Unlike Renetil, Hak was never formally linked to the resistance movement, and its strategy of using Indonesian law to defend the rights of its clients drew criticism from some quarters of that movement. But by its reliance on the language of law and human rights, it provided a vital avenue of resistance to Indonesian rule and helped to garner international sympathy for the cause of East Timor, especially among more moderate groups. Aniceto Guterres, interview, Dili, September 26, 2008.

53. On the strategy and planning of this demonstration, see Gomes, "The East Timor Intifada"; Constancio Pinto, "The Student Movement and the Independence Struggle in East Timor: An Interview," in *Bitter Flowers, Sweet Flowers: East Timor, Indonesia, and the World Community*, ed. Richard Tanter, Mark Selden, and Stephen Shalom (New York: Rowman and Littlefield, 2001), 31–41.

54. Arnold Kohen, *From the Place of the Dead: The Epic Struggles of Bishop Belo of East Timor* (New York: St. Martin's Press, 1999), 145.

55. On the details of these events, and the general pattern of short-term detention and ill-treatment of peaceful demonstrators at this time, see Amnesty International, "East Timor: Short-term Detention and Ill-treatment" (London: Amnesty International, January 1990), "East Timor: Amnesty International Statement to the UN Special Committee on Decolonization" (London: Amnesty International, August 1990), 5, and "East Timor:

Update on Human Rights Concerns since August 1990" (London: Amnesty International, January 1991), 2–3).

56. The international reaction to the Santa Cruz massacre is spelled out in more detail in Geoffrey Robinson, "Human Rights in Southeast Asia: Rhetoric and Reality," in *Southeast Asia in the New World Order*, ed. David Wurfel and Bruce Burton (New York: Macmillan, 1996).

57. For details of the charges and sentencing, see Amnesty International, "Indonesia/East Timor: The Suppression of Dissent" (London: Amnesty International, 1992).

58. Many years later, Ali Alatas used the same phrase in the title of his book about Indonesia's struggles to retain East Timor (*The Pebble in the Shoe: The Diplomatic Struggle for East Timor* [Jakarta: Aksara Karunia, 2006].)

59. "Interview with Mário Carrascalão," 21–22.

60. Amnesty International, *East Timor—Violations of Human Rights: Extrajudicial Executions, "Disappearances," Torture, and Political Imprisonment, 1975–1984* (London: Amnesty International, 1985).

61. Gusmão declared, for example, that the CNRM, formed in 1987, "was committed to building a free and democratic nation, based on respect for the freedoms of thought, association and expression, as well as complete respect for Universal Human Rights" (cited in Webster, "Non-State Diplomacy," 14).

62. Gama, "The War in the Hills," 99.

63. Among the most prominent of the new groups were the U.S.-based East Timor Action Network, the East Timor Human Rights Centre in Australia, and Parliamentarians for East Timor, a network linking legislators in more than forty countries, including Canada, Japan, Portugal, the United Kingdom, and Australia. Solidarity groups also began to form in non-Western countries, including Malaysia, the Philippines, Thailand, Brazil, Mozambique, and India. The most credible of the older groups still functioning included the Lisbon-based A Paz é Possível em Timor-leste (Peace Is Possible in East Timor), the Australian Council for Overseas Aid, the Catholic Institute for International Relations and Tapol in London, and the East Timor Research Project in Washington, DC.

64. Summarizing the logic of Indonesian solidarity groups at this time, one scholar writes that "for young activists, the driving force of the movement, East Timor became an inspiring example of resistance to the Suharto regime as well as evidence of the regime's misdeeds. One young activist spoke of 'two peoples against a common enemy'" (Webster, "Non-State Diplomacy," 24).

65. Nug Kacasungkana, interview, Dili, September 25, 2008.

66. José Luís de Oliveira, interview, Dili, September 25, 2008; Nug Kacasungkana, interview, Dili, September 23 and 25, 2008; Aniceto Guterres, interview, Dili, September 26, 2008. See also George J. Aditjondro, *Welcoming the Rising Sun at the Top of Ramelau* (Jakarta: Yayasan HAK and Fortilos, 2000), 249–60.

67. Webster, "Non-State Diplomacy," 24.

68. See Geoffrey Gunn, *East Timor and the United Nations: The Case for Intervention* (Lawrenceville, NJ: Red Sea Press, 1997), which contains a useful collection of UN and other documents related to the East Timor question.

69. The UN Special Rapporteur on Torture visited the territory in 1991 and issued a report in time for the 1992 meeting of the Human Rights Commission. The commission passed a consensus statement on human rights in East Timor that year and a stronger one in 1993. In 1994, the UN Special Rapporteur on Extrajudicial, Summary, or Arbitrary Executions visited East Timor, and issued a highly critical report later that same year.

70. Excerpt from "Reflections of the East Timorese Religious," cited in Archer, "The Catholic Church in East Timor," 122.

71. During a religious gathering in Dili in October 1981, for example, Monsignor Lopes spoke openly about the terrible massacre at Lacluta. Summoned by Indonesian military authorities later that day, he told them, "I feel an urgent need to tell the whole world, as I did this afternoon, about the genocide being practiced in Timor, so that when we die, at least the world knows we died standing" (cited in Rowena Lennox, *Fighting Spirit of East Timor: The Life of Martinho da Costa Lopes* [London: Zed Books, 2000], 174).

72. Arnold Kohen, Testimony before the Commission on Reception, Truth, and Reconciliation in East Timor (CAVR), Dili, March 15, 2008, 10.

73. The most complete account of Bishop Belo's life and work is Kohen, *From the Place of the Dead*.

74. Letter from Bishop Belo to UN Secretary-General Xavier Perez de Cuellar, February 11, 1989. This position was not new. In a letter from December 1984, Belo had written, "Despite all forces against us, we continue to hold and to disseminate that the only solution to the East Timor conflict is a political and diplomatic one, and this solution should include, above all, the respect for the right of a people for self-determination. . . . As long as this is not implemented, there will not be a peaceful solution for East Timor" (cited in Archer, "The Catholic Church in East Timor," 125).

75. Cited in CAVR, *Chega!* chapter 7.1, 73–74.

76. "This arrangement," Archer writes, "meant that, throughout the occupation, the Catholic Church was the *only* local institution that communicated independently with the outside world, maintained institutional connections with an international structure, and could therefore guard for itself a certain independence from the Indonesian authorities" ("The Catholic Church in East Timor," 126).

77. Gusmão was found guilty of rebellion and the illegal possession of firearms, and sentenced to life imprisonment on May 21, 1993. His sentence was later commuted to twenty years by President Suharto. On Gusmão's capture and trial, and for a translation of his defense speech, see Amnesty International, "East Timor: Unfair Political Trial of Xanana Gusmão" (London: Amnesty International, July 1993).

78. The letter is reproduced in Amnesty International, "Indonesia and East Timor: Seven East Timorese Still in Danger" (London: Amnesty International, July 5, 1993), appendix I.

79. Sword's own account of these events underscores the degree to which they were designed to capture the attention of an international audience. See Kirsty Sword Gusmão, *A Woman of Independence: A Story of Love and the Birth of a New Nation* (Sydney: Macmillan, 2003), 56–66.

80. See Amnesty International, "Indonesia & East Timor: Seven East Timorese Seek Asylum" (London: Amnesty International, June 23, 1993), and "Indonesia and East Timor: Seven East Timorese Still in Danger."

81. See Amnesty International, "Indonesia & East Timor: The 12 November Protests" (London: Amnesty International, 1994), "Indonesia & East Timor: Update on the 12 November Protests" (London: Amnesty International, 1994), and "Indonesia and East Timor: Human Rights in 1994—A Summary" (London: Amnesty International, January 1995).

82. The committee also said it had awarded the prize to the two men "for their work towards a just and peaceful solution to the conflict in East Timor . . . [and] to honour their sustained and self-sacrificing contributions to a small but oppressed people" (Norwegian Nobel Institute, "The Nobel Peace Prize for 1996," October, 11, 1996).

83. "Open Letter to President Suharto," *Kabar dari Pijar*, September 11, 1997.

84. Underlining the importance of this development, in April 1998 Gusmão declared from his prison cell that "unity is the best form of resistance!" (cited in Webster, "Non-State Diplomacy," 25).

CHAPTER FIVE: MOBILIZING THE MILITIAS

1. This idea was proposed to Habibie by Foreign Minister Alatas in early June 1998. See Ali Alatas, *The Pebble in the Shoe: The Diplomatic Struggle for East Timor* (Jakarta: Aksara Karunia, 2006), 135.

2. Geoffrey Robinson, diary, August 1998.

3. Alatas, *The Pebble in the Shoe*, 141–42.

4. On the UN-sponsored negotiations, see Ian Martin, *Self-Determination in East Timor: The United Nations, the Ballot, and International Intervention*, International Peace Academy Occasional Paper (London: Lynne Rienner Publishers, 2001), 26–29; Jamsheed Marker, *East Timor: A Memoir of the Negotiations for Independence* (Jefferson, NC: McFarland and Company, Inc., 2003); Alatas, *The Pebble in the Shoe*.

5. The initial announcement was made on January 27, 1999, by Foreign Minister Alatas and Minister of Information Yunus Yosfiah (see *Kompas*, January 27, 1999).

6. On Howard's letter and Habibie's response to it, see Don Greenlees and Robert Garran, *Deliverance: The Inside Story of East Timor's Fight for Freedom* (Crows Nest, NSW: Allen and Unwin, 2002), chapter 5. For the full text of Howard's letter, see Tim Fischer, *Seven Days in East Timor: Ballot and Bullets* (St Leonards, NSW: Allen and Unwin, 2000), 10–14.

7. Martin, *Self-Determination in East Timor*, 22–24.

8. In another bizarre indication of U.S. reluctance to embrace a serious policy shift, in early February 1999 the State Department invited longtime East Timor activist Arnold Kohen to a meeting to request his support for a private U.S. effort "to hold conflict-resolution sessions between militias and pro-independence forces." U.S. officials at the meeting "agreed that the only real solution was to disband and disarm the militias (and that the Indonesian Army was behind the violence), but no policy changes were made" (Arnold Kohen, Testimony before the Commission on Reception, Truth, and Reconciliation in East Timor [CAVR], Dili, March 15, 2004, 15).

9. From the outset, Alatas had flatly rejected the idea of a referendum, and he made a point of reiterating that position during a visit to Jakarta by Secretary Albright in March 1999 (*Kompas*, January 28, 1999; Agence France-Presse, March 4, 1999; see also Alatas, *The Pebble in the Shoe*, 141, 164–65).

10. Cited in John Taylor, *East Timor: The Price of Freedom* (London: Zed Books, 1999), 179.

11. For an insider's view of Habibie's thinking on the issue, see the interview with his presidential adviser, Dewi Fortuna Anwar, in "The Ties That Bind," Australian Broadcasting Corporation, broadcast, February 14, 2000, available at http://www.abc.net.au/4corners/stories/s99352.htm.

12. Samuel Moore, "The Indonesian Military's Last Years in East Timor: An Analysis of Its Secret Documents," *Indonesia* 72 (October 2001): 9–44.

13. The agreements consisted of three related documents: Annex I—Agreement between the Republic of Indonesia and the Portuguese Republic on the Question of East Timor (the main agreement); Annex II—Agreement Regarding the Modalities for the Popular Consultation of the East Timorese through a Direct Ballot (the modalities agreement); and Annex III—East Timor Popular Consultation (the security agreement). The

full text of the agreements is provided in United Nations, Secretary-General, "Question of East Timor: Report of the Secretary-General," May 5, 1999.

14. These points had originally been included in a letter to President Habibie, dated April 30, 1999, but when Foreign Minister Alatas refused to accept the letter, they were put into a memorandum submitted to both governments. For the text of the letter and a summary of the memo, see Marker, *East Timor*, 152–55.

15. See Martin, *Self-Determination in East Timor*, 31–33. Alatas later wrote that "the idea of allowing foreign troops onto Indonesian soil at this stage . . . was anathema not only to President Habibie and the Government but also to the Indonesian public. In short, the Indonesian responsibility for security during the popular consultative process was non-negotiable" (*The Pebble in the Shoe*, 180).

16. In the same press conference one of the principal UN negotiators, Jamsheed Marker, explained the lack of discussion as follows: "We have not found it necessary under the present circumstances to send in a peacekeeping force, to parachute a whole lot of Blue Helmets down there. We don't think the situation calls for that" (cited in United Nations, Secretary-General, Press Release, SG/SM/6966, April 23, 1999). For Marker's later account of the negotiations on this question, see Marker, *East Timor*, 139, 151–55.

17. "The Price of Independence," *Financial Times*, September 7, 1999.

18. A former secretary-general of Apodeti, Francisco Carvalho, reportedly showed Australian journalists a document, dated June 24, 1998, said to be an Apodeti report on a meeting with military officers at which plans for creating a militia force were laid out. See Australian Broadcasting Corporation, "A License to Kill," *Four Corners*, March 15, 1999, transcript, 11.

19. Australia, Defence Intelligence Organization, "Current Intelligence Briefing," March 4, 1999. The content of this leaked document was reported by Australian Broadcasting Corporation radio on April 23, 1999, and subsequently cited in East Timor International Support Center, "Indonesia's Death Squads: Getting Away with Murder," occasional paper no. 2 (Darwin: ETISC, May 1999), 53.

20. For a complete list and summary of the activities of the militias in each district, see Geoffrey Robinson, *East Timor 1999: Crimes against Humanity. A Report Commissioned by the UN Office of the High Commissioner for Human Rights* (Jakarta: Elsam and Hak, 2006), 112–58, 234.

21. Sector A covered the eastern districts of Baucau, Viqueque, Lospalos, and Manatuto; Sector B covered the central districts of Dili, Liquiçá, Ermera, and Aileu; and Sector C covered the western districts of Ainaro, Maliana, Suai, and Oecussi. See Komando Pasukan Pejuang Integrasi, Letter from Eurico Guterres to Governor of Nusa Tenggara Timur, 55/SP/MK-AT/VI/1999, June 30, 1999.

22. Douglas Kammen, "Master-Slave, Traitor-Nationalist, Opportunist-Oppressed: Political Metaphors in East Timor," *Indonesia* 76 (October 2003): 69–85.

23. Robinson, *East Timor 1999*, 83.

24. Cited in "Timor Coup Planned," *Age*, June 22, 1999.

25. Cited in SBS (Australia), "Timor Terror Fund," *Dateline*, February 16, 2000, transcript, 34.

26. Cited in Australian Broadcasting Corporation, "A License to Kill," 6.

27. United Nations, *Situation of Human Rights in East Timor*, December 10, 1999, 12.

28. Mário Pinto da Costa, Letter to Komandan [Aitarak], March 30, 1999.

29. Several senior military officers have reiterated this claim in their memoirs. See, for example, Brigadier General Tono Suratman, *Merah Putih: Pengabdian and Tanggung*

Jawab di Timor Timur (Jakarta: Lembaga Pengkajian Kebudayaan Nusantara, 2000); Zacky Anwar Makarim, Glenny Kairupan, Andreas Sugono, and Ibnu Fatah, *Hari-Hari Terakhir Timor Timur: Sebuah Kesaksian* (Jakarta: PT Sportif Media Informasindo, 2003).

30. Lafaek Saburai, "Re: Operasi Pembersihan," Front Pembersihan Timor Timur Milisi Sayap Kiri Darah Merah, 024/Ops/R/III/1999, March 11, 1999. An English translation of this document is appended to East Timor Action Network, "Subject: Operasi Sapu Jagad—Indonesia's Military Plan to Disrupt Independence," ref. doc. FAIO-1999/10/21.

31. For a more detailed analysis of this document, see Geoffrey Robinson, "The Fruitless Search for a Smoking Gun: Tracing the Origins of Violence in East Timor," in *Roots of Violence in Indonesia: Contemporary Violence in Historical Perspective*, ed. Freek Colombijn and J. Thomas Lindblad (Leiden: KITLV Press, 2002), 246–47.

32. The direct involvement of high-ranking TNI authorities in the distribution of weapons was summarized in an indictment filed against eight senior Indonesian officials by East Timor's deputy general prosecutor for serious crimes in February 2003. The indictment directly implicated Major General Kiki Syahnakri, Major General Zacky Anwar Makarim, Colonel Tono Suratman, and Lieutenant Colonel Yayat Sudrajat. Democratic Republic of Timor-Leste, Deputy General Prosecutor for Serious Crimes, Indictment of Wiranto et al., Dili, February 22, 2003.

33. "Up in Arms," *Far Eastern Economic Review*, February 18, 1999.

34. Cited in East Timor International Support Center, "Indonesia's Death Squads," 12. Damiri made a similar remark shortly before the April 6 attack on the Liquiçá church, noting that the military had supplied weapons to a "limited number" of militia groups. See "Timor Needs No Foreign Soldiers," *Indonesian Observer*, April 5, 1999.

35. "KSAD Jelaskan Soal Sipil Dipersenjatai," *Media Indonesia*, February 2, 1999.

36. Cited in East Timor International Support Center, "Indonesia's Death Squads," 13.

37. "Crossbows and Guns in East Timor," *Economist* 350, no. 8106 (February 13, 1999): 40.

38. East Timor International Support Center, "Indonesia's Death Squads," 12.

39. Ibid., 10.

40. Australian Broadcasting Corporation, "A License to Kill," 5.

41. Kodim 1628/Baucau, "Daftar: Nominatif Anggota Kompi Khusus Pusaka, Kodim 1628/Baucau," February 3, 1999.

42. Kodim 1630/Viqueque, "Daftar: Nominatif Pemegang Senjata Team Makikit," undated, but found at Kodim 1630/Viqueque on November 28, 1998.

43. Korem 164/Wira Dharma, Danrem/WD to Dandim 1627–1639, Dansatgas Tribuana, and others, Secret Telegram No. TR/46/1999, February 2, 1999.

44. Cited in Kevin O'Rourke, *Reformasi: The Struggle for Power in Post-Soeharto Indonesia* (Sydney: Allen and Unwin, 2002), 352.

45. Korem 164/Wira Dharma, Danrem 164/WD to Dandim 1627–1639 and others, Secret Telegram No. TR/41/1999, January 28, 1999.

46. Cited in Marker, *East Timor*, 140.

47. In the statement, Gusmão declared that "the situation has reached an intolerable limit in East Timor. Therefore, I am compelled to authorize the Falintil guerillas to undertake all necessary action in defense of the population of East Timor against the unprovoked and murderous attacks of armed civilian groups and ABRI. . . . I also authorize a general popular insurrection against the armed militia groups who have been killing the population with impunity under the indifferent eye of the international commu-

nity" (cited in CNRT, "Falintil Resumes Their Mission in Defense of the People of East Timor," press statement, Jakarta, April 5, 1999).

48. For a detailed account of this attack, see Robinson, *East Timor 1999*, 159–63.

49. Rafael dos Santos, deposition recorded and compiled in Sydney, Australia on October 27–28, 1999, 8.

50. Cited in East Timor International Support Center, "Indonesia's Death Squads."

51. Korem 164/Wira Dharma, Dan Sat Gas Pam Dili to Dan Rem Up, Kasi Intel Rem 164/WD, and others, Secret Telegram No. STR/200/1999, April 17 (18?), 1999.

52. The video footage was held by the Serious Crimes Unit in Dili. According to unconfirmed accounts, the other officers included Major General Zacky Anwar Makarim and Major General Adam Damiri.

53. UNTAET, District Human Rights Office—Dili, "Key Cases of HRVs/Abuses in Dili District," September 2002, District Human Rights Office—Dili, "Dili Chronology," Dili, 2002.

54. For a detailed account of this incident, see Robinson, *East Timor 1999*, 166–70.

55. The denials became even more emphatic after the terrible violence of September 1999. Testifying before the Ad Hoc Human Rights Tribunal in Jakarta, Suratman categorically denied that the military had ever supplied weapons to the militias. "We never gave them weapons," he said. See "Tono Bantah Keterlibatan TNI dan Polri," *Media Indonesia*, October 23, 2002.

56. This was "The Agreement to End Conflict and the Endeavour to Create Peace in East Timor," Dili, April 21, 1999.

57. The governor's demands were echoed by the speaker of East Timor's provincial parliament, Armindo S. Mariano, who said at the same meeting that disloyal civil servants would be fired (see Kodim 1627/Dili, "Laporan hasil pertemuan di Gada Paksi," Dandim 1627 (Lt. Col. Endar Priyanto) to Danrem 164/WD and others, June 23, 1998).

58. See Gubernur Timor Timur, "Tindakan terhadap PNS yang terlibat organisasi/ kegiatan yang menentang Pemerintah RI," Circular No. 200/827/Sospol/V/1999, May 28, 1999.

59. Mário Pinto da Costa, Letter to Komandan [Aitarak], March 30, 1999.

60. For details of government funding for the socialization campaign and the militias, see Robinson, *East Timor 1999*, 97–110.

61. The indictment of General Wiranto and seven other senior Indonesian officials, issued by East Timor's deputy general prosecutor for serious crimes, alleges that the total figure diverted into the socialization campaign was Rp.52 billion, or 60 percent of East Timor's Regional Development Budget (see Republic of Timor-Leste, Deputy General Prosecutor for Serious Crimes, Indictment of Wiranto et al., paragraph 28).

62. A copy of the governor's letter sent to the Bupati of Liquiçá is dated May 21, 1999, and another copy of the letter, addressed to all Bupatis, is signed but undated (see Gubernur Timor Timur, Letter to All Bupatis concerning "Proposal," May 1999).

63. See Gubernur Timor Timur, Letter to Bupati of Oecussi, June 1999, and Letter to Bupati of Lautem, May 21, 1999.

64. Gubernur Timor Timur, Letter to All Provincial Heads of Department (*Kakanwil*) in East Timor, May 1999. The governor's letter was copied to several key officials, including the armed forces commander, the minister of foreign affairs, and the minister of finance.

65. Gubernur Timor Timur, Letter to All Bupatis concerning "Proposal," May 1999.

66. The FPDK was formally established on January 27, 1999, and the BRTT was set up in April 1999 (see Martin, *Self-Determination in East Timor*, 43).

67. That relationship was symptomatic of a more general phenomenon. As Ian Martin writes, "The links between the local administration, the FPDK, the militia, and the TNI were so close that they constituted a single operation to counter pro-independence activities and ensure a pro-autonomy vote" (*Self-Determination in East Timor*, 43).

68. For details, see Robinson, *East Timor 1999*, 107–8.

69. The English here is not an exact translation of the Indonesian, but these were the titles used in official correspondence and documents.

70. Representatives from the government, the TNI, the police, and each of the two proautonomy parties were ranged against just two delegates from the CNRT/Falintil. The sole CNRT representative present at the signing of the agreement, Leandro Isaac, was brought to the venue from a police station where he had taken refuge after his house had been attacked. UNAMET was entirely excluded from the KPS as were local NGOs and other civil society groups. On the composition and weaknesses of the KPS, see Martin, *Self-Determination in East Timor*, 30–31, 70.

71. TP4 OKTT probably stands for Tim Pengamanan Pelaksanaan [or Penyuksesan] Penentuan Pendapat Otonomi Khusus Timor Timur, or Team for the Security and Implementation [or Success] of the Popular Consultation on Special Autonomy in East Timor. It appears to have been established by Presidential Decision No. 43, May 18, 1999. See Tentara Nasional Indonesia, Order by Armed Forces Chief of General Staff (Lt. Gen. Sugiono) on Behalf of TNI Commander (Gen. Wiranto), "Surat Perintah No. Sprin/14 096/VI/1999," June 4, 1999; Order by TNI Commander (Gen. Wiranto), "Surat Perintah No. Sprin 1180/P/VI/1999," June 16, 1999. The TP4 OKTT team comprised the ministers of foreign affairs, home affairs, defense, and justice as well as the national chief of police and the head of BAIS (Badan Strategis Intelijen, or Strategic Intelligence Agency). Martin, *Self-Determination in East Timor*, 42.

72. They included H. R. Garnadi, a retired army major general, with a background in military intelligence, and Brigadier General Glenny Kairupan, who had served as deputy Korem commander in East Timor in the mid-1990s, and who reportedly had a Kopassus background. A third member, Police Colonel Andreas Sugianto, had served as the chief of police in East Timor in 1994–96, and had worked closely with a number of TNI officers who played key roles in 1999, including Mahidin Simbolon and Kiki Syahnakri.

73. The BIA was renamed BAIS in April 1999.

74. Makarim was formally ordered to deploy to East Timor as a member of TP4 OKTT on June 4, 1999. The order (Surat Perintah No. Sprin/1096/VI/1999) was issued under the authority of the TNI commander, General Wiranto. He and Major General Syahnakri were members of a team sent by TNI headquarters to investigate the Liquiçá church massacre in April 1999. Greenlees and Garran, *Deliverance*, 126–27.

75. For a list of eighty senior officers and officials suspected of responsibility for crimes against humanity committed in 1999, see Robinson, *East Timor 1999*, 229–31.

CHAPTER SIX: BEARING WITNESS—TEMPTING FATE

1. UNAMET, Political Affairs Office, "Weekly Sitrep #1 (27 June–4 July [1999])," 3–4.

2. The main district offices were located in the towns of Dili, Liquiçá, Ermera, Maliana, Suai, Baucau, Lospalos, Viqueque, and the enclave of Oecussi. Smaller auxiliary offices were set up in Same, Manatuto, and Aileu. On the formation and deployment of UNAMET, see Ian Martin, *Self-Determination in East Timor: The United Nations, the Ballot,*

and International Intervention, International Peace Academy Occasional Paper (London: Lynne Rienner Publishers, 2001), 37–42.

3. A detailed account of one such operation is provided in UNAMET, Political Affairs Office, "Report on UNAMET Retrieval of Hostages from Falintil and Observation of Joint TNI/Militia Operations—15 June 1999," June 16, 1990.

4. The problem was made clear in the Indonesian police report on the Liquiçá massacre of April 6, 1999. In a section called "Obstacles Encountered," the report noted that the "army support for the pro-integration group strongly influenced the investigation process" (see Kepolisian Daerah Timor Timur, Direktorat Reserse, "Laporan Penanganan Kasus Liquisa," Dili, April 15, 1999, 9).

5. Martin, *Self-Determination in East Timor*, 71.

6. For a detailed discussion of the TNI's counterinsurgency repertoire, see chapters 2 and 3 in this volume; see also Geoffrey Robinson, "*Rawan* Is as *Rawan* Does: The Origins of Disorder in New Order Aceh," *Indonesia* 66 (October 1998): 127–56.

7. TNI soldiers were also directly implicated in rape and sexual slavery. For further detail, see United Nations, *Situation of Human Rights in East Timor*, December 10, 1999, 9–11. See also Geoffrey Robinson, *East Timor 1999: Crimes against Humanity. A Report Commissioned by the UN Office of the High Commissioner for Human Rights* (Jakarta: Elsam and Hak, 2006), 33–34, 171–73, 194–97.

8. See "Case Studies: Major Human Rights Incidents," in Robinson, *East Timor 1999*, 159–202.

9. Roughly half (684) of all killings in 1999 occurred in the four westernmost districts: 229 in Bobonaro, 190 in Covalima, 183 in Liquiçá, and 82 in Ermera (see Robinson, *East Timor 1999*, chapter 9).

10. Fewer than one-fifth (213) of all killings in 1999 occurred in the six easternmost districts: 27 in Manufahi, 28 in Aileu, 30 in Viqueque, 32 in Manatuto, 43 in Baucau, and 53 in Lautem (see ibid.).

11. See UNAMET, Political Affairs Office, "Report on 29 June Incident in Maliana," July 5, 1999, "Report on the Liquiçá Incidents of 4 July," July 12, 1999.

12. UNAMET, Political Affairs Office, "Report on the Liquiçá Incidents of 4 July," 3.

13. With only five or six officers based at headquarters in Dili and a similar number serving in the district offices, the Political Affairs Office was one of UNAMET's smallest and most tightly knit units. While we did not agree on every point, on certain key questions a consensus did emerge.

14. UNAMET, Head of Mission, "Weekly Report," June 14, 1999, 1–2.

15. United Nations, Secretary-General, "Question of East Timor: Report of the Secretary-General," June 22, 1999.

16. "UNAMET's objective assessment today," he explained, " is that the necessary security situation for the peaceful implementation of the consultation process does not exist; that there is as yet no sign of effective action on the part of the Indonesian authorities to create it; and that the Secretary-General's security assessment, due next week, cannot be expected to be positive. In this context, I recommend—for political, security, and practical reasons—that we announce now that UNAMET is temporarily suspending its electoral preparations" (UNAMET, Head of Mission, "Recommendation to Suspend Electoral Preparations," July 5, 1999).

17. UNAMET, Head of Mission, "Security Conditions for the Operational Phase of the Popular Consultation," July 8, 1999.

18. Jim Della Giacoma, interview, Washington, DC, October 2000. Della Giacoma is

a former UN staff member who attended most of the meetings on East Timor at the UN Secretariat in 1999.

19. All of these tendencies were in evidence at a meeting with the Japanese parliamentary vice minister for foreign affairs in Dili on August 15, 1999. Discussing the possible consequences of a proindependence victory, the UNAMET record of the meeting states that "Ambassador Marker did not foresee much antagonism. [The two sides] had been talking about reconciliation and not retribution." On the question of guaranteeing security during and after the ballot, the same record says: "Ambassador Marker noted that the Indonesian Government had been extremely cooperative, even though they still had a lot to do. He added that the Indonesian authorities were fully committed to the process." On the efficacy of diplomatic pressures, about which the Japanese delegation had expressed some doubt, the record notes that "Ambassador Marker said that demarches by important governments, including Japan's had made a difference." See UNAMET, Political Affairs Office, "Note to the File: Meeting with the Japanese Parliamentary Vice-Minister for Foreign Affairs," August 15, 1999, 2.

20. Before traveling to Jakarta, Martin first met representatives of the Indonesian Task Force in Dili to express his grave concern about the attacks and their possible ramifications for the conduct of the consultation. Reporting on that meeting, Martin wrote to New York that "while the usual undertaking was given to improve the security provided for UNAMET personnel, they did not adequately address my concerns regarding Indonesia's obligations to ensure the necessary conditions exist for the conduct of the Consultation" (see UNAMET, Head of Mission, "Weekly Report," July 5, 1999, 1).

21. The document, prepared by UNAMET's Political Affairs Office, was "Report on 29 June Incident in Maliana." A second document, "Report on the Liquiçá Incidents of 4 July," also prepared by the Political Affairs Office, was submitted to Indonesian government officials on July 12, 1999.

22. See, for example, United Nations, Security Council, "Statement by the President of the Security Council," June 29, 1999; United Nations, Secretary-General, "Question of East Timor: Report of the Secretary-General," July 20, 1999.

23. Suratman reported this to UNAMET's chief military liaison officer, Brigadier Rezaqul Haider, during a meeting on July 14, 1999. See UNAMET, Military Liaison Office, "Record of Conversation. Meeting between Brigadier Reuq [sic], CMLO UNAMET and Colonel Tono Suratman, Comd Korem 164," July 14, 1999.

24. United Nations, Secretary-General, "Question of East Timor: Report of the Secretary-General," July 20, 1999.

25. UNAMET, Head of Mission, "Weekly Report," July 19, 1999, 1.

26. UNAMET, Head of Mission, "Security Conditions for the Operational Phase of the Popular Consultation—Update," July 14, 1999, 2–3.

27. The letter is referred to in United Nations, Secretary-General, "Question of East Timor: Report of the Secretary-General," July 20, 1999, 3.

28. The registration centers affected in the first ten days were in Zumalai (four), Maliana (three), Cassa (one), and Lolotoe (one). For details, see UNAMET, Political Affairs Office, "Weekly Sitrep #3 (12–18 July)," July 18, 1999, and "Weekly Sitrep #4 (26 July–1 August)," August 1, 1999.

29. See UNAMET, Political Affairs Office, "Assessment of Security Conditions in East Timor," July 9, 1999.

30. UNAMET, Political Affairs Office, "Weekly Sitrep #3 (12–18 July)," 1.

31. At the end of ten days, the total number registered was 239,893, of which 233,716 were in East Timor. See UNAMET, Head of Mission, "Weekly Report," July 26, 1999, 1.

32. These incidents in late July and early August, along with dozens of others, are described in UNAMET, Political Affairs Office, "Weekly Sitrep #4 (26 July–1 August 1999)," and "Weekly Sitrep #5 (2 August–8 August 1999)," August 8, 1999.

33. On July 30, for example, the head of mission met the military commander for region IX, General Adam Damiri. UNAMET, Political Affairs Office, "Weekly Sitrep #4 (26 July–1 August 1999)." On August 2, Civpol commissioner Mills met with the regional police commander, Colonel Timbul Silaen, to voice concern about police inaction over the recent violence in Dili. UNAMET, Head of Mission, "Weekly Report," August 2, 1999.

34. H. R. Garnadi, "Gambaran unum apabila Opsi I gagal," Nomor: M.53/Tim P4-OKTT/7/1999, Dili, July 3, 1999, 3.

35. Ibid., 4.

36. Ibid., 4.

37. João Tavares, "Instruksi . . . Tentang Kesiapan dan Kesiagaan Pasukan Pejuang Integrasi (Milisi) Dalam Menyikapi Perkembangan Situasi dan Kondisi di Timor-Timur," No. 010/INS/PPI/VII/1999, July 17, 1999.

38. Ibid.

39. Several copies of this document came to UNAMET at about the same time, together with a letter dated August 3, 1999, addressed to the vice secretary of the Internal Political Front (Frente Politica Interna) of the CNRT.

40. The Indonesian Task Force had written to UNAMET proposing a registration/polling site at Atambua, in West Timor, on June 21, 1999, but the issue was not pursued with any vigor until late July. See UNAMET, Head of Mission, "Weekly Report," June 28, 1999, 4.

41. Additional resources were diverted to registration centers in the border districts of Maliana, Covalima, and Oecussi, to which an estimated 9,200 potential registrants were to be transported. See UNAMET, Electoral Section, "Weekly Report (27 July–2 August 1999)," 2.

42. Electoral officials hoped that some 400,000 might register, and by August 2 the total was already 400,525. After the close of registration on August 6, the preliminary total was 446,666 registered, of which 433,576 were in East Timor. For detailed registration statistics, see UNAMET, Electoral Office, "Summary of Voter Registration," August 9, 1999. Following a review the figures were revised, with the total number registered increased to 451,792, of which 438,513 had registered inside East Timor. See UNAMET, Political Affairs Office, "Weekly Sitrep #7 (16 August–22 August 1999)," August 22, 1999, 5.

43. UNAMET, Political Affairs Office, "Weekly Sitrep #5 (2 August–8 August)," 7.

CHAPTER SEVEN: THE VOTE

1. UNAMET, Political Affairs Office, "Weekly Sitrep #6 (9 August—15 August 1999)," August 15, 1999, 6. On August 11, the parties approved a set of regulations on the code's implementation that called, among other things, for the establishment of Regional Campaign Coordination Committees, comprised of representatives of the two contending sides, UNAMET, and the Indonesian police. In Jakarta, party leaders agreed to additional guidelines on the conduct of the campaign.

2. Other key provisions of the agreements included the following: campaigning to take place only during the designated campaign period (Sections D and E-c); the United Nations to be solely responsible for the information campaign (Section E-a); campaign-

ing to be conducted in a peaceful and democratic manner (Section E–c); both sides to have an equal opportunity to disseminate their views (Section E–c); participation by government officials, use of public funds, and recourse to pressure of office to be prohibited. United Nations, "Agreement regarding the Modalities for the Popular Consultation of the East Timorese through a Direct Ballot," Annex II, in United Nations, Secretary-General, "Question of East Timor: Report of the Secretary-General," May 5, 1999.

3. UNAMET, Political Affairs Office, "Weekly Sitrep #5 (2 August–8 August 1999)," August 8, 1999, 7. When the campaign period began on August 14, the CNRT had offices in only eight of the thirteen districts. There were still no offices in the districts of Liquiçá, Ermera, Aileu, Bobonaro, and Manufahi. UNAMET, Political Affairs Office, "Weekly Sitrep #6 (9 August–15 August)," August 15, 1999, 7. And with just one week remaining before the vote, there were still no CNRT offices in three districts. See UNAMET, Political Affairs Office, "Weekly Sitrep #7 (16 August–22 August)," August 22, 1999, 7. See also UNAMET, Political Affairs Office, "Status of CNRT Offices in East Timor (22 August 1999)," August 22, 1999.

4. See UNAMET, Political Affairs Office, "Weekly Sitrep #5 (2 August–8 August)," 7.

5. CNRT, National Political Commission, "Directive No. 1/99, 7 July 1999."

6. For a firsthand account of CNRT campaigning, see Fernando de Araújo, "The CNRT Campaign for Independence," in *Out of the Ashes: The Destruction and Reconstruction of East Timor*, ed. James J. Fox and Dionisio B. Soares (Adelaide, Australia: Crawford House Publishing, 2000), 106–25. Araújo, a student activist who had been jailed in 1992 for his proindependence activities and was released in March 1998, was a member of the Campaign Planning and Coordination Commission with special responsibility for media relations. On Araújo's arrest and trial, see Amnesty International, "Indonesia/East Timor: Fernando de Araújo—Prisoner of Conscience" (London: Amnesty International, May 1992).

7. See UNAMET, Joint Operations Center, "Report on Incidents in Central Dili: 26th of August 1999," August 27, 1999, 2.

8. UNAMET, Electoral Commission, "Statement Minuted on Friday, 27 August 1999," August 27, 1999.

9. For details on Dare II, see Ian Martin, *Self-Determination in East Timor: The United Nations, the Ballot, and International Intervention*, International Peace Academy Occasional Paper (London: Lynne Rienner Publishers, 2001), 67–68.

10. Komisi Perdamaian dan Stabilitas, "Kesepakatan Bersama Conselho Nasional da Resistência Timorense (CNRT) dan Falintil, dan Pro-Integrasi dalam Rangka Penentuan Pendapat di Timor-Timur," Jakarta, June 18, 1999.

11. Martin, *Self-Determination in East Timor*, 70–73. For an account of the UNAMET visit to the first cantonment site, at Uai Mori, see UNAMET, Political Affairs Office, "Meeting between UNAMET and Falintil Deputy Commander Taur Matan Ruak," July 26, 1999.

12. UNAMET, Political Affairs Office, "Selected Comments of Mahidi Leader, Cancio de Carvalho at Cantonment Ceremony, Cassa, Ainaro, 18 August 1999," August 19, 1999.

13. UNAMET, "Press Release," August 19, 1999. See also Martin, *Self-Determination in East Timor*, 69.

14. Xanana Gusmão, "Now Is the Time to Build the Future! Reconciliation, Unity, and National Development in the Framework of the Transition towards Independence," Jakarta, [August 24?] 1999.

15. The speakers included Falur, the Falintil commander for region 3; Guterres, the

deputy commander of the PPI; Colonel Silaen, the regional police commander; and Colonel Muis, the East Timor military commander. See UNAMET, "Remarks Made at the Ceremony Announcing the Agreement Reached by Pro-Integration Forces and Falintil, UNAMET Headquarters, Dili, Sunday, 29 August 1999"; Martin, *Self-Determination in East Timor*, 77–78.

16. James Fox, "Ceremonies of Reconciliation as Prelude to Violence in Suai," in *Violent Conflicts in Indonesia: Analysis, Representation, Resolution*, ed. Charles A. Coppel Coppel (London: Routledge, 2006), 174–79.

17. UNAMET, Joint Operations Center. "Daily Log," August 29, 1999.

18. UNAMET, Civilian Police Office, "Interview conducted at UNAMET HQ on Sunday the 29th of August 1999, by Superintendant Pim Martinsson, Inspector Peter Burt, and Anthony Goldstone (Political)." August 29, 1999. A second man interviewed by UNAMET, Inacio da Silva, admitted to kicking Placido Meneses. According to the report of that interview, his action had been "an emotional reaction to the fact that his brother, Adelino da Silva, had been one of those killed on Thursday, 26 August during clashes in Kuluhun involving pro-independence and pro-autonomy supporters and BRIMOB."

19. In a message issued on the morning of the vote, Gusmão alluded to the previous day's incident, writing, "I order the youth and youth leaders to be in control of their emotions, to refrain from provocation and resist the temptation to respond to provocation. I am aware that some youth have allowed themselves to get out of control and this cannot continue" ("Let Us Free Our Beloved Homeland, Our Beloved East Timor," Jakarta, August 30, 1999).

20. UNAMET, Civilian Police Office, "Interview Conducted at UNAMET HQ on Sunday the 29th of August 1999, by Superintendant Pim Martinsson, Inspector Peter Burt, and Anthony Goldstone (Political)," August 29, 1999.

21. For a contemporary account of the events of voting day, see UNAMET, Political Affairs Office, "Summary of Developments as of 18:00 hours, 30 August 1999," August 30, 1999.

22. Speaking to journalists in January 2000, Makarim said, "In our prediction, we would either lose or win by a slight margin.... But only 21 per cent voted in favour of Indonesia's continued rule in East Timor.... It was really disappointing" (*South China Morning Post*, January 5, 2000).

23. The first account of the murders at Atsabe was recorded in UNAMET, Political Affairs Office, "Summary of Developments as of 18:00 hours, 30 August 1999," 3–4. Further details became known as UNAMET conducted investigations over the next few days and weeks. The relevant reports include UNAMET, Civpol, Ermera Regional Commander, "Murder of Locally Employed UNAMET Staff," August 30, 1999; UNAMET, Civpol, "Report of Incident at Bobo Leten, Atsabe, Ermera on 30 August 1999," September 21, 1999; UNAMET, Political Affairs Office, "Notes on the Atsabe Investigation," August 31, 1999.

24. See UNAMET, Political Affairs Office, "Notes on the Atsabe Investigation."

25. For an account of events in Maliana in the days after the ballot, see UNAMET, Political Affairs Office, "Report on the Incidents in Maliana, 30 August to 3 September," September 4, 1999.

26. See Peter Bartu, "The Militia, the Military, and the People of Bobonaro," in *Bitter Flowers, Sweet Flowers: East Timor, Indonesia, and the World Community*, ed. Richard Tanter, Mark Selden, and Stephen Shalom (New York: Rowman and Littlefield, 2001), 73–90.

27. During the siege, Alatas reportedly said, "Some rogue elements have been noted. . . . We have had, in the past, difficulties with rogue elements" (cited in *Time International* 154, no. 11 [September 20, 1999]).

28. UNAMET, Political Affairs Office, "Incidents on 3 and 4 September Which Led to the Relocation to Dili of UNAMET Staff from Aileu, Ainaro, Maliana, Liquiçá, and Same Regencies," [September 5] 1999.

29. One near exception to the rule occurred in the course of the evacuation from Liquiçá, on September 4, 1999. In that case, a UNAMET convoy was repeatedly ambushed and fired on by militias, police, and the TNI as it left the compound. One U.S. Civpol was seriously wounded, and the vehicles were riddled with bullet holes, but there were no fatalities. See UNAMET, Political Affairs Office, "Attack on UNAMET Staff in Liquiçá, 4 September 1999," September 4, 1999. A second near exception occurred in Baucau on September 7 when Brimob troops fired directly on the UNAMET compound, with apparent intent to kill or injure UN staff. In that case too, however, there were no injuries.

Chapter Eight: A Campaign of Violence

1. UNAMET, Political Affairs Office, "Situation Report," September 6, 1999, and "Overview Sitrep, 5–6 September," September 6, 1999.

2. UNAMET, Political Affairs Office, "Overview Sitrep, 5–6 September."

3. For a detailed account of the attack on Bishop Belo's residence, see Geoffrey Robinson, *East Timor 1999: Crimes against Humanity. A Report Commissioned by the UN Office of the High Commissioner for Human Rights* (Jakarta: Elsam and Hak, 2006), 182–84.

4. Sister Margarida, interview, Dili, September 8, 1999; UNAMET, Political Affairs Office, "Attack on Bishop Belo's Residence, 6 September 1999," September 8, 1999.

5. The bishop was evacuated from Baucau to Darwin on September 7, and from there he flew to Lisbon, where he received an emotional reception. Arnold Kohen, telephone conversation, September 12, 1999.

6. Senior CNRT figures in Dare included Leandro Isaac, Fernando de Araújo, and David Ximenes.

7. Robinson, *East Timor 1999*; Amnesty International, "East Timor: The Terror Continues" (London: Amnesty International, September 24, 1999), and "East Timor—As Violence Descended: Testimonies from East Timorese Refugees" (London: Amnesty International, October 1999).

8. UNAMET, Political Affairs, "Situation Report—Update on Humanitarian Affairs," September 6, 1999.

9. The exact number who fled to Indonesia was difficult to establish, mainly because they dispersed to so many locations. Early estimates were around 200,000, but a consensus later emerged that the number was closer to 270,000. See Amnesty International, "East Timor: Building a New Country Based on Human Rights" (London: Amnesty International, July 2000), 31.

10. Unless otherwise noted, this account is drawn from Robinson, *East Timor 1999*, 184–88. The human rights organization, Yayasan HAK, placed the number killed between fifty and two hundred. The indictment issued in this case said that "between 27 and 200 civilians were killed during the attack" (see Democratic Republic of Timor-Leste, Deputy General Prosecutor for Serious Crimes, Indictment against Egidio Manek et al., Dili, February 28, 2003, 232).

11. Democratic Republic of Timor-Leste, Deputy General Prosecutor for Serious

Crimes, Indictment against Col. Herman Sedyono, et al., Dili, February 28, 2003, 42. The indictment also named fourteen TNI personnel who took part in the killings at the church.

12. Unless otherwise noted, this account is drawn from Robinson, *East Timor 1999*, 188–92.

13. Higher estimates announced in the weeks and months after the massacre appear to reflect the number of people killed in the surrounding area at about this time, only some of whom were actually killed at the police station on September 8. At least thirteen people who fled the scene were killed the next day in nearby Mulau, and two more were killed at or near the police station on September 10. In all, at least seventy-one people were killed in Maliana subdistrict alone in the period September 2–29.

14. UNTAET interview with witness "FG-1," November 12, 1999, cited in Robinson, *East Timor 1999*, 190.

15. A Western journalist reported in 2001 that several other children—Renato Gonçalves (twelve), Victorino Lopes (eleven), and Francisco Barreto (ten)—had been killed in the police station massacre. See Mark Dodd, "Widows Who Share a Legacy of Murder," *Suara Timor Lorosae*, August 10, 2001. This report would appear to be in error. Several children were killed in Maliana, along with their father, on the morning of September 8, but they were not killed at the police station.

16. Those reportedly killed at the police station included Lourenço Gomes, a high-level clandestine figure; Manuel Barros, a well-known proindependence leader; Julio Barros, the camat of Maliana; Domingos Pereira, the head of Ritabou Village; and Damião, the former head of Tapo Village.

17. They included Domingos P. Gonçalves, a TNI soldier. Filomeno Guterres, a police officer, was killed at or near the station on September 10, 1999. UNTAET interview with witness "FG-1," November 12, 1999, cited in Robinson, *East Timor 1999*, 190.

18. Teresinha de Jesus Calao, interview by Jill Jolliffe, November 16, 1999, cited in Robinson, *East Timor 1999*, 190.

19. Testimony of Victor dos Reis, in joint deposition, March 17, 2000. See also Duarte Barros, interview by Jill Jolliffe, November 11, 1999, cited in Robinson, *East Timor 1999*, 191.

20. Interview of witness "FB-1" by UNAMET, October 29, 1999, cited in Robinson, *East Timor 1999*, 191.

21. UNAMET, Political Affairs Office, "Sitrep," September 7, 1999.

22. Arnold Kohen, personal communication, August 15, 2008.

23. The attack on the bishop's residence and the ICRC generated considerable alarm at UN headquarters in New York. Jim Della Giacoma, former UN Department of Political Affairs desk officer for East Timor, interview, Washington DC, October 2000.

24. UNAMET, Political Affairs Office, "Sitrep," September 7, 1999, 2.

25. Geoffrey Robinson, desk diary, September 8, 1999.

26. For an early attempt to answer these questions, see Harold Crouch, "The TNI and East Timor Policy," in *Out of the Ashes: Destruction and Reconstruction of East Timor*, ed. James J. Fox and Dionisio Babo Soares (Adelaide, Australia: Crawford House Publishing, 2000), 151–79.

27. Cited in Joseph Nevins, *A Not-So-Distant Horror: Mass Violence in East Timor* (Ithaca, NY: Cornell University Press, 2005), 6.

28. UNAMET, Political Affairs Office, "Sitrep," September 7, 1999.

29. Explaining the recommendation several months later, Martin wrote, "It was only

in the context of a decision for total staff evacuation that we could ever have got a decision to take the local staff" (personal communication, July 26, 2000).

30. UNAMET, Political Affairs Office, "Sitrep," September 7, 1999.

31. The four were Cantier-Aristide, Stewart, and myself of the Political Affairs Office and Burgess of Humanitarian Affairs.

32. The decision, which was made by the secretary-general, was communicated to Security Council members during an informal consultation on East Timor at around noon on September 8 (Della Giacoma, interview).

33. On the evening of September 9, Annan also called Gusmão in Jakarta and told him that he was determined to keep the United Nations in East Timor (ibid.).

34. United Nations, Secretary-General, Telegram to Ian Martin, re: Message of Support, September 9, 1999.

35. I later learned that as early as September 7, Japan had taken a strong position in favor of international intervention at meetings in New York. At a meeting of the Core Group, Japan said that it would approach Habibie directly with a threat to end economic cooperation (Della Giacoma, interview). For details of these and other international reactions, see Reuters and Agence France-Presse, September 8, 1999.

36. "The Price of Independence," *Financial Times*, September 7, 1999.

37. "Ergo: No U.S. Dorm Cleaners for Timor," *Washington Post*, September 10, 1999.

38. UNAMET, Political Affairs Office, "Militia Attack against UNAMET Staff on Logistical Mission," September 9, 1999.

39. Robinson, desk diary, September 10, 1999.

40. UNAMET, Political Affairs Office, "Notes on the Militia Incursion," September 10, 1999.

41. UNAMET, Joint Operations Center, "Interoffice Memo re: Advice from MLO at DanRem HQ," September 10, 1999.

42. Robinson, desk diary, September 10, 1999.

CHAPTER NINE: INTERVENTION

1. "The Price of Independence," *Financial Times*, September 7, 1999. In a tragic irony, the author of this story, Sander Thoenes, was killed by TNI soldiers in Dili on September 21, 1999 (see Geoffrey Robinson, *East Timor 1999: Crimes against Humanity. A Report Commissioned by the UN Office of the High Commissioner for Human Rights* (Jakarta: Elsam and Hak, 2006), 197–201.

2. Among other things, a Mahidi militia commander was reported to have said: "UNAMET has no force. It is like a woman. How does it dare to come unarmed and tease Indonesia?" And "Why do you believe UNAMET? Where will its force come from? The whole of East Timor is surrounded by Indonesian Armed Forces by sea or by land. So, everyone will be hanged and killed" (CNRT-Falintil, Frente Politica Interna [FPI], Secretariat for Information and Security, Region 3, Letter to UNAMET, July 16, 1999).

3. The speaker was New Democratic Party MP Svend Robinson (Agence France-Presse, August 12, 1999).

4. One member of the delegation, Jim McGovern (D-MA), told reporters that an armed international peacekeeping force was vital, adding, "I think we should have had it in there already." The other two members stressed that Indonesia should be made to live up to its responsibility to maintain order, or suffer severe consequences. See "U.S. Warns Indonesia over Political Violence," *New York Times*, August 28, 1999.

5. For criticisms and threats at the Paris meeting, see Agence France-Presse, July 27, 1999. For expressions of concern in late August, see *Australian Financial Review*, August 19, 1999.

6. "U.S. Warns Indonesia over Political Violence," *New York Times*, August 28, 1999.

7. Article 42 of Chapter VII of the UN Charter (1945) stipulates that where other measures have proved to be inadequate, the Security Council "may take such action by air, sea or land forces as may be necessary to maintain or restore international peace and security." *Charter of the United Nations*, available at http://www.un.org/aboutun/charter/chapter7.shtml.

8. The relevant Security Council resolution authorized a Civpol component of 460 personnel and an MLO component of up to 300 personnel. On the question of security, it stressed "the continuing responsibility of Indonesia to maintain peace and security in East Timor in the interim phase." United Nations, Security Council, Resolution No. 1262, August 27, 1999.

9. Remarkably, some DPKO officials even raised objections to the early deployment of additional *unarmed* Civpol and MLO personnel. Again, the grounds were as much political as logistical. Jim Della Giacoma, interview, Washington, DC, October 2000.

10. The report on Srebrenica, for example, referred to "the gulf between mandate and means; the inadequacy of symbolic deterrence in the face of a systematic campaign of violence; the pervasive ambivalence within the United Nations regarding the use of force in the pursuit of peace; [and an] institutional ideology of impartiality even when confronted with attempted genocide" (United Nations, Secretary-General, *Report of the Secretary-General Pursuant to General Assembly Resolution 53/55, 1998: The Fall of Srebrenica* [November 15, 1999].)

11. *New York Times*, September 6, 1999.

12. As the United Nations' report on Rwanda noted, "For the government of the United States, the events in Mogadishu were a watershed in its policy toward peace-keeping. By May 1994, when the genocide in Rwanda began, President Clinton had enacted PDD 25, a directive which placed strict conditions on U.S. support for UN peacekeeping" (United Nations, *Report of the Independent Inquiry into the Actions of the United Nations during the 1994 Genocide in Rwanda* [December 15, 1999].)

13. Throughout 1999, U.S. military officials in Washington, DC, and at the embassy in Jakarta had consistently downplayed any criticism of the TNI, and strongly opposed any measures that would upset good relations between the two militaries (Ed McWilliams, political counselor at the U.S. Embassy in Jakarta from 1996 to July 1999 and thereafter at the Department of State, interview, Washington, DC, July 3, 2003; see also Allan Nairn, "US Complicity in Timor," *Nation*, September 27, 1999, available at http://www.thenation.com/doc/1990927/nairn/print).

14. The official reportedly said peacekeepers were out of the question because of "objections in the UN and because it would have serious geo-political implications" (*Australian Financial Review*, August 29, 1999).

15. These documents are analyzed in Desmond Ball, "Silent Witness: Australian Intelligence and East Timor" (Canberra: Strategic and Defence Studies Centre, Australian National University, 2001).

16. It is also noteworthy that on her visit to Jakarta in March 1999, Secretary Madeleine Albright had appeared to acquiesce in Alatas's rejection of the idea of a peacekeeping force (Agence France-Presse, March 4, 1999).

17. After congressional committees had cut a peacekeeping budget request from $738 to $500 million, and had rejected outright a request for $107 million to support

current missions in East Timor and Kosovo, Holbrooke said: "The tragedy is that by lagging behind in funding peacekeeping operations, we . . . contribute to conditions in which peacekeeping fails and refugee and relief assistance is then required" (*New York Times*, July 21, 2000).

18. United States, Congress, Letter to U.S. Secretary of State, Madeleine Albright, April 12, 1999.

19. *Age* (Melbourne), April 1, 1999.

20. In March 1999, Australia said it was doubling its rapid reaction forces and would have a second battalion ready for action by the end of June, bringing the total number of troops available to between six and seven thousand (Reuters, April 14, 1999). From June these troops were reportedly carrying out exercises near Darwin (*Independent*, September 2, 1999).

21. "Downer on East Timor Violence," Australian Broadcasting Corporation, August 27, 1999, available at http://www.abc.net.au/pm/stories/s47370.htm.

22. Cited in "East Timor's Killers Target Priests, Student Leaders," *Washington Post*, September 10, 1999. A few days later, Pope John Paul II spoke out publicly, saying, "I repeat my appeal to the responsible political and military parties and the international community to listen to the cries of the weak and defenceless and help them soon" (cited in Patrick A. Smythe, *"The Heaviest Blow": The Catholic Church and the East Timor Issue* [New Brunswick, NJ: Transaction Publishers, 2004], 198–99).

23. In Lisbon, for example, there were up to one million people demonstrating in the streets in early September 1999 (Arnold Kohen, personal communication, August 18, 2008).

24. Ian Martin, *Self-Determination in East Timor: The United Nations, the Ballot, and International Intervention*, International Peace Academy Occasional Paper (London: Lynne Rienner Publishers, 2001), 103–4.

25. On this point, see Asfane Bassir Pour, "Le combat solitaire de Kofi Annan," *Le Monde*, October 31, 1999.

26. Jim Della Giacoma, interview, Washington DC, October 2000.

27. Astri Suhrke, "Annan Showed What One Leader Can Achieve," *International Herald Tribune*, August 31, 2000.

28. In an interview given after key powers had started to change their positions, Annan said that he had been surprised by the weakness of the response of major powers, including the United States, in the early days of the crisis. While he welcomed their eventual involvement, he said, "I wish the pressure had come sooner" (cited in "Annan Warns Indonesians That Inaction May Lead to Criminal Charges," *New York Times*, September 11, 1999).

29. Della Giacoma, interview.

30. Arnold Kohen, testimony before the Commission on Reception, Truth, and Reconciliation in East Timor (CAVR), Dili, March 15, 2004, 16.

31. "UN Says 200,000 Driven from Homes in East Timor," *New York Times*, September 8, 1999.

32. "Rights Body Wants Deployment of UN Force," *Jakarta Post*, September 9, 1999; "East Timor—U.S. to Use Economic Threats," *Los Angeles Times*, September 9, 1999.

33. "Militias in Timor Menace Refugees at UN Compound," *New York Times*, September 11, 1999.

34. At a press briefing in Canberra in May 2000, Blair said, "There were only two people in that meeting so I am not going to characterize what went on" (cited in Don Greenlees and Robert Garran, *Deliverance: The Inside Story of East Timor's Fight for Freedom*

[Crows Nest, NSW: Allen and Unwin, 2002], 244). In early 2008, Blair declined my own request for an interview to discuss this and other questions about U.S. policy toward Indonesia.

35. Blair reportedly met Wiranto on April 8, 1999, just two days after the Liquiçá church massacre. According to one source, who cites U.S. government documents, Blair had instructions to tell Wiranto that the militia terror strategy had to stop, but failed to do so (Nairn, "US Complicity in Timor"). On the other hand, some Western diplomats are convinced that Blair's meeting with Wiranto was decisive in changing the Indonesian position (Ambassador Paul Heinbecker, permanent representative of Canada to the United Nations, New York, October 24, 2003).

36. Martin, *Self-Determination in East Timor*, 108–9.

37. "Clinton Demands End of Violence in East Timor," *New York Times*, September 10, 1999.

38. Della Giacoma, interview.

39. United Nations, Secretary-General, "Statement on East Timor," September 10, 1999. The next day Annan made similar remarks before the Security Council (see United Nations, Secretary-General, Press Release, "Kofi Annan Says Time Has Come for Indonesia to Seek International Community's Help to Bring Order and Security to East Timor," September 11, 1999).

40. United Nations, Secretary-General, "Statement on East Timor." As of September 7, the secretary-general had already received some sixty thousand email messages calling for urgent UN action in East Timor. The volume was so great that the United Nations' Department of Public Information had to set up a separate server solely for messages relating to East Timor (Della Giacoma, interview).

41. "Indonesia Assisting Militias, U.S. Says," *New York Times*, September 11, 1999.

42. United States, President Clinton, "Remarks to American and Asian Business Leaders in Auckland," September 12, 1999, *Weekly Compilation of Presidential Documents* 35, no. 37 (September 20, 1999), 1727–28; emphasis added.

43. As one close observer has written, "A series of furious editorials in the *Washington Post* by editorial page editor Fred Hiatt severely chastised both the administration and National Security Adviser Berger for the stance they had taken and virtually demanded a reversal of policy" (Kohen, Testimony before the CAVR, 16). By Kohen's account, the chief lobbyist for the U.S. Catholic Bishops Conference considered those letters to be "the angriest he had seen in his thirty years on the U.S. Bishops' staff" (personal communication, August 15, 2008). Republican support for intervention in East Timor appears to have been driven, in some considerable measure, by the efforts of Ronald Reagan's national security adviser, William Clark, himself a Catholic Republican. According to Kohen, who knew him well, Clark "single-handedly got the Republicans to support the intervention" (ibid.).

44. Among those who met at the summit to coordinate strategy were U.S. secretary of state Albright, British foreign secretary Robin Cooke, Australian foreign minister Downer, Canadian foreign minister Lloyd Axworthy, and New Zealand foreign minister Don McKinnon (Martin, *Self-Determination in East Timor*, 107).

45. Ibid., 109.

46. Cited in ibid., 108.

47. Ibid.

48. The total bailout package for Indonesia was worth $47 billion (Agence France-Presse, September 11, 1999).

49. United Nations, Security Council, *Report of the Security Council Mission to Jakarta*

and Dili, 8 to 12 September 1999, September 14, 1999. The delegation was composed of Ambassador Martin Andjaba (Namibia) as chair, Ambassador Jeremy Greenstock (United Kingdom), Ambassador Danilo Turk (Slovenia), Ambassador Hasmy Agam (Malaysia), and Minister Alphons Hamer (Netherlands).

50. According to one account of the meeting, the head of the delegation, Martin Andjaba, told Wiranto: "We don't believe you. You are not convincing us" (cited in "Cry from Beseiged City: Don't Forget East Timor," *New York Times*, September 12, 1999; see also Martin, *Self-Determination in East Timor*, 110).

51. Greenstock described the scene in Dili as a "Potemkin operation," and in an echo of UNAMET's own earlier assessment, said, "It illustrates that you can never know whether these people are going to switch it on or switch it off" (cited in "Jakarta Concedes a Loss of Control over Timor Forces," *New York Times*, September 12, 1999).

52. The UN Security Council mission later wrote that it "had the distinct impression" that Wiranto "had not been prepared for the extent of the destruction" in Dili and that "accurate first-hand information may well have contributed to the change in Government policy" (*Report of the Security Council Mission to Jakarta and Dili*, 5; see also "UN Says Jakarta Is Easing Opposition to Peacekeepers," *New York Times*, September 12, 1999).

53. UNAMET, Political Affairs Office, "The Destruction of East Timor since 4 September," September 11, 1999. Quite unexpectedly, this briefing paper was included as an appendix to the Security Council delegation's report of September 14, 1999.

54. United Nations, Security Council, Press Release, "Security Council Hears 52 Speakers in Open Debate on Situation in East Timor," September 11, 1999.

55. Cited in "Indonesia Invites a UN Force to Timor," *New York Times*, September 13, 1999. For the full text of Habibie's announcement in Indonesian, see "Indonesia-L Detik Teks Pidato H," available at http://www.hamline.edu/apakabar/basisdata/1999/09/12/0145.html.

56. Heinbecker, interview.

57. Cited in *Financial Times*, September 7, 1999.

58. Michael Harvey, former political officer at the Canadian mission to the United Nations, telephone interview, New York, October 29, 2000.

59. For a sense of the arguments made in favor of international intervention at the turn of the century, see Brian Urquhart, "In the Name of Humanity," *New York Review of Books* 47, no. 7 (April 27, 2000), 19–22; Bernard Kouchner, "Establish a Right to Intervention against War, Oppression," *Los Angeles Times*, October 18, 1999; Michael Walzer, "Arguing for Humanitarian Intervention," in *The New Killing Fields: Massacre and the Politics of Intervention*, ed. Nicolaus Mills and Kira Brunner (New York: Basic Books, 2002), 19–36.

60. See, for example, United Nations, Secretary-General, "We the Peoples: The Role of the United Nations in the 21st Century," April 3, 2000; Bill Clinton, Speech to UN General Assembly, September 21, 1999.

61. United Nations, Secretary-General, "We the Peoples," 48.

62. See, for example, Stanley Hoffman, "Principles in the Balkans but Not in East Timor?" *New York Times*, September 11, 1999. On the other hand, some observers took the view that the intervention in Kosovo should be seen as an exception rather than the rule. See, for example, Ronald Steel, "East Timor Isn't Kosovo, *New York Times*, September 12, 1999.

63. On September 10, for example, the Portuguese ambassador to the United Nations, Antônio Monteiro, said that since Indonesia had broken its promise, the Security

Council should be free to act: "Do you believe that anyone else in this world from now on will ever believe that the United Nations is capable of keeping an agreement respected if this happens to East Timor?" (cited in "Annan Warns Indonesians That Inaction May Lead to Criminal Charges," *New York Times*, September 11, 1999).

64. The report on UN peace operations singled out the visit to East Timor as "an example of effective Council *action* at its best: *res, non verba*" (see United Nations, *Report of the Panel on United Nations Peace Operations,* August 17, 2000, xiv).

65. According to the desk officer for East Timor at the UN Department of Political Affairs in New York, the "subtext" to all discussions about East Timor in 1999 was the memory of UN failure in Rwanda and Srebrenica: "The parallels were on everyone's mind, and were often discussed over a beer at the end of the day" (Della Giacoma, interview).

66. United Nations, Secretary-General, Press Release, SG/SM/7263 AFR/196, December 16, 1999.

Chapter Ten: Justice and Reconciliation

1. For details of these incidents, see Geoffrey Robinson, *East Timor 1999: Crimes against Humanity. A Report Commissioned by the UN Office of the High Commissioner for Human Rights* (Jakarta: Elsam and Hak, 2006), 192–94, 201–2.

2. For an assessment of these efforts, see Hansjorg Strohmeyer, "Making Multilateral Interventions Work: The UN and the Creation of Transitional Justice Systems in Kosovo and East Timor," *Fletcher Forum for World Affairs Journal* 25 (Summer 2001): 107–24.

3. For a biting critique of the international role in derailing justice for the crimes committed in East Timor, see Joseph Nevins, *A Not-So-Distant Horror: Mass Violence in East Timor* (Ithaca, NY: Cornell University Press, 2005), 157–78.

4. On the experience of other postconflict societies with justice and reconciliation, and more specifically with truth commissions, see Priscilla Hayner, *Unspeakable Truths: Confronting State Terror and Atrocity* (New York: Routledge, 2002).

5. These were Security Council resolutions 1264 (September 15, 1999) and 1272 (October 25, 1999), and UN Commission on Human Rights resolution 1999/S-4/1 (September 27, 1999).

6. These were the UN Special Rapporteur on extrajudicial, summary, or arbitrary executions, the Special Rapporteur on the question of torture, and the Special Rapporteur on violence against women, its causes and consequences. Their report, *Situation of Human Rights in East Timor,* was issued on December 10, 1999.

7. The commission was mandated to "gather and compile systematically information on possible violations of human rights and acts which might constitute breaches of international humanitarian law committed in East Timor since January 1999." United Nations, *Report of the International Commission of Inquiry on East Timor to the Secretary-General,* January 2000, 1.

8. When they heard about the planned visit, many East Timorese activists and political leaders were angry. Some took the view that the delegation should not be welcomed, and that sensitive information and eyewitnesses should not be made available to the delegates. The suspicion about the motives of the Indonesian delegation was understandable. After all, the same body had failed utterly to curtail or even speak out against the rampant violations that had occurred in the preceding months and years. Some commission members, in fact, had been part of the Indonesian government apparatus that had openly supported pro–Indonesian campaigning and militia violence. It was widely sus-

pected that the inquiry had been set up primarily to undermine demands for an international tribunal.

9. The United Nations arguably also had legal responsibilities under the UN Charter in connection with its central role in the process of East Timor's decolonization.

10. Moreover, under the May 5 Agreements, the United Nations effectively became the administering authority in East Timor after the ballot. As such it arguably had a legal obligation, similar to the obligation of a state, to bring to justice the perpetrators of crimes against humanity.

11. UN Security Council resolution 1272 (October 25, 1999) stated clearly that the council "*condemns* all violence and acts in support of violence in East Timor . . . and *demands* that those responsible be brought to justice." UN Commission on Human Rights resolution 1999/S-4/1 (September 27, 1999) affirmed that the international community would exert every effort to ensure that those responsible for the crimes committed in East Timor would be brought to justice.

12. United Nations, *Report of the International Commission of Inquiry on East Timor to the Secretary-General*, paragraphs 146–47.

13. Ibid., 2.

14. Ibid., paragraph 153.

15. United Nations, *Situation of Human Rights in East Timor*, December 10, 1999, 14; emphasis added.

16. For international reactions to the September 2000 killings, see *New York Times*, September 19, 2000; *Jakarta Post*, September 10, 2001.

17. *Washington Post*, April 11, 2001; *Christian Science Monitor*, May 7, 2001. Apparently responding to UN and other international pressure, in November 2001 Indonesia's Supreme Court increased the sentences of three of the men to between five and seven years. (Anthony Goldstone, personal communication, June 10, 2009).

18. *Los Angeles Times*, July 31, 2001.

19. Shortly after Indonesian president Megawati Sukarnoputri's visit to the United States in September 2001, the Indonesian minister of justice and human rights announced that the East Timor trials would begin in December 2001. Some human rights observers believed that the move came in response to U.S. pressure to show progress on that front, in order to smooth the way for renewed military relations (Lucia Withers, Amnesty International researcher for Indonesia and East Timor, personal communication, London, September 30, 2001).

20. *Los Angeles Times*, July 31, 2001.

21. On a number of occasions after September 11, 2001, the Bush administration sought the resumption of military cooperation with Indonesia in the name of the "war on terror." That argument won some support in Congress. See, for example, "Congress Moves to Renew Military Ties with Indonesian Military," *East Timor Estafeta* 8, no. 1 (Winter 2002–3), available at http://www.etan.org/estafeta/02/winter02/1milties.htm.

22. According to one account, "A UN legal expert said that the [Indonesian] courts—and the Attorney General's office—were so corrupt and unprofessional it might be difficult to meet international standards of justice" (*New York Times*, October 22, 2000).

23. See, for example, Brigadier General Tono Suratman, *Merah Putih: Pengabdian and Tanggung Jawab di Timor Timur* (Jakarta: Lembaga Pengkajian Kebudayaan Nusantara, 2000); Zacky Anwar Makarim, Glenny Kairupan, Andreas Sugono, and Ibnu Fatah, *Hari-Hari Terakhir Timor Timur: Sebuah Kesaksian* (Jakarta: PT Sportif Media Informasindo, 2003); Colonel Muh. Nur Muis, "Kecurangan UNAMET Selama Jajak Pendapat di

Timor-Timur Pada Tahun 1999" (paper prepared for workshop on Masalah Kecurangan UNAMET, Jakarta, October 6, 2000). For a "legal analysis" of the "international conspiracy" that led to the proindependence vote and the violence, see Suhardi Somomoeljono, *Analisa Juridis Mengenai Konspirasi Internasional Atas Wilayah Timor-Timur* (Jakarta: Dewan Pimpinan Pusat Himpunan Advocat/Pengacara Indonesia, May 2000).

24. The court was established by Presidential Decree No. 96/2001.

25. For example, by the time he was brought to trial in 2002, the former regional military commander, Major General Damiri, had assumed the powerful post of assistant for operations to the armed forces chief of general staff. In that position he played a central role in organizing the TNI military operations in Aceh that began in May 2003.

26. For a detailed analysis of the trials, see David Cohen, *Intended to Fail: The Trials before the Ad Hoc Human Rights Court in Jakarta* (New York: International Center for Transitional Justice, 2003).

27. See "Indonesia Wants to Acquit General in Human Rights Case," *New York Times*, June 8, 2003.

28. Amnesty International, *Indonesia and Timor Leste: International Responsibility for Justice* (London: Amnesty International, April 2003), 1. This document also contains a useful summary of Amnesty International's principal concerns with the trial process.

29. National Alliance for an International Tribunal for East Timor, Letter to the UN High Commissioner for Human Rights, March 13, 2003.

30. See "An International Tribunal Must Be Established for East Timor: A Statement from U.S. Religious Leaders and Organizations," available at http://www.etan.org/action/action2/relig.htm.

31. Cited in "Lt. Col. Endar Priyanto," *Masters of Terror*, available at http://yayasanhak.minihub.org/mot/booktoc.htm.

32. U.S. ambassador Ralph L. Boyce, cited in "Indonesia Wants to Acquit General in Human Rights Case," *New York Times*, June 8, 2003.

33. The statute was UNTAET, Regulation No. 2000/15, "On the Establishment of Panels with Exclusive Jurisdiction over Serious Criminal Offences," June 6, 2000. The serious crimes over which these panels had jurisdiction were genocide, war crimes, crimes against humanity, murder, sexual offenses, and torture.

34. After East Timor's independence on May 20, 2002, the Serious Crimes Unit began to operate under the legal authority of the general prosecutor of the Democratic Republic of Timor-Leste (Democratic Republic of Timor-Leste, Deputy General Prosecutor for Serious Crimes, Serious Crimes Unit, "Serious Crimes Update V/03," Dili, May 28, 2003).

35. Ibid.; United Nations, Security Council, "Summary of the Report to the Secretary-General of the Commission of Experts to Review the Prosecution of Serious Violations of Human Rights in Timor-Leste (then East Timor) in 1999," May 26, 2005, 3, Annex I of UN Security Council document S/2005/458, July 15, 2005.

36. In May 2003, 169 of 247 indictees were in Indonesia (see Democratic Republic of Timor-Leste, Deputy General Prosecutor for Serious Crimes, Serious Crimes Unit). In May 2005, the figure was 339 of 391 indictees (see United Nations, Security Council, "Summary of the Report to the Secretary-General of the Commission of Experts," 4). In August 2006, the UN Security Council renewed the mandate of the Serious Crimes Unit to investigate but not to prosecute such crimes (United Nations, Security Council, Resolution 1704 [August 25, 2006]).

37. Australian Broadcasting Corporation Radio, February 25, 2003.

38. Cited in Patrick Burgess, "East Timor's Community Reconciliation Procedures: A Valuable New Addition to the Reconciliation Tool-kit," draft paper, 2004, 8.

39. Associated Press, *WorldStream*, May 17, 2004.

40. President Gusmão was especially cautious in this regard. Prime Minister Mari Alkatiri called for the establishment of an international tribunal in a neutral third country (see "East Timor PM Wants International Tribunal to Try Indonesian Officers," Associated Press, May 30, 2003).

41. For a useful summary of the problems facing East Timor's judiciary in 2003, see Judicial System Monitoring Programme, "JSMP Background Paper on the Justice Sector" (paper prepared for the Timor-Leste and Development Partners Meeting, Dili, June 2003).

42. In May 2003, for example, the House International Relations Committee supported a Foreign Relations Authorization Bill (HR 1950) that, among other things, called for "justice for crimes against humanity and war crimes committed in East Timor," criticized the Jakarta trials as inadequate, and urged the State Department to "consider alternative mechanisms of justice for East Timor, including the establishment of an ad hoc international tribunal" (U.S. Congress, HR 1500, 108th sess., sec. 721, May 2003).

43. United Nations, Secretary-General, Letter to the President of the Security Council, January 11, 2005.

44. Paul van Zyl, International Center for Transitional Justice, interview, September 25, 2003. The idea of a Commission of Experts was already being discussed within the United Nations in late 2003, but did not gain traction until late 2004, when both the Jakarta and Dili trials had run their course.

45. United Nations, Security Council, "Summary of the Report to the Secretary-General of the Commission of Experts," 6.

46. Ibid., 6.

47. Ibid., 8.

48. The report was submitted to the Office of the High Commissioner for Human Rights in July 2003 (see Geoffrey Robinson, *East Timor 1999: Crimes against Humanity. A Report Commissioned by the UN Office of the High Commissioner for Human Rights* [Jakarta: Elsam and Hak, 2006]). That office formally conveyed the report to the CAVR later the same year, but declined to make it public. The report was finally published in early 2006, as an annex to the CAVR's final report, and by the human rights organizations Elsam and Hak.

49. Robinson, *East Timor 1999*, preface, chapter 12.

50. The CAVR was established under UNTAET regulation 10/2001 (July 13, 2001), but it was not a UN body. Its final report, *Chega!* was published in early 2006, and is available at http://www.cavr-timorleste.org/en/chegaReport.htm.

51. Nug Kacasungkana, CTF staff, interview, Dili, September 23, 2008.

52. On June 22, for example, President Gusmão and Prime Minister Alkatiri sent identical letters to the secretary-general in which they "stated the need for both Indonesia and Timor Leste, as nascent democracies, to find a balance between the competing principles of justice and achieving peace and stability" (United Nations, Secretary-General, *Report of the Secretary-General on Justice and Reconciliation for Timor-Leste*, S/2006/580, July 26, 2006, 8).

53. "RI, Timor Leste to announce commission members next week," *Jakarta Post*, July 9, 2005.

54. The report noted, for example, that in his statement to the Security Council

(January 23, 2006) and his address to the diplomatic corps (February 9, 2006), President Gusmão had explained that "the Government's policy placed emphasis on restorative justice as the most appropriate tool of response to past human rights violations, instead of punitive justice, which is impracticable, tedious and counterproductive within the context of the bilateral and multilateral relations that Timor-Leste enters into with other countries" (United Nations, Security Council, *Report of the Secretary-General on Justice and Reconciliation for Timor-Leste*, 6).

55. Ibid., 11, 8.

56. Ibid., 12–13.

57. United Nations, Security Council, Resolution No. 1704, August 25, 2006, 2, 8.

58. Worse still, in the view of some observers, Gusmão went out of his way to support Wiranto, who had been indicted for crimes against humanity, in his bid for the presidency in 2004.

59. A UN official in Jakarta at the time, and who had served with UNAMET in 1999, saw the consequences of these positions firsthand. In his effort to convince foreign embassies in Jakarta of the need to support the cause of justice for the crimes of 1999, he was repeatedly told that Gusmão himself did not support such efforts (Colin Stewart, head of political affairs, UN Integrated Mission in Timor-Leste, interview, Dili, September 24, 2008).

60. Carsten Stahn, a legal officer in the Office of the Prosecutor of the International Criminal Tribunal for Yugoslavia, writes that "the combined justice and reconciliation formula" established in East Timor may be regarded as "an innovative and promising mechanism for restoring peace and justice in a postwar society" ("Accommodating Individual Criminal Responsibility and National Reconciliation: The UN Truth Commission for East Timor," *American Journal of International Law* 94, no. 4 [October 2001]: 966).

61. Cited in Burgess, "East Timor's Community Reconciliation Procedures," 21.

62. Cited in ibid., 23.

63. Cited in ibid.

64. According to a CTF publication disseminated in Dili in January 2006, the commission's main purpose was to "establish the conclusive truth in regard to the events prior to and immediately after the popular consultation in 1999," with a view to "promoting true reconciliation and friendship." Among other things, it had a mandate to "recommend appropriate measures to heal the wounds of the past," inter alia, by recommending "amnesty for those who cooperate fully in revealing the truth" (Commission on Truth and Friendship of Indonesia and Timor-Leste, "Questions and Answers," Denpasar, [2005]).

65. Paul van Zyl, "Transitional Truth-Seeking: A Comparative Perspective on South Africa, East Timor, and Indonesia," in *Beginning to Remember: The Past in the Indonesian Present*, ed. Mary S. Zurbuchen (Seattle: University of Washington Press, 2001).

66. Aniceto Guterres, human rights lawyer and East Timorese member of the CTF, interview, Dili, January 24, 2006.

67. "NGOs Slam RI-Timor Leste Commission Meeting," *Jakarta Post*, July 24, 2007; Asian Centre for Human Rights, "Indonesia—East Timor CTF: Why the UN Must Boycott it," *ACHR Weekly Review* 178/07, August 1, 2007; Megan Hirst, "Too Much Friendship, Too Little Truth: Monitoring Report on the Commission of Truth and Friendship in Indonesia and Timor-Leste," (Jakarta:, International Center for Transitional Justice, February 2008); Indonesian Non-Governmental Coalition for International Human Rights Advocacy, "CTF a Failure If It Lacks Transparency: Rights Group," April 7, 2008.

68. Commission of Truth and Friendship, *Per Memoriam Ad Spem: Final Report of the Commission of Truth and Friendship (CTF), Indonesia–Timor-Leste* (Denpasar, March 31, 2008).

69. For a summary of the commission's conclusions, see ibid., xiii–xviii.

70. As the commission itself acknowledged, the concept of institutional responsibility "is not recognized in criminal law" (ibid., iii).

71. Aniceto Guterres, CTF commissioner, interview, Dili, September 25, 2008; Kacasungkana, interview.

72. Guterres, interview, September 25, 2008; Kacasungkana, interview.

73. Leigh-Ashley Lipscombe, CTF staff, interview, Dili, September 26, 2008; Dionisio Babo Soares, CTF commissioner, interview, Dili, September 24, 2008.

74. Kacasungkana, interview.

75. Guterres, interview, September 25, 2008; Kacasungkana, interview; Soares, interview.

76. As the CTF report explained, "Determining individual responsibility is not the mandated task of this Commission" (Commission of Truth and Friendship, *Per Memoriam Ad Spem*, xiii).

77. Guterres, interview, September 25, 2008; Soares, interview; Atul Khare, special representative of the secretary-general, UN Integrated Mission in Timor-Leste, interview, Dili, September 29, 2008.

78. Kacasungkana, interview.

Chapter Eleven: Conclusions

1. For an elaboration of this argument in the cases of Aceh and East Timor, see Geoffrey Robinson, "*Rawan* Is as *Rawan* Does: The Origins of Disorder in New Order Aceh," *Indonesia* 66 (October 1998): 127–56, and "People's War: Militias in Indonesia and East Timor," *South East Asia Research* 9, no. 3 (November 2001): 271–318.

2. Ben Kiernan, *The Pol Pot Regime: Race, Power, and Genocide in Cambodia under the Khmer Rouge* (New Haven, CT: Yale University Press, 1996).

3. For that argument, see T. David Mason and Dale A. Krane, "The Political Economy of Death Squads: Toward a Theory of the Impact of State-Sanctioned Terror," *International Studies Quarterly* 33, no. 2 (June 1989): 175–98.

4. See Bruce Campbell, "Death Squads: Definition, Problems, and Historical Context," in *Death Squads in Global Perspective: Murder with Deniability*, ed. Bruce Campbell and Arthur D. Brenner (New York: St. Martin's Press, 2000), 16–18.

5. For variations on this argument, see David Rieff, *A Bed for the Night: Humanitarianism in Crisis* (New York: Simon and Schuster, 2002); William Shawcross, "Protection of Civilians in Conflict," in *World in Crisis: The Politics of Survival at the end of the Twentieth Century*, ed. Médecins Sans Frontières (New York: Routledge, 1999), 1–15; Michael Ignatieff, *Virtual War: Kosovo and Beyond* (New York: Metropolitan Books, 2000); Amnesty International, *"Collateral Damage" or Unlawful Killings? Violations of the Laws of War by NATO during Operation Allied Force* (London: Amnesty International, June 2000).

6. That problem was captured by Colin Powell's comment on U.S. military operations in Afghanistan in 2001 that "the NGOs are such a force multiplier for us, such an important part of our combat team" (cited in Samantha Power, "First Do No Harm," *Los Angeles Times Book Review*, October 6, 2002, 5).

7. See, for example, David Chandler, "International Justice," *New Left Review* 6 (November–December 2000): 55–66.

8. For expressions of this view, see United Nations, Secretary-General, "We the Peoples: The Role of the United Nations in the 21st Century," April 3, 2000; Brian Urquhart, "In the Name of Humanity," *New York Review of Books* 47, no. 7 (April 27, 2000): 19–22; Geoffrey Robertson, *Crimes against Humanity: The Struggle for Global Justice* (New York: New Press, 2000); Bernard Kouchner, "Establish a Right to Intervention against War, Oppression," *Los Angeles Times*, October 18, 1999; Michael Walzer, "Arguing for Humanitarian Intervention," in *The New Killing Fields: Massacre and the Politics of Intervention*, ed. Nicolaus Mills and Kira Brunner (New York: Basic Books, 2002), 19–36.

9. For a trenchant critique of the United Nations' failings that highlights this problem, see William Shawcross, *Deliver Us from Evil: Peacekeepers, Warlords, and a World of Endless Conflict* (New York: Simon and Schuster, 2000).

10. Gary Jonathan Bass argues, for example, that the influence of NGOs on the establishment of international ad hoc tribunals for Rwanda and the former Yugoslavia in the mid-1990s was limited to their role in encouraging a handful of liberal, Western governments that favored the idea anyway (*Stay the Hand of Vengeance: The Politics of War Crimes Tribunals* [Princeton, NJ: Princeton University Press, 2000], 33).

11. See, for example, Rachel Brett, "The Role and Limits of Human Rights: NGOs and the United Nations," in *Politics and Human Rights*, ed. David Beetham (Oxford: Blackwell, 1995), 96–110; William Korey, *NGOs and the Universal Declaration of Human Rights: "A Curious Grapevine"* (New York: St. Martin's Press, 1998); Robertson, *Crimes against Humanity*.

12. For a review and analysis of truth commissions, see Priscilla Hayner, *Unspeakable Truths: Confronting State Terror and Atrocity* (New York: Routledge, 2002).

A NOTE ON SOURCES

WHILE THE EVENTS that are the principal focus of this book are relatively recent, the available sources for their study are unusually rich. In addition to a growing body of secondary materials and memoirs published since 1999, the key sources include a remarkable collection of Indonesian army, police, and militia documents—including secret orders, briefings, budgets, and operational plans. Many of these documents were collected in 1999 by UNAMET or rescued from burning buildings by the local NGO Yayasan HAK at the height of the violence. Others were gathered in later years by various investigative agencies and judicial bodies, including the Serious Crimes Unit of the General Prosecutor of the Republic of Timor-Leste, the Human Rights Office of UNTAET, and the CTF. The relevant sources also include a wide array of UN documents from 1999, such as Security Council resolutions, reports by the secretary-general, weekly situation reports prepared by UNAMET's Political Affairs Office, briefings prepared for the UN staff in New York by the UNAMET head of mission in Dili, and four substantial UN reports written between late 1999 and 2006. Another important body of materials are the testimonies, interviews, and documents gathered over three years by East Timor's CAVR, and used in the preparation of its final report, *Chega!* Now stored in the CAVR archives in Dili, with digital copies of many holdings also in the British Library, this collection includes transcripts and audio recordings of the eight national public hearings held by the CAVR on different aspects of the violence experienced during the Indonesian occupation, and dozens of interviews with key political figures. Also valuable are the official indictments and testimonies generated by the judicial proceedings related to the events of 1999—specifically, the ad hoc human rights trials in Jakarta and the serious crimes process in Dili.

Unfortunately, at the time of writing, most of these important materials had yet to be systematically archived or made available to the public for research purposes. For that reason, most were borrowed by the author from the collections of the bodies or institutions named above. Unless otherwise indicated, therefore, copies of the documents listed as "primary sources" in the bibliography are in the author's possession.

BIBLIOGRAPHY

PRIMARY SOURCES

CNRT. "Falintil Resumes Their Mission in Defense of the People of East Timor." Press statement, Jakarta, April 5, 1999.
———. Letter to UNAMET, Political Affairs Office, September 1, 1999.
CNRT-Falintil, Frente Politica Interna (FPI), Secretariat for Information and Security, Region 3. Letter to UNAMET, July 16, 1999.
CNRT, National Political Commission. "Directive No. 1/99, 7 July 1999."
da Costa, Mário Pinto. Letter to Komandan [Aitarak], March 30, 1999.
"Declassified British Documents Reveal U.K. Support for Indonesian Invasion and Occupation of East Timor, Recognition of Denial of Self-Determination, 1975–1976." National Security Archive. Available at http://www.gwu.edu/~nsarchiv/NSAEBB/NSAEBB174/indexuk.htm.
Democratic Republic of Timor-Leste, Deputy General Prosecutor for Serious Crimes. Indictment against Wiranto et al., Dili, February 22, 2003.
———. Indictment against Col. Herman Sedyono et al., Dili, February 28, 2003.
———. Indictment against Egidio Manek et al., Dili, February 28, 2003.
———. Serious Crimes Unit. "Serious Crimes Update V/03." Dili, May 28, 2003.
Departemen Pertahanan-Keamanan Republik Indonesia. "Petunjuk-Pelaksanaan, Nomor: Juklak/06/V/1976, tentang Kegiatan di Bidang Operasi Tempur, Tahun 1976–1977," May 17, 1976.
———. "Keputusan Menteri Pertahanan-Keamanan/Panglima Angkatan Bersenjata, Nomor: Kep/23/X/1978, tentang Normalisasi Penyelenggaraan Pertahanan-Keamanan di Daerah Timor-Timur dan Pembubaran Kodahankam Tim-Tim," October 12, 1978.
———. "Petunjuk-Pelaksanaan, Nomor: Juklak/02/V/1979, tentang Kegiatan Operasi di Daerah Timor Timur Dalam Tahun 1979–1980," May 11, 1979.
———. *Doktrin Pertahanan Keamanan Negara.* Jakarta, 1991.
dos Santos, Rafael. Deposition recorded and compiled in Sydney, Australia on October 27–28, 1999.
Garnadi, H. R. "Gambaran unum apabila Opsi I gagal." Nomor: M.53/Tim P4-OKTT/7/1999. Dili, July 3, 1999.
Gubernur Timor Timur. Letter to All Bupatis concerning "Proposal," May 1999.
———. Letter to All Provincial Heads of Department (*Kakanwil*) in East Timor, May 1999.
———. Letter to Bupati of Lautem, May 21, 1999.
———. "Tindakan terhadap PNS yang terlibat organisasi/ kegiatan yang menentang Pemerintah RI." Circular No. 200/827/Sospol/V/1999. May 28, 1999.
———. Letter to Bupati of Oecussi, June 1999.
Gusmão, Xanana. "Now Is the Time to Build the Future! Reconciliation, Unity, and National Development in the Framework of the Transition towards Independence." Jakarta, [August 24?] 1999.
———. "Let Us Free Our Beloved Homeland, Our Beloved East Timor." Jakarta, August 30, 1999.

Japan, Embassy to Indonesia. "Political News Round-Up." August 31, 1999.

Kepolisian Negara Republik Indonesia. "Tinjauan Strategis Pembangunan Kekuatan dan Kemampuan Komando Antar Resort Kepolisian 15.3 Timor Timur, Tahun 1978–1983." Dili, March 1978.

———, Daerah Timor Timur. "Rencana Operasi Hanoin Lorosae II." Dili, August 15, 1999.

———, Daerah Timor Timur, Direktorat Reserse. "Laporan Penangan Kasus Liquisa." Dili, April 15, 1999.

Kodim 1627/Dili. "Laporan hasil pertemuan di Gada Paksi." Dandim 1627 (Lt. Col. Endar Priyanto) to Danrem 164/WD and others. June 23, 1998.

Kodim 1628/Baucau. "Daftar: Nominatif Anggota Kompi Khusus Pusaka, Kodim 1628/Baucau." February 3, 1999.

Kodim 1630/Viqueque. "Daftar: Nominatif Pemegang Senjata Team Makikit." Undated, but found at Kodim 1630/Viqueque on November 28, 1998.

Komandan Komando Pasukan Aitarak Sector B. "Permohonan Dispensasi." Letter from Eurico Guterres to Dandim 1627/Dili and others. No. 46/PD/MK-AT/VI/1999. June 22, 1999.

Komando Pasukan Pejuang Integrasi. Letter from Eurico Guterres to Governor of Nusa Tenggara Timur. No. 55/SP/MK-AT/VI/1999. June 30, 1999.

Komisi Perdamaian dan Stabilitas. "Kesepakatan Bersama Conselho Nasional da Resistência Timorense (CNRT) dan Falintil, dan Pro-Integrasi dalam Rangka Penentuan Pendapat di Timor-Timur." Jakarta, June 18, 1999.

Komisi Penyelidikan Pelanggaran Hak Asasi Manusia (KPP-HAM). *Laporan Penyelidikan Pelanggaran Hak Asasi Manusia di Timor Timur.* Jakarta, January 31, 2000.

Korem 164/Wira Dharma. Danrem 164/WD to Dandim 1627–1639 and others. Secret Telegram No. TR/41/1999. January 28, 1999.

———. Danrem 164/WD to Dandim 1627–1639, Dansatgas Tribuana, and others. Secret Telegram No. TR/46/1999. February 2, 1999.

———. Dan Sat Gas Pam Dili to Dan Rem Up. Kasi Intel Rem 164/WD. Secret Telegram No. STR/200/1999. April 17 (18?), 1999.

———. "Rencana Operasi Wira Dharma-99." Operational plan prepared by East Timor Sub-Regional Military Command (Korem 164). Dili, July 1999.

Korem 164/Wira Dharma, Seksi Intel. "Petunjuk Tehnis tentang Desa." Juknis/01-A/IV/1982. Dili, 1982.

———. "Petunjuk Teknis tentang Cara Babinsa/Team Pembina Desa Dalam Memobongkar Jaringan Pendukung GPK." Dili, 1982.

———. "Petunjuk Tehnis tentang Cara Mengamankan Masyarakat Dari Pengaruh Propaganda GPK." Juknis/04-B/IV/1982. Dili, 1982.

———. "Prosedur Tetap tentang Razia Daerah Pemukiman." Protap/01-A/VII/1982. Dili, 1982.

———. "Rencana Penyusunan Kembali Rakyat Terlatih." Dili, 1982.

———. "Petunjuk Tehnis tentang Kegiatan Babinsa." Juknis/06/IV/1982. Dili, July 1982.

———. "Petunjuk Tehnis tentang Sistem Keamanan Kota dan Daerah Pemukiman." Juknis/05/I/1982. Dili, July 1982.

———. "Prosedur Tetap tentang Cara Interogasi Tawanan." Protap/01-B/VII/1982. Dili, July 1982.

Krieger, Heike, ed. *East Timor and the International Community: Basic Documents.* Cambridge: Cambridge University Press, 1997.

National Alliance for an International Tribunal for East Timor. Letter to the UN High Commissioner for Human Rights, March 13, 2003.

Pemerintah Kabupaten Daerah Tingkat II Dili. "Pengamanan Swakarsa (PAM Swakarsa) dan Ketertiban Kota Dili." Dili, April 1999.

Saburai, Lafaek. "Re: Operasi Pembersihan." Front Pembersihan Timor Timur Milisi Sayap Kiri Darah Merah. No. 024/Ops/R/III/1999. March 11, 1999.

Tavares, João. "Instruksi . . . Tentang Kesiapan dan Kesiagaan Passukan Integrasi (Milisi) Dalam Menyikapi Perkembangan Situasi dan Kondisi di Timor-Timur." No. 010/INS/PPI/VII/1999. July 1999.

Tentara Nasional Indonesia. Telegram from Lt. Gen. Johny Lumintang to Regional Military Commander (Pangdam) General Adam Damiri. "Surat Telegram kepada Pangdam IX." May 5, 1999.

———. Letter from Ermera District Military Commander Lt. Col. Muhammad Nur to Bupati of Ermera. "Permohonan Uang Saku PAM Swakarsa." June 1999.

———. Order by Armed Forces Chief of General Staff (Lt. Gen. Sugiono) on Behalf of TNI Commander (Gen. Wiranto). "Surat Perintah No. Sprin/1096/VI/1999." June 4, 1999.

———. Order by TNI Commander (Gen. Wiranto). "Surat Perintah No. Sprin 1180/P/VI/1999." June 16, 1999.

———. Secret telegram from Chief of Staff, Kodam IX/Udayana (Brig. Gen. Mahidin Simbolon) to Armed Forces Commander (Gen. Wiranto). July 6, 1999.

UNAMET. "Press Release." August 19, 1999.

———. "Remarks Made at the Ceremony Announcing the Agreement Reached by Pro-Integration Forces and Falintil, UNAMET Headquarters, Dili, Sunday, 29 August 1999."

UNAMET, Civilian Police Office. "Interview Conducted at UNAMET HQ on Sunday the 29th of August 1999, by Superintendant Pim Martinsson, Inspector Peter Burt, and Anthony Goldstone (Political)." August 29, 1999.

———. Ermera Regional Commander. "Murder of Locally Employed UNAMET Staff." August 30, 1999.

———. "Report of Incident at Bobo Leten, Atsabe, Ermera on 30 August 1999." September 21, 1999.

UNAMET, Electoral Commission. "Statement Minuted on Friday, August 27, 1999." August 27, 1999.

UNAMET, Electoral Office. "Weekly Report." June 14, 1999.

———. "Weekly Report (27 July–2 August 1999)."

———. "Summary of Voter Registration." August 9, 1999.

UNAMET, Head of Mission. "Weekly Report." June 14, 1999.

———. "Weekly Report." June 28, 1999.

———. "Recommendation to Suspend Electoral Preparations." July 5, 1999.

———. "Weekly Report." July 5, 1999.

———. "Security Conditions for the Operational Phase of the Popular Consultation." July 8, 1999.

———. "Security Conditions for the Operational Phase of the Popular Consultation—Update." July 14, 1999.

———. "Weekly Report." July 19, 1999.

———. "Weekly Report." July 26, 1999.

———. "Weekly Report." August 2, 1999.

UNAMET, Joint Operations Center. "Report on Incidents in Central Dili: 26th of August 1999." August 27, 1999.

————. "Daily Log." August 29, 1999.

————. "Interoffice Memo re: Advice from MLO at DanRem HQ." September 10, 1999.

UNAMET, Military Liaison Office. "Weekly Sitrep." July 14–16, 1999.

————. "Record of Conversation. Meeting between Brigadier Reuq [sic], CMLO UNAMET, and Colonel Tono Suratman, Comd Korem 164." July 14, 1999.

UNAMET, Political Affairs Office. "Report on UNAMET Retrieval of Hostages from Falintil and Observation of Joint TNI/Militia Operations—15 June 1999." June 16, 1999.

————. "Weekly Sitrep #1 (27 June–4 July [1999])."

————. "Report on 29 June Incident in Maliana." July 5, 1999.

————. "Assessment of Security Conditions in East Timor." July 9, 1999.

————. "Report on the Liquica Incidents of 4 July." July 12, 1999.

————. "Weekly Sitrep #3 (12–18 July 1999)." July 18, 1999.

————. "Meeting between UNAMET and Falintil Deputy Commander Taur Matan Ruak." July 26, 1999.

————. "Weekly Sitrep #4 (26 July–1 August 1999)." August 1, 1999.

————. "Weekly Sitrep #5 (2 August–8 August 1999)." August 8, 1999.

————. "Weekly Sitrep #6 (9 August–15 August 1999)." August 15, 1999.

————. "Note to the File: Meeting with the Japanese Parliamentary Vice-Minister for Foreign Affairs." August 15, 1999.

————. "Selected Comments of Mahidi Leader, Cancio de Carvalho at Cantonment Ceremony, Cassa, Ainaro, 18 August 1999." August 19, 1999.

————. "Status of CNRT Offices in East Timor (22 August 1999)." August 22, 1999.

————. "Weekly Sitrep #7 (16 August–22 August 1999)." August 22, 1999.

————. "Summary of Developments as of 18:00 hours, 30 August 1999." August 30, 1999.

————. "Notes on the Atsabe Investigation." August 31, 1999.

————. "Report on the Incidents in Maliana, 30 August to 3 September." September 4, 1999.

————. "Attack on UNAMET Staff in Liquica, 4 September 1999." September 4, 1999.

————. "Incidents on 3 and 4 September Which Led to the Relocation to Dili of UNAMET Staff from Aileu, Ainaro, Maliana, Liquica, and Same Regencies." [September 5] 1999.

————. "Overview Sitrep, 5–6 September." September 6, 1999.

————. "Situation Report." September 6, 1999.

————. "Situation Report—Update on Humanitarian Affairs." September 6, 1999.

————. "Sitrep." September 7, 1999.

————. "Attack on Bishop Belo's Residence, 6 September 1999." September 8, 1999.

————. "Militia Attack against UNAMET Staff on Logistical Mission." September 9, 1999.

————. "Notes on the Militia Incursion." September 10, 1999.

————. "The Destruction of East Timor since 4 September." September 11, 1999.

United Nations. "Decolonization: Issue on East Timor." August 1976.

————. *Situation of Human Rights in East Timor.* December 10, 1999.

————. *Report of the Independent Inquiry into the Actions of the United Nations during the 1994 Genocide in Rwanda.* December 15, 1999.

———. *Report of the International Commission of Inquiry on East Timor to the Secretary-General.* January 2000.

———. *Report of the Panel on United Nations Peace Operations.* August 17, 2000.

United Nations, Commission on Human Rights. Resolution No. 1999/S-4/1. September 27, 1999.

United Nations, Secretary-General. Press Release. SG/SM/6966. April 23, 1999.

———. "Memorandum" [to the governments of Indonesia and Portugal]. May 4, 1999.

———. "Question of East Timor: Report of the Secretary-General." May 5, 1999.

———. "Question of East Timor: Report of the Secretary-General." June 22, 1999.

———. "Question of East Timor: Report of the Secretary-General." July 20, 1999.

———. Telegram to Ian Martin, re: Message of Support. September 9, 1999.

———. "Statement on East Timor." September 10, 1999.

———. Press Release. "Kofi Annan Says Time Has Come for Indonesia to Seek International Community's Help to Bring Order and Security to East Timor." September 11, 1999.

———. *Report of the Secretary-General Pursuant to General Assembly Resolution 53/55, 1998: The Fall of Srebrenica.* November 15, 1999.

———. Press Release. SG/SM/7263 AFR/196. December 16, 1999.

———. "We the Peoples: The Role of the United Nations in the 21st Century." April 3, 2000.

———. Letter to the President of the Security Council. S/2005/96. January 11, 2005.

———. *Report of the Secretary-General on Justice and Reconciliation for Timor-Leste.* July 26, 2006.

United Nations, Security Council. "Statement by the President of the Security Council." June 29, 1999.

———. Resolution No. 1262. August 27, 1999.

———. Press Release. "Security Council Hears 52 Speakers in Open Debate on Situation in East Timor." September 11, 1999.

———. *Report of the Security Council Mission to Jakarta and Dili, 8 to 12 September 1999.* September 14, 1999.

———. Resolution No. 1264. September 15, 1999.

———. Resolution No. 1272. October 25, 1999.

———. "Summary of the Report to the Secretary-General of the Commission of Experts to Review the Prosecution of Serious Violations of Human Rights in Timor-Leste (then East Timor) in 1999." May 26, 2005. Annex I of UN Security Council document S/2005/458, July 15, 2005.

———. Resolution No. 1704. August 25, 2006.

UNTAET. Regulation No. 2000/15. "On the Establishment of Panels with Exclusive Jurisdiction over Serious Criminal Offences." June 6, 2000.

———, District Human Rights Office—Dili. "Dili Chronology." 2002.

———, District Human Rights Office—Dili. "Key Cases of HRVs/Abuses in Dili District." September 2002.

UNTAET, Political Affairs Office. *Briefing Book on Political Affairs and Human Rights.* Dili, November 1999.

United States, Agency for International Development. "Situation Report No. 1, October 19, 1979: East Timor, Indonesia—Displaced Persons."

United States, Congress. HR 1500, 108th sess., sec. 721, May 2003.

———. Letter to U.S. Secretary of State, Madeleine Albright, April 12, 1999.

United States, Department of State, Telegram 1579 from U.S. Embassy Jakarta to Secretary of State, on "Ford–Suharto Meeting," December 6, 1975, "East Timor Revisited: Ford, Kissinger, and the Indonesian Invasion, 1975–76," document 4, National Security Archive, available at http://www.gwu.edu/~nsarchiv/NSAEBB/NSAEBB62/.

United States, President Clinton. "Remarks to American and Asian Business Leaders in Auckland," September 12, 1999. *Weekly Compilation of Presidential Documents* 35, no. 37 (September 20, 1999): 1727–28.

United States, White House. Memorandum of Conversation between President Ford and President Suharto, July 5, 1975. National Security Archive, "East Timor Revisited: Ford, Kissinger, and the Indonesian Invasion, 1975–76," document 1. Available at http://www.gwu.edu/~nsarchiv/NSAEBB/NSAEBB62/.

Way, Wendy, ed. *Documents on Australian Foreign Policy: Australia and the Indonesian Incorporation of Portuguese Timor, 1974–1976.* Canberra: Department of Foreign Affairs and Trade, 2000.

SECONDARY SOURCES

Aditjondro, George J. "Ninjas, Nanggalas, Monuments, and Mossad Manuals: An Anthropology of Indonesian State Terror in East Timor." In *Death Squad: The Anthropology of State Terror*, ed. Jeffrey A. Sluka, 158–88. Philadelphia: University of Pennsylvania Press, 1998.

———. *Welcoming the Rising Sun at the Top of Ramelau.* Jakarta: Yayasan HAK and Fortilos, 2000.

Alatas, Ali. *The Pebble in the Shoe: The Diplomatic Struggle for East Timor.* Jakarta: Aksara Karunia, 2006.

Amnesty International. *East Timor—Violations of Human Rights: Extrajudicial Executions, "Disappearances," Torture, and Political Imprisonment, 1975–1984.* London: Amnesty International, 1985.

———. "East Timor: Short-term Detention and Ill-treatment." London: Amnesty International, January 1990.

———. "East Timor: Amnesty International Statement to the UN Special Committee on Decolonization." London: Amnesty International, August 1990.

———. "East Timor: Update on Human Rights Concerns since August 1990." London: Amnesty International, January 1991.

———. "East Timor: Amnesty International Statement to the UN Special Committee on Decolonization." London: Amnesty International, August 1991.

———. "East Timor: The Santa Cruz Massacre." London: Amnesty International, November 14, 1991.

———. "East Timor: After the Massacre." London: Amnesty International, November 21, 1991.

———. "Indonesia/East Timor: The Suppression of Dissent." London: Amnesty International, 1992.

———. "Indonesia and East Timor: Santa Cruz—The Government Response." London: Amnesty International, February 1992.

———. "Indonesia/East Timor: East Timor Human Rights Protesters Charged with Subversion." London: Amnesty International, March 27, 1992.

———. "Indonesia/East Timor: Fernando de Araújo—Prisoner of Conscience." London: Amnesty International, May 1992.

————. "East Timor: 'In Accordance with the Law.' Statement before the UN Special Committee on Decolonization." London: Amnesty International, July 1992.

————. "Indonesia and East Timor: A New Order? Human Rights in 1992." London: Amnesty International, 1993.

————. "Indonesia: 'Shock Therapy'—Restoring Order in Aceh, 1989–1993." London: Amnesty International, 1993.

————. "Indonesia and East Timor: Seven East Timorese Seek Asylum." London: Amnesty International, June 23, 1993.

————. "Indonesia and East Timor: Seven East Timorese Still in Danger." London: Amnesty International, July 5, 1993.

————. "East Timor: Unfair Political Trial of Xanana Gusmão." London: Amnesty International, July 1993.

————. "Indonesia and East Timor: Political Prisoners and the Rule of Law." London: Amnesty International, 1994.

————. "Indonesia and East Timor: The 12 November Protests." London: Amnesty International, 1994.

————. "Indonesia and East Timor: Update on the 12 November Protests." London: Amnesty International, 1994.

————. "Indonesia: 'Operation Cleansing'—Human Rights and APEC." London: Amnesty International, 1994.

————. "Indonesia and East Timor: Human Rights in 1994—A Summary." London: Amnesty International, January 1995.

————. Urgent Action 33/95. London: Amnesty International, February 13, 1995.

————. "Paramilitary Attacks Jeopardise East Timor's Future." London: Amnesty International, April 16, 1999.

————. "East Timor: Seize the Moment." London: Amnesty International, June 21, 1999.

————. "East Timor: The Terror Continues." London: Amnesty International, September 24, 1999.

————. "As Violence Descended: Testimonies from East Timorese Refugees." London: Amnesty International, October 1999.

————. "Collateral Damage" or Unlawful Killings? Violations of the Laws of War by NATO during Operation Allied Force. London: Amnesty International, June 2000.

————. "East Timor: Building a New Country Based on Human Rights." London: Amnesty International, July 2000.

————. Indonesia and Timor Leste: International Responsibility for Justice. London: Amnesty International, April 2003.

Anderson, Benedict. "Testimony for the Subcommittee on International Organizations and the Subcommittee on Asian and Pacific Affairs of the Committee on International Relations of the U.S. House of Representatives." Washington, DC, February 6, 1980.

————. "East Timor: Some Implications." In East Timor at the Crossroads: The Forging of a Nation, ed. Peter Carey and G. Carter Bentley, 137–47. Honolulu: University of Hawaii Press, 1995.

————. "Gravel in Jakarta's Shoes." In The Spectre of Comparisons: Nationalism, Southeast Asia, and the World, 131–38. London: Verso Press, 1998.

Araújo, Fernando de. "The CNRT Campaign for Independence." In Out of the Ashes: The Destruction and Reconstruction of East Timor, ed. James J. Fox and Dionisio B. Soares, 106–25. Adelaide, Australia: Crawford House Publishing, 2000.

Archer, Robert. "The Catholic Church in East Timor." In *East Timor at the Crossroads: The Forging of a Nation*, ed. Peter Carey and G. Carter Bentley, 120–33. Honolulu: University of Hawaii Press, 1995.

Australian Broadcasting Corporation. "A License to Kill." *Four Corners*. March 15, 1999.

Ball, Desmond. "Silent Witness: Australian Intelligence and East Timor." Canberra: Strategic and Defence Studies Centre, Australian National University, 2001.

Barker, Joshua. "State of Fear: Controlling the Criminal Contagion in Suharto's New Order." *Indonesia* 66 (October 1998): 7–42.

Bartu, Peter. "The Militia, the Military, and the People of Bobonaro." In *Bitter Flowers, Sweet Flowers: East Timor, Indonesia, and the World Community*, ed. Richard Tanter, Mark Selden, and Stephen Shalom, 73–90. New York: Rowman and Littlefield, 2001.

Bass, Gary Jonathan. *Stay the Hand of Vengeance: The Politics of War Crimes Tribunals*. Princeton, NJ: Princeton University Press, 2000.

Berrigan, Frida. "Indonesia at the Crossroads: U.S. Weapons Sales and Military Training—A Special Report." New York: Arms Trade Resource Center, October 2001.

Bertrand, Jacques. *Nationalism and Ethnic Conflict in Indonesia*. New York: Cambridge University Press, 2004.

Bourchier, David. "Crime, Law, and Authority in Indonesia." In *State and Civil Society in Indonesia*, ed. Arief Budiman, 177–211. Papers on Southeast Asia. Clayton, Victoria: Monash University, 1990.

Boxer, C. R. "Portuguese Timor: A Rough Island History: 1550–1960." *History Today* 10, no. 5 (May 1960): 349–55.

———. *Fidalgos in the Far East, 1550–1770*. London: Oxford University Press, 1968.

———. *The Portuguese Seaborne Empire, 1415–1825*. New York: Alfred A. Knopf, 1969.

Brass, Paul R. *Theft of an Idol: Text and Context in the Representation of Collective Violence*. Princeton, NJ: Princeton University Press, 1997.

Brett, Rachel. "The Role and Limits of Human Rights: NGOs and the United Nations." In *Politics and Human Rights*, ed. David Beetham, 96–110. Oxford: Blackwell, 1995.

Browning, Christopher. *Ordinary Men: Reserve Police Battalion 101 and the Final Solution in Poland*. New York: Harper Perennial, 1998.

Burgess, Patrick. "East Timor's Community Reconciliation Procedures: A Valuable New Addition to the Reconciliation Tool-kit." Draft paper, 2004.

Campbell, Bruce. "Death Squads: Definition, Problems, and Historical Context." In *Death Squads in Global Perspective: Murder with Deniability*, ed. Bruce Campbell and Arthur D. Brenner, 1–26. New York: St. Martin's Press, 2000.

Cardoso, Luis. *The Crossing: A Story of East Timor*. London: Granta Books, 2000.

Carey, Peter. "Third World Colonialism, the *Geraçao Foun*, and the Birth of a New Nation: Indonesia through East Timorese Eyes, 1975–1999." *Indonesia* 76 (October 2003): 23–67.

Carey, Peter, and G. Carter Bentley, eds. *East Timor at the Crossroads: The Forging of a Nation*. Honolulu: University of Hawaii Press, 1995.

Castro, Gonçalo Pimenta de. *Timor: Subsidios Para a Sua História*. Lisbon: Agência Geral das Colónias, 1944.

CAVR. "Massacres. National Public Hearing, 19–21 November 2003." Dili: CAVR, 2005.

———. *Chega!* Dili: CAVR, 2006. Available at http://www.cavr-timorleste.org/en/chegaReport.htm.

Chauncey, Helen, Jane Clayton, and Rachael Grossman. "Showcase Garrison." *Southeast Asia Chronicle* 58–59 (December 1977): 5–11.

Chomsky, Noam. "East Timor, the United States, and International Responsibility:

'Green Light' for War Crimes." In *Bitter Flowers, Sweet Flowers: East Timor, Indonesia, and the World Community*, ed. Richard Tanter, Mark Selden, and Stephen Shalom, 127–47. New York: Rowman and Littlefield, 2001.

Cohen, David. *Intended to Fail: The Trials before the Ad Hoc Human Rights Court in Jakarta*. New York: International Center for Transitional Justice, 2003.

Columbijn, Freek, and Thomas Lindblad, eds. *Roots of Violence in Indonesia: Contemporary Violence in Historical Perspective*. Leiden: KITLV Press, 2002.

Commission of Truth and Friendship. "Questions and Answers." Denpasar [2005].

Conboy, Ken. *Kopassus: Inside Indonesia's Special Forces*. Jakarta: Equinox, 2003.

Correia, A. Pinto. *Timor de Lés a Lés*. Lisbon: Agência Geral das Colónias, 1944.

Cribb, Robert, ed. *The Indonesian Killings, 1965–1966: Studies from Java and Bali*. No. 21. Clayton, Victoria: Monash Papers on Southeast Asia, 1990.

———. "From Petrus to Ninja: Death Squads in Indonesia." In *Death Squads in Global Perspective: Murder with Deniability*, Bruce B. Campbell and Arthur D. Brenner, 181–202. New York: St. Martin's Press, 2000.

Crouch, Harold. *The Army and Politics in Indonesia*. Ithaca, NY: Cornell University Press, 1978.

———. "The TNI and East Timor Policy." In *Out of the Ashes: Destruction and Reconstruction of East Timor*, ed. James Fox and Dionisio Babo Soares, 151–79. Adelaide, Australia: Crawford House Publishing, 2000.

———. *Per Memoriam Ad Spem: Final Report of the Commission of Truth and Friendship (CTF), Indonesia–Timor-Leste*. Denpasar, March 31, 2008.

Davidson, Katherine. "The Portuguese Colonisation of Timor: The Final Stage, 1850–1892." PhD diss., University of New South Wales, 1994.

Dunn, James. "The Timor Affair in International Perspective." In *East Timor at the Crossroads: The Forging of a Nation*, ed. Peter Carey and G. Carter Bentley, 59–72. Honolulu: University of Hawaii Press, 1995.

———. *Timor: A People Betrayed*. Sydney: ABC Books, 2001.

East Timor Action Network. "Subject: Operasi Sapu Jagad—Indonesia's Military Plan to Disrupt Independence." Ref. doc. FAIO-1999/10/21.

East Timor International Support Center. "Indonesia's Death Squads: Getting Away with Murder." Occasional paper no. 2. Darwin: ETISC, May 1999.

Evans, Grant. "Portuguese Timor." *New Left Review* 91 (May–June 1975): 67–79.

Fein, Helen. "Genocide: A Sociological Perspective." *Current Sociology* 38, no. 1 (Spring 1990): 1–126.

———. "Revolutionary and Anti-revolutionary Genocides: A Comparison of State Murders in Democratic Kampuchea, 1975–1979, and in Indonesia, 1965–1966." *Comparative Studies in Society and History* 35, no. 4 (October 1993): 796–823.

Felgas, Hélio A. Esteves. *Timor Português*. Lisbon: Agência Geral do Ultramar, 1956.

Fischer, Tim. *Seven Days in East Timor: Ballot and Bullets*. St Leonards, NSW: Allen and Unwin, 2000.

Forbes, H. O. "On Some Tribes of the Island of Timor." *Journal of the Anthropological Institute of Great Britain and Ireland* 13 (1884): 402–30.

Fox, James. "Ceremonies of Reconciliation as Prelude to Violence in Suai." In *Violent Conflicts in Indonesia: Analysis, Representation, Resolution*, ed. Charles A. Coppel, 174–790. London: Routledge, 2006.

Fretilin. "What Is Fretilin? The Revolutionary Front for an Independent East Timor Explains Its Aims in a Question and Answer Format." Sydney: Campaign for an Independent East Timor, 1974.

Gama, Paulino. "The War in the Hills, 1975–1985: A Fretilin Commander Remembers." In *East Timor at the Crossroads: The Forging of a Nation*, ed. Peter Carey and G. Carter Bentley, 97–105. Honolulu: University of Hawaii Press, 1995.

Gomes, Donaciano. "The East Timor Intifada: Testimony of a Student Activist." In *East Timor at the Crossroads: The Forging of a Nation*, ed. Peter Carey and G. Carter Bentley, 106–8. Honolulu: University of Hawaii Press, 1995.

Greenlees, Don, and Robert Garran. *Deliverance: The Inside Story of East Timor's Fight for Freedom*. Crows Nest, NSW: Allen and Unwin, 2002.

Gross, Jan T. *Neighbors: The Destruction of the Jewish Community in Jedwabne, Poland*. New York: Penguin Books, 2002.

Gunn, Geoffrey. *East Timor and the United Nations: The Case for Intervention*. Lawrenceville, NJ: Red Sea Press, 1997.

Gusmão, Kirsty Sword. *A Woman of Independence: A Story of Love and the Birth of a New Nation*. Sydney: Macmillan, 2003.

Hainsworth, Paul, and Stephen McCloskey, eds. *The East Timor Question: The Struggle for Independence from Indonesia*. London: I. B. Tauris, 2000.

Harris, Mark. "Heroes of Integration." MA thesis, School of Oriental and African Studies, 2001.

Hartung, William D. "U.S. Arms Transfers to Indonesia, 1975–1997: Who's Influencing Whom?" New York: Arms Trade Resources Center, March 1997.

Hayner, Priscilla. *Unspeakable Truths: Confronting State Terror and Atrocity*. New York: Routledge, 2002.

Hill, Helen. *The Timor Story*. 2nd ed. Fitzroy, Victoria: Timor Information Service, 1976.

————. "Fretilin: The Origins, Ideologies, and Strategies of a Nationalist Movement in East Timor." MA thesis, Monash University, 1978.

Hinton, Alexander L. "Why Did You Kill? The Cambodian Genocide and the Dark Side of Face and Honor." *Journal of Asian Studies* 57, no. 1 (February 1998): 93–118.

Hirst, Megan. "Too Much Friendship, Too Little Truth: Monitoring Report on the Commission of Truth and Friendship in Indonesia and Timor-Leste." Jakarta: International Center for Transitional Justice, February 2008.

Hoadley, J. Stephen. "The Future of Portuguese Timor." Occasional Paper no. 27. Singapore: Institute of Southeast Asian Studies, March 1975.

Ignatieff, Michael. *Virtual War: Kosovo and Beyond*. New York: Metropolitan Books, 2000.

Institute for Policy Studies. "Background Information on Indonesia, the Invasion of East Timor, and U.S. Military Assistance." Washington, DC: Institute for Policy Studies, May 1982.

"Interview with Mário Carrascalão." *Indonesia* 76 (October 2003): 1–22.

Jonassohn, Kurt, and Karin Solveig Bjornson. *Genocide and Gross Human Rights Violations in Comparative Perspective*. London: Transaction Publishers, 1998.

Jolliffe, Jill. *East Timor, Nationalism, and Colonialism*. St Lucia: University of Queensland Press, 1978.

————. *Cover-up: The Inside Story of the Balibo Five*. Melbourne: Scribe Publications, 2001.

Judicial System Monitoring Programme. "JSMP Background Paper on the Justice Sector." Paper prepared for the Timor-Leste and Development Partners Meeting, Dili, June 2003.

Kammen, Douglas. "Master-Slave, Traitor-Nationalist, Opportunist-Oppressed: Political Metaphors in East Timor." *Indonesia* 76 (October 2003): 69–85.

Kiernan, Ben. *The Pol Pot Regime: Race, Power, and Genocide in Cambodia under the Khmer Rouge.* New Haven, CT: Yale University Press, 1996.

Kohen, Arnold. *From the Place of the Dead: The Biography of Bishop Carlos Ximenes Belo of East Timor.* New York: St. Martin's Press, 1999.

———. Testimony before the Commission on Reception, Truth, and Reconciliation in East Timor (CAVR). Dili, March 15, 2004.

"The Kopassus-Militia Alliance." *Tapol Bulletin,* 154 no. 5 (November 1999). Available at http://www.gn.apc.org/tapol/154nkopa.htm.

Korey, William. *NGOs and the Universal Declaration of Human Rights: "A Curious Grapevine."* New York: St. Martin's Press, 1998.

La Rocque, Gene R. "Our Interests Are Not at Stake." *Southeast Asia Chronicle* 74 (August 1980): 9–10.

Lawless, Robert. "The Indonesian Takeover of East Timor." *Asian Survey* 16, no. 10 (October 1976): 948–64.

Lennox, Rowena. *Fighting Spirit of East Timor: The Life of Martinho da Costa Lopes.* London: Zed Books, 2000.

Lowry, Bob. *Indonesian Defence Policy and the Indonesian Armed Forces.* Canberra: Strategic and Defence Studies Centre, Australian National University, 1993.

Makarim, Zacky Anwar, Glenny Kairupan, Andreas Sugono, and Ibnu Fatah. *Hari-Hari Terakhir Timor Timur: Sebuah Kesaksian.* Jakarta: PT Sportif Media Informasindo, 2003.

Mann, Michael. *The Dark Side of Democracy: Explaining Ethnic Cleansing.* New York: Cambridge University Press, 2004.

Marker, Jamsheed. *East Timor: A Memoir of the Negotiations for Independence.* Jefferson, NC: McFarland and Company, Inc., 2003.

Martin, Ian. *Self-Determination in East Timor: The United Nations, the Ballot, and International Intervention.* International Peace Academy Occasional Paper. London: Lynne Rienner Publishers, 2001.

Mason, T. David, and Dale A. Krane. "The Political Economy of Death Squads: Toward a Theory of the Impact of State-Sanctioned Terror." *International Studies Quarterly* 33, no. 2 (June 1989): 175–98.

McVey, Ruth. "The Post-Revolutionary Transformation of the Indonesian Army, Part I." *Indonesia* 11 (April 1971): 131–76.

———. "The Post-Revolutionary Transformation of the Indonesian Army, Part II." *Indonesia* 13 (April 1972): 147–81.

Midlarsky, Manus I. *The Killing Trap: Genocide in the Twentieth Century.* Cambridge: Cambridge University Press, 2005.

Moore, Samuel. "The Indonesian Military's Last Years in East Timor: An Analysis of Its Secret Documents." *Indonesia* 72 (October 2001): 9–44.

Moynihan, Daniel Patrick. *A Dangerous Place.* Boston: Little, Brown, 1978.

Muis, Colonel Muh. Nur. "Kecurangan UNAMET Selama Jajak Pendapat di Timor-Timur Pada Tahun 1999." Paper prepared for workshop on Masalah Kecurangan UNAMET, Jakarta, October 6, 2000.

Nairn, Allan. "US Complicity in Timor." *Nation,* September 27, 1999. Available at http://www.thenation.com/doc/1990927/nairn/print.

Nasution, Abdul Haris. *Fundamentals of Guerrilla Warfare.* New York: Praeger, 1965.

National Security Archive. "CIA Stalling State Department Histories on Indonesia." Available at http://www.gwu.edu/~nsarchiv/NSAEBB/NSAEBB52/#FRUS.

Nevins, Joseph. *A Not-So-Distant Horror: Mass Violence in East Timor.* Ithaca, NY: Cornell University Press, 2005.

Niner, Sarah, ed. *To Resist Is to Win! The Autobiography of Xanana Gusmão*. Richmond, Victoria: Aurora Books, 2000.

———. "A Long Journey of Resistance." In *Bitter Flowers, Sweet Flowers: East Timor, Indonesia, and the World Community*, ed. Richard Tanter, Mark Seldon, and Stephen Shalom, 15–29. New York: Rowman and Littlefield, 2001.

Noor, Machmuddin, et al. *Lahirnya Propinsi Timor Timur*. Jakarta: Badan Penerbit Almanak Republik Indonesia, 1977.

Norwegian Nobel Institute. "The Nobel Peace Prize for 1996." October, 11, 1996.

O'Rourke, Kevin. *Reformasi: The Struggle for Power in Post-Soeharto Indonesia*. Sydney: Allen and Unwin, 2002.

Pélissier, René. *Le Crocodile et les Portugais*. Orgeval, France: privately printed, 1996.

Peluso, Nancy Lee. "Passing the Red Bowl: Creating Community Identity through Violence in West Kalimantan, 1967–1997." In *Violent Conflicts in Indonesia: Analysis, Representation, Resolution*, ed. Charles Coppel, 106–28. New York: Routledge, 2006.

Pinto, Constancio, and Matthew Jardine. *East Timor's Unfinished Struggle: Inside the Timorese Resistance*. Boston: South End Press, 1997.

———. "The Student Movement and the Independence Struggle in East Timor: An Interview." In *Bitter Flowers, Sweet Flowers: East Timor, Indonesia, and the World Community*, ed. Richard Tanter, Mark Selden, and Stephen Shalom, 31–41. New York: Rowman and Littlefield, 2001.

Pour, Julius. *Moerdani: Profil Prajurit Negarawan*. Jakarta: Yayasan Kejuangan Panglima Besar Soedirman, 1993.

Power, Samantha. *"A Problem From Hell": America and the Age of Genocide*. New York: Basic Books, 2002.

———. "First Do No Harm." *Los Angeles Times Book Review*, October 6, 2002. Available at http://articles.latimes.com/2002/oct/06/books/bk-power6.

———. "Increasing the Cost of Genocide." In *The New Killing Fields: Massacre and the Politics of Intervention*, ed. Nicolaus Mills and Kira Brunner, 245–64. New York: Basic Books, 2002.

Ramos-Horta, José. *Funu: The Unfinished Saga of East Timor*. Trenton, NJ: Red Sea Press, 1987.

Republic of Indonesia. "East Timor: Building for the Future." Jakarta: Department of Foreign Affairs, July 1992.

Rieff, David. *A Bed for the Night: Humanitarianism in Crisis*. New York: Simon and Schuster, 2002.

Robertson, Geoffrey. *Crimes against Humanity: The Struggle for Global Justice*. New York: New Press, 2000.

Robinson, Geoffrey. *The Dark Side of Paradise: Political Violence in Bali*. Ithaca, NY: Cornell University Press, 1995.

———. "Human Rights in Southeast Asia: Rhetoric and Reality." In *Southeast Asia in the New World Order*, ed. David Wurfel and Bruce Burton, 74–99. New York: Macmillan, 1996.

———. "*Rawan* Is as *Rawan* Does: The Origins of Disorder in New Order Aceh." *Indonesia* 66 (October 1998): 127–56.

———. "Indonesia: On a New Course?" In *Coercion and Governance: The Declining Political Role of the Military in Asia*, ed. Muthiah Alagappa, 226–56. Stanford, CA: Stanford University Press, 2001.

———. "People's War: Militias in East Timor and Indonesia." *South East Asia Research* 9, no. 3 (November 2001): 271–318.

———. "The Fruitless Search for a Smoking Gun: Tracing the Origins of Violence in East Timor." *Roots of Violence in Indonesia: Contemporary Violence in Historical Perspective*, ed. Freek Columbijn and Thomas Lindblad, 243–76. Leiden: KITLV Press, 2002.

———. *East Timor 1999: Crimes against Humanity. A Report Commissioned by the UN Office of the High Commissioner for Human Rights*. Jakarta: Elsam and Hak, 2006.

———. "People Power: A Comparative History of Forced Displacement in East Timor." In *Conflict, Violence, and Displacement in Indonesia: Dynamics, Patterns, Experiences*, ed. Eva Lotta Hedman, 87–118. Ithaca, NY: Cornell South East Asia Program, 2008.

Rocamora, Joel. "The Uses of Hunger." *Southeast Asia Chronicle* 74 (1980): 11–16.

Rockwell International. "The Bronco Workhorse: Ask Thailand About It." Advertisement, reprinted in *Southeast Asia Chronicle* 63 (July—August 1978): 25.

Ryter, Loren. "Pemuda Pancasila: The Last Loyalists of Suharto's New Order?" *Indonesia* 66 (October 1998): 45–74.

Scharfe, Sharon. *Complicity: Human Rights and Canadian Foreign Policy—The Case of East Timor*. Montreal: Black Rose Books, 1996.

Schulte Nordholt, Henk. "A Genealogy of Violence." In Colombijn and Lindblad, eds. *Roots of Violence in Indonesia*, ed. Freek Columbijn and Thomas Lindblad, 33–61. Leiden: KITLV Press, 2002.

Shawcross, William. "Protection of Civilians in Conflict." In *World in Crisis: The Politics of Survival at the end of the Twentieth Century*, ed. Médecins Sans Frontières, 1–15. New York: Routledge, 1999.

———. *Deliver Us from Evil: Peacekeepers, Warlords, and a World of Endless Conflict*. New York: Simon and Schuster, 2000.

Sidel, John T. *Riots, Pogroms, and Jihad: Religious Violence in Indonesia*. Ithaca, NY: Cornell University Press, 2006.

Simpson, Brad. "'Illegally and Beautifully': The United States, the Indonesian Invasion of East Timor, and the International Community, 1974–1976." *Cold War History* 5, no. 3 (August 2005): 281–315.

———. *Economists with Guns: Authoritarian Development and U.S.-Indonesian Relations, 1960–1968*. Stanford, CA: Stanford University Press, 2008.

Sluka, Jeffrey A., ed. *Death Squad: The Anthropology of State Terror*. Philadelphia: University of Pennsylvania Press, 1998.

Smythe, Patrick A. *"The Heaviest Blow": The Catholic Church and the East Timor Issue*. New Brunswick, NJ: Transaction Publishers, 2004.

Soeharto. *Pikiran, Ucapan, dan Tindakan Saya*. Jakarta: PT Citra Lamtoro Gung Persada, 1988.

Somomoeljono, Suhardi. *Analisa Juridis Mengenai Konspirasi Internasional Atas Wilayah Timor-Timur*. Jakarta: Dewan Pimpinan Pusat Himpunan Advocat/Pengacara Indonesia, May 2000.

Spores, John C. *Running Amok: A Historical Inquiry*. Athens: Ohio University Monograph Series, 1988.

Stahn, Carsten. "Accommodating Individual Criminal Responsibility and National Reconciliation: The UN Truth Commission for East Timor." *American Journal of International Law* 94, no. 4 (October 2001): 952–66.

Straus, Scott. *The Order of Genocide: Race, Power, and War in Rwanda*. Ithaca, NY: Cornell University Press, 2006.

Strohmeyer, Hansjorg. "Making Multilateral Interventions Work: The UN and the Creation of Transitional Justice Systems in Kosovo and East Timor." *Fletcher Forum for World Affairs Journal* 25 (Summer 2001): 107–24.

Suratman, Brigadier General Tono. *Merah Putih: Pengabdian dan Tanggung Jawab di Timor Timur.* Jakarta: Lembaga Pengkajian Kebudayaan Nusantara, 2000.

Tambiah, Stanley. *Levelling Crowds: Ethnonationalist Conflicts and Collective Violence in South Asia.* Berkeley: University of California Press, 1996.

Tanter, Richard. "Intelligence Agencies and Third World Militarization: A Case Study of Indonesia, 1966–1989," PhD diss., Monash University, 1991.

Tanter, Richard, Mark Selden, and Stephen Shalom, eds. *Bitter Flowers, Sweet Flowers: East Timor, Indonesia, and the World Community.* New York: Rowman and Littlefield, 2001.

Tanter, Richard, Gerry van Klinken, and Desmond Ball, eds. *Masters of Terror: Indonesia's Military and Violence in East Timor.* New York: Rowman and Littlefield, 2006.

Taylor, John G. *Indonesia's Forgotten War: The Hidden History of East Timor.* London: Zed Books, 1991.

———. "The Emergence of a Nationalist Movement in East Timor." In *East Timor at the Crossroads: The Forging of a Nation,* ed. Peter Carey and G. Carter Bentley, 21–41. Honolulu: University of Hawaii Press, 1995.

———. *East Timor: The Price of Freedom.* London: Zed Books, 1999.

Tilly, Charles. *The Politics of Collective Violence.* Cambridge: Cambridge University Press, 2003.

Turner, Michele. *Telling East Timor: Personal Testimonies, 1942–1992.* Kensington: New South Wales University Press, 1992.

Urquhart, Brian. "In the Name of Humanity." *New York Review of Books* 47, no. 7 (April 27, 2000): 19–22.

Valentino, Benjamin. *Final Solutions: Mass Killing and Genocide in the Twentieth Century.* Ithaca, NY: Cornell University Press, 2004.

Van Dijk, Kees. "The Good, the Bad, and the Ugly. Explaining the Unexplainable: Amuk Massa in Indonesia." In *Roots of Violence in Indonesia: Contemporary Violence in Historical Perspective,* ed. Freek Columbijn and Thomas Lindblad, 277–97. Leiden: KITLV Press, 2002.

van Klinken, Gerry. *Communal Violence and Democratization in Indonesia: Small Town Wars.* London: Routledge, 2007.

———. "Communal Conflict and Decentralization in Indonesia." Occasional Papers Series, no. 7. Brisbane: University of Queensland. Australian Centre for Peace and Conflict Studies, July 2007.

van Zyl, Paul. "Transitional Truth-Seeking: A Comparative Perspective on South Africa, East Timor, and Indonesia." In *Beginning to Remember: The Past in the Indonesian Present,* ed. Mary S. Zurbuchen, 324–42. Seattle: University of Washington Press, 2001.

Wallace, Alfred Russel. *The Malay Archipelago: The Land of the Orang-utan and the Bird of Paradise.* London: Macmillan and Co., 1869.

Walzer, Michael. "Arguing for Humanitarian Intervention." In *The New Killing Fields: Massacre and the Politics of Intervention,* ed. Nicolaus Mills and Kira Brunner, 19–36. New York: Basic Books, 2002.

Weatherbee, Donald E. "Portuguese Timor: An Indonesian Dilemma." *Asian Survey* 6, no. 12 (December 1966): 683–95.

Webster, David. "Non-State Diplomacy: East Timor, 1975–99." *Portuguese Studies Review* 11, no. 1 (Fall–Winter 2003): 1–28.

Weitz, Eric D. *A Century of Genocide: Utopias of Race and Nation.* Princeton, NJ: Princeton University Press, 2003.

Wessel, Ingrid, and Georgia Wimhofer, eds. *Violence in Indonesia.* Hamburg, Germany: Abera, 2001.

MEDIA

Age
Agence France-Presse
Australian Broadcasting Corporation
Australian Financial Review
Christian Science Monitor
Economist
Editor
Far Eastern Economic Review
Financial Times
Guardian (London)
Independent
Jakarta Post
Kompas
Los Angeles Times
New York Times
Reuters
South China Morning Post
Special Broadcasting System
Suara Karya
Tempo
Time International
Washington Post

INDEX

HUMAN RIGHTS AND CRIMES AGAINST HUMANITY
Edited by Eric D. Weitz

THIS SERIES PROVIDES a forum for publication and debate on the most pressing issues of modern times: the establishment of human rights standards, and at the same time, their persistent violation. It features a broad understanding of human rights—one that encompasses democratic citizenship as well as concerns for social, economic, and environmental justice. Its understanding of crimes against humanity is similarly broad, ranging from large-scale atrocities like ethnic cleansings, genocides, war crimes, and various forms of human trafficking, to lynchings, mass rapes, and torture. Some books in the series are more historically oriented, and explore particular events and their legacies. Others focus on contemporary concerns, like instances of forced population displacements or indiscriminate bombings. Still others provide serious reflection on the meaning and history of human rights, or the reconciliation efforts that follow major human rights abuses. Chronologically, the series runs from around 1500, the onset of the modern era marked by European colonialism abroad and the Atlantic slave trade, to the present. Geographically, it takes in every area of the globe. It publishes significant works of original scholarship and major interpretations by historians, human rights practitioners, legal scholars, social scientists, philosophers, and journalists. An important goal is to bring issues of human rights and their violations to the attention of a wide audience, and stimulate discussion and debate in the public sphere as well as among scholars and in the classroom. The knowledge that develops from the series will also, we hope, help promote human rights standards and prevent future crimes against humanity.